A FRATERNITY
OF ARMS

A Fraternity of Arms

· · · · · · · · · · · · ·

AMERICA AND
FRANCE IN THE
GREAT WAR

ROBERT B. BRUCE

 University Press of Kansas

All photographs are from the collection of the U.S. Army Military History Institute, Carlisle Barracks, Carlisle, Pennsylvania.

Published by the University Press of Kansas (Lawrence, Kansas 66049), which was organized by the Kansas Board of Regents and is operated and funded by Emporia State University, Fort Hays State University, Kansas State University, Pittsburg State University, the University of Kansas, and Wichita State University

British Library Cataloguing in Publication Data is available.

The paper used in this publication meets the minimum requirements of the American National Standard for Permanence of Paper for Printed Library Materials Z39.48-1984.

Library of Congress Cataloging-in-Publication Data

Bruce, Robert B. (Robert Bowman), 1963–
  A fraternity of arms : America and France in the Great War / Robert B. Bruce.
    p. cm. — (Modern war studies)
  ISBN 0-7006-1253-X (cloth : alk. paper)
  1. World War, 1914–1918—United States.
2. World War, 1914–1918—France. 3. United States—Military relations—France. 4. France—Military relations—United States.
5. World War, 1914–1918—Campaigns—France. I. Title. II. Series.
D570.B77 2003
940.4'0973—dc21
                    2003000116

Printed in the United States of America
10 9 8 7 6 5 4 3 2 1

To the American volunteers of the
Légion étrangère and *Escadrille Lafayette*
who died for France in the Great War

CONTENTS

• • • • • • • • • • • • • •

TABLES, ILLUSTRATIONS, AND MAPS

• • • • • • • • • • • • • • •

Tables

Illustrations

Maps

PREFACE

• • • • • • • • • • • • • •

This book began as a result of my lifelong passions for the history of the U.S. Army, the history of the French army, and the history of the Great War. Throughout my study of these areas, I was struck by how closely the military efforts of France and the United States were linked during World War I and how close the two republics were at that time. I have always been troubled by the popular image, so widely held in America, of a historically acrimonious relationship between the two nations, when in fact this is a relatively recent development. In this book I examine Franco-American military relations during World War I, a time when Americans viewed France as a historical and natural ally in what President Woodrow Wilson portrayed as a struggle between democracy and monarchical tyranny. I hope that this book will shed light on a time when the French army and the U.S. army fought side by side in a common cause, against a common enemy, and were indeed, in the words of one French soldier of the Great War, "not just allies, but friends."

World War I was a major turning point in the history of the United States and marked its emergence as a world military power. Although American economic dominance and the strength of the U.S. Navy had helped to raise the United States to the status of an international power during the period from 1898 to 1917, the nation lacked the ability to wage a major military conflict on land. The U.S. Army in 1917 was essentially a nineteenth-century frontier constabulary designed more for chasing bandits than for engaging in modern industrialized warfare. Yet with America's entry into the Great War, the U.S. Army was thrust into the maelstrom of modern warfare on the European continent, where the most technologically and militarily advanced nations in the world had waged war on one another for almost three years.

On the eve of America's entry into World War I, the U.S. Army numbered approximately 135,000 officers and men, less than one-tenth the size of the smallest of the major European combatants. Besides manpower shortages, the United States possessed virtually no heavy artillery, tanks, or combat aircraft and had no experience in modern warfare. As a consequence of these deficiencies, America needed a tremendous amount of support and advice in order to establish a significant military force in Europe. Fortunately for the United States, it would not be fighting alone in this immense undertaking because World War I marked the first time since the American Revolution that the nation waged war as a member of a military coalition.

Although it was officially an "associated power" of the Allies, the United States enjoyed a special bilateral military relationship with France, under the overall aegis of the Entente alliance; and the close association between the armies of the two republics was significant in the development and maturation of the United States as a major military power in the early twentieth century and played a critical role not only in America's military contribution to the war but also in the ability of France to continue fighting during 1917 and 1918.

The Franco-American military relationship in World War I began with a group of American volunteers, whose quest for adventure, thirst for glory, and love for France inspired them to volunteer to fight in the French army. During the period of American neutrality, from 1914 to 1917, hundreds of Americans volunteered to fight for France. Many enlisted in the French Foreign Legion, but the most famous of the American volunteers were the men of the Escadrille Lafayette, an all-American pursuit squadron formed by the French Service Aéronautique. The colorful pilots of the Escadrille Lafayette, with their lion cub mascots and gaudy uniforms, were an elite group and became international celebrities. Through their service they generated among the American people an admiration and support for the cause of France in the Great War. Moreover, their extraordinary combat record inspired among French military leaders and the French people themselves an admiration and respect for the martial capabilities of Americans at a time when few Europeans held U.S. soldiers in high regard.

These volunteers raised interest within the United States for the cause of France and resurrected images of America's military alliance with

France in the American Revolution. From this humble and unofficial beginning, the Franco-American military relationship became a formal one when the United States declared war on the German Empire in April 1917. Although America had entered the conflict, it not only lacked an army with which to prosecute the war but also modern weapons to arm it and the instructors to train it. Both France and Great Britain sent military missions to the United States shortly after America entered the war in the hopes of securing the lion's share of the country's potentially vast military resources for their nations. Marshal Joseph Joffre, heading the French mission, offered to provide weapons and instruction in modern warfare to the nascent American Expeditionary Forces (AEF) that would be sent to fight in Europe. Joffre succeeded in convincing the Wilson administration, and the American people, to entrust the AEF to the care and training of the French army rather than to the British. Joffre's visit and the agreement he signed with U.S. Secretary of War Newton D. Baker laid the foundation for the Franco-American military relationship in the Great War and established France, rather than Britain, as America's principal military partner in the conflict.

America's entry into the war came at a most propitious time for France; with the failure of the Nivelle offensive during the very month Joffre was in the United States, the French army and nation entered into the most perilous stage of the entire war. France suffered through massive labor strikes and food shortages as defeatist politicians argued for surrender, and mutiny erupted in the French army. Yet the arrival of the first U.S. contingent, led by General John J. Pershing, gave France a tremendous morale boost during this most dire period of crisis. The arrival of the first Americans, and the promise that hundreds of thousands more were on their way, greatly encouraged the French people and their army to continue the struggle.

I argue that France played the dominant role in arming and training the AEF in World War I. American soldiers went into battle equipped with French artillery, French automatic rifles, French machine guns, French tanks, and French aircraft. In addition, French instructors trained in whole or in part approximately 80 percent of the U.S. soldiers who served in combat during the war. The United States reciprocated by providing raw materials and financial assistance to a French nation desperately in need of both commodities.

The Franco-American military relationship was not always a smooth one, and indeed one of the severest challenges occurred during winter 1917–1918. The French, impatient over the length of time it was taking to assemble a complete American army, argued that U.S. soldiers should be amalgamated into the French army by battalions. The relationship was greatly strained during this time, and the United States almost decided to develop a closer military association with Britain. Yet the special bilateral military relationship between France and the United States survived, through a combination of compromise and America's realization of the numerous detrimental effects a closer military association with Britain would have on the development of an autonomous U.S. military presence on the western front.

The AEF entered into serious combat for the first time in 1918 in the French sectors of the western front under French leadership. American divisions served under French corps, French army, and French army group command. Indeed, I demonstrate that virtually every "American" engagement of World War I was a Franco-American military operation. The battles waged by the Franco-American forces in summer 1918, and in particular their magnificent defensive stand and counteroffensive at the Second Battle of the Marne, proved the deadly combat efficiency of these combined forces. This victory marked the turning point in the course of the war and demonstrated the significance of the Franco-American military contribution to the Allied effort in 1918.

Although the French exercised command over U.S. divisions, during the course of the war they also provided the Americans with ever greater authority as they supported and encouraged the development and deployment of an autonomous American force responsible for its own sector of the western front. Yet even after U.S. military autonomy was achieved, with the establishment of the U.S. First Army, this army was in fact a Franco-American force, containing entire French divisions, French corps, French artillery batteries, French armored units, and French aircraft. Moreover, its operations were supported by and waged in conjunction with French armies at every step.

Throughout the chapters that follow, I demonstrate that in sharp contrast to modern images of Franco-American relations, during World War I a mutual bond of affection existed between the French and American soldiers as well as the French and American people. During the war the American people viewed France as a fellow democracy in a world still dominated by kings and emperors, and they held a deep respect for the historical and contemporary achievements of the French army and its leaders. Americans also cherished the memory of French assistance during the American Revolution, which had been a decisive factor in winning U.S. independence. The French people in turn saw America not only as a fellow democracy but also as their deliverers at a time when their entire nation seemed on the verge of collapse.

American soldiers respected the experience and professionalism of their French trainers, and the French admired the enthusiasm and fighting abilities of the American soldiers. Many of the Americans developed close personal friendships with their French counterparts. Indeed, the commander of the AEF, General John J. Pershing, became a close friend of his French counterpart, General Philippe Pétain, and their personal relationship did much to help promote a harmonious professional rapport between the two armies. In all cases, the friendship between the people and the armies of the two republics was based on a mutual respect and appreciation for the abilities and accomplishments of the other. The military efforts of both nations were inextricably entwined throughout America's involvement in the war. Indeed, it is impossible to fully comprehend America's participation in the conflict without understanding the special military relationship that existed between the United States and France during the war.

ACKNOWLEDGMENTS

● ● ● ● ● ● ● ● ● ● ● ● ● ●

This book would not have been possible without the guidance and support of numerous individuals. I would like to thank Dr. Donald J. Mrozek of the Department of History at Kansas State University for his tireless support of the project and the many hours he invested in reading the manuscript and offering invaluable advice on writing, researching, and exploring the issues that I investigate. He has always personified to me what a professor and mentor should be, and I owe him more than I could ever repay for his support and advice throughout my academic career. I would also like to extend a special thanks to Colonel Robert A. Doughty, professor and chair of the Department of History, USMA, West Point. Colonel Doughty provided me with wonderful insights on military and political affairs in France during World War I, and his tremendous knowledge of the French army proved to be an invaluable resource. Colonel Doughty's challenging critiques of my work and his constant support for the project enabled the manuscript to evolve into the book you now see. A special thank you also goes to Dr. James S. Olson, chair of the Department of History at Sam Houston State University, for the time and financial assistance that the department provided to support the research and writing of this book, and for his encouragement and support of military history at SHSU. I would also like to thank all the individuals who took the time to read through the manuscript and to offer their suggestions and support, including Dr. Jack M. Holl, Dr.

George Kren, Dr. Dennis Showalter, Dr. David Graff, and Dr. Leonard Smith, as well as the anonymous reviewers whose advice was so helpful in writing this book. An early version of chapter 2 was published in the *Journal of Military History* in April 2002, and I want to thank Bruce Vandervoort for his encouragement and support for the article and the advice of the anonymous reviewers of JMH.

A special thanks goes out to the staff of the Service Historique de l'Armée de Terre (SHAT), at the Château de Vincennes, especially M. Gibiat and Mme. Bernard, for their advice and help in researching the vast French archival holdings on World War I. As those who have been there know, SHAT is an absolutely fabulous place to research and work, and during my visits there I was treated with the utmost courtesy, respect, and genuine friendliness. I also wish to thank M. Robert, the manager of the brasserie *Le Drapeau,* located just across the street from the Château de Vincennes, where I always had breakfast during my time there. The courtesy and warmth he and his staff displayed to my wife and me during our trips to France form one of the most pleasant memories of my research for the book.

I would like to extend my thanks to the staff of the National Archives and Records Administration, especially to Mitchell Yockelson, for their assistance and advice in my research, as well as to the staff of the Library of Congress and the U.S. Army Military History Institute for their help.

Finally, I would like to thank my dear wife, Dr. Susannah U. Bruce, for her critical commentary and advice on the manuscript as well as for her love, support, and devotion during the years I spent working on the book.

CHAPTER 1

• • • • • • • • • • • • •

American Volunteers in France, 1914–1917

When the Great War erupted in Europe in 1914, President Woodrow Wilson adopted a policy of strict neutrality for the United States. Sensing that in spite of his official pronouncements, partisan emotions among America's large and varied ethnic population of immigrants and first-generation Americans could boil over, Wilson urged American citizens to be "neutral in fact as well as in name" and "impartial in thought as well as in action." Yet even before Wilson had issued his proclamation, some American citizens had already decided for themselves that they would volunteer to take part in the war.[1]

On 2 August 1914, Paul and Kiffin Rockwell, two brothers from a wealthy family, lunched with friends in Atlanta, Georgia. The Rockwells were from Asheville, North Carolina, and their maternal and paternal grandfathers had been officers in the Confederate States Army during the Civil War. These old soldiers had both enjoyed regaling their grandsons with tales of their heroic exploits during the war. Kiffin had studied at the Virginia Military Institute and Washington and Lee University, and Paul had attended Wake Forest and Washington and Lee. The brothers were working as freelance writers for the *Atlanta Constitution* in 1914 while considering what else life might have to offer them.[2]

News from overseas was grim that Sunday. The Rockwells and their friends agreed that a general European war seemed inevitable. As they speculated on the possible European nations that would be drawn into this conflict, Paul Rockwell later recalled that he and Kiffin both agreed "how interesting it would be to go over and fight for France." Although neither of the brothers had ever been to France, or even spoke French for that matter, they had both read a great deal of military history, and their favorite period of study was the Napoleonic Wars. Their interest in those campaigns had resulted in a strong admiration for France as well as in romantic ideals about what service and combat would be like with the French army. Moreover, the two men hungered for adventure and fame, and they perceived that the war in Europe offered them an opportunity to satisfy both these desires. While their friends quickly turned the conversation to a discussion of the poker game played the evening before, Paul and Kiffin mulled over issues deeper than card games.[3]

After lunch, Kiffin took his older brother aside and told him that he had been thinking a great deal about the events in Europe and had already made up his mind to join the French army. The brothers talked late into the night about serving in the inevitable conflict, and Paul recalled, "We became more and more inflamed at the thought of what a general European war must be, and of the possibility of our country being drawn into it." Kiffin was convinced that the war would eventually engulf the whole world but that America would probably remain neutral at first. As Paul later wrote, "We then and there decided to offer our services to our favorite among the [combatant] nations—France."[4]

On Monday, 3 August 1914, Kiffin Rockwell wrote to the French consul in New Orleans:

> I desire to offer my services to the French Government in case of actual warfare between France and Germany, and wish to know whether I can report to you at New Orleans and go over with the French reservists who have been called out, or must I go to France before enlisting? I am twenty-one years old, and have had military training at the Virginia Military Institute. I am very anxious to see military service, and had rather fight under the French flag than any other, as I greatly admire your nation. If my services can be used by your country, I will bring my brother, who also desires to fight for the French flag.[5]

His letter is revealing in that it is devoid of any rhetoric, such as fighting for democracy and civilization, or even of any expressions of undying devotion to France. Rather, he states that he is "anxious to see military service," with all the romantic visions he believed such service would entail, and this in all likelihood was his prime motivating factor. Had the United States entered the war in 1914, or if the Rockwell brothers had thought that was a strong possibility, they probably would have stayed in America.

Yet even if this had been the case, one must still address the issue of why, among all the belligerent nations, they chose to offer their services to France. I believe that if one accepts that their primary motivation for service was romance and glory, then their historical vision of the French army, based on their study of the Napoleonic Wars, had a tremendous impact on their decision. The aura of *"la gloire,"* which surrounded the Napoleonic legend, exerted a powerful influence on both the Rockwells and no doubt fed their romantic and adventurous beliefs of what war would be like as a French soldier. Thus, it was not so much out of affection for France per se that they decided to join the French army; rather, it was because they believed that it offered the greatest prospects to achieve their true goals of romantic adventure.

In no way does this assessment belittle the Rockwells' motivation for service. Indeed, it serves as a powerful illustration of how some Americans who studied military history believed the French army possessed a certain mystique that set it apart from other armies. This belief also helps to explain why after America's intervention in the war professional American army officers, many of whom were also enamored of the historical image of the French army, were inclined to accept its tutelage.

On 4 August 1914 the Rockwell brothers learned that war had begun. Concerned about reports of the difficulty in finding passage to Europe now that hostilities had been formally declared, the two brothers decided not to wait on a formal reply to their inquiry from the French consulate. Instead, they cabled New York to obtain tickets on the first available American vessel headed for Europe. On 7 August Paul and Kiffin Rockwell set sail on the SS *St. Paul,* bound for France to pursue their visions of glory.

Even before the Rockwell brothers sailed, other Americans, who were already in France when the war began, had also determined to join the French army to fight in the Great War. The U.S. ambassador to France in 1914, Myron T. Herrick, was a prominent figure in the Republican Party and an avid Francophile. Herrick, a holdover from the Taft administration, was in the process of handing over his office to his Democratic successor, William Graves Sharp, when the beginning of hostilities delayed both his departure and the transfer of his responsibilities.[6]

Shortly after the outbreak of war, Herrick was in his office when his secretary informed him that a group of young American men wished to see him. The young men informed Herrick that they wanted to enlist in the French army and to join the fight, but they wanted to make sure they had the legal right to do so. Herrick explained the international laws forbidding the participation of citizens from neutral countries in an armed conflict and America's own restrictions on this subject. It was clear to Herrick after he read the law to the young men that this was not what they had wanted to hear, and it grieved him personally to have to throw a damp towel on their ardor. Herrick, who personally longed for America to enter the war at France's side, suddenly burst out with his true feelings. He recalled, "I brought my fist down on the table saying, 'That is the law boys; but if I was young and stood in your shoes, by God I know mighty well what I would do.' At this they set up a regular shout, each gripped me by the hand and then they went rushing down the stairs as though every minute was too precious to be lost."[7]

Soon after leaving Herrick's office, these young Americans formed an ad hoc organization, the American Volunteer Corps. On 21 August 1914 the corps marched through the streets of Paris carrying a large American flag that had been signed by all the Americans who were volunteering to fight for France.[8] Alan Seeger, a graduate of Harvard University and a romantic young writer and poet, carried the U.S. flag in the parade, which culminated at the Hôtel des Invalides, the sacred shrine of the French army. Here the men were mustered into the Légion étrangère, the French Foreign Legion, the elite and fabled French army unit composed of foreign volunteers. The French government, eager to welcome foreigners into the Legion's ranks, amended the terms of service from the normal five-year enlistment to one that would last "for the duration of the war."[9]

The Americans who volunteered that summer were a mixed group, although a surprisingly large number of them were quite wealthy. Paul Rockwell later commented, "A number of the volunteers possessed independent fortunes. Almost every one of them gave up a good situation with excellent promise for the future, to undergo hardships and risks for France."[10] Shortly after his arrival in France, Kiffin Rockwell wrote to his mother, "The American branch [of the Foreign Legion] is quite a mixture, but there are several fine fellows. Yale, Harvard, Michigan, Columbia, Cornell and several other schools are represented by graduates. There are two or three college professors and two lawyers."[11]

It is beyond the scope of this book to discuss in detail all the American volunteers who served with the French army during the Great War. Nevertheless, it is helpful to examine several of the more prominent individuals in order to gauge why Americans volunteered for service with the French army. Moreover, given the celebrity status that many of them later achieved, they provide important case studies of how their service impacted French and American perceptions of one another during this period.

Although there were numerous exceptions, one cannot help but be struck by the disproportionate number of wealthy and educated young men from elite American families who served in the Foreign Legion and in the Escadrille Lafayette during World War I. Tall, burly, mustachioed William Thaw came from a wealthy Pittsburgh family and had studied briefly at Yale, among other elite universities, before learning to fly in 1913 and living the life of a millionaire playboy piloting a flying boat on the French Riviera. When the war came, Thaw, eager for a new adventure, joined the Foreign Legion and was instrumental in recruiting other Americans to join. Thaw was later one of the chief organizers, and original pilots, of the Escadrille Lafayette.[12]

Victor Chapman, another Legionnaire who also later flew in the Escadrille Lafayette, was a tall, pious, and quiet young man from a wealthy New York family. According to Chapman's father, Victor's greatest desire seemed to be to help those less fortunate than himself. He graduated from Harvard and studied architecture at the École des Beaux-Arts in Paris, where his family occasionally spent time, before deciding that he really wanted to become an artist, a decision that did not please his stern father, John J. Chapman. In August 1914, John Chapman took his wife and Victor from France to England to escape the war. Victor was visibly disturbed by his father's decision, which he deemed as cowardly, and in London boldly announced that he was returning to France to join the Foreign Legion. The two quarreled, and John Chapman accused Victor of seeking an escape from "his serious duties" as a man, browbeating his son into compliance. But Victor's stepmother intervened, announcing that she would rather see Victor "lying on the battlefield than see that look [of submission] on his face." Victor was on his way to France within the week.[13]

Kenneth Weeks, who volunteered for the Foreign Legion in the opening days of the war, was a graduate of the Massachusetts Institute of Technology and the École des Beaux-Arts. Weeks had left the profession of engineering to dedicate his life to writing and had moved to Paris permanently in 1910. His widowed mother, Alice Weeks, was in the process of setting up a music school in Greenwich Village, New York, when the war broke out. Mrs. Weeks could not bear to be so far from her youngest son while he was in the service, so she moved to Paris in January 1915. Eventually, she "adopted" all the Americans serving in the French Foreign Legion as her own and became known to them as Maman Légionnaire.

Not all the American volunteers came from such illustrious backgrounds. For example, Bert Hall was a vagabond and rogue whose global wanderings, and escapes from his numerous ex-wives, had taken him to Paris, where he was working as a taxi driver when the war broke out.[14] Raoul Lufberry, who became the leading ace of the Escadrille Lafayette, was born in France, but early in life he became a citizen of the world. He served with the U.S. Army in the Philippine Insurrection, then wandered to India, China, and throughout Europe. He was in France working as a mechanic with a barnstorming troupe of flyers when war came, and being both sympathetic to the cause of France and a lover of high adventure, he immediately joined the Service Aéronautique.[15]

What motivated these Americans to fight for France in the Great War? Many years after it, Eugene Bullard, an African-American boxer from Georgia who joined the Foreign Legion in 1914 and later became an ace with the Service Aéronautique, replied to a reporter's question on why he volunteered by saying, "Well, I don't rightly know but it must have been more curiosity than intelligence."[16] Edwin C. Parsons, who served as a fighter pilot with the Escadrille Lafayette, and even after America's entry into the war remained with the Service Aéronautique, wrote of the volunteers: "Some sought adventure, others revenge, while a pitiful few actually sacrificed themselves in the spirit of purest idealism. The adventurer fought and died side by side with the idealist."[17] Edward Morlae, an American who joined the French Foreign Legion shortly after the outbreak of war, perhaps best summed up the various motivating factors for himself and others when he wrote in 1916: "Some of us who volunteered for the war loved fighting, and some of us loved France. I was fond of both."[18]

By all accounts, the poet Alan Seeger was among the most idealistic of the American volunteers. Seeger was a young romantic from a wealthy New England family who had graduated from Harvard University in 1912. He saw glory and honor in war and believed that by fighting for France he was also fighting for America's ideals of freedom and democracy. In his view, America had become so corrupted by pacifism that it failed to realize the tremendous importance of the global struggle raging all around it and the inevitable necessity of American involvement in that conflict. Seeger's literary talents soon found an outlet when as early as 1914 he began publishing articles in American newspapers and magazines about the Foreign Legion and the Great War. However, his true voice was found in poetry. Although his best-known verse is "I Have a Rendezvous with Death," he wrote many other poems as well, and through his writings he soon became one of the most famous Americans serving in the Foreign Legion.

Seeger expressed his views on why Americans fought for France in his "Ode in Memory of the American Volunteers Fallen for France." He composed this work for a special Memorial Day ceremony held in Paris at the Place des États-Unis on 31 May 1916 and was bitterly disappointed when he failed to receive permission from his commanding officer to attend the ceremony and read the poem in person. The French clerk who processed Seeger's leave papers apparently confused America's Memorial Day with Independence Day, and thus the leave was issued for the Fourth of July instead of 31 May.[19]

Seeger's poem recalls the sacrifices of soldiers in the American Civil War and expresses his dismay that since that glorious time Americans have "somewhat fallen and gone astray," because they were not fighting for the "bright flag of freedom" in the Great War. He writes that the Americans who fell for France died as a sacrifice for their own country's honor, conjuring up an almost Christ-like image of the death of the few for the salvation of many. The third stanza is perhaps the most revealing:

Yet sought they neither recompense nor praise,
Nor to be mentioned in another breath
Than their blue coated comrades whose great days
It was their pride to share—ay, share even to the death!
Nay, rather, France, to you they rendered thanks
(Seeing they came for honor, not for gain),
Who, opening to them your glorious ranks,
Gave them that grand occasion to excel,
That chance to live the life most free from stain
And that rare privilege of dying well.[20]

Seeger's entire poem is filled with romantic images of war, heroism, and the glory of dying in battle. And though he lauds comradeship with the French soldiers and thus by extension with France, the final line offers perhaps the truest glimpse into his motivation for service. The "rare privilege of dying well" reveals not only Seeger's romantic image of death but also his philosophy of life. His poetry suggests the underlying theme that it is far better to find a glorious death on the battlefield as a young man than to meet an anonymous end to existence in one's bed as an old one. Although the poem speaks volumes about his motivation for service in the Great War, it still fails to address the rationale for why, if adventure and a glorious death were his goals, he chose to serve with the French army rather than with one of the other belligerents.

In 1916 Seeger wrote "A Message to America," his attempt not only to explain why he volunteered to fight for France but also why his own countrymen should be taken to task for not joining the fight, which he believed was as much America's as it was France's:

But I have given my heart and hand
To serve, in serving another land,
Ideals kept bright that with you are dim;
Here men can thrill to their country's hymn,
For the passion that wells in the Marseillaise
Is the same that fires the French these days,
And, when the flag that they love goes by,
With swelling bosom and moistened eye
They can look, for they know that it floats there still
By the might of their hands and the strength of their will,
And through perils countless and trials unknown
Its honor each man has made his own. [21]

Seeger saw France as the nation that most embodied America's own ideals of freedom and democracy, which, if not abandoned, were in his view taken for granted in America. With "The Marseillaise" he alludes to the ideals of *liberté, égalité, et fraternité* that embodied the French Revolution and that he saw as the common revolutionary bond ideologically joining the United States and France. He believed America had neglected this democratic heritage when it had failed to enter a war he saw as being waged to preserve the very ideals for which it was supposed to stand. Thus, although his motivation for service in the Great War was in all likelihood inspired by a thirst for adventure, his decision to serve with the French army, instead of the British, Russian, Italian—or even German, for that matter—was ideologically based.

Seeger saw France as a fellow republic in a world dominated by monarchies; by fighting for France, he was also fighting to preserve democracy. Significantly, his ideology and motivation for service is reflected in President Woodrow Wilson's pronouncement in his war message to the U.S. Congress in 1917 that the United States needed to intervene in the war to "make the world safe for democracy." Although Seeger detested Wilson, he certainly shared his point of view regarding democracy and believed that, among the combatant nations, it was France that most embodied the democratic ideals so important and precious to the United States.

Initially, the French placed the Americans, along with all other foreign volunteers who volunteered to fight for France in 1914, in the Légion étrangère. Ivy League graduates, playboy millionaires, and starry-eyed idealists motivated to fight for France and democracy in the Great War found themselves serving with hardened mercenaries whose loyalty was to the Legion and who felt no patriotic stirrings over the great events engulfing Europe. The men of the Legion fought because they were told to, and whether they fought against Bedouins in North Africa, Black Flag revolutionaries in Indochina, or Germans in Europe made little difference to them. The mingling of two such disparate groups inevitably led to internal conflict within the Legion's ranks and the disillusionment of many of the American volunteers.[22]

Kosta Todorov, a Bulgarian volunteer, wrote, "Idealists who had come to defend the principles of the French Revolution marched in the same ranks with professional soldiers indifferent to all ideas and values save one—the honor of the Legion and its fighting prestige." A veteran sergeant of the Legion once berated his new recruits: "Fools! So you've come to fight for freedom and civilization? Words, empty words!" The veteran Legionnaires, their bodies adorned with obscene tattoos and their uniforms decorated with campaign ribbons and medals from French colonial wars, certainly made a distinct yet not always unfavorable impression on the volunteers. Todorov recalled that the veterans "all drank heavily, talked their own colonial slang, knew the field-service regulations by heart, were crack marksmen, bore up easily under prolonged marches, and had as much contempt for other regiments as for civilians."[23]

Despite the admiration many of the new recruits felt for these veterans, the Legion essentially failed to amalgamate the idealistic volunteers and adventurers with the hardened mercenaries who formed the core of the organization. The historian Douglas Porch has noted that the American volunteers in particular found it difficult to adjust to life in the Legion. He argues that the French government and army seriously erred in assigning all foreign volunteers to the Legion and should have considered placing these men into the regular French army.

Many Americans, such as the Rockwell brothers, had expected to be placed in the regular army and were somewhat dismayed to find themselves in the Foreign Legion instead. After a short time with the Legion, Paul Rockwell was seriously injured and sent back to Paris to recuperate.[24] Meanwhile, his brother Kiffin became increasingly disillusioned with service in the Legion and wrote to Paul on 26 December 1914: "Bill Thaw left day before yesterday to join an aviation corps. The English [Legionnaires] expect to be transferred to the English Army soon; they took the names of all the English, and Rapier wanted to add my name. I had rather stay with France but sometimes feel that this is a d—— rotten outfit, and I had best transfer, being handicapped by not speaking French."[25] Kiffin later wrote Paul, "If you can get me into a French regiment, get busy, for I want out of the Legion. This regiment is no good; the officers are no good. It is just luck I am not dead, owing to their d——d ignorance and neglect."[26]

These letters are revealing: they demonstrate that even in the face of disillusionment with service in the Foreign Legion, Kiffin Rockwell remained determined to stay with the French army rather than transfer to the British army. Unlike Seeger, Rockwell does not identify with any particular ideological cause other than his own thirst for adventure and glory. He was determined to stay in the army of the nation that most embodied those ideals for him, in spite of his disillusionment with the Foreign Legion. Certainly one could argue that because he was with the Legion, he was able to detach his feelings for France from his experiences. Thus, he blamed the less than ideal situation he found himself in while still hoping that the romantic adventure he sought could be found in the regular French army.

Since his injury, Paul Rockwell had been desperately trying to receive medical clearance to resume his duties at the front. On 1 February 1915 Kiffin Rockwell advised his brother to cease trying to come back to active duty with the infantry:

> There is no romance or anything to the infantry. It is not a question of bravery, it is a question of being a good day laborer. So if you don't want to leave the service, get into something that requires education and not brute strength. . . . As far as fighting goes, we are always in danger of our lives but don't get a chance to protect ourselves, as this is mostly an artillery war. Of course, the infantry sometimes does fierce fighting, but seldom, and I believe it possible to go through the war without ever taking part in the kind of fighting we imagined we would do.[27]

Kiffin Rockwell was an adventurer, not an idealist. He was motivated more by a thirst for glory than by a love for France, yet his service is still significant in terms of understanding American perceptions of the French army at the time of the war. Despite Rockwell's disillusionment with service in the Foreign Legion, he still refused to transfer to a different army. For Rockwell and many other Americans, there was a mystique that surrounded the French army that simply could not be found elsewhere. Hence, American idealists and adventurers served side by side and, while each pursued separate goals of personal fulfillment, each fought for the same country, France.

After months of inactivity, Kiffin Rockwell at last got his chance for glory on 9 May 1915, when the Foreign Legion took part in the greatest battle they had yet fought in the war. General Joseph Joffre had launched the French army in a massive offensive against the German positions in Champagne, and in May he decided to commit the Legion to the battle.

Rockwell and the other Americans were abuzz with excitement over the imminent engagement and were thrilled when on the eve of the attack the French officers of the Legion appeared in full-dress uniform, their chests covered in medals, armed only with a sword or swagger stick. For Kiffin Rockwell and other American volunteers, it seemed as if their romantic visions of the French army were personified in these officers.[28]

At dawn, 9 May, the French artillery opened fire on the German lines to prepare the way for the Legion's attack, with what Kiffin Rockwell later described to his brother as "the damnedest bombardment imaginable," and at 1000 hours the Foreign Legion went over the top:

At ten o'clock I saw the finest sight I have ever seen. It was men from the *Premier Étranger* crawling out of our trenches, with their bayonets glittering against the sun, and advancing on the Boches. There was not a sign of hesitation. They were falling fast, but as fast as men fell, it seemed as if new men sprang up out of the ground to take their places. One second it looked as if an entire section had fallen by one sweep of a machine-gun. . . . We scrambled out, and from then on it was nothing but a steady advance under rifle, machine-gun and artillery fire. We certainly had the Boches on the run, but at the same time they were pouring the lead at us. . . . To think of fear or the horror of the thing was impossible. All I could think of was what a wonderful advance it was, and how everyone was going up against that stream of lead as if he loved it.[29]

For Kiffin, the attack was the closest thing to the sort of warfare he had hoped for since he had arrived in France, and even the loss of so many comrades did not detract from his exhilaration of at last being in battle. Indeed, Rockwell himself was felled with a serious wound to his thigh during the assault. Yet the letter reveals that in his mind, given his romantic views on warfare, the heavy casualties merely added to the glory of the experience.

The Legion saw heavy fighting in Champagne during spring and autumn 1915, and the American volunteers suffered heavy casualties in these engagements. Paul Pavelka, one of the veterans of the battles, wrote to Alice Weeks, whose son Kenneth had been reported missing in action during the fierce fighting of early autumn:

Our company has lost 160 men, and the most of these were killed. . . . All of our officers fell, and there remained no one to command us. I have not even a scratch on me only my clothes are torn to shreds by pieces of shrapnel. One shell burst about 2 meters in front of me, and I received the full charge on my steel [helmet], with which we are equipped. My rifle was demolished in my hands, and the overcoat torn to pieces. I wish you could see me in my present state. No one in B. 2 seems to know anything of what has happened to Kenneth. At present I am with [Frank] Musgrave. Only us two being left here, who speak English.[30]

After Kenneth Weeks was reported missing in action by the French army, his distraught mother used her money and influence in a desperate attempt to locate her son. After failing to make headway with the French authorities, she turned to her own government. The U.S. government was intent on preserving its image as a disinterested neutral and thus essentially adopted a "don't ask, don't tell" policy regarding the American volunteers. When Alice Weeks visited the U.S. embassy in Paris to see if they could assist her in finding her son, Robert Bliss, the first secretary, told her, "Mrs. Weeks, this embassy knows nothing about those Americans who have volunteered in the Foreign Legion . . . and makes it a point to know nothing about them."[31]

Kiffin Rockwell's wound during the assault on 9 May required him to be sent to the rear for what became an extended period of recuperation. While recovering from his injury, he witnessed a disturbing scene that convinced him that he had to get out of the Foreign Legion. A group of severely wounded Legionnaires were being discharged because the French army doctors had deemed them to be permanently disabled. A Legion officer accosted the men as they prepared to leave. As Rockwell later wrote,

Because these men were going to get out of it through the doctors, the Commandant was sore as hell. He lined them up, some of them could hardly walk, and cursed them out. He told them they were not worth a ———, that they disgraced the Legion, and that they only came here for *la gamelle*. Now, we have heard that from sergeants and such all the time. But for a Commandant to tell men who have ruined themselves for life out of a love for France and the principles she is fighting for, I think it is going a little too far.[32]

Significantly, Rockwell describes his fellow Legionnaires' motivation for service as being "a love for France." It is noteworthy that an adventurer, and by this time a somewhat cynical one, recognized that a love for France was a prime factor in motivating many men to volunteer for service with the Legion. Perhaps Rockwell also felt some stirrings of this emotion himself, which would certainly help to explain at least in part his decision to remain with the French army even though he wanted out of the Legion.

Other American volunteers were becoming equally disillusioned with the Legion in 1915. The morale problem was so acute that the French army finally relented on its policy of placing all foreign volunteers in the Legion and allowed some American Legionnaires to transfer to the 170th *Régiment de Ligne* of the regular French army. Known as *les Hirondelles de Mort* (the Swallows of Death), the 170th was an elite infantry regiment, and American volunteers faithfully and bravely served in this unit even after the United States entered the war in April 1917.[33]

Though some Americans left the Legion, others chose to stay and finally helped to spur an effective amalgamation of the wartime volunteers with the old Legion.[34] Among those who opted to stay was Alan Seeger. He was at first ecstatic over the prospect, as he put it, of "the privilege of entering a French regiment. . . . After a year of what I have been through, I feel more and more the need of being among Frenchmen, where the patriotic and military tradition is strong, where my good will may have some recognition, and where the demands of a sentimental and romantic nature like my own may be gratified."[35] Seeger, like Rockwell, still held a romantic vision of the French army, even after service in the trenches with the Foreign Legion had proved to be somewhat of a disappointment to his romantic visions of warfare. In the end, however, he decided that the Legion had become his home and that he wanted to remain with it. He wrote that since the Legion had proven itself in the battles of 1915, the prospects "of seeing great things is better than ever" and "perhaps the greatest glory will be here."[36]

After the bloody fighting in Champagne, the French Foreign Legion was withdrawn to a quiet sector for a long period of rest that extended through the first half of 1916. In early 1915, the Legion had numbered 21,887 men, but by 1916 there were only 10,683 serving, with 3,316 on the western front. The heavy losses the Legion sustained in Champagne forced the French army to restructure all the Legionnaires in France into one unit, the Régiment de Marche de la Légion Étrangère, or RMLE.[37]

On 21 February 1916 the Germans launched a great offensive against Verdun, but the Legion was still recuperating from its losses and thus was not sent to join the battle, much to Seeger's disappointment. He was bitter over being left out of the fighting at Verdun and wrote, "I should really like to go there, for after the war I imagine Frenchmen will be divided into those who were at Verdun and those who were not."[38] Seeger here expresses concern over which group of Frenchmen he will be placed with, although in other letters and diary entries he reverts to calling himself an American. This is a curious and significant conflict in national identity that other American volunteers also struggled with, even after the United States entered the war in 1917.

In summer 1916, the French high command transferred the Foreign Legion north to the valley of the Somme to take part in the great battle that would begin there on 1 July. Seeger was thrilled at the prospect for action: "We go up to the attack tomorrow. This will probably be the biggest thing yet. We are to have the honor of marching in the first wave. . . . I am glad to be going in the first wave. If you are in this thing at all it is best to be in to the limit. And this is the supreme experience."[39]

Seeger's regiment was kept out of the fighting until 4 July, when his unit was ordered to attack the village of Belloy-en-Santerre. He was thrilled at the coincidence of fighting in the greatest battle he had yet participated in on the anniversary of American independence. He was in the first wave as the Legionnaires charged the German positions with fixed bayonets. German machine-gun fire soon forced the men to seek cover, but they gathered themselves and then rushed forward once more, capturing the German frontline trenches. A fellow Legionnaire recalled glimpsing Seeger: "His tall silhouette stood out on the green of the cornfield. He was the tallest man in his section. His head erect, and pride in his eye, I saw him running forward, with bayonet fixed. Soon he disappeared and that was the last time I saw my friend."[40]

Seeger was horribly wounded by a German machine gun and died slowly; eyewitnesses who saw his body reported he had stripped off his equipment and overcoat in a vain attempt to dress his wounds. He also had time to stick his rifle, with bayonet fixed, into the ground, as was the general custom of the French army in World War I to inform the stretcher bearers that a wounded man was close by. Thus did Alan Seeger keep his "rendezvous with Death, at midnight in some flaming town."[41] The French army cited the Foreign Legion for gallantry in the attack on Belloy-en-Santerre in an Order of the Day:

Under the energetic command of its chief, Lieutenant-Colonel Cot, the Régiment de Marche de la Légion Étrangère, ordered, the 4th of July, 1916 to take a village strongly occupied by the enemy, threw itself forward to the attack with a remarkable vigor and spirit, conquered the village with the bayonet, broke the desperate resistance of the Ger-

mans and opposed itself afterwards to all the counter-attacks of the reinforcements brought up during the night of the 4th to the 5th of July.
Captured seven hundred and fifty prisoners, including fifteen officers
and took many machine-guns.[42]

A total of nine American volunteers were slain during the storming of
Belloy-en-Santerre, more than in any other single engagement of the
French Foreign Legion during the Great War. In total the Legion lost 25
officers and 844 men killed, wounded, and missing in this battle, which
has been described by Douglas Porch as "one of the most glorious in Legion history."[43]

In death, Seeger achieved his dream of fame. He was already somewhat known, thanks to his articles in various newspapers and journals;
and a collection of his poetry was posthumously published in late 1916
and a collection of his letters and his diary in May 1917. "I Have a Rendezvous with Death" became an instant sensation with the American
public, but his romantic imagery was no longer in vogue in the literary
world, and the critics who were already moving away from romanticism
gave him poor reviews. Yet T. S. Eliot, Seeger's classmate at Harvard, reviewed his work for the magazine the *Egoist,* writing, "The work is well
done, and so much out of date as to be almost a positive quality. It is high-
flown, heavily decorated and solemn, but its solemnity is thorough
going, not a mere literary formality. Alan Seeger, as one who knew him
can attest, lived his whole life on this plane, with impeccable poetic dignity; everything about him was in keeping."

Whatever the critics thought, the average American was enthralled by
Seeger's story and his poetry, and he provided the United States with one
of its first martyrs for the cause, long before American troops actually became engaged in the war. American book and newspaper publishers ad-
vertised the writings of other Legionnaires by saying that the author had
served with Seeger or had been good friends with him, even when this
was not the case. Seeger became a hero in France and in the United States,
and the fact that he died while serving with the French army was viewed
by many Americans as a selfless act of service, which made his death
even more noble and thus more honorable.

The French army recognized the tremendous boon that the American
poet's death had been for Franco-American relations and sought to capitalize on it. On Christmas Day 1916 the French army posthumously
awarded Seeger the Croix de Guerre and issued a formal citation honor-
ing him: "A young legionnaire, enthusiastic and energetic, with a pas-
sionate love for France. Volunteered at the beginning of hostilities and

proved during the course of the campaign to have admirable courage. Gloriously fell on 4 July 1916."[44] Seeger was not the only American in the Foreign Legion to be decorated for gallantry, of course. Although their numbers were small, probably just over 150 served in battle with the Legion on the western front, 8 won the Légion d'honneur, 21 the Medaille Militaire, and 52 the Croix de Guerre. Moreover, Americans were mentioned in over 100 citations in the French army's Orders of the Day.[45]

The service of these volunteers in the ranks of the Foreign Legion helped to establish a positive, indeed laudatory, image of the American fighting man in the minds of the leadership of the French army. This belief, established during the period of American neutrality, had major spillover effects after U.S. intervention in the war, when the French soldiers quickly accepted their new allies as equals and as deserving of respect.

The American volunteers serving in the Legion certainly earned the respect of the French army and attracted some attention in America as well. Yet a different group of American volunteers in French service succeeded in capturing the imagination of neutral America and served to galvanize sympathy and support for the French cause. These men were a group of adventurous young American pilots, many recruited from the ranks of the Foreign Legion, who called themselves the Escadrille Américaine.

There is some controversy over who first conceived of putting together an all-American volunteer flying squadron to fight for France in the Great War, but most sources credit Norman Prince, from Pride's Crossing, Massachusetts, with the idea. Like many other American volunteers fighting for France, Prince came from an elite New England family. He had spent many vacations in France before the war, where he enjoyed hunting near the town of Pau and developed a fluency in the French language and a love for the French people.[46] With the outbreak of war, Prince immediately decided to offer his services to France; however, he had no particular inclination to join the Foreign Legion. Instead, he hoped to enlist in the Service Aéronautique to serve as a pilot.[47] He had several difficulties to overcome in order to achieve this dream, not the least of which was that he did not know how to fly. Wisely, he enrolled in a flight school in the United States and learned how before taking passage to France in January 1915.[48]

Once in France, Prince discovered that other Americans were already serving as pilots and observers with the Service Aéronautique, and he quickly decided that it would be wonderful to join these men together into an all-American squadron. There is no evidence that his idea was based on any notion of fostering American support for France or hastening U.S. intervention. Apparently, he was primarily motivated by a sense of adventure and perhaps a desire to be among Americans who shared his own values. Yet despite his family connections and wealth, he initially failed in his attempts to secure French governmental support for his scheme.

The French government was concerned that the Wilson administration might be angered by the formation of an American flying squadron since Germany could interpret such an action as a violation of the nation's declared stance of neutrality, thus placing Wilson in a compromising situation. The French also were concerned that their active encouragement of American citizens to volunteer to fight for France might antagonize and alienate the administration. Although there was only a slim hope, at least in 1915, of the United States becoming involved in the war, France still received valuable economic assistance from American financial firms and purchased large amounts of raw materials from the United States. Thus, the French government did not want to jeopardize either present or future American support with any action that it believed would initially bring only a modicum of military benefit but that could possibly result in a tremendous amount of political damage.

There was certainly a historical precedent on which the French might base their fears. In 1792 the new French minister to the United States, Edmond Charles Genet, came to America to encourage the U.S. government to honor the Franco-American alliance of 1778 and to join the French Republic as an ally in the War of the First Coalition. When the Washington administration announced that America would remain neutral, Genet had openly, and successfully, roused the American people to support France. He recruited American volunteers for an army to attack British and Spanish colonial holdings in North America and the Caribbean. He also helped to outfit American privateers and issued them letters of marque to attack British and Spanish ships. Even though many American people enthusiastically supported Genet, his actions angered and alienated the administration, contributing to Washington's decision to abrogate the original Franco-American alliance.[49]

Thus Prince faced a daunting task in attempting to win French governmental support for his scheme, yet in early 1915 he found an unexpected source of help from the American physician Dr. Edmond Gros, who headed the volunteer American ambulance units serving in France. Gros was thoroughly acquainted with both the language and customs of the French, and from his office in Paris, he soon joined the fight to impress upon the government and military the advantages of forming an American flying squadron. He determined that he needed financial backing in order to help facilitate the establishment of the squadron and so decided to approach the wealthiest American in France, William K. Vanderbilt, who was living in Paris.[50]

Vanderbilt and his wife had already contributed both time and money to supporting American medical assistance to the French army. During the Battle of the Marne in September 1914, the Vanderbilts had converted the American Hospital in Paris, which they had founded before the war as a medical facility for American jockeys working in France, into a military hospital. They also spent considerable money outfitting hospital trains, purchasing ambulances for the French army, and even improving railway facilities in Paris to expedite the movement of wounded French soldiers to the various hospitals located in the capital. When informed of the plan to establish an all-American flying squadron, Vanderbilt was elated. He believed that the vital interests of the United States were at risk in the war and that France especially needed and deserved American support. He was furious that President Wilson had kept America neutral and firmly believed that the establishment of an American flying squadron could be a powerful catalyst to U.S. intervention. Vanderbilt told Gros that he would do everything in his power to use his formidable connections in the French government and the army to help to establish the squadron.[51]

Gros and Prince won a powerful friend to their cause when they succeeded, with the help of Vanderbilt, in convincing the undersecretary of the French Ministry of Foreign Affairs, Jarousse de Sillac, of the worthiness of their idea. De Sillac was a powerful man with influential connections in both the French government and the army and was also a great admirer of the United States. He agreed with Gros and Prince that the all-American squadron would provide the Service Aéronautique with an excellent group of pilots and give France a tremendous propaganda tool for encouraging American popular support.

Paul Rockwell also became involved in the formation of the squadron. After he received a medical discharge from the Foreign Legion in early 1915, he had become a driver in a volunteer ambulance company with the French army. His unit operated out of Paris, and when not ferrying wounded men, he spent considerable time and effort trying to extricate his brother from the Legion and transferred to the French army. When he heard of the attempts to form an all-American flying squadron, he quickly became an avid supporter of the plan. Somehow, he also managed to find the time to fall in love with and marry the daughter of Georges Leygues, a member of the French Chamber of Deputies and president of the Foreign Affairs Committee.[52] Paul Rockwell soon convinced Leygues of the benefits of an all-American squadron and of the suitability of his brother Kiffin as a pilot for the unit. Leygues thus joined the growing list of powerful individuals within the French government who supported the scheme.[53]

With such enthusiasm steadily growing, de Sillac organized a meeting of the squadron's supporters, which was held on 8 July 1915. During the course of the meeting, the French politicians and the squadron's American advocates managed to convince the head of the Service Aéronautique, General Auguste Hirschauer, of the merits of the plan. At the conclusion of the meeting Hirschauer announced that he would give the orders for the formation of a flying squadron to be named the Escadrille Américaine. He noted that there were many details still to be worked out, however, and thus an official Franco-American Committee was formed that day from the various people attending the meeting and charged with hammering out the final arrangements of the scheme. The committee, although unofficial and composed entirely of American and French volunteers, had the blessing and cooperation of the French Ministry of Foreign Affairs, the Chamber of Deputies, and the army.[54]

It was several months before the plan for the squadron was formally adopted by the French commander in chief, General Joseph Joffre, and work on the final arrangements continued through autumn 1915 and into the new year. Nevertheless, General Hirschauer's assent had opened the doors of French military aviation to American volunteers, and Americans serving in the Foreign Legion and the Ambulance Service were soon being welcomed into French flying schools, even though the Escadrille Américaine as yet existed only on paper.

Kiffin Rockwell was one of those accepted into the flight school at Alvord in autumn 1915, as were his fellow Legionnaires William Thaw, Bert Hall, and Victor Chapman. Most of the Americans were ecstatic to "at last be among gentlemen," as Rockwell put it, and to be treated as such by their trainers. This was indeed a welcome change from the harsh life of a Legionnaire. Military aviation was still in its infancy in 1915, and the aircraft used for training purposes were usually outdated models that had outlived their usefulness at the front. The Americans were taught how to fly using various training models of the Maurice Farman and the Blériot, at that time the standard training aircraft of the French Air Service. Edwin C. Parsons learned to fly in Blériots:

[The motor] always presented elements of surprise, for it was a single valve with no carburetor. Raw gas was fed directly into the cylinders, and with a very disconcerting habit of popping one of those valves quite frequently, fire generally resulted, which was likely to cause the pilot considerable embarrassment. . . . The unfortunate pilot sat with half his body projecting above the fuselage, with no protection against the full blast of the propeller stream. The whirling stick was only a couple of feet in front of his nose.[55]

Behind Parson's somewhat comic description of the aircraft he learned to fly was a bitter truth: in these primitive flying machines death could come as surely as in the trenches at the front. Shortly after his arrival for flight training at Alvord, Kiffin Rockwell discovered this reality when he witnessed a horrible training accident in which three men were killed, including the flight instructor and a mechanic.[56]

Yet just as the volunteer pilots were winning their wings and well on their way to realizing their dream of an all-American flying squadron, the whole project almost fell apart. Norman Prince, William Thaw, and several others received leave to return home to visit their families for the 1915 Christmas holiday after they had completed their training. For the American flyers, it was a great time for visiting family and friends and for regaling them with their exploits while stuffing themselves with the American food they universally seemed to miss. And because of the elite social status of their families in the community, and the sheer colorfulness of their stories of service with the French Foreign Legion and as volunteer pilots with the Service Aéronautique, the local press quickly transformed the American pilots into celebrities.[57]

The volunteers did not escape the notice of the German government and its U.S. representatives, who sent agents to follow the Americans and track their movements, as they were suspected of attempting to drum up popular support for France. William Thaw was sitting in a New York City barbershop when, to his amazement, the German ambassador to the United States, Count Johann von Bernstorff, entered. Von Bernstorff informed Thaw that it would be best if he and the other American pilots voluntarily interned themselves for the remainder of the war, before they caused an international incident. Thaw gave von Bernstorff an unprintable reply, before calmly turning his back on the German and walking out of the shop. The German ambassador subsequently filed a formal protest with U.S. Secretary of State Robert Lansing, declaring his outrage at the presence of what he termed these "French officers" in the neutral United States.[58]

The editor of the vehemently pro-German New York newspaper *Fatherland*, George S. Viereck, picked up the story and printed on the front page an open letter to Lansing: "These men, though of American birth, are officers in active service in the French army, and it would be a gross violation of American neutrality if they were not at once detained so as to prevent their return to the front."[59]

Fortunately for the American volunteers, Lansing was in no mood to receive any form of protest from von Bernstorff. Only three weeks earlier the U.S. Secret Service had uncovered a German plot to undermine American munitions production through various schemes, including sabotage. The evidence indicated that two members of von Bernstorff's embassy staff were behind the plot, and on 1 December 1915 Lansing formally requested that the men in question be dismissed and sent back to Germany. In addition to the State Department's rebuttal of the official German protest, virtually all the American newspapers that covered the incident expressed their opinion that Viereck was out of line. After all, Viereck himself was under investigation for anti-American activities, and it had been while following him that the Secret Service agents had first uncovered information regarding the German sabotage plot.[60]

While Lansing mulled over how to deal with the American volunteers, Thaw and the others decided to make the issue moot by immediately returning to France before the furor jeopardized the formation of the Escadrille Américaine. The historian Philip Flammer wrote that the "Christmas leave incident" gave the Franco-American Committee charged with overseeing the establishment of the squadron "cause for some satisfaction and some concern. On the one hand, an aggressive move by the State Department could easily cancel the whole program. On the other, the idea of an all-American squadron had virtually received a public vote of confidence."[61]

Flammer also points out that although there were certainly military factors to be considered, "political motives were the primary factor behind French recognition of the new squadron." He argues that a pursuit squadron, the most glamorous of the flying squadrons, was formed with the express purpose of gaining high visibility for the Americans in the hope of galvanizing U.S. support for the French cause.[62]

Undoubtedly, the French government's decision to form the Escadrille Américaine was a politically motivated attempt to win American popular support during the war. At the same time, the vast majority of the volunteers themselves, although most of them certainly hoped to see the United States enter the war on the side of France, joined for a variety of reasons that rarely included encouraging U.S. intervention in the conflict.

Meanwhile in France, the civilian population had become quite excited over the volunteer pilots, as Kiffin Rockwell soon discovered. During a training flight, he became lost in a dense fog. Running low on fuel, he spotted a village and landed his aircraft on the outskirts of town in the middle of the night. The sound of his plane attracted the attention of the local populace, and to his surprise hundreds of people turned out to see him. When the locals learned that he was an American they were overjoyed, and he was immediately quartered as a distinguished guest in the home of the mayor. Rockwell stayed in the village for three days waiting for the fog to lift, and he wrote to his mother that the villagers treated him royally and followed him en masse everywhere he went in town. He wrote that when the weather finally cleared and he prepared to leave, the whole village turned out to see him off. As he made his way through the crowd, he finally arrived at his aircraft to find it covered in flowers, notes, and love letters from the French girls of the village.[63]

This incident reveals the attitude of the French people toward the American volunteers. Certainly at this time villagers would have been curious about any airplane that had landed near their town, but the fact that the pilot was an American no doubt was a second reason for wonder, since, in this case, no one in the town had ever seen an American before. Indeed, many American volunteer pilots reported similar experiences when they were forced to crash land. The incidents became so numerous that they gave rise to what the volunteers called *pannes de châteaux*, (château breakdowns). According to Edwin Parsons,   ·

> [An American pilot] would disappear for anywhere from three days to a week and come back with a smug face and a tale of having made a forced landing, but fortunately, oh so fortunately, near a big château, where he was royally entertained and lived on the fat of the land all the time he was waiting for the repair crew. Some of the alibis for château landings were works of art. Dirt in the carburetor, wing flutter, rainstorm, anything served. Of course, motors *were* bad, and there *are* a lot of châteaux in France, but it was a strange coincidence that when a pilot had to land, it was always within easy hailing distance of a château.[64]

The evidence is rather overwhelming that at an early and as yet unofficial stage of American military involvement, French civilians developed a sincere affection and admiration for these pilots. These sentiments were later transferred to the U.S. soldiers who arrived in France after America's declaration of war and who were a tremendous assistance in the establishment and maintenance of the special bilateral military relationship that existed between the two republics during the conflict.

After many delays the French army officially activated Escadrille N-124, the Escadrille Américaine, on 16 April 1916; four days later it became operational.[65] William Thaw was commissioned as a lieutenant in the French army and thus became the senior American officer in the squadron. He was the first to admit, however, that he and the other volunteers lacked the experience necessary to be in charge of a fighter squadron. Therefore, the French high command, on Thaw's recommendation, appointed Captain Georges Thénault as the commanding officer, a position he held throughout the squadron's existence.

Thénault had first met Norman Prince and William Thaw while he was on leave in Paris in January 1916. He had been thrilled with their idea for the formation of an American squadron and was soon introduced to the various distinguished members of the American community in Paris and the French politicians backing the scheme. Thénault recalled that he was "delighted" when the news was officially announced of his appointment to command the squadron, and he quickly secured the appointment of another French officer, Lieutenant Alfred de Laage de Meux, as the deputy commander. Thénault and de Meux were the only French pilots in the Escadrille Américaine, although the ground crews and mechanics were French.[66]

The fact that French officers commanded the American squadron suggests that perhaps the French army lacked faith in the ability of the Americans to assume positions of responsibility. But it was Thaw who recommended Thénault for the post. It is also important to bear in mind that the American pilots volunteered for action and excitement, not for paperwork. The various administrative duties required of a commanding officer and his second were anathema to these Americans. They wanted to fly for France, they wanted to kill Germans, and they wanted to achieve glory and fame in the process. Therefore the paperwork and responsibilities that command involved were no more appealing to them than the drudgery of being a mechanic.

In order to gain some experience, the squadron was assigned to Luxeuil-les-Baines, in the relatively quiet Vosges sector of the western front. After several weeks of uneventful missions over the front, Kiffin Rockwell was on a lone patrol on 16 May when he spotted a two-seat German observation plane below him; edging his Nieuport-11 into a steep dive, he pounced on it. The German aircrew spotted Rockwell, and as the pilot took evasive action, the gunner opened fire on him. Bullets streaked past Rockwell, but he continued to bore in on the German plane until he was only thirty meters away, at which point he let loose a fatal burst of machine-gun fire that killed both the observer and the pilot. Their plane wavered and then plunged straight toward the ground, exploding on impact and sending up a long column of thick black smoke.

Because it crashed behind French lines and several observers on the ground had witnessed Rockwell's fight, he was officially credited with the first kill for the Escadrille Américaine.[67]

News of the American's first victory rapidly reached Paris, where ecstatic French military and political officials congratulated Paul Rockwell on the achievement of his brother and the squadron. In honor of the occasion, Paul sent Kiffin a special reserve bottle of aged bourbon that he had been hoarding for some time. Kiffin promptly offered to share it with the rest of the squadron, but his fellow pilot Victor Chapman immediately offered a suggestion typical of his romantic nature. Chapman said that it should be dubbed The Bottle of Death, and from that point on anyone who shot down a German would be entitled to a belt from the bottle, with Kiffin, naturally, having the first honor. The other pilots quickly agreed, and William Thaw was designated to watch over the bourbon.[68]

Shortly after Rockwell's victory, the French transferred the squadron to Bar-le-Duc and committed it to the monumental struggle raging at Verdun. The Germans had attacked there on 21 February, intent on dragging the French army into a grinding battle of attrition on unfavorable ground, where, as General Erich von Falkenhayn put it, they could "bleed France to death."[69] Thus began the Battle of Verdun; France suffered approximately 400,000 casualties during the ten months that it lasted.[70]

French military aviation came of age during the Battle of Verdun as the Service Aéronautique massed almost half of all French fighter squadrons there. German aircraft had won initial air superiority over the battlefield in the opening weeks, as their aircraft at first ruled the skies, accurately directing the massive artillery bombardment decimating the French soldiers on the ground. Rising to meet this challenge, the French Air Service assigned Commandant Jean Baptiste Marie Charles de Tricornet de Rose to assemble the best fighter squadrons available and to hurl them into the battle. De Rose was a pioneer of military aviation and is referred to by the French as the father of the fighters. He commanded the first squadron of *avions de chasse* ever assembled, and his daring and genius for aerial tactics had earned him widespread recognition as one of the foremost aerial commanders of the war.

General Henri-Philippe Pétain, commanding the French Second Army at Verdun, ordered Commandant de Rose to "clear the sky above Verdun." To fulfill his mission de Rose gathered together the best fighter pilots in the French Air Service, including Charles Nungesser, Jean Navarre, and George Guynemer. De Rose organized fighter squadrons and taught them to fly as a team rather than as individuals. Thus, the air battle over Verdun marked the end of the era of the lone ace that had dominated the first years of the war and ushered in the new age of squadron flying and squadron tactics.[71]

One could say that the decision to assign the American squadron to Verdun was a further way for the French government to turn the service of the American volunteers into a propaganda coup. However, the French army clearly recognized that the skies over Verdun were no place for such publicity stunts and would never have agreed to it if the officers had not truly believed that the Americans were excellent pilots. There would have been no propaganda value gained at all if they were shot out of the sky. Therefore, regardless of the initial reasoning behind the formation of the Escadrille Américaine, the French believed unquestionably that their American squadron could hold its own.

Flying with the Escadrille Américaine at Verdun was James Rogers McConnell, who had left his job as a land and industrial agent for his father's railroad company in 1915 to volunteer to drive an ambulance in France. McConnell served with distinction as an ambulance driver with the French army throughout 1915 and was awarded the Croix de Guerre for gallantry in action. During his time as a driver, he became much more than merely pro-French. Writing in 1915 to a young Frenchwoman in Paris with whom he had become infatuated, he expressed his disdain for the British effort in the war but stated his belief that France, along with Russia, would be able to "crush Germany" within a year: "We French will be the ones that will administer the final touch, as is fitting and proper, for France from the first to the last has fought the whole war. I'm glad to note that Americans are beginning to realize it . . . [but] they are just waking up to the truth."[72]

Significantly, McConnell, an American of Scottish ancestry, referred to himself as "we French" and spoke of Americans in the third person. Like many other American volunteers, his vision of his nationality was increasingly formed not by his own history but by his experiences in service with the French, a people whom he loved, respected, and admired. He was also tremendously proud of his service with the French army, a force he considered to be "the finest army in the world."[73]

McConnell volunteered for the Service Aéronautique in late 1915 and was thrilled when he was accepted. He was sent to train at Pau, where he was breveted as a pilot on 6 February 1916 and soon assigned to the nascent Escadrille Américaine. Along with most of his fellow-squadron members, he gained his first experience in aerial warfare in the skies over Verdun.[74]

The utter devastation of the Verdun battlefield disturbed McConnell. He wrote of the eerie sensation of flying over the battle where he knew men were bravely fighting and dying, yet all he could see were puffs of white smoke and small flashes. Occasionally, one of the heavy shells would pass uncomfortably close to his aircraft, and his plane would be rocked back and forth by the projectile on its way to a target below. "It is very weird to see the endless fall of shells," he wrote to his French friend, "[and it] makes one wonder how men can stand in the face of such fire."[75]

Far more deadly for McConnell, however, was the fighting going on above the ground. He wrote of seeing German observation planes moving in the distance during his sortie over Verdun and then noted "little black specks. They are the guarding Fokkers. One watches and forgets the fight below for one's sphere is the air and there will be something coming out of it before long."[76]

In the skies over Verdun the Escadrille Américaine emerged as one of the elite fighter squadrons of the French Air Service, and in the process the Americans became almost overnight international celebrities. The appeal of these pilots among the American press was easily understandable: besides fighting at Verdun with the French army, they were also a colorful group of characters who made for excellent copy. They dressed in unique uniforms of their own design, which did not even match those of other squadron members, and ignored Service Aéronautique regulations. Their aircraft were decorated with the squadron insignia of an American Indian in full warbonnet and with other personal symbols. McConnell's plane, for example, was decorated with the emblem of the Hotfoot Society, an exclusive student club he had belonged to during his college days at the University of Virginia.

Early on in the squadron's existence the Americans purchased a mascot, a male lion cub that McConnell christened Whiskey. After a few months with their new mascot, they decided that Whiskey was lonely, so they bought a female lion cub, which they naturally named Soda. Whiskey and Soda soon became as famous as the squadron members themselves and were a featured attraction at the Escadrille Américaine's base at Bar-le-Duc during the Battle of Verdun. Reporters from around the world and even curious *poilus* (French soldiers) would gather at the airfield to gawk at these colorful American volunteers and their lion cub mascots. Although Soda got along fine with her mate, she was somewhat cantankerous and mean to the American pilots. Whiskey, on the other hand, was a bundle of energetic friendliness. He was never penned up or placed in a cage but was allowed to roam free around the base. He was in fact quite tame, and Raoul Lufberry was Whiskey's favorite pilot.

Lufberry would return from a mission and then spend hours playing and wrestling with Whiskey in the fields around the squadron's aerodrome; he could call Whiskey much as one could call a dog. He also taught the lion an infamous trick. Lufberry would get Whiskey to lie down in some bushes behind the squadron's barracks while he and other pilots would assemble behind some shrubbery across from the lion and wait for one of the many sightseers to pass by. When an unsuspecting victim walked past them, Lufberrry would give a signal to Whiskey, and the lion would leap out and pounce on its startled and frightened prey, easily knocking even large men to the ground with his huge paws. Whiskey would then stand over his conquest and emit a ferocious roar, as the trembling passerby braced himself to be eaten alive at any moment. Lufberry and the others would then emerge, hardly able to walk from laughing, and save the unfortunate soul. Edwin Parsons recalled that the stunt "was an unfailing source of amusement."[77]

Such colorful antics, combined with a formidable reputation for fighting prowess, soon made the pilots of the Escadrille Américaine legends in their own time, as American newspapers carried daily accounts of the squadron's activities at the front. Yet fame did not come without a price. Victor Chapman, one of the original pilots of the squadron, had been recovering from a head wound suffered in an earlier engagement. On 23 June 1916 he was flying to a nearby airbase to bring a present to a friend in a hospital when he saw two of his fellow squadron members under attack by German fighters. Although he was under strict orders not to engage in combat until his wound was properly healed, he dove straight into the fray, and in the swirling dogfight that ensued he was shot down and killed, becoming the first member of the Escadrille Américaine to die in combat.[78]

Kiffin Rockwell and Victor Chapman had become best friends during their time with the Escadrille, and Kiffin wrote to his brother Paul informing him of Chapman's death. Kiffin requested that Paul delay notifying the newspapers until Chapman's family had been told but then to make sure that "every paper in the world pay a tribute to him." Kiffin added that he and Norman Prince were going up the next day to "do our best to kill one or two Germans for him."[79]

Kiffin later wrote to Victor's stepmother, informing her that her son had "died the most glorious death, and at the most glorious time of life to die, especially for him with his ideals." He hastened to add that Victor was not really dead, because "he is alive every day in this *Escadrille* and has a tremendous influence on all our actions."[80]

The death of Victor Chapman made headlines across the United States, and since 1916 was also a presidential election year, the advocates of preparedness soon seized upon his image as a martyr for the cause. Former president Theodore Roosevelt, America's foremost advocate for preparedness and even for outright intervention on behalf of the Allies, used the occasion to write a fitting eulogy for a man he believed personified the ideals for which he himself stood. Roosevelt stated that Chapman possessed "that combination of dauntless courage and of devotion to great ideals which is essential to the best type of citizenship." He also took the opportunity to attack the Wilson administration's neutralist stance and praised all the pilots of the Escadrille Américaine "who have shown that courage and idealism are not dead among us."[81]

Roosevelt's article was in many ways an attempt to achieve political gain for the Republican Party by playing on the growing sympathy for France being generated by the service of the volunteer pilots. Certainly the French had hoped that the squadron would inspire these very feelings among the American people, and by extension their leaders, and thus it would appear that in many ways they were successful. The squadron was also militarily successful, which further enhanced its effect on the American public. By the time of America's intervention in the war, these pilots wore the *fourragere* (shoulder braid) of a unit that had been cited twice in a French army Order of the Day, a distinction shared by only one other French pursuit squadron, the elite *Cigognes*. Therefore, although the French had established the squadron for propaganda reasons, military success was an integral part of its political role.

The French government certainly did all they could to emphasize the significance of the Escadrille Américaine. On 4 July 1916, the same day Alan Seeger was killed in action at Belloy-en-Santerre, a large celebration was held in Paris to commemorate American Independence and to recall the Franco-American military alliance that had proved so crucial to the American victory in the Revolution. Captain Georges Thénault and several American pilots represented the squadron at a special ceremony conducted at the tomb of Lafayette in Picpus Cemetery.[82]

Shortly afterward, the French army briefly assigned Charles Nungesser, one of the greatest French aces of the war, to the Escadrille Américaine, where he participated in several patrols with the Americans and recorded a kill during his short stay. His assignment was highlighted by an already omnipresent international news media that covered every detail of the squadron's actions, and the journalists had a field day with stories regarding Nungesser's comments on the quality and superb fighting abilities of the American pilots. By summer 1916 the Escadrille Américaine had become not only an elite fighter squadron but also a powerful propaganda tool for garnering the support of the American public.[83]

The Germans also noted how the squadron quickened American popular support for France and were greatly angered by its presence on the western front. In fall 1916 the German government lodged formal diplomatic protests with both the French government and the Wilson administration, stating that the Escadrille Américaine represented a breach of American neutrality and demanding that the squadron be immediately disbanded. By this time, however, it had become so famous and popular with the American public that the Wilson administration turned a blind eye to the matter. The French government, however, anxious not to offend the administration, decided that the name of the squadron should be changed. William Thaw quickly came up with the new title, the Escadrille Lafayette. This name conjured up images of the old military relationship between France and America and the spirit of adventure and idealism that had motivated Lafayette to come to America to fight in the Revolution, a spirit the American pilots shared.[84]

The members of the Escadrille Lafayette soon tired of their celebrity status and often complained about the overwhelming publicity, much of it exaggerated, which they generated. Kiffin Rockwell, deeply saddened by the loss of his friend and flying a grueling number of sorties, began to grow bitter about his service in the squadron. He was especially angry at how difficult it was to receive official recognition for a kill. During summer 1916 he shot down many Germans but received no credit because they fell behind German lines where there were no witnesses, as required by French army regulations, to confirm the kill. He angrily wrote to his brother: "I have had about twenty fights lately, sometimes going as close as ten meters to the Germans. . . . But I haven't had the luck to have one of them smash to pieces in our trenches, so as far as thanks go [I] could not have done anything."[85]

Kiffin Rockwell was shot down and killed on 23 September while in pursuit of a German observation aircraft that had ventured over French lines. He was the second American of the Escadrille to die, and the recognition given his death was every bit as grand as Chapman had received. Captain Georges Thénault was the first to break the news to the squadron. He returned from the scene of the crash and convened the pilots in the briefing room, where, with tears welling in his eyes, he announced, "The best and bravest of us all is no more."[86] Rockwell would not be the last of the American pilots to die. Four of the original seven (Chapman, Rockwell, Prince, and McConnell) were killed in action during the course of the war, as were many of those who followed them into the ranks of the squadron.

James McConnell was the last American volunteer pilot to die during the period of American neutrality. Although he had been hospitalized for some time from a back injury he had sustained in a crash, he persuaded Thénault to allow him to fly when the squadron became desperately short of pilots in March 1917, just weeks before America's declaration of war. McConnell became involved in a swirling dogfight and, no doubt extremely hampered by his back injury, he was outmaneuvered and shot down.

Among McConnell's personal effects was a letter he had written in case of his death: "My burial is of no import. Make it as easy as possible for yourselves. I have no religion and do not care for any service. If the omission would embarrass you I presume I could stand the performance. Good luck to the rest of you. God damn Germany and *vive la France.*"[87]

After the war, the French did not forget the service of the Americans who volunteered to fight with the Foreign Legion and the Escadrille Américaine. In Paris, at the Place des États-Unis, a memorial was erected to the memory of all the American volunteers who fought for France. Dedicated on the Fourth of July, 1923, the memorial was funded through popular subscription and private donations from the people of France and its colonies. Atop the monument stands a lifesize bronze figure of an American in French uniform, facing west and beckoning his countrymen to come and join the fight. The base of the memorial, appropriately constructed from Lorraine stone, is covered by the writings of Alan Seeger and also has the bronze figures of a French *poilu* and an American doughboy embracing in front of a winged goddess of victory. Engraved in gold letters on the memorial are the names of the American volunteers who died for France in the Great War.[88]

General Charles Mangin, one of France's greatest heroes of World War I and the president of the Comité du Monument aux Volontaires Américains, stated that the sculpture testified to French gratitude for American service, which had constituted a "fresh and lasting bond between the two countries." Mangin concluded his remarks at the dedication of the memorial by saying, "Should the cause of Civilization be threatened again, he would again come forward, the American Volunteer of 1914, and his arm of bronze would move to beckon his country on! Ye sublime soldiers of idealism, who have passed away, we swear ever to remain worthy of you."[89]

On the Fourth of July, 1928, a massive monument, paid for by donations from various French and American individuals and organizations, was erected to the memory of the Escadrille Lafayette just outside Paris on land donated by the French government. The memorial is emblazoned with the famous Indianhead emblem of the squadron, which is carved into the stone of the monument, as are the figures of the squadron's lion cub mascots Whiskey and Soda. Within the monument is a crypt that contains the remains of the squadron members who died during the Great War.[90]

American volunteers who joined the Légion étrangère and the Escadrille Lafayette did so mainly from a spirit of romantic adventure. Nevertheless, they believed that their needs for such an experience would best be met by the French army rather than by the army of any other European nation. This association of glory and romance with the French army was reinforced in the minds of the American public through the service of these colorful volunteers. Moreover, their service resulted in a tremendous amount of sympathy and admiration among the American public for France and assisted in swaying the neutral nation to join the French cause.

The French agreed to the formation of the Escadrille Américaine for political reasons in the hope that the unit would be a great propaganda tool in encouraging just such support. Yet the decision also reflected the tremendous confidence the French had in the ability of Americans to fight, not only as soldiers in the trenches but also as fighter pilots, a role previously reserved exclusively for the elite pilots of the Service Aéronautique. Before America's entry into the war, most Europeans had a rather dim view of the military capabilities of Americans. But the French perspective marked a major difference of opinion. French appraisal was based on the impressive record the American volunteers compiled in the Foreign Legion and in the Escadrille Lafayette. After the United States declared war, French respect for the military capabilities of American soldiers helped them to establish an immediate and close rapport with the AEF. This friendship was based on the mutual respect and admiration the soldiers of the two republics felt and was instrumental in the success of the military relationship between France and the United States during the Great War.

CHAPTER 2

• • • • • • • • • • • • • •

America Embraces France: Joffre and the French Mission to the United States

Premier Alexandre Ribot summoned the French Chamber of Deputies to meet in special session on 5 April 1917 and formally announced to the representatives of the Third Republic that President Woodrow Wilson had requested that the U.S. Congress declare war on Germany. It was apparent that the measure would pass overwhelmingly; thus, the United States would soon be entering World War I on the side of the Allies. The American ambassador to France, William Graves Sharp, was invited to appear as a special guest of honor at the proceedings. Sharp watched from his position in the Diplomatic Gallery as the deputies filed silently into the chamber in a somber and dramatic ceremony. As he observed the procession, he noted the vacant desks marked with wreaths commemorating those members who had fallen in battle. He later wrote, "The scene at the Chamber was historic and lacked nothing in the elements of the dramatic to make an unforgettable impression upon the minds of all those in attendance."[1]

Ribot spoke to the gathered deputies, his voice trembling with emotion, and praised Wilson's war message to Congress, noting that the president's speech "makes everyone realize that the struggle is truly a struggle between the spirit of freedom of modern societies and the spirit of domination of societies still enslaved to military despotism."[2]

As the French premier spoke, nearly every sentence was punctuated by applause and cheers from the assembled deputies. Ribot spoke of the ideology of democracy that bound the great republics of the United States and France together and made several references to their alliance during the American Revolution, a theme that would often be repeated throughout the course of American involvement in the Great War. At his first mention of "Amérique," the deputies rose in unison and turned toward Sharp, the lone American representative present, bowing and cheering, a performance they repeated several times during the course of the premier's speech. Sharp later wrote, "It was indeed the culmination of a time to which all France had looked in eager, and often yearning, expectancy for nearly two years. A people, not slow to evince their emotions of pleasure and of gratitude, gave vent in the following few days to an unrestrained joy over the turn of events."[3]

The news of America's entrance into the war electrified Paris. The atmosphere in the French capital changed overnight from despondency to ebullient joy not seen since the heady days of August 1914. In the weeks following Ribot's address, there were numerous manifestations of both official and unofficial French sentiment for America. The Ribot government proclaimed 22 April 1917 "United States Day" and many festivities were held throughout Paris in celebration of the occasion. The American flag was flown over the Hôtel de Ville in Paris and from the top of the Eiffel Tower, as planes towing large French and American flags circled overhead. A huge crowd attended a gathering in Paris held at the statue of George Washington in the Place d'Iéna, where a wreath was laid at the foot of the American hero in a ceremony rife with symbolism. The almost tangible feeling in the air was that after a long and nightmarish struggle, the sacrifices of the French people had not been in vain. At that moment the United States meant more to France than merely a new ally in the war; it symbolized salvation.[4]

On 8 April 1917 the French general Robert Nivelle, commander in chief of the Armies of the North and Northeast, made the first effort toward establishing a military relationship between France and the United States when he sent a message of welcome to Major General Hugh Scott, the U.S. Army chief of staff: "The French Army has heard with the deepest emotion the noble and moving words addressed by President Wilson to the American Congress. Her joy is immense on hearing that Congress has declared war with Germany. She recalls the memory of military fraternity sealed more than a century ago by Lafayette and Rochambeau on American soil and which will be made still tighter on the battlefields of Europe."[5] A flattered General Scott replied to Nivelle, "The memory of Lafayette and Rochambeau form one of the most cherished traditions of the American people, and the Army of the United States is eager to take its place side by side with the Armies of France and her Allies now fighting so nobly for democracy and the liberty of the world."[6]

Shortly after the special session in the Chamber of Deputies, Ribot informed Sharp that the French would be sending a mission to the United States "for the purpose of discussing the technical organization of [America's] overseas forces." Sharp learned that the senior military representative of the mission would be Marshal Joseph Jacques Césaire Joffre, the former commander in chief of the French army and a man whom Sharp greatly admired and respected.[7]

Joffre was born in 1852 to a family of humble origins, but he had shown promise early on and won admission to the illustrious École polytechnique in Paris. The Franco-Prussian War of 1870–1871 interrupted his studies when he and his classmates were mustered into the army to assist in the defense of Paris. Joffre served with the artillery during the siege of Paris; and following the war, he returned to his studies, graduated, and entered the army as an engineer officer.[8] After several years spent in metropolitan France, he sought action, and promotion, through overseas service in his country's expanding colonial empire. He served with distinction in campaigns in Indochina and Madagascar and led the expedition that captured the legendary African city of Timbuktu, in the process securing much of western Africa for France. His accomplishments and strongly republican political ideology enabled him to survive the turmoil of the Dreyfus affair and the *affaire des fiches*, which shook the French army's officer corps to its very foundation, and his star continued to rise throughout the years before the Great War.[9] After serving in a series of increasingly important positions, Joffre was named chief of staff of the French army in 1911, a post that converted to commander in chief when the war erupted in 1914.[10]

During the war Joffre emerged as a good commander, who nevertheless, like his contemporaries, struggled to come to grips with the massive industrialized conflict in which he found himself. Although his initial offensive in August 1914 was a failure, he displayed superior capabilities in holding his defeated army together during the subsequent retreat before turning to make a stand before Paris. Under Joffre's command the French army rallied along the Marne, contained the enemy advance, and fell upon the exposed flank of the overextended Germans. His ensuing counteroffensive drove the German army backward and ended their hopes of a quick victory in the west. The French victory at the Battle of the Marne electrified the world; it was immediately hailed as one of the great battles of history. Although other French commanders had played their part in achieving the success, and General Sir John French and the British Expeditionary Force (BEF) had also played an important role, the accolades for the triumph were heaped upon Joffre, who quickly became an international celebrity and was widely regarded as the greatest of the Allied commanders during the early years of the Great War.[11]

Joffre's reputation as the victor of the Marne was tarnished the following year after a series of French offensives in Artois and Champagne cost France over 1 million casualties yet failed to achieve the elusive breakthrough of the German line along the western front. The failures produced criticism from the French press and the government, and Joffre reacted strongly to both. He banned the distribution of certain newspapers in the French army's zone of operations and refused to allow politicians, including government ministers on occasion, access to the trenches. He created a virtually autonomous fiefdom for himself along the western front and in the process not only angered his opponents in the Chamber of Deputies but also alienated former supporters. For his part, Joffre increasingly believed that the enemy within was just as real as the Germans at the front and thought that his measures regarding security and censorship were necessary to preserve order and good morale among his men and to keep his latest military plans from appearing as front-page news before they even began.[12]

Throughout 1915 Joffre's relations with the government grew worse. By that winter he had pinned his career, and France's hopes for victory, on a massive Anglo-French offensive along the Somme, to be launched sometime in summer 1916. The attack was to be coordinated with a Russian offensive in the east, and Joffre hoped that this concerted action by all the Allied armies would destroy the Central Powers. But the Germans upset his plans when they struck at Verdun in February 1916, and the French army found itself drawn into a vicious battle of attrition that soon devoured the reserve divisions and supplies that Joffre had stockpiled for his own attack. Although the German offensive was contained, the French press alleged that Joffre had allowed the defenses of the Verdun sector to run down and that he had ignored warnings of an impending German assault there, charges that led to a direct attack on him in the Chamber of Deputies. The ultimately successful defense of Verdun enabled him to fend off these critics, at least for a time, but the incident made the forthcoming battle along the Somme assume an even greater importance for him.

The Anglo-French offensive at the Somme, launched in July 1916, involved only half the original French force that Joffre had planned for it, a result of the grueling attritional contest at Verdun, and although the French scored some tactical successes in their sector, neither they nor the British were able to deliver the promised breakthrough. This new failure prompted the political opposition to Premier Aristide Briand's government and Joffre's political enemies to renew their assaults on both men. As deputies began to speak out ever more forcefully against Briand's government, they increasingly used Joffre's alleged shortcomings as evidence of how the war was being mishandled.

As the Briand ministry slid toward complete collapse in autumn 1916, the premier attempted to deflect fire from his critics by taking the previously unthinkable step of removing the powerful Joffre from his position. Briand believed that relieving the victor of the Marne outright could severely damage French morale. He therefore decided to assign Joffre to a new position that would ease him out of power without causing a crisis of confidence in the government. Joffre was told that he was going to be promoted to a new position that would allow him to focus exclusively on military affairs in France instead of all French operations throughout the various theaters of war. He was suspicious and protested vociferously that he was still capable of fulfilling all his duties as commander in chief.[13] But with the Briand government collapsing, no politician was willing to sacrifice his career to save him, and Joffre found himself politically isolated. In December 1916 he was promoted to the rank of maréchal, the first such individual to be so exalted by the Third Republic, and named "technical military adviser to the government," with all the intended vagueness about his exact responsibilities that such a title implied. Joffre at first hoped he would still retain some control over the French army, but this was not to be. He was relieved of all duties at the front and sent to Paris, where he was given a spacious office and nothing to do. It appeared to be a premature end to a distinguished military career, but there yet remained one final assignment, and one last glimpse of fleeting glory, for Marshal Joffre.[14]

Joffre was summoned to the office of France's new premier, Alexandre Ribot, on 1 April 1917 and informed that the French government was preparing to send a joint political/military mission to the United States, then on the brink of entering the war. Ribot told Joffre that the former premier and current minister of justice René Viviani, a Republican Socialist and longtime antagonist of Joffre, would head the political contingent and that Minister of War Paul Painlevé had proposed that Joffre should head the military mission. Ribot informed him that he was the best person for the job because the marshal had considerable prestige in the United States and that "in France and throughout the world [Joffre] was the representative of the French Army."[15]

Having been treated poorly, in his view, by the previous government, Joffre was at first hesitant to go. Yet after a short while he relented and decided that perhaps he could accomplish something worthwhile in America that his present duties, which were virtually ceremonial, prevented him from doing in France. Joffre also concluded that "if our new Allies saw only political men [i.e., Viviani] arriving amongst them they might not get a complete and accurate idea concerning the military situation." He was further concerned to learn that Great Britain was sending a similar mission to the United States; thus, there would be competition for the potentially vast amounts of military resources that America could provide to the allied war effort. Joffre therefore agreed to accept the assignment.[16]

The French ambassador to the United States, Jean Jules Jusserand, informed U.S. Secretary of State Robert Lansing on 5 April that the French wished to send a mission to the United States, and Lansing so informed President Wilson the following day, stating that the French government wants "to express to you and to the American people the friendship and appreciation of the French Republic." Lansing had been informed on the same day by the British ambassador that they also wished to send a mission headed by the former prime minister, and current foreign secretary, Arthur James Balfour. Wilson was not eager to receive either delegation because he believed himself and his cabinet far too busy with urgent matters regarding mobilizing the nation for war to take time for what he deemed to be nothing more than diplomatic niceties. Nevertheless, Lansing was able to persuade him that it would be a good idea to receive both delegations to see what assistance they could offer to help ready the nation for war, and Wilson agreed.[17]

In the days that followed Jusserand's initial proposal, Ambassador Sharp was able to clarify further for the Wilson administration the important nature of the French mission. Lansing then instructed Sharp to "please inform the [French] Foreign Office that this Government is deeply gratified to learn of the proposed visit of Viviani, Marshal Joffre and the distinguished party that will accompany them." Subsequently, Jusserand telegraphed Paris: "The project of the Government of the Republic is accepted with great satisfaction by President Wilson." The French mission to the United States was soon on its way.[18]

As the mission's purpose would be to solicit American military support, Jusserand took care to keep the U.S. Army informed regarding the visit. After Wilson's formal acceptance, Jusserand immediately notified

Major General Scott that Marshal Joffre would like to meet with him personally to discuss various military matters relating to America's entry into the war. The visits of the French and British missions to the United States in 1917 have often been portrayed by historians as Allied missions, suggesting that they had a common agenda and worked in conjunction with each other. In fact, there was never any attempt by either the British or the French to coordinate their efforts. To the contrary, it is clear that from the moment of America's entry into the war the French rapidly moved on both the diplomatic and the military level to establish a unique bilateral military relationship with the United States that excluded the British.[19]

Joffre and the French mission set sail from Brest aboard the French cruiser *Lorraine II* on 15 April. The marshal spent most of his time during the voyage studying the U.S. military and attempting to formulate an idea of what form of assistance he could reasonably ask for. There were no guarantees that the United Sates would even commit a ground force to the war. American grievances against the German Empire revolved around Germany's violation of neutral rights on the high seas, and the powerful U.S. Navy was quite capable of addressing this issue. The economic power of the United States could also prove to be an invaluable asset to a French economy faltering under the strain of total war and desperately in need of loans and subsidies. However, the French government and military leadership believed that it was absolutely vital to their cause that the United States also send a powerful army to fight on the western front.

The U.S. Army numbered just over 135,000 officers and men on 6 April 1917, but with a total population of approximately 120 million, the available manpower was enormous. Therefore, Minister of War Paul Painlevé and General Robert Nivelle quickly agreed that the best method for utilizing American soldiers would be to amalgamate them directly into the French army. Just eleven days prior to America's entrance into the war Painlevé had notified the French military attaché in Washington, Colonel P. Vignal, that although the Americans would probably want to send their own expeditionary corps to Europe, he was afraid this would take too much time. Painlevé ordered Vignal to stress to the Americans that "it is desirable to send with little delay, small units, companies or battalions of volunteers." Painlevé estimated that at least 500,000 American volunteers should be sent in this fashion to serve in the French army.[20]

General Nivelle readily agreed to this proposal, mainly because it was as much his idea as Painlevé's. Nivelle informed the minister of war that he would organize the new volunteers into anywhere from 150 to 200 battalions of infantry, which he would amalgamate directly into his regiments to bring the depleted ranks of the French army up to full strength.

Nivelle pointed out that this plan had the decided benefit of providing France with immediate military assistance while they waited on the formation of the American expeditionary corps.[21]

On 13 April, Colonel James A. Logan, the head of the American military mission in Paris, informed the U.S. War Department of the French plan, which he dubbed the "Nivelle scheme." Logan informed his superiors that "all of the French are somewhat afraid of the efficiency of our military organization" and that consequently they were not confident that the United States could actually field a powerful military force on the western front in a reasonable amount of time. Nivelle had personally met with Logan and stressed that time was of the essence, confiding that the French had already lost over 2 million men killed, permanently disabled, or captured. Nivelle argued that the immediate shipment of raw American troops to be incorporated as individuals or perhaps as small units (companies or battalions) directly into the French army was absolutely necessary from the French point of view. Logan quickly asserted that this proposition would never be acceptable to the United States and strongly urged that the French reconsider their position.[22]

Painlevé was disappointed by Logan's stance against amalgamation and cabled the French military attaché in Washington that "after informal consultations with the [American] Military Mission now in France, [the Nivelle Scheme] has little chance of being adopted." Yet Painlevé was not prepared to abandon the idea just yet, hastily adding, "You can, nevertheless, if you deem it advisable, take the matter up again as it has the advantage of permitting important American contingents to enter the line on our front very rapidly." Clearly, then, even though the French government knew their proposal would be unpopular with the Americans, they still hoped that the French mission could persuade the Wilson administration to accept it.[23]

Fortunately for the United States, and in the long run for France, Joffre was adamantly opposed to Nivelle's plan. Joffre was informed of the French government's proposal for amalgamation before his departure, although he apparently was not told of Painlevé's meeting with Logan. As Joffre studied both his government's proposal and the American military, he recognized that the plan, though certainly beneficial to France, would be unacceptable to the United States. He believed that the Americans would insist on having their own army. He later wrote, "Upon reflection, the [French proposal] could not be defended for a single minute. No great nation having a proper consciousness of its own dignity—and America perhaps less than any other—would allow its citizens to be incorporated like poor relations in the ranks of some other army and fight under a foreign flag."[24]

Joffre therefore decided that the French needed to accept the fact quickly that the United States would want its own army. Rather than insisting on mere replacements for its army, France should provide assistance to the U.S. Army in the form of training, equipment, and advisers. Joffre later wrote that this form of assistance would help prepare the Americans to "play a role commensurate with their strength" on the western front. He also decided that, with Anglo-French rivalries for American assistance being rather acute at that point, he would seek for this new U.S. Army to fight beside the French rather than alongside the British.[25]

Joffre knew the immediacy of the danger that confronted France during spring 1917 and concluded that speeding along America's military commitment to the western front was essential to his country's survival. While en route to the United States he received the first reports of General Nivelle's highly touted offensive in Champagne. Joffre scanned the official communiqué and read between the lines of the news it contained. His head sank, and turning to one of his aides, he commented, "Things are not going very well." The French army had suffered a catastrophic defeat, and its morale plummeted to a dangerously low point. By the end of April, unbeknownst to Joffre, mutiny had broken out in several divisions, and by late May approximately 50 percent of the divisions were either in open mutiny against their officers or conducting sit-down strikes and refusing to attack. Although he did not know the full details of the disaster unfolding along the western front, he knew that France was teetering near the precipice of defeat and believed that the very survival of his nation depended on the success of his mission. He therefore determined that while he would counsel the French government to show patience, he would at the same time press upon American political and military leaders the necessity for sending at least a token force to France as soon as possible.[26]

On 24 April, the *Lorraine II* arrived at Hampton Roads, Virginia, and was greeted with full military fanfare by the U.S. Navy's North Atlantic Squadron, including the battleship USS *Pennsylvania*, the flagship of Admiral Henry T. Mayo, the commander of the squadron. Mayo and his staff visited the French mission aboard the *Lorraine II*, and they were soon followed by a distinguished group of dignitaries that included French Ambassador Jusserand, Assistant Secretary of State Breckinridge Long, Assistant Secretary of the Navy Franklin D. Roosevelt, and U.S. Army Chief of Staff General Hugh Scott. Joffre was most impressed by the Americans and later wrote, "From the very moment of our arrival, the deference and courtesy which were shown to us, on the one hand, and, on the other, the impression of order, power, and majesty produced by the warships which lay beside us gave me the feeling that America had espoused our cause with all her heart and that she was preparing to enter the struggle with manly resolution."[27]

On 25 April, Joffre and the French mission transferred to Wilson's presidential yacht *Mayflower* for the trip up the Potomac to Washington, D.C. As the vessel passed George Washington's home at Mt. Vernon, Joffre and the entire French mission stood at the salute while the band aboard ship played the "Star Spangled Banner" in honor of the great American military and political leader who had done so much to forge the first Franco-American military alliance during the American Revolution. Many times during the French mission's visit, the legacy of the American Revolution was referred to with great respect and reverence and the names of Washington and Lafayette invoked repeatedly, as if to seek a blessing on this renewed union of the two nations.

Arriving in Washington, Joffre was surprised by the wildly enthusiastic crowds who greeted the French delegation. All the schools, public buildings, and offices had been closed in the city in honor of the French visit, and thousands poured into the streets to greet the dignitaries, especially to catch a glimpse of Joffre, who was assuredly the most famous member of the delegation. The American public knew much about the victor of the Marne but knew little of the complex political machinations that had resulted in his relief from command. Thus Joffre, who had fallen somewhat into disrepute among his own countrymen, arrived in America to a hero's welcome.[28]

The French delegation was placed into two cars, with Viviani and his political advisers in the lead car and Joffre, accompanied by Major General Hugh Scott, in the second. The cars were escorted down Pennsylvania Avenue by two troops of U.S. cavalry to the frenzied cheers of the crowd. Joffre was immediately recognizable to the spectators because of the numerous photographs of him that had been published in American newspapers, both during the course of the war and in the days just prior to his arrival in Washington; thus, he was singled out for their attention and adulation. People along the sidewalks cheered and waved at the marshal, while passing drivers caught in the motorcade hung out the windows of their cars yelling, blowing whistles, and blaring their horns, adding to the general cacophony. An atmosphere of near hysteria seemed to have swept over the city's populace, and it all appeared to be directed at Joffre.[29]

Presidential aide Thomas W. Brahany, witnessing the French mission's motorcade and the frenzied scene in the streets it provoked, noted, "The greeting was more spontaneous and warmer than that given the British Commission on Sunday [22 April]. There can be no doubt of the deep affection of the people of this country for the French. The hero of the day was Marshal Joffre. . . . Everybody wanted to see the man who planned the battle of the Marne and probably never before has Washington given such a tribute to a foreign visitor as that represented in today's greeting.[30]

An editorial in the *New York Evening Post* summed up the day's activities: "It was a tribute not alone to the genius of Marshal Joffre—but a greeting to France, the country that had aided America when she was in need, a reflection of a national desire to repay in some measure an historic debt."[31]

Indeed, Joffre became an overnight sensation in the United States. Because General Scott was closely associated with the visit of the French mission he was soon deluged with requests from friends, acquaintances, and even complete strangers for photographs or mementos of Joffre and pleas to have the French marshal visit them. Typical of these letters was one received by Scott from his friend Palmer C. Ricketts, director of the Rensselaer Polytechnic Institute in Troy, New York: "My wife is crazy to see Joffre. . . . The understanding is that [he] is to be in New York at the end of this week and as I have some business anyway there I thought I could take her down and she might cast her eye upon him if I had any idea what they are going to do. . . . I know, of course, that he will be just as busy there as he is in Washington, but I want her to see him if she can. . . . We have a French flag out as well as one of our own in front of our house." Such letters are indicative of the pro-French frenzy in America that had been provoked by Joffre's visit and the entrance of the United States into the Great War.[32]

The accolades that the American people heaped upon Joffre had the unforeseen consequence of adding to the natural friction between the French civil and military representatives in the delegation. Indeed, during Joffre's tenure as commander of the French army, he and Viviani had often been antagonists. On the voyage to America the two men saw each other only when they dined at the captain's table, and even then they rarely spoke. As Viviani, a proud man with a fragile ego, witnessed the enthusiastic outpouring of acclaim granted to his rival, relations between the two men became even more strained. President Wilson's close adviser, Edward M. House, chatting with the mission's interpreter Émile Hovelaque shortly after the delegation's arrival, was informed of the differences between Joffre and Viviani. Hovelaque told House that Viviani was a socialist who had "no sympathy with military men or their methods" and consequently the two men were "continually quarrelling over the most trivial matters." Hovelaque blamed the arguments entirely on Viviani, who he asserted had become exceedingly jealous over the reception the American people had given to Joffre.[33]

On 27 April Joffre delivered a brief speech, through an interpreter, to the officers of the U.S. Army War College. He informed the gathering that he realized they were the elite of the army. He expressed his hope that these officers would soon be leading their soldiers into battle "side by side with those of [Joffre's] own country" who were "fighting now for what is right and just in Europe." His brief comments provoked thunderous applause from the officers, who were clearly highly motivated by the prospect of active service in France.[34]

After his brief remarks to the War College, Joffre went into a confidential conference with Major General Hugh Scott and other high-ranking officers. As late as 3 April, Scott had been opposed to sending American forces to fight in Europe and was especially wary of "entangling alliances" with European powers.[35] Yet since Joffre's arrival in Washington, Scott had become somewhat enamored of the French marshal, describing him as "a delightful man in every way."[36] Perhaps sensing that the Wilson administration was leaning toward the idea of sending an American force overseas, Scott had begun to warm to the idea of Franco-American military cooperation. Joffre stressed to Scott that the most important subject to discuss was the establishment of a cooperative relationship between the two armies. The marshal did not mention the British or Allied armies, but he emphasized the immediate need to establish a bilateral military relationship between France and the United States.[37]

Joffre stressed that time was essential, and although he realized it would take many months to build a powerful American army, he strongly urged that the United States send over at least a token force of one division as soon as possible. He proposed that this division be sent to France to undergo advanced training in modern warfare from instructors provided by the French army. Joffre realized that this American division would "lack many essential things, grenades, machine guns, trench mortars, infantry cannon, etc., [but] the French could make up everything which such a division would lack." He envisioned that this token division would represent the first phase of Franco-American military cooperation and would provide the foundation on which a powerful American army could eventually be built up in Europe, with French guidance and assistance.[38]

Joffre informed Scott that he believed it would be best to place these initial forces under overall French command but only until an actual American army was established in France. Scott then inquired if the

French intended to keep this nascent American army together or to scatter its units among the French forces. Joffre immediately replied that by all means the Americans should be kept together as "it was bad to divide an army." Scott and the other American officers were very much impressed by Joffre's knowledge of and experience in modern warfare and his friendly and cordial personality. The conference ended on a positive note, and a potentially powerful opponent to Franco-American military cooperation had been completely won over by Joffre's arguments and force of personality.[39]

In his meetings with Scott, as well as in later conferences with Secretary of War Newton D. Baker, Joffre urged the Americans to adopt a national plan for compulsory military service. He believed that this was the best and most efficient way to raise a large army in the shortest possible time. The marshal's call for American adoption of conscription did not come as a shock to the Wilson administration or to the U.S. Army high command. American military leaders had been urging such a course of action on the administration for several weeks, and a bill was even then before Congress concerning this very issue. Wilson and Baker both supported the plan, but they faced strong opposition in Congress, where critics vociferously denounced the practice of conscription as being unworthy of a great democracy. Wilson's congressional opponents claimed that conscription was "another name for slavery" and that a draft would "Prussianize America" by making it stoop to the level of the autocratic dictatorships that were the avowed enemy in this war. Joffre's position was delicate. As a foreigner, he did not wish to appear to be lobbying for the draft bill, yet at the same time he deemed the matter critical to the ultimate success of American military intervention in the war.[40]

While in Washington, Joffre stayed at the home of Henry White, a former U.S. ambassador to France and a strong Wilson supporter. With a congressional vote on conscription imminent, White arranged to entertain opponents of the bill at dinner parties where Joffre appeared as a guest of honor. After dinner many of these congressmen pressed him to give his views on the necessity for the pending legislation. With the assistance of an interpreter, Joffre stated his belief that such a step was vital if the United States was going to field a large army, and he spoke at great length on the benefits of and necessity for a national conscription act. He also held impromptu press conferences during which he spoke about the necessity for conscription. Joffre later claimed to have won over many converts for conscription among both the recalcitrant congressmen and the American press, and when the draft bill passed both houses of Congress by a large majority he took great pride in his part in aiding its passage. Many prominent French officers and government officials also credited him with having a significant impact on the final passage of the bill.[41]

There is no question that Joffre provided the Wilson administration and other conscription advocates with a powerful spokesman for the draft legislation. The fact that he was the representative of a fellow democracy that had used conscription to augment its army directly refuted Wilson's congressional opponents who charged that such policies were practiced only by autocratic governments. Moreover, Joffre's formidable military experience and international reputation as an expert on military affairs also lent considerable weight and credence to the position of the Wilson administration and to those congressional leaders who supported the bill.

Joffre, and indeed all the senior political and military leadership of France, viewed American adoption of conscription as positive and tangible proof that the United States was firmly committed to fielding a large army and sending it to France. He later wrote, "The consequences of this measure, adopted with such amazing rapidity, were destined to have a decisive influence upon the issue of the war."[42]

In the days following the passage of the conscription bill, Joffre quickly moved to impress upon Wilson, Baker, Scott, and other American political and military leaders the urgent need to send a token contingent of American forces to France as soon as possible. He realized that it would take many months before the U.S. Army was ready to assume an active role on the western front. Yet with the spirits of the French people and their army at perhaps their lowest ebb of the entire war, he hoped that even a small force of American soldiers in France would provide a desperately needed boost to morale, and the sooner they arrived the better.

Wilson's confidant Edward M. House met privately with Joffre on 30 April and had a short but quite frank and open discussion on the situation in Europe. Joffre emphasized that France had suffered grievous losses in the war and stressed to House the urgent need to send American soldiers to France as soon as possible. He explained that these men would need only rudimentary training in the United States, as the French could provide the advanced instruction. Even though he spent only a short time with the marshal, House was impressed with him and wrote in his diary that evening: "[Joffre] seems to have a well ordered mind, and appears to be the type of General well suited to the French in the time of stress which they were under when he was in general command." Joffre's steady and calm bearing reminded House of General Ulysses S. Grant, a comparison that seemed to please the French marshal.[43]

On 30 April President Wilson met with Viviani and the political representatives of the French mission at the White House. If Viviani and Joffre were antagonists in private, they still shared a common goal during their mission to the United States: to convince the Wilson administration of the necessity of sending American soldiers to France as soon as possible. In an emotional, forceful, and exuberant display of oratory, Viviani put forth his arguments for an American ground contingent to serve on the western front. Having already received reports from both Baker and Scott of Joffre's plans for military cooperation between the United States and France, Wilson was receptive to Viviani's proposals. The president spoke of France with great affection and of the suffering it had endured during the war and assured Viviani that he intended to establish full cooperation between the two nations on military matters.[44]

Viviani and Jusserand reported to the French government that they had accomplished a great success and that Wilson had promised to send one division of troops to France in the very near future, with more detachments following at intervals. Joffre then made a public statement to the American press corps, obviously with Wilson's blessing, advocating that the United States send an expeditionary force to France at the earliest possible moment. The Wilson administration withheld making a formal announcement on the subject at the time, even though privately it had already been agreed upon. Wilson apparently engaged Joffre as a point man for this project, and given the popularity of the marshal with the American people, it enabled him to ease the idea gradually into the public forum while dodging potential criticism from his political opponents. Indeed, Theodore Roosevelt, Wilson's fiercest opponent and critic, hailed Joffre's call for American troops: "I most earnestly hope that the request of General [sic] Joffre to the American people that we, at the earliest possible moment, send American troops to the front will be granted."[45]

On 1 May Joffre and Viviani appeared before the U.S. Senate. Significantly, only Joffre had been specifically invited by the senators, but Viviani insisted that the invitation applied to all the members of the mission, and he crashed the special session. He came armed with a speech that he delivered in French, with the assistance of an interpreter, which the senators politely applauded. After Viviani had finished, however, the Senate chambers suddenly began to resound with the chant of "Joffre, Joffre, Joffre!" as first the senators and then the crowd in the gallery joined in. An embarrassed Joffre, who had no prepared statement, finally appeared before the rostrum and simply stated, "I do not speak English." The senators and the crowd in the gallery ignored that and continued to chant his name. Joffre hesitated as he looked around the exuberant chamber and struggled to come up with an appropriate comment.

Finally, he raised his large right hand and shouted, "Vivent les États-Unis!" and then came to attention and saluted the senators. No speech or act could have had a more electrical effect. The senators and the spectators went wild as the shouts of "Joffre" were redoubled, echoing off the walls of the august chamber as the distinguished senators cheered "like college boys at a football game."[46]

Joffre went to the White House the following day for a meeting with Wilson to discuss the military aspects of Franco-American cooperation in the war. Joffre again emphasized the need for an immediate display of American involvement through the dispatch of a division to France as soon as possible and stressed that Wilson should not concern himself if the troops he sent were not fully trained. He informed the president that the American division "could leave the United States almost immediately and complete its training in France within the space of a month. After this period of intense training, it could gradually take its place in one of the more secure sectors of the front."[47]

In terms of transporting the force, Joffre urged Wilson to consider the advantages of landing the American troops directly in France instead of routing them through England, as had been contemplated. He also emphasized that the man who would eventually command the American forces in France (as yet unnamed) and his staff should be sent to France ahead of this first contingent of American troops. The future American commander thus could see to it that quarters for his men were secured and training areas established beforehand and could have a chance to inspect the sector that the American forces would occupy on the western front. Wilson agreed in principle with Joffre's proposals but expressed some concern, and perhaps a trace of embarrassment, when he admitted to Joffre, "I fear that, in the case of the present war, our army does not have enough artillery." Joffre said it would not be a problem: "France can provide all you need for the first division, from trench cannon from 58 to 75[mm], all the way to the heavy artillery which you lack. We are also in a position to give you grenades, machine guns, and the special weapons [trench mortars, flame-throwers, and so on] which you don't have."[48]

Joffre informed Wilson that the French mission would soon be departing for a tour of the United States but that he would leave behind several staff officers to help hammer out the details of French support for the nascent American Expeditionary Forces with the U.S. War Department. Although it was apparent to Joffre that Wilson had little interest in military matters, the marshal was nevertheless favorably impressed with the president's keen intellect and sincere desire to better understand the important military issues under consideration. Joffre left the meeting with "the conviction that the plans whose general outline I had just explained to [Wilson] met with his approval and that nothing I had proposed ran counter either to his patriotism or his good sense."[49]

Before the French mission began its tour, it was received by the House of Representatives on 3 May and given a reception that almost defies description. The Speaker of the House was unable to get out a single word, so loud and boisterous were the enthusiastic shouts and wild animated bursts of applause from the members and the visitors in the gallery. After numerous failures to bring the House to order, the Speaker finally gave up trying to deliver his prepared speech and allowed the members to file by the French mission and personally extend their best wishes amid the general acclaim and tumult of the crowd. Joffre later wrote, "Such scenes leave an impression which nothing can ever obliterate."[50]

The odd men out in this rapidly evolving bilateral military relationship between France and the United States were the members of the British mission. Anglo-American relations during the first years of World War I, though not warm, were initially cordial. However, British interference with American trade, both through their naval blockade of Germany and with sanctions against American companies dealing with the Central Powers, resulted in a decline in relations between the two countries that became acute during 1916. Wilson's increasingly hostile attitude toward the British prompted Secretary of State Robert Lansing to fear that the president would retaliate so forcefully to British interference that the United States would find itself aligning with the Germans. Although the French were sometimes lumped together with their British Allies in Wilson's anger, the fact that British actions were more overt, even confrontational, continued to make them a special target of the president's ire. It was not until Germany renewed its policy of unrestricted submarine warfare on 31 January 1917 that Wilson relented in his outrage against British interference with American economic activity.[51]

Many American policymakers also viewed the British with distrust and suspicion. The British Empire's powerful navy and its dominion over Canada made it the only Great Power that could realistically project its military might into the Western Hemisphere. As such, American military and political leaders viewed Britain as a potential threat to U.S. national security. The British alliance with Japan, a nation that the United States increasingly viewed as a major threat to its interests in Asia, caused many nightmarish scenarios to evolve in the minds of senior U.S. policymakers during the years of American neutrality. Indeed, as recently as December 1916, just four months before the visit of the French and British missions, General Scott had testified before the Senate Military Affairs Committee that the U.S. Army had to be built up in order to defend against a possible Anglo-Japanese invasion from Canada.[52]

During the course of the Great War this fear of a potential Anglo-American conflict kept relations between the two nations cool and distant. Although the British Royal Navy and the U.S. Navy directly cooperated in the war against the German U-boats, there was tension. Admiral William S. Benson, the U.S. Navy's chief of naval operations during the war, instructed his subordinate, Rear Admiral William Sims, who was assigned command of American naval forces in Europe: "Don't let the British pull the wool over your eyes. It is none of our business pulling their chestnuts out of the fire. We would as soon fight the British as the Germans."[53]

The British also viewed the United States with a certain distrust that was greatly exacerbated by the American campaign to increase the number of capital ships in their navy during the course of U.S. involvement in the war. The British wanted the Americans to focus their shipbuilding efforts on antisubmarine craft such as destroyers, but the U.S. Navy insisted on building new battleships and cruisers as well. With the German High Seas Fleet effectively bottled up after Jutland, the British openly wondered about the meaning of this American naval buildup. Indeed, the First Lord of the British Admiralty concluded that the United States was not thinking of the needs of the current conflict but was preparing for a future war against Japan or Great Britain. American naval planners considered the greatest danger America would face in the postwar world to be a conflict with the island empires of Britain and Japan, and the U.S. Navy prepared for just such a war throughout much of the interwar period. Though relations between France and the United States were at times strained, at no point did either country look upon the other as a potential adversary in a future war.[54]

There was also a deep feeling of hostility expressed toward the British Empire by the politically powerful Irish-American population and its large numbers of supporters in the United States. Although this animosity had a long history, it had reached a new level of outrage following Britain's suppression of the Irish Easter Rising in April 1916. Subsequently, the British government disregarded a formal petition from the U.S. Senate and a personal request from President Wilson requesting leniency for the leaders of the rebellion and instead executed most of them. The severity of the British suppression of the Irish revolt generated a tremendous amount of outrage in America, and in the months that followed a broad range of American society embraced the cause of Irish independence.[55]

Senators and congressmen repeatedly brought up the need for Irish Home Rule in their discussions with Lord Balfour during the British mission's visit, and American cities with large Irish-American populations sent delegations to Washington to seek audiences with the British mission to advocate Irish independence.[56] Under increasing pressure from Congress, Wilson and Lansing also urged upon the foreign secretary the need for British recognition of an independent Ireland. One newspaper account summed up the general attitude of many Americans by observing that Irish Home Rule was "scarcely second in importance to the triumph of democracy in Russia."[57] Speaker of the House Champ Clark urged Balfour to press upon British Prime Minister David Lloyd George the necessity for Irish independence and informed him, "Nothing will add more to the enthusiasm of America in the war than the settlement of the Irish Question."[58]

Thus, the attitude of the American public toward the British delegation was reserved, and nowhere did it approach the wild outbursts of enthusiasm that greeted Joffre and the French. Secretary of State Lansing met with Balfour and the British mission on 5 May 1917 and later recalled, "I thought it advisable to tell Mr. Balfour very frankly that the sympathy of the American people was far greater for France than for Great Britain, that there still lingered in the minds of our people the old feeling that the British Empire was our hereditary foe."[59] The members of the British mission could not help but notice the difference between the ambivalent way the American public reacted to them as opposed to the wildly enthusiastic reception that greeted the French. American newspapers commented that even the British "themselves [realized] that the public sentiment in the United States is more friendly to France than to Great Britain." A staff member of the British mission was quoted as saying, "The ties that bind the American and French people are closer and for that reason we Britishers feel the French are entitled to the highest honors and the greatest consideration."[60]

In 1917 most Americans did not perceive the British Empire as the embattled champion of democracy, as it was later portrayed. To the contrary, large segments of American society viewed Great Britain as an imperialistic nation whose actions, at least in Ireland, endangered democracy instead of promoting it. Significantly, unlike popular sentiment in America during World War II and the Cold War, during the Great War the American people looked upon France rather than Britain as America's traditional ally and as the foreign nation that most embodied the American ideals of democracy and freedom.

In addition to the political, historical, and sentimental reasons that attracted the Americans to the French, Joffre's proposals for how American soldiers could best be used were infinitely more palatable to the Wilson administration than the British scheme. General G. T. M. Bridges, the military representative of the British mission, presented a proposal that called for 500,000 American men (not soldiers) to be shipped immediately to military depots in England. These men were to be given nine weeks of training and then sent to serve as British soldiers in the depleted battalions of the British army. The British government argued that the formation and training of an independent American army could continue while these 500,000 men made an immediate contribution to the Allied war effort.[61]

Unlike Joffre, who had quickly realized that the similar position initially taken by the French government would never be acceptable to the United States, Bridges continued to attempt to promote his government's enlistment scheme to the Wilson administration. Despite Bridges's urgings, Secretary of War Baker (supported by Wilson) refused all suggestions for allowing American citizens to serve in the British army.

There were many reasons behind the administration's insistence on an autonomous American force in the field, a position that was shared by the American military high command and then enforced in Europe by General John J. Pershing. Certainly one of the most important was the concern over how the American people would react to their young men being in effect conscripted into foreign armies to fight under foreign flags. Aside from national pride, there was also the professional pride of the U.S. Army to consider, whose officers considered it a grievous insult that they would be simply dismissed as inconsequential.

The opinions of American officers regarding the British were also influenced to some degree by the historical ties between the French army and the U.S. Army. On a tour of George Washington's home and tomb at Mt. Vernon, Virginia, the only public event that was jointly attended by the British and French missions, there was some open joking among the American officers, including Major General Scott, regarding the British presence at the event. Scott remarked on the irony of seeing a former British prime minister and a British general paying homage to Washington alongside a marshal of France and a former French premier. Scott noted, "It is not remarkable that the French should be engaged in this, but the sight of such participation by the English has never been seen before, and would no doubt be a surprise to Washington if he knew about it."[62]

Once the Wilson administration had made its position on amalgamation clear to the British mission, General Bridges changed his tactics. His next move was to attempt to convince U.S. military and political leaders that if the United States insisted on sending its own expeditionary force, then that force should more closely associate itself with the British.

Bridges wrote to Major General Scott: "We have been told that the sentiment in this country is in favor of fighting with and for the French. We understand this sentiment. I think I have made it clear there are serious military disadvantages, and you will be sacrificing some of your efficiency for this sentiment."[63]

Bridges's intimation that an American decision to have its expeditionary force assigned to the French sector was based on "sentiment" instead of on military "efficiency" significantly reflects the British impression of the reception the American people, and their representatives in Congress, granted to the French mission. Nevertheless, the British believed (and hoped) that the U.S. government and military would make their choice with their head rather than with their heart, and it was to the Wilson administration's cold and logical side that the British made their appeal.

The nation's frenzied outburst of affection for France in May had a dramatic impact on the administration's decision regarding the deployment of the nascent AEF. Secretary of War Baker informed the British mission "that the likelihood was that our first expeditionary forces would cooperate more directly with the French." Baker later reported to President Wilson: "I think popular sentiment in our own country would approve cooperation with the French first rather than with the English." Wilson replied that he completely agreed with Baker on this issue and informed the secretary of war that in his meetings with the French mission, "I allowed General [sic] Joffre to take it for granted that such a force would be sent just as soon as we could send it."[64]

Joffre and the French mission left Washington by special train on 3 May for a whirlwind tour of the Midwest and the Northeast. Hundreds of American cities had issued invitations to the French mission and from these the French had selected those that were deemed the most practical in terms of travel time. The mission's tour was scheduled to begin in Chicago, a plan that concerned some members of the Wilson administration, who went so far as to warn Joffre that his reception there would probably be much cooler than what he had received in Washington.[65]

Chicago would be difficult because it had one of the largest German-American populations of any city in the United States. Chicago's Mayor William "Big Bill" Thompson called it "the sixth largest German city in the world" and openly opposed the extension of an invitation to the French mission to visit the city. At a press conference held on 27 April to announce his opposition, Thompson asked the gathered reporters, "Are these distinguished visitors here to encourage the doing of things to make our people suffer further or have they some other purpose? Our national officers seem to have their minds set on seeing how much they can spend and how much food they can ship out of the country. It is about time they considered the firesides at home." A reporter shot back, "We are a part of this war now," to which Thompson responded, "Are we?" That the mayor of one of America's largest cities would be so hostile toward U.S. intervention, three weeks after America's declaration of war, speaks volumes as to the initially ambivalent attitude of some Americans toward U.S. participation in this European conflict.[66]

Thus, the necessity for the French mission to rally American popular support for the war in general, and for France in particular, was a vitally important component of its visit. Indeed, one could even argue that President Wilson in part supported the French mission's tour of the United States in the hope that it would be able to encourage the support of the American people for the war effort. The former American ambassador to Germany was already barnstorming the country on just such a mission, speaking of the dangerous power of Imperial Germany and what needed to be done to meet this threat to democracy. However, he was being received with a polite, but hardly enthusiastic, response from the general public. Perhaps Wilson hoped that Joffre and the French would have more success.[67]

On 4 May the French mission arrived by train in Chicago and then proceeded by motorcade to the auditorium where they would make a formal appearance. Given the controversy that surrounded the visit, Joffre was understandably apprehensive about what sort of reception he would receive and was therefore shocked to see the massive crowds that turned out to cheer him. Newspapers that day announced in huge headlines, "Chicago Waves French Banner; It's Joffre Day," and "City Unites to Cry Vive la France." The populace turned out in full force to greet Joffre and the French.[68]

Many businesses closed early and the superintendent of Chicago's public schools announced that all schools would devote a portion of their classes to a study of the historical ties between France and the United States, with a special emphasis on Lafayette and the American Revolution. The public schools also conducted a program consisting of the singing of patriotic songs, a discussion of the importance of the French mission and its members, and readings from President Wilson's war message to Congress. At the conclusion of the program, the approximately 300,000 children were released from class early so that they could take part in the festivities surrounding the arrival of the mission.[69]

A tremendous throng of people lined the streets to get a glimpse of Joffre. The marshal waved to the crowd as onlookers shouted, "Papa Joffre!" "Hurrah for the French!" "Just hang on a bit longer. We're coming!" and

"We're with you general, we're with you!" Small children waving French and American flags shrilled out *"Vive la France!"* as Joffre's car slowly rolled by; the marshal responded to the children with a grandfatherly smile and then a stern salute, which delighted the crowd of onlookers.[70]

Throughout Chicago it was amply demonstrated that Mayor Thompson had been completely out of step with the vast majority of his constituents. As a skilled politician, however, Thompson had sensed the popular mood of the city and quickly reversed his position. On the day before Joffre's arrival, Thompson stated that his previous remarks were merely a big misunderstanding, and he unabashedly crashed his way onto the official welcoming committee put together by the city council. The press could not resist such a tempting target, and the *Chicago Daily Tribune* declared, "Big Bill Begins Learning to Say 'Bonjour.'"[71]

Outside the auditorium, a large crowd milled, hoping to catch a glimpse of the French mission. Tickets to the event had been quickly sold out and scalpers wandered outside the building selling them at prices ranging from fifteen to three hundred dollars, a princely sum in 1917.[72] Those fortunate enough to make it inside saw two large American flags stretched out to form a backdrop for the stage, with a French flag between them. On the white center stripe of the French tricolor, the word "Marne" had been stitched vertically in large bold letters.

The recently converted Mayor Thompson appeared and addressed the crowd, but they responded with jeers, whistling, and boos.[73] Somewhat shaken, he beat a hasty retreat while the Chicago band tried unsuccessfully to get the crowd in better spirits with various tunes, including "Onward Christian Soldiers" and "Tipperary," but the audience remained reserved. Then the band began to play "La Marseillaise," and as the stirring strains of the French national anthem filled the hall, Viviani and Joffre walked onto the stage. Although Viviani entered first, it was clearly Joffre who was the object of the crowd's affection. The hall suddenly began to resound with wild applause, as one reporter noted, "just as the crowds had cheered during the day wherever they got a glimpse of the hero of the Marne."[74]

The crowd produced a large number of French and American flags and began energetically waving them. Then the audience began to sing "La Marseillaise," and the tune was quickly picked up until the whole auditorium was belting it out at the top of their lungs, pronouncing the French words with more enthusiasm than skill.[75] It was only with great difficulty that Viviani was able to begin his speech. Speaking of 1914, when the Germans had reached the gates of Paris, he said, "While the enemy were temporarily successful as Fate was again against us, we withdrew until our

general had completed his plans of defense." Gesturing toward Joffre, Viviani continued, "He then gave us the order, '*En Avant!*' Then our soldiers, with blood in their eyes and determination in their hearts,
responded bravely." Joffre, overcome by the emotion of the moment,
wiped tears from his eyes with his large fist and then impulsively rose
and embraced his old antagonist, an act that brought the crowd roaring
to its feet amid an absolute frenzy of cheering. The auditorium exploded
into a sea of red, white, and blue, as American and French flags were
waved with equal intensity while the chant of "Joffre! Joffre!" resounded
through the building. It was indeed Joffre who captured the hearts of the
crowd and who most represented France and the French army to the
American people. More important, from the point of view of the French
mission's work, the American people were rallying to the cause of France,
personified by Joffre, and the tour was off to a better start than anyone in
the mission possibly could have envisioned.[76]

The mission's visit to Chicago set the tone for the rest of their tour. From
Chicago, it traveled to Springfield, Illinois, where huge crowds turned out,
as one Illinois newspaper observed, to give "vocal demonstration of welcome and the war spirit of Illinois." The French flag was flown just beneath the American flag atop the Illinois Statehouse dome, marking the
first time that any foreign colors had been so honored. Before heading
east, the French stopped in St. Louis, Missouri, where the city also gave
them an enthusiastic welcome. Speakers dwelled on the French origins of
the city and its French name and, sensitive to possible concerns over the
large German-American community who lived there, proclaimed the loyalty of the city to the nation and the cause of democracy. Toasts were
raised in honor of the French visitors, and both Viviani and Joffre showed
remarkable restraint in not being openly amused that the toasts, in an
America rapidly adopting prohibition, were made with water.[77]

Throughout the tour, the pattern of the French mission's appearances
remained the same: Joffre was the star attraction, and the various cities
where the French stopped seemed to compete with one another in show-
ering honors on the marshal. In Philadelphia, he was presented with a
marshal's baton made with wood taken from one of the rafters of Independence Hall. Joffre called the baton "a piece of real liberty" and extended to the gathered crowd "the greetings of the French army and an
expression of happiness in having the cooperation of the Americans."[78]

Although Joffre occasionally made brief remarks during the tour, he
was not an accomplished orator, and he felt especially uncomfortable addressing large crowds through an interpreter. However, he played a far
more important role as a symbol. His massive frame, his marshal's uni-

form and cape, and his large moustache made him instantly recognizable to the crowds. To many Americans he personified the cause of France and the heroism of the French army. The fact that he rarely spoke during the tour merely served to enhance his mystique in the eyes of the American public, who took him to be a brooding intellect with much on his mind, and the press often made comparisons to Ulysses S. Grant.[79]

At the end of the tour, an exhausted Joffre arrived in Boston, where his motorcade proceeded through a vast throng that police estimated at over 500,000 people, described as the largest single turnout for any event in the history of the city. An official welcome was given at the Massachusetts Statehouse, where a special joint session had been called. After being repeatedly cheered and praised, Joffre at length was coaxed to speak to the gathered legislators with the assistance of an interpreter: "I have heard several times in the course of our journey: 'Everybody loves you here.' In my turn, I shall tell you that we all love America. From now on, America and France are two sisters, bound with the links of a deep and enduring friendship. From this friendship will come at first the help and the aid which you will send to us; and, when peace is concluded, there will also spring from it an eternal friendship which will bind forever the two republics, France and America."[80]

Later that same day, Joffre attended a reception at Boston's historic Faneuil Hall. Only ten days earlier the city's mayor, James M. Curley, had addressed a gathering of 1,500 prominent Irish Americans in this very hall and denounced British rule of Ireland as an affront to democracy. At that same meeting the boisterous crowd had cheered lustily when another speaker read aloud the tonnage of British shipping sunk by German submarines.[81] The attitude toward the French was markedly different. Mayor Curley praised the French mission as he spoke of the American Revolution and the historic building in which they were gathered. He then added, "But Faneuil Hall is today no greater as an institution in the minds of lovers of liberty than is the distinguished guest of Boston. Every tradition and every aspect of love that make Faneuil Hall a treasure has been represented by Marshal Joffre in stopping the mad march of the Germans to Paris." The Boston press hailed the event and called Joffre "The Savior of Democracy in the Cradle of Liberty."[82]

At a later public function on the Boston Commons, Joffre was presented with a gift of $175,000, collected by schoolchildren and private citizens of New England for the war orphans of France. Money collected by private American citizens for these orphans had been presented to the French mission at virtually every stop of the tour, but this was the largest amount yet received, and Joffre was visibly moved by the gesture. He informed the huge crowd, estimated at over 100,000, that of "all the kindnesses showered by you on France, none touches us so deeply as what you are doing for the orphans of our heroic dead. Our children are our most precious possession, our joy and our hope, and there is no surer way to our hearts than to help these little ones, the most pitiful victims of this war for the liberation of the world. In their name, in the name of the soldiers of France, I thank you."[83]

Joffre returned to Washington, D.C., from his triumphal tour for one last meeting on 14 May with Secretary of War Baker, Chief of Staff General Scott, and their respective staffs. The final touches were made on the agreement that outlined the details of Franco-American military cooperation, laying out the program Joffre described to his superiors in Paris as the plan by which "the American army will be organized for the war."[84]

The agreement Joffre and Baker signed called for the U.S. Army to dispatch an expeditionary force "equivalent to a division" to France as soon as possible. It would be deployed in the French zone of operations, where it would begin training under French tutelage. It was agreed that the commander of the American force would determine when his men were ready to move up to the front.[85] As to the organization of the new U.S. Army, the Americans would adopt a "large combat unit similar to the type recognized as the best adapted to modern warfare; that is, an army corps with 2 divisions of 3 or 4 regiments each."[86] As these units were formed, they would receive preliminary training in the United States before being shipped to France, where they would "complete their training in the camps of the French army zone in the same manner as the expeditionary corps."[87]

On 20 May, while en route to France, Joffre prepared his formal report to Minister of War Paul Painlevé on the results of the mission's visit to America. In addition to including the formal agreement he had signed with Baker, he explained in detail his decision-making process in determining what military assistance he could reasonably ask for from the Americans. He informed Painlevé that he believed France needed "to concede from the beginning that the United States was capable of organizing a large army, that such was its desire, and that it would take any measures to that end."[88]

Joffre explained the current lack of readiness of the U.S. Army for modern war and informed him of the promises he had made to the Americans regarding French support in the form of equipment and training. Yet he encouraged the French war minister to put aside any doubts that the Americans were unwilling or unable to field a large army. The Americans, he wrote, would eventually prove instrumental in "hastening the victorious end of the war."[89]

Joffre expressed optimism for the success of the newly forged Franco-American military relationship and confidence that the Americans could successfully raise and organize a large army for overseas service. He did not believe they would be ready for active operations in 1917 but assured his government that the U.S. Army would provide "an enormous contribution to the 1918 campaign," as long as France did everything in its power to assist the United States in this monumental undertaking. He concluded his report: "The watchword that has come to me from the lips of the highest authorities, the most prominent men, and the masses is: 'For France, to the last dollar, to the last man.' The country and the Government merit our complete confidence; we have no Allies who are such friends. There is no sacrifice we should refuse to make in order to have their army join ours on the French front."[90] Ambassador Sharp was ecstatic over the news of the military agreement and wrote, "France and America were again brothers in arms for the defense of humanity and the liberty of mankind."[91]

Once again in France, Joffre was decorated by Painlevé for the tremendous success of the mission and praised by the French press and numerous political figures for his diplomatic skill. He quickly convinced the government to accept his proposals for military assistance to the Americans and obtained its assent for the construction of an autonomous American force, with French support, to serve with the French army on the western front. The agreement was thus completely accepted and widely distributed throughout various French government ministries and the army's high command. Painlevé was so impressed by the marshal's achievements that he named Joffre "Inspector General of American Troops." Joffre's initial responsibility in this new post was to convince the new commander of the French army, General Philippe Pétain, who had replaced the failed Nivelle only a few weeks earlier, of the wisdom of the plan.[92]

Joffre met with Pétain on 11 June and discussed in detail the agreement he had concluded with the Americans. As expected, Pétain balked at the idea of equipping and training an autonomous American army. Although he agreed to the general principle of American military autonomy, he did not believe that given the current crisis, the French could afford to wait on the construction of such a force. He therefore championed Nivelle's original scheme, arguing for individual American volunteers or battalions to be brought over to augment the French army directly. Joffre bluntly stated that such a plan was completely unacceptable to the Americans and that such measures could fatally delay the formation of the powerful American army that both he and Pétain knew to be essential for victory. Joffre also cautioned that reneging on the agreement could throw the Americans into the arms of the British. These arguments struck home, and at length Pétain relented, stating that he firmly agreed with the marshal on these matters and would do his best to implement them.[93]

Joffre, through the French mission's visit to America, securely established the foundation of the military relationship between France and the United States in the Great War, a relationship that proved vital to the military efforts of both nations. His work ensured that the United States would send an army to Europe to fight with the French, joining the military forces of the two great republics on the field of battle. Thus, contradictory to current perceptions and prejudices regarding Franco-American relations, the U.S. policy in the Great War was to establish its primary military relationship with the French rather than with the British.

The bonds of friendship that joined France and the United States during the war extended beyond the halls of power in Washington, D.C., and even beyond the military relationship between the two armies. As evidenced by the public's response to Joffre and the French mission, the American people in 1917 expressed a strong and heartfelt affection for France. They gave full vent to that affection as they welcomed the symbol of both France and the French army, Marshal Joffre.

Through his charm, intellect, and fame as the victor of the Marne, Joffre swayed not only U.S. political and military leaders to his agenda but also evoked a great outpouring of American public support for France. His ability to inspire the public for the war effort should not be overlooked. No democracy can effectively wage war without the support of its people. Joffre proved to be tremendously effective in rousing a martial spirit in the American people and in moving them to embrace France as a natural and historical ally in what the public viewed as a great struggle between democracy and autocracy. Although the United States had not had close military ties with France since the American Revolution, by the time Joffre and the French mission left America, the Wilson administration had committed itself to sending a powerful expeditionary force to France to fight beside the French army, and the American people enthusiastically supported this plan. Thus it was Joffre, more than any other individual, who established Franco-American military relations in 1917 and ensured that America's primary military relationship during the Great War would be with France.

CHAPTER 3

• • • • • • • • • • • • • •

The Arrival of the American Expeditionary Forces in France and the Crisis in French Morale, April–July 1917

Shortly after President Wilson pledged to Marshal Joffre and the French military mission that the United States would immediately send an expeditionary force to France, the president charged U.S. Secretary of War Newton D. Baker with appointing a suitable commander for the force. Baker was a small bookish man whose uninspiring physical presence concealed an intellect of the first order. A former student of Wilson's at Johns Hopkins University, he had made a name for himself in politics as mayor of Cleveland, Ohio, and as a progressive Democrat who had campaigned hard for Wilson in 1912 and again in 1916. Nevertheless, Baker, and many political insiders in Washington, had been surprised when Wilson had appointed him secretary of war in 1916. He had been involved with various pacifist organizations and informed Wilson that he had virtually no knowledge of military affairs other than the history of the American Civil War. Still, Wilson thought Baker was the best man for the job because of his intellect, good judgment, and loyalty to the administration. In the words of the historian Donald Smythe, Baker was "competence personified."[1]

Baker quickly narrowed the field of candidates for the position of commander of the AEF to two people: Major General Leonard Wood and Major General John J. Pershing.[2] Although both men were the same age, Wood had seniority in rank, and he also possessed an outstanding military record.[3] He had won the Medal of Honor for his role in capturing the Apache chief Geronimo in 1886 and had commanded the U.S. First Volunteer Cavalry Regiment (the Rough Riders) in the Spanish-American War, later serving as military governor of Cuba and as military governor of Moro Province in the Philippines. From 1910 to 1914 he had been the chief of staff of the U.S. Army, and he was widely recognized in both the United States and Europe as America's foremost military leader. Despite these qualifications for the post, he had two serious drawbacks in the eyes of President Wilson and Secretary of War Baker.[4]

The first concern was Wood's health, which had been steadily deteriorating ever since a freak accident he had suffered in Santiago, Cuba, while serving as military governor there.[5] While attending military maneuvers with Wood in Plattsburg, New York, in late 1916, Baker had noticed the general's poor health, which created in the secretary's mind an unfavorable impression of Wood's suitability for command. After World War I, Baker wrote to General Peyton C. March, who had served as chief of staff of the U.S. Army during most of America's involvement in the war, regarding the choice between Wood and Pershing for command of the AEF: "The last time I saw Wood before I made the selection he had a sham battle for my benefit and walked with me up a little mountain to get a place to view the battle. While walking up there he panted and labored so obviously that I came to the conclusion that his health was bad, and when I later came to make the decision between Pershing and Wood that recollection influenced the choice."[6]

The second major concern, and arguably the more influential one, was Wood's outspoken criticism of the Wilson administration and his involvement in partisan political activity with the Republican Party. During the period of American neutrality, from 1914 to 1917, Wood was a strong advocate of the preparedness movement and had been the driving force behind the establishment of camps in Plattsburg, New York, to provide ad hoc universal military training to American citizens. The White House tolerated Wood's extracurricular activities both because of his powerful Republican political connections in Washington and the widespread popular support his actions seemed to have among the American people. In August 1915, however, Wood aroused Wilson's anger when he invited the preparedness movement's leading advocate, and the Wilson administration's leading critic, former president Theodore Roosevelt, to come to

Plattsburg to address the volunteers. Roosevelt used the occasion to deliver a thunderous denunciation of the Wilson administration; from that point Wood was, for all intents and purposes, forever removed from Wilson's mind as a candidate for any high post.[7]

With Wood out of the running, Major General John J. Pershing remained as the best candidate for the post, and indeed to Baker he seemed to be the ideal commander. Pershing possessed everything that Wood lacked. Pershing's health was not an issue; he was in excellent physical shape. Moreover, he was as apolitical as any general officer of the U.S. Army could be, and although his influential father-in-law was a leading Republican senator, Pershing had always steered clear of partisan politics. Like Wood, Pershing had also strongly disagreed with the Wilson administration's handling of foreign affairs; however, unlike his competitor, he had kept his own counsel on these matters and had refrained from openly expressing his opinions, either to his superiors or to the press.

On 3 May 1917 Pershing received a telegram from his father-in-law, Senator F. E. Warren of Wyoming, a powerful and influential Republican member of the Senate Armed Services Committee, that simply stated, "Wire me to-day whether and how much you speak, read and write French."[8] Pershing immediately cabled back, "Spent several months in France nineteen eight studying language. Spoke quite fluently; could read and write very well at that time. Can easily reacquire satisfactory working knowledge."[9] Pershing, who at that time was serving as commanding general of the U.S. Army's Southern Department, knew full well the importance of this exchange of telegrams. Ever since the U.S. declaration of war against the German Empire on 6 April 1917, every senior officer in the U.S. Army had been eagerly awaiting word whether and when the United States would be sending over an expeditionary force to fight in France. Pershing knew that he was being considered for the post of commander in chief and could not help but interpret the telegram as a sign that his candidacy was moving swiftly forward.

Baker ordered Pershing to report to the War Department in Washington, D.C., where he arrived on 10 May. He was informed by the secretary of war that he had been chosen as commander in chief of the American Expeditionary Forces that were being formed to fight in France. Although in May he could only begin to guess at the task that lay before him, Pershing had just become the commander of what would in time be the largest army yet fielded by the United States. To his fellow Americans and their French allies, Pershing would come to personify the AEF and with good reason. It was to be built from the ground up under his direction and his supervision. Perhaps no other commanding general in American history was ever given as much authority to place his own indelible mark on an American army. Any discussion of the AEF in World War I has to begin with Pershing.

Pershing was born on 13 September 1860 in Laclede, Missouri. He entered West Point in 1882, and although he was destined for a military career, he originally harbored hopes of using the experience as a springboard into law school. The curriculum at the U.S. Military Academy was rigorous, and for Pershing the most difficult subject, ironically, was French. He never mastered the language, and indeed it was a constant source of frustration for him. The subject failed to yield to his normal solid study habits, and his grades in the subject dropped precipitously. His fellow classmate, Avery Andrews, later wrote, "I never knew Pershing to show any sign of fear, but probably his nearest approach thereto was his cadet attitude toward his instructor in French."[10] Pershing's poor marks in the subject brought him perilously close to a "deficiency" in French. In order to deal with this problem, he gave up first his dinner hour to use it as time for studying the subject and then, when that failed, he also devoted his Saturday afternoons (which were designated as leisure hours) to work on it. Gradually, the hard work paid off, and he was able to maintain passing grades in the language.[11]

Perhaps because of his intense and difficult struggles with the language, Pershing, unlike many of his fellow cadets and his instructors, had little interest in France or the history of the French army. It is ironic that the man who would be most responsible for establishing the U.S. Army's relationship with the French army in the Great War would have only scant knowledge of that nation's military history and its armed forces.

Pershing graduated from West Point in 1886, ranked thirtieth in a class of seventy-seven, and chose the cavalry as his branch of service. For many West Point graduates in the 1880s, the cavalry *was* the U.S. Army, since it offered the most promise for action on the western frontier and thus was the surest path to career advancement. In 1898 Pershing accepted a post as a white officer with the Black Tenth Cavalry Regiment and was sent to Cuba during the Spanish-American War. On 1 July of that year his regiment took part in the most famous action of the war, the assault on San Juan Hill and Kettle Hill. Pershing and his troopers charged on foot side by side with the famous First U.S. Volunteer Cavalry, the Rough Riders, and together the two regiments stormed the fortified heights overlooking the strategic port of Santiago. He later served with distinction in the Philippines and as an observer with the Imperial Japanese Army during the Russo-Japanese War.[12]

In 1916 the Wilson administration assigned Pershing to lead the difficult punitive expedition into Mexico to look for the Mexican revolutionary leader Pancho Villa. Although the expedition was ultimately unsuccessful, Pershing's tact in handling the potentially explosive situation in Mexico won him approval in the eyes of the Wilson administration and played a large part in Baker's decision to make him commander of the AEF.[13]

Baker and Wilson both had the utmost confidence in Pershing, but the French had only scant information about the new American commander. The French, like many Americans, had expected Leonard Wood to be named to the post, and they had to scramble somewhat to find out information about Pershing, a relative unknown. The French ambassador, Jean Jules Jusserand, notified his government of the appointment and briefed the Ministry of Foreign Affairs on Pershing's military background and experience. Jusserand reported that Pershing had distinguished himself in Cuba, the Philippines, and in the expedition against Villa and was by all accounts an excellent soldier. The French ambassador also informed his government that Wilson and Baker had the utmost confidence in Pershing, even though he was a member of the Republican Party.[14]

On 22 May 1917 the steamship *Baltic* set sail from New York City bound for Europe carrying the newly designated commander in chief of the as yet nonexistent AEF and his personal staff.[15] Pershing was sent to France by the Wilson administration to comply with Marshal Joffre's request that the commander of the AEF be sent over as soon as possible in order to establish immediately a liaison with the French government and military authorities. More important, as Acting Chief of Staff Major General Tasker H. Bliss said, "General Pershing's expedition is being sent abroad on the urgent insistence of Marshal Joffre and the French Mission that a force, however small, be sent to produce a moral effect. We have yielded to this view and a force is being sent solely to produce a moral effect."[16]

Traveling with Pershing was his chief of staff James G. Harbord. Like Pershing, Harbord was a cavalry officer, but he was not a West Point graduate. He had graduated from Kansas State Agricultural College (now Kansas State University) in 1886. In 1889 he enlisted as a private in the U.S. Army and began a slow and steady rise through the ranks until he was selected in 1891 for an officer's commission. He served with distinction as a staff officer and an adjutant general under General Wood in Cuba from 1899 to 1901 and developed a close and enduring friendship with Wood. Harbord was assigned to the Philippines in 1902 and served in various administrative posts there until 1914. It was in the Philippines that he first met Pershing, and the two men developed a great mutual respect. Harbord had an outstanding reputation for hard work and loyalty that made him a highly sought-after staff officer as the U.S. Army began to mobilize for war in 1917. He was Pershing's immediate choice for the position of chief of staff of the AEF.[17]

The voyage of the *Baltic* to Europe was hardly an easy passage, as the vessel zigzagged its way through the treacherous waters of a North Atlantic teeming with German submarines. Allied ships had been going down at an alarming rate since the kaiser's decision to resume unrestricted submarine warfare on 31 January 1917. Indeed, on the *Baltic*'s voyage to New York to pick up the distinguished American party, German torpedoes had narrowly missed it on two separate occasions, so precautions such as strict blackouts and frequent lifeboat drills were part of the daily routine of the American passengers on board. Harbord recorded in his diary, "A piece of dark paper is fastened over every porthole; all doors are kept closed at night and smoking or lighting a match on deck is strictly forbidden."[18] Moreover, the Americans wore civilian clothes, since it was assumed that if the vessel was torpedoed and it sank, the Germans would fire on lifeboats containing men in uniform.[19]

Other than worrying over a German submarine attack, the main pursuit of the American officers aboard the *Baltic* was learning, or relearning, French, an endeavor that consumed virtually all their free time. Harbord later remembered, "There was much brushing up on long-forgotten French and classes were organized where much violence was done to that beautiful language."[20] Pershing placed Colonel Benjamin Alvord, a former French instructor at West Point, in overall charge of the French language classes, and Pershing himself was a frequent participant. Also serving as French instructors were Major Robert Bacon, the former U.S. ambassador to France and the former secretary of state in the Roosevelt administration, and Captain George S. Patton Jr. Patton wrote to his wife Beatrice: "I have worked over five hours a day on French ever since we started and am one of the best on the boat which does not speak well for the others."[21] On 5 June Harbord recorded his struggles with learning the French language in his diary: "We are trying to learn '*La Marseillaise*' in the French, to read it if we cannot sing it, so that on occasion in France we shall be able to join in the chorus."[22]

On 8 June the *Baltic* docked in Liverpool, England, so Pershing and his staff could be greeted and wooed by the British military and political leadership before setting off for France. The Americans were given a military reception by British officers, assembled honor guards, and political dignitaries; although the official response was cordial, the British people themselves did not turn out to see the Americans. There was virtually no one at the docks, except for the official delegation and a small gathering of reporters. A royally commissioned train took the Americans from Liverpool to London, where again British dignitaries greeted them but no crowds. Pershing later recalled, "Our appearance on the streets [of London] attracted little attention."[23]

Beginning with King George V and continuing down the chain of command, British leaders repeatedly attempted to circumvent the Wilson administration's decision to place the AEF with the French army rather than with the British. Virtually every British leader Pershing spoke with during his brief stay in England made his own pitch to try to convince Pershing of the folly of Wilson's decision and the wisdom of the AEF serving with the British army. Pershing was given an audience with King George V, who spoke at length of his joy that "Anglo-Saxon peoples were at last united in a common cause." The British monarch added, "It has always been my dream that the two English-speaking nations should some day be united in a great cause, and to-day my dream is realized. Together we are fighting for the greatest cause for which peoples could fight. The Anglo-Saxon race must save civilization."[24]

After his audience with the king, Pershing paid a visit to General Sir William Robertson, chief of the Imperial General Staff. Pershing recalled, "Like all the British officials, he was much in favor of having our army serve with or near their forces. He pointed out that we were both Anglo-Saxons, spoke the same language, and gave other reasons to support his views." The inside joke, which the commander of the AEF had the good graces to keep from his British suitors, was that the Pershing (or Pfoershing) family was a combination of French Huguenot and German ancestors who had immigrated to America from Alsace in the eighteenth century.[25] Pershing asked for help from the British in shipping his soldiers to Europe but remained adamant that the American troops would be placed with the French. He noted that once this had been made clear to the British, their attitude toward him noticeably cooled. Robertson and the other British officers in attendance were dismayed by this "curious American penchant for the French," and Pershing left the meeting on less than cordial terms with his British hosts.[26]

The constant British references to the United States as being an Anglo-Saxon nation, though perhaps resonating among certain social elites in the United States, belied the fact that in 1917 the nation was ethnically diverse as a society. At the time of the Great War, of a total population of approximately 120 million people, fewer than 18 million Americans were of Anglo-Saxon ancestry, and America was still in the throes of a massive wave of immigration from southern and eastern Europe that had begun approximately thirty years earlier and that continued into the 1920s.[27]

The British leadership thus revealed a certain amount of ignorance about the American people, for although there were aspects of American social and cultural systems that reflected a heavy English influence, the population itself had undergone a radical transformation since colonial times. Southern, central, and eastern European ethnic groups, none of whom had any particular affinity for England, were numerous. The large and vocal Irish-American population was anti-English and had joined with German Americans, also a large and vocally Anglophobic group, in opposing American entry into the war from 1914 to 1917.[28]

It was absolutely hopeless for the British to try to persuade Pershing to go against his own government on any issue. Wilson and Baker had the utmost faith and confidence in him, feelings that he reciprocated, and their professional relationship was a strong one founded on mutual respect for the other's spheres of authority. Wilson and Baker had given Pershing tremendous authority in all matters military, and he respected and appreciated that fact by steering as far away as he could from political entanglements. As far as he was concerned, the British were discussing a nonissue; the Wilson administration had decided to place his forces with the French and that was the end of the matter. Heavy-handed attempts to conjure up an illusion of some sort of natural bond between the British and Americans because of their shared language had absolutely no impact on Pershing.

Pershing and his staff boarded a cross-channel steamer and arrived in Boulogne, France, on 13 June. The French greeted the American officers with all the pomp and ceremony that they could muster. A French honor guard was drawn up along the dock, and as the Americans pulled alongside, a large military band struck up the "Star-Spangled Banner." Pershing and his staff came to attention and stood at the salute as the band played, at that time, the unofficial American national anthem over and over. James G. Harbord noted, "Even [Pershing], who stands like a statue, growled over the number of times they played it." At last the band finished, but before the officers could relax, the musicians struck up "La Marseillaise" and played this at least an equal number of times, much to the consternation of the Americans.[29]

When the songs ended, a prestigious French military and civil delegation came on board officially to welcome the Americans to France. Harbord wrote that the French soldiers with "their funny little steel helmets and whiskers of various types" certainly looked strange but admitted that he probably made a similar impression on the French. Harbord was clean-shaven, which struck the French as odd because during the Great War virtually every French officer and soldier wore moustaches and some sported a full beard. Harbord commented, "International relations may stand the strain of my carrying out the wifely injunction to shave daily, but [the French] think I am a chaplain."[30]

Harbord's remark that the French helmets were "funny looking" is particularly interesting in assessing the impact of the French on his later service with their army. When Harbord received a combat command in summer 1918, a brigade and later a division under overall French corps and army command, he eschewed the regular-issue U.S. helmet, patterned after the British style, and instead wore a French helmet. In 1918 he even posed for an official portrait, which was later used as a frontispiece for one of his books, wearing the same "funny little" French helmet that he had joked about when he first arrived in France. This incident provides a strong statement on the change in his opinion of the French army during his service in the war from one of mockery to one of respect and great pride in having served with them.[31]

Although certainly there were similarities between the French and British receptions of the Americans, there was also an important difference between the two. In England, only military and political officials had gathered to greet them, but in France the local townspeople of Boulogne had gathered in large numbers to witness the arrival of the first American soldiers on French soil. Pershing was moved by the large crowd and was also somewhat embarrassed that he had no more to offer to the French nation at that moment other than himself and his staff. He later recalled, "It was a significant and solemn moment and I am sure that each one of us silently wished that our Army might have been more nearly ready to fulfill the mission that loomed so large before us."[32]

After the ceremonies at the dock, Pershing and his officers were driven through the streets of Boulogne, and large crowds turned out to see and cheer them. A special train then whisked them to Paris, where they arrived at the Gare du Nord later that same day. Awaiting them on the platform were various dignitaries, including Joffre and Viviani as well as French Minister of War Paul Painlevé, Chief of Staff of the French Army General Ferdinand Foch, and the U.S. ambassador to France, William Graves Sharp. Unlike in Boulogne, the ceremonies at the Paris station were brief and informal and consisted mainly of Pershing being introduced to the distinguished members of the welcoming committee. Once again though, massive crowds turned out to see the Americans and lined the route of the motorcade from the station to the Hôtel Crillon, which had been designated as temporary headquarters for the AEF. Pershing reported that "the wildly enthusiastic reception" from the crowds reflected the "deep feeling existing among French people over our participation in this war."[33]

Pershing and his staff were paired off in automobiles with various French dignitaries and then driven straight into a maelstrom of patriotic pandemonium. In sharp contrast to England, where Pershing and the Americans had "attracted little attention" on the streets of London, Paris went wild with a frenzied outpouring of emotion. It seemed as if the entire population of the city had turned out, as dense crowds lined the streets waving French and American flags, cheering and lauding their new allies. The naturally reserved Pershing was completely taken aback by the reception. At several points, the crowds surged past the police and into the streets, blocking the motorcade. French women dashed up to the automobiles, leaped onto the running boards, and even climbed into the cars, attempting, with some success, to kiss and embrace the American officers.[34]

Harbord later wrote to his wife that the people of Paris "cheered and shouted and wept as only a French crowd can do. My [car] was half-swamped in roses; shouts of 'Vive l'Amérique' filled the evening air; people crowded near and elbowed each other to touch my hand; pretty girls smiled at [this] old American soldier; and Colonel de Chambrun kept saying, 'Salute Colonel, salute. It is for you.'" For Pershing, the scene was moving but also disturbing. He later wrote of the reception he had received in Paris: "It was most touching and in a sense most pathetic. It brought home to us as nothing else could have done a full appreciation of the war-weary state of the nation and stirred within us a deep sense of the responsibility resting upon America."[35]

After being allowed a brief time to settle in at the Hôtel Crillon, Pershing and his staff, at the request of the French army and government, began a series of public appearances designed to bolster French morale. Pershing's first stop was the place that had so impressed him when he had first visited Paris as a young officer in 1899, the Hôtel des Invalides. Built by King Louis XIV as an old soldiers' home for the veterans of his wars, the complex of buildings had been greatly expanded during the reign of Emperor Napoleon I. In 1840 Napoleon's body was brought to the Invalides and encased in a mammoth sarcophagus that was placed beneath the dome of the chapel of St. Louis, named for Louis IX, the crusading French king who had been canonized by the Roman Catholic Church. By 1917 the Invalides had been made the home of the Musée de l'Armée and the entire complex of buildings transformed into a stirringly romantic tribute to the French army.[36]

Pershing was escorted into the crypt of the Invalides, where priceless mementos of the great French emperor's reign were kept, including Napoleon's uniforms, medals, and sword. The sword was carefully taken from its case and offered to the commander of the AEF, "as if to transmit some of the genius of the great captain," Pershing later recalled. Pershing did not quite know what to do, so he stood rigidly at attention and then bent forward and gently kissed the sacred blade. This act was received with great acclaim by the gathered French officers and dignitaries and made a profound impression on the officers of his own staff, who were taken aback, yet pleased and moved, by Pershing's romantic gesture.[37]

Unlike some American officers, Pershing had no great affection for, or interest in, Napoleon and his campaigns. One might be tempted, then, to consider Pershing's action as merely a political act of showmanship meant to impress his new allies. Yet it is difficult simply to dismiss his gesture as shallow because he was not given to displays of emotion, either public or private, and was not by nature a showman of any sort. In the cold and sober light of reflection, Pershing omitted from his memoirs the fact that he had kissed the blade, saying merely that it was offered to him. It is indeed plausible that the emotion and excitement of those first days in Paris, and the tumultuous reception, may have simply overwhelmed the stoical professional soldier. He later wrote of his visit to the Invalides and Napoleon's crypt: "So much of French sentiment and tradition are associated with this tomb and its treasures that every one who visits there with Frenchmen must share their feelings of profound emotion. This incident, more than any other connected with my reception, impressed me with the martial spirit of the French people."[38]

The French martial spirit was sorely in need of bolstering in June 1917. Unbeknownst to Pershing and his staff, the French nation and army were passing through the direst period of danger in the history of the Third Republic. After enduring nearly three years of sacrifice and bloodshed on an unprecedented scale, the nation appeared to have reached the end of its physical and spiritual strength when the greatly anticipated and highly publicized Nivelle Offensive met with disaster in April 1917.

In order to understand the conditions in France and the state of the French army in June, it is important to understand what had transpired there in the two months after America entered the war. The events from April to June of that year demonstrate that France was in desperate need of American assistance and that even the token gesture of Pershing's arrival had an immediate impact on the restoration of French morale just when the nation was on the brink of defeat.

At the time of America's entry into the war, General Robert Nivelle was the commanding general of the French army.[39] He was a lively and boisterous commander who had first risen to fame as the supposed architect of the French tactical victories at Verdun in October and December

1916. His Second Army had succeeded in retaking Ft. Douaumont and Ft. Vaux and had pushed the Germans back almost to the original positions they had occupied when they had first begun their massive effort against Verdun in February. Nivelle was given credit by the French government for the victories and was deemed a genius for developing the "rolling barrage" as a means of providing continuous artillery fire-support for advancing troops. This governmental acclaim purposefully overlooked the fact that his superior, the army group commander General Pétain, had actually formulated the battle plans for the offensives and had contributed far more to the victory at Verdun than Nivelle had.[40]

However, Pétain had made many enemies in the French government, enemies who were not eager to strengthen his hold on the army or his popularity with the people by acclaiming him the victor of Verdun. Nivelle, on the other hand, had ingratiated himself with the politicians of the Third Republic, inviting them to visit his headquarters and charming them with his wit and his apparent interest in their ideas. French politicians made wonderful speeches on the floor of the Chamber of Deputies, singing Nivelle's praises. Meanwhile, Pétain, like Joffre, neither liked nor trusted politicians anywhere near the front, and he made no secret of his disdain for the armchair strategists of the chamber. Thus, in December 1916, when Joffre was relieved of command by the French government, it was Nivelle who was named as his replacement and not Pétain, a decision that displeased many in the French army.[41] Although Joffre supported Nivelle's promotion, it was an unpopular decision with a large segment of the French officer corps. The French writer Gabriel Terrail observed that Nivelle was "commander in chief by choice of the government, not by the acclamation nor even the tacit assent of all his subordinates."[42]

Primarily, the government had named Nivelle because he promised that he would deliver a victorious conclusion to the war in 1917, something neither Joffre nor Pétain was rash enough to do. Nivelle announced, "I have the formula for victory," and he loudly, and indiscreetly, proclaimed that he would break the stalemate on the western front and end the war in a single dramatic offensive. He essentially intended to do with armies what he had done with regiments at Verdun, coordinate rolling artillery barrages with advancing infantry to form an irresistible force capable of breaking through the German defense system. Nivelle's plan called for a massive concentric attack against the German salient in Champagne, along the Aisne River and the Chemin des Dames ridge. He intended to strike a blow of "supreme violence" that would rupture the German front lines within twenty-four hours, whereupon he would unleash his "mass of maneuver," twenty-seven divisions of infantry and cavalry that would pour through the breach, breaking open the German defense system on the western front. Nivelle's plan, as he explained to eager politicians in his headquarters, with broad sweeping movements of his hands over the map, would liberate virtually all of occupied France in a matter of weeks and carry the fight into Germany itself.[43]

Many Frenchmen, soldiers and civilians alike, believed Nivelle's promises, if for no other reason than because they wanted to believe. After nearly three years of suffering horrific casualties and with little to show for the tremendous sacrifice, the French were desperate for a military leader capable of leading them to the final victory that would end the war. Colonel Jean de Pierrefeu, a French staff officer at GQG, recalled that after meeting Nivelle for the first time he wondered, "Was this the man destined by Fate to be the savior of his country? . . . Was this the miraculous soldier whom so many Frenchmen awaited, and who would restore order to democracy after having conquered the enemy?"[44]

Unfortunately for France, Nivelle's plan of attack went awry almost from the start because of a serious defect. Due to the massive scale of the operation, the French were unable to provide the same concentration of artillery fire along the whole front that they had achieved during their limited offensives at Verdun. And Pétain had been the real architect of those victories. His mastery in forging the artillery into a unified force capable of hammering the enemy into submission and achieving fire superiority over the battlefield had proven the key to French success there. But now Nivelle was out from under Pétain's shadow, and guidance, and Nivelle's grandiose plan, though an imitation of the Verdun offensives, failed to provide the concentration of firepower so important to Pétain's proven methods of war.

Nivelle was also terribly indiscreet in his comments regarding the operation. In his effort to take the troops into his confidence, his plan of operation was distributed down to company level. In some ways this boosted French morale, but secret details of the forthcoming operation began to show up in the soldiers' letters, much to the dismay of French intelligence officers. Nivelle himself also spoke far too freely to the French and foreign press regarding the operation. Such indiscretion meant that German intelligence officers did not have to work very hard to discern that a major offensive was in the offing and where and when the French would strike.[45]

Armed with this information, the Germans moved quickly to prepare themselves for Nivelle's assault. They used the first months of 1917 to build the strongest fortified position in the world (*Siegfried Stellung*, nicknamed the Hindenburg Line by the Allies) behind their front line along the north-central sector of the western front. Their new defense system implemented everything they had learned in nearly three years of trench warfare. The Hindenburg Line was not just one trench line but in actuality was an in-depth defensive system, in some locations as many as five layers deep. These defensive works consisted of steel-reinforced concrete bunkers and trenches laced together by a web of interlocking defensive fire from machine guns and supporting artillery that created a zone of death, where no attacker could long survive. Massive belts of barbed wire, hundreds of feet wide and eight feet high, were placed before the frontline trench as well as in between the successive defensive lines, and German gunners methodically zeroed in their artillery on all the likely avenues of advance. It was without question the best constructed and, in 1917, the best defended trench system ever devised during the Great War.[46]

With their new defense system constructed, Field Marshal Paul von Hindenburg and General Erich Ludendorff executed a series of carefully planned and flawlessly executed tactical withdrawals that began on 9 February 1917 and continued in phases through March. In a little over one month of secretive, retrograde movements, the Germans completely withdrew their forces from the vulnerable salient that Nivelle had intended to strike and moved into the carefully prepared defensive positions of the Hindenburg Line. The one area of the intended offensive where the Germans did not fall back was the Chemin des Dames ridge, which they instead heavily reinforced by carefully placing their troops in newly built defensive positions on its reverse slope while leaving a sparsely occupied front line.[47]

In mid-March, as the French high command became dimly aware that something was amiss, patrols sent forward to occupy the now abandoned salient discovered that the retreating Germans had converted the area into a wasteland. Every building had been demolished, every orchard cut down, forests burned, wells and reservoirs poisoned, roads and bridges destroyed, and booby-traps placed everywhere to kill or maim the unwary. French troops took up a slow pursuit of the retreating Germans, and as they moved through this scene of desolation, they soon ran into the new defense system looming before them.[48]

In light of these new developments along the sector of the proposed offensive, several senior French commanders openly argued that Nivelle should cancel the attack, or at the very least postpone the assault until a new plan of operations could be devised. These arguments were not sent to Nivelle but to certain members of the French government, including the new war minister, Paul Painlevé.

As the controversy over Nivelle's offensive began to build within the high command, Premier Aristide Briand's government suddenly collapsed in March under heavy pressure from the French Left, mainly French Socialists, Radical Socialists and Radical Republicans. This group was furious over Briand's failure to be more forceful in his dealings with the French army, an issue brought to a crisis when the Left had become incensed over insults, both real and imagined, hurled in their direction by Minister of War General Hubert Lyautey. In the parliamentary upheaval that followed, the aged finance minister Alexandre Ribot became the new premier and the prudent mathematician Paul Painlevé became the new minister of war. Painlevé was hardly the antimilitary republican that the Left had sought for the post, but he was certainly no friend of General Nivelle, and that sufficed. Indeed, in December 1916 Painlevé had refused the post of minister of war in Briand's government because he had insisted that he would accept only if Pétain, not Nivelle, was named commander in chief of the French army.

When reports of the German withdrawal reached Painlevé's desk, the new minister of war began to develop serious reservations about Nivelle's offensive. It was clear that the tactical situation along the western front had changed dramatically and that the strategic situation had changed as well. In March 1917 Russia was convulsed by revolution, and although the provisional government that replaced the czar appeared willing to continue the war, it was apparent that little could be expected from the Russian army in the way of a major offensive that year.[49] Painlevé believed that the peripheral theaters of war along the Italian front and in the Balkans offered little support for the French armies on the western front. Italy was feeling the strain of war after its army had bashed itself senseless for two years against the Austrian strongholds in the Alps, and the Allied forces based at Salonika were simply too few in number and lacked the logistical support necessary to make a serious threat to the Central Powers in the Balkans. Thus, Painlevé concluded that Britain and France could attack on the western front, according to Nivelle's plan, but that if they did so they would be facing an undistracted German army capable of bringing its full might to the battlefield.[50]

Meanwhile, the news that the United States had broken diplomatic relations with Germany and appeared to be on the brink of entering the war promised to be the event that, in time, would offset the collapse of Russia and tip the scales irrevocably in favor of the Allies. Therefore, it was clear to Painlevé that the wise course would be to delay taking the offensive until the Americans could arrive in force and that there was no need for Nivelle to strike immediately in an all-or-nothing attempt to win the war.[51]

Painlevé met with Nivelle on 22 March to discuss what changes the general was making in his plans based on the new information, only to be astonished to learn that he was not contemplating any changes. Instead of pinching off a salient, Nivelle explained, his armies would simply break through the enemy line in a frontal assault. He pointed out that the German position along the Chemin des Dames remained unchanged from when the original plan had been conceived; thus, there was no reason to cancel the attack in that sector. Besides, Nivelle argued, his formula would work, regardless of the tactical situation confronting it. Only minor details regarding shifting the jumping-off points for the attack needed to be made. Surprised, Painlevé pointed out to Nivelle that intelligence reports indicated the Germans were expecting the attack and that although they had not withdrawn from the Chemin des Dames, their defenses there had been heavily reinforced. "I do not fear numbers," Nivelle said. "The greater the numbers the greater the victory."[52]

Nivelle's confidence in the operation appeared to be unshakable, but other commanders were beginning to have grave doubts about the operation. On the same day that Painlevé met with Nivelle, General Micheler, commanding the Reserve Army Group (GAR), whose forces were charged with launching the main offensive operation along the Chemin des Dames, wrote to the minister of war. He pointed out that the new German positions were strong, established in depth, and held in great strength and that he did not believe there was a realistic chance of achieving a breakthrough. Painlevé then summoned Micheler, to speak to him in person on these matters. Micheler, invited to speak freely, stated that although Nivelle's initial plan had merit, the new situation along the front had changed everything. Instead of the concentric attacks against an exposed enemy salient that the original plan had set out, the German withdrawals now forced the French essentially to make a frontal assault against carefully prepared and strongly held positions. Consequently, Micheler believed that there was little hope of achieving the type of breakthrough and rapid exploitation that Nivelle had envisioned for the operation.[53]

A profoundly disturbed Painlevé sought out the opinions of other French generals; as he did so his level of concern grew. General Pétain, commander of the Central Army Group (GAC), joined the swelling ranks of critics and informed the minister of war that the attack as designed was folly and urged that its objectives be reduced to a more realistic goal of obtaining a local tactical success. Pétain warned that Nivelle's attempt to achieve a massive breakthrough along a broad sector of the front would lead only to slaughter.[54]

As protests mounted and the day of the attack grew nearer, the highest governmental and military officials in France met at Compiègne on 6 April to discuss the forthcoming offensive. Among others attending the meeting were Premier Ribot; President Raymond Poincaré; Painlevé, representing the government; and Nivelle and his four army group commanders, representing the French army. At the meeting Poincaré and Painlevé both urged Nivelle to reconsider his offensive and pointed out that with the American declaration of war (which became official that day), the United States would soon contribute a mighty army to the Allied cause. Thus the French ministers argued that there was no need to risk the last manpower reserves France had on a chancy offensive. Nivelle listened in silence then tersely replied, "The offensive alone can give victory; the defensive gives only defeat and shame." Frustrated, Poincaré and Painlevé turned to the assemblage of senior officers and asked their opinions about the coming battle.[55]

In the presence of their commander in chief, the French officers, critical when cloaked in anonymity, now gave evasive answers that essentially supported Nivelle, except for Pétain. When asked by Poincaré and Painlevé for his opinion on the operation's chances for success, Pétain stated that he believed the French army could possibly rupture the German defenses but that there would be no point to it, as they lacked sufficient reserves to exploit such a breakthrough on the scale that Nivelle envisioned. Pétain asked, "Have we five hundred thousand fresh troops to make an advance? No. Then it is impossible."[56]

Nivelle, furious, interrupted Pétain and began blurting out historical examples from the campaigns of Napoleon to support his position. Pétain later recalled that he had to contain his amusement at such a dire moment, as Nivelle hopelessly confused the facts of the campaigns to the point that it became apparent he knew little about the Napoleonic Wars. Nivelle was angered by what he quite rightly interpreted as a lack of support for his plan, both from the government and his immediate subordinates. Dramatically, he offered to resign, a move that apparently neither Painlevé nor Poincaré were prepared for. All of France knew about the impending offensive, as did everyone in Germany for that matter, and the troops were just days away from launching the attack. For the commander in chief of the French army to resign his post on the eve of the great battle was unthinkable. The political repercussions from such an event could be enough to bring the new Ribot government crashing down almost before it had begun to govern.[57]

Sensing that his threat to resign had achieved its desired affect, Nivelle once more became the charmer and promised that he would not allow the battle to turn into another grim attritional struggle like Verdun or the Somme. To this end, he vowed that if he were not successful within forty-eight hours, he would cancel the remainder of the operation. At this point, Painlevé and Poincaré decided that perhaps the prudent course to follow was to let Nivelle have his battle. After all, he just might be correct, and this could be the decisive moment of the war. If he was wrong, they reasoned, how much harm could possibly be done in forty-eight hours? The French politicians and most of the French army commanders backed down, much to Pétain's visible disgust, and Nivelle was granted permission to proceed with his offensive.[58]

The divisive arguments among the French high command were virtually unknown in the frontline trenches. The correspondence of the common French soldiers in the weeks leading up to the attack reveal that they were generally in high spirits; in particular, the divisions chosen to lead the assault demonstrated a high level of morale. Nivelle's promise to achieve victory within forty-eight hours or to halt the offensive had spread to the ranks, and this news lent an even greater degree of confidence to the frontline *poilus*. Indeed, it appears that Nivelle's promise had an intoxicating effect on many French soldiers, and even battle-hardened veterans allowed themselves to dream of victory and the long sought-for end of the war.[59]

After a brief but violent preparatory artillery barrage, the French *poilus* went over the top on 16 April in a driving storm of snow mixed with freezing rain and hurled themselves against the Hindenburg Line and the heavily fortified German positions along the Chemin des Dames ridge. To their dismay, the French assault battalions quickly discovered that the initial bombardment had failed to open sufficient gaps in the vast belts of barbed wire. As the troops struggled through the twisted maze of wire entanglements at an agonizingly slow pace, German machine guns and artillery, carefully emplaced and well protected, began to exact a frightful toll.[60]

Nivelle's formula of using rolling artillery barrages to support the infantry quickly broke down as the fires moved forward according to a rigid timetable based on overly optimistic estimates of how much ground the infantry could cover in the initial assault. Because the frontage of the offensive was much broader than that of the French counteroffensives at Verdun, the French artillery fire was more widely dispersed and consequently far less effective than it had been the previous autumn. Unlike at Verdun, German defenses were well constructed and deeply held, and, again unlike at Verdun, the Germans were not taken by surprise.

When the infantry advance bogged down in the face of heavy German resistance, the *poilus* watched in dismay as their artillery fire rolled remorselessly forward according to the timetable and left them stranded in

No Man's Land, facing heavily entrenched Germans. Aerial observation, which had been critical to coordinating these types of barrages in Nivelle's previous attacks, was poor due to the foul weather and the suddenly resurgent Imperial German air force.[61]

The German air force, which had lost control of the skies over Verdun, had regained its footing by spring 1917. The introduction of their new Albatross D-III fighter aircraft enabled the Germans to inflict massive losses on both the French Service Aéronautique and the British Royal Flying Corps, during what the British dubbed Bloody April. Exemplifying German mastery of the air during this offensive is the grim statistic that during this one month the German ace Manfred von Richtofen (the Red Baron) scored twenty-one kills, or roughly one-fourth of his total kills for the entire war. In the face of these catastrophic losses, neither the Royal Flying Corps nor the Service Aéronautique was able to provide adequate air support to Nivelle's offensive.[62]

Deprived of proper aerial reconnaissance to locate German guns and troop concentrations and lacking aerial observation to direct the fire of their gunners, the French were unable to coordinate closely the rolling barrages with the advancing infantry; consequently, Nivelle's formula broke down within hours of the opening of the attack. Yet the French infantry displayed remarkable élan and tenacity in their attacks and succeeded in clawing out a toehold in the German defenses—but at a frightful cost in casualties. As reports filtered in of the failure of the initial attacks to achieve the anticipated breakthrough, Nivelle ignored his promise to break off the offensive within forty-eight hours and instead committed wave after wave of infantry to the increasingly futile assaults.[63]

Nivelle demanded that his subordinates display an aggressive spirit, and commanders such as General Charles Mangin, commanding the French Sixth Army, complied with his wishes, only to see their forces chewed to pieces by the Germans. Nivelle's imprudent and badly coordinated attacks achieved only minimal gains at an exorbitant cost in lives, and he soon had squandered what was left of the cream of the French army. During the week of 16–23 April, the French army lost approximately 32,000 men killed and 85,000 wounded. Even Nivelle's confidence was at last shaken. Desperate for a solution, he sought out the advice and support of his former chief, Pétain.[64]

On 27 April Nivelle asked Pétain if he would be willing to join his staff as an adviser, but Pétain curtly refused. He had no intention of joining the staff of an individual whose ability to command the French army he seriously questioned. It is also distinctly possible that Pétain, who could clearly see that Nivelle's star was sinking, was already considering the possibility that the French government might ask him to replace Nivelle. Regardless, Nivelle was clearly dismayed by the rebuff and left Pétain's headquarters a thoroughly dejected man who knew of no other way to salvage his career except to continue the attacks and hope that through sheer force of will he could drive through the German lines. However, events were rapidly beginning to overtake Nivelle.[65]

By late April French military intelligence had become increasingly disturbed by the defeatist nature of letters being sent home by French soldiers, many of whom had reached the limits of human endurance. After being raised to such lofty heights by the heady promises of victory, the army's morale plummeted dangerously as the battle turned into yet another slugging match with minimal gains for exorbitant casualties. Confidence in Nivelle all but disappeared. The infantry, who bore the brunt of the casualties, wrote bitterly of the incompetence of the artillery and armor that was supposed to have supported them and heaped insults on the French Air Service, which they deemed not only to be inept but also to be cowardly.[66]

The German positions along the Chemin des Dames were deemed impregnable by *les bonnes hommes,* and they began to think that after nearly three years of horrific losses for virtually no gains, perhaps the entire German defensive system along the western front was too strong to be broken. Indeed, perhaps the war itself simply could not be won. Pessimism as to the outcome of the war and anger at those in charge of the army and the government became more and more widespread among the rank and file. It was apparent that in spite of official attempts to cover it up, the Nivelle offensive had achieved little other than to add to the already prodigious pile of dead *poilus.* French soldiers writing home described the offensive as "disastrous," "a screw up," "a fiasco," and "a butchery," among other more vulgar terms. It was obvious to any who cared to see that the French army had reached its breaking point.[67]

On 29 April a French infantry battalion refused to go back into the line, and on 3 May the Second Colonial Division mutinied en masse when the men learned that they were being sent back to the front instead of to a rest area, as had been promised to them. After several days, the mutineers were eventually coerced into going back to the front lines by being told that they were letting down their comrades in the trenches, who were expecting to be relieved, and that they were breaking faith with their fellow soldiers. Inspired by this loyalty, the Second Colonial Division finally marched to the front, but its mutiny went unpunished, as there were simply too many men involved to isolate and blame a small group of ringleaders. After the troops had left, pacifist and Communist leaflets were found strewn throughout their barracks. As the morale of the army continued to plummet, the government forced Nivelle to halt his offensive on 9 May. But by that time the damage had already been done. The body and the spirit of the army lay shattered on the slopes of the Chemin des Dames. By the first week of June perhaps as many as 50 percent of the divisions were in various stages of indiscipline and actual mutiny.[68]

As the military situation became increasingly critical in the trenches, the French home front also suddenly turned volatile. In May a series of crippling strikes broke out in Paris, Toulouse, and other large manufacturing areas. The predominantly female factory workers went out on strike for higher wages and better working conditions and to protest the sudden increases in food prices that had occurred that month. France had suffered through strikes in every year of the war, but these were by far the largest in terms of factories affected and number of workers on strike; for the first time the labor stoppages affected war production in a significant way. Moreover, these strikes seemed to have revolutionary overtones, as Socialist and Communist agitators worked to incite the crowds, and volleys of rocks hurled at the gendarmes were accompanied by cries of "Down with war!" "Down with the Republic!" and "Long live the Worker's International!"[69]

The French high command was dismayed to learn that the frontline soldiers had quickly found out about the strikes. Wild rumors about them soon swept through the disillusioned ranks, fed by subversives and agitators who the French high command charged were in the pay of international Socialists, Communists and the Germans. The rumors were numerous and varied, but some of the more persistent were that the government was using colonial soldiers to break up the labor strikes. Stories abounded that these colonials had abused French women and fired upon striking workers. Other reports came back that agitators were trying to persuade soldiers to start a rebellion against the government and that they were spreading claims that a revolution had already broken out in Paris.[70]

None of these events had actually occurred, at least not yet, and the hardened French veteran looked as much askance at these rumors of revolution from the Left as much as he did promises of victory and appeals to his patriotism by the French army and the Right. Nevertheless, the combination of mutiny in the trenches and a serious workers' revolt on the home front created a dangerous combination of conditions that simply had to be confronted if France was to survive.

On 15 May Painlevé took the first dramatic step toward rectifying the situation by relieving Nivelle of command and replacing him with the hero of the common soldier and one of the handful of military leaders still admired by the French people, Philippe Pétain. Painlevé believed that no other man could win back the confidence of the soldiers and rally the army to the defense of the Republic; and the Ribot government, despite its misgivings regarding his reputation and alleged antirepublican attitude, grudgingly agreed. As Pétain's biographer Stephen Ryan has argued: "Pétain was popular in the army and his military theories had been proved sound; he was the only leader in whom the army would have confidence at the moment. It was plain enough that Pétain as commander of the French armies represented less of a danger to French political liberties than did a loss of the war."[71] The great Free French leader of World War II, arguably the greatest French statesman of the modern era, Charles de Gaulle, best summed up the moment of crisis in the French army in 1917 when he wrote, "On the day when France had to choose between ruin and reason, Pétain was promoted."[72]

In the post–World War II era, Pétain has been viciously attacked by critics who have never forgotten or forgiven his role as leader of Vichy France from 1940 to 1944. Whatever his conduct during the terrible years of German occupation, it should never be forgotten that Pétain was one of the greatest Allied commanders of World War I. It was Pétain who had been the true victor at Verdun, and it was he who rallied the army and the nation through the grave crisis in morale in 1917 and who led the army to ultimate victory in 1918. That he was unable to accomplish these same feats as an eighty-four-year-old man in 1940 should not obscure the magnificent courage, wisdom, compassion, and leadership he demonstrated during the Great War.[73]

On being named the new commanding general of the French army, Pétain made suppression of the mutiny and the recovery of the army's morale and physical strength his top priorities. To this end he implemented a series of sweeping reforms. The first step he took was an obvious one, the restoration of military law and the swift punishment of those involved in the mutinies. Some of the senior officers in the army argued for a massive and brutal crackdown on the mutineers, but Pétain did not favor such a harsh course of action; the government would never have allowed it anyway. Instead, he showed leniency to all but the most hardcore mutineers and revolutionaries.[74]

For many years wild stories circulated regarding the number of French soldiers executed for their role in the mutinies, including ridiculous tales of entire regiments being marched into No Man's Land and shelled to death by their own artillery.[75] In fact, of the thousands of men directly involved in instigating the acts of "collective indiscipline" (as the official French army phrase went), 554 of them were condemned to death by courts-martial, but the death sentence was actually carried out in only

50 of these cases. The other condemned men, as well as those mutineers who received a prison sentence, were shipped off to hard labor battalions in North Africa. Pétain quickly decided, however, that merely punishing ringleaders was not enough to restore discipline. The soldiers of France had many legitimate complaints that needed to be addressed if morale was to be restored, and to this end he made numerous significant changes in policy that directly affected his men.[76]

Pétain swiftly addressed the issue of military leave, a subject that had been virtually ignored throughout the war by the high command, yet it was a major cause of discontent among the men. The granting of permission (leave) to soldiers had been haphazardly organized throughout the war (some men had not seen their families since they entered military service), with the result that by 1917 morale was greatly suffering, given the isolation of the soldiers from their families. Pétain's new plan guaranteed each soldier seven days of leave every four months, and he immediately began ordering divisions to implement this, in cycles of course, so as to provide not only rest for the men but also immeasurable solace from once more seeing their families and loved ones.[77]

Pétain also took steps to take care of his men, once they received permission, to protect them from war profiteers who sold food and drink at exorbitant prices and from organized gangs of antiwar Leftists who prowled train stations handing out their defeatist pamphlets. To this end, he ordered leave camps to be set up with telegraph offices so that the men could communicate with their families, railroad timetable bulletin boards to assist the men in finding trains home, dining halls, showers, latrines, and canteens providing free food and drink run by various charitable organizations. These camps and the nearby train stations were vigorously patrolled by military police who either arrested or ran off the Leftist political agitators seeking to undermine the men's fighting spirit. Various pacifist, communist, and defeatist newspapers and journals were banned from the zone of the armies, and Pétain urged the government to crack down on these agitators, who were doing immeasurable harm to the fighting spirit and morale of his men.[78]

Pétain also demanded that the government order the railway companies to better regulate their trains and to establish more regular passenger schedules, and more frequent stops, in the areas near the front where soldiers boarded trains to go home. Previously, it was not uncommon for a soldier to spend his entire leave stranded at a train station waiting to go home. Pétain found this inexcusable, and through a series of meetings with government ministers and railway officials, positive steps were taken to ensure that this situation would not continue.[79]

The new commanding general also addressed the universal complaint among the soldiers regarding the quantity and quality of their food. He ordered officers to pay particular attention to the training of cooks and demanded that officers themselves be thoroughly informed as to the food their troops were entitled to, how that food should be prepared, how it should be distributed, and all the other "practical aspects of catering." Dismayed by the lack of proper nutrition for his men, he also wrote to the minister of food and demanded that 100 truckloads of green vegetables be sent to the front each day, even if it meant rationing the civilian population.[80]

The establishment of a regular system of leave and the improved quantity and quality of food worked wonders, but perhaps more important was Pétain's determination to reform French tactical doctrine. Shortly after assuming command, he published a series of directives in rapid order that spelled out in detail how he would implement his theories of firepower on the battlefield, spending shells rather than lives, and utilize to the utmost advantage the latest weapons and technology to maximize the fighting power of the French army on the battlefield while keeping the physical and mental health of his troops foremost in his mind. He also implemented a vast training program for the officer corps to indoctrinate them in his tactical concepts and to train them to use the new weapons available to the fullest advantage.[81]

Pétain was not content merely to sit back and watch to see if his reforms would take effect. Instead, he determined personally to tell the soldiers what he had done, what he was going to do, and how things were going to be run differently now that he was in command. To this end, he began a remarkable tour of the front lines, speaking to virtually the entire French army, one division at a time. Arriving at an assembly area, he would inspect a chosen regiment and have the men break ranks and gather around his automobile while he climbed up on the hood of his car and spoke to them. He was not overly affectionate or fatherly toward the troops but spoke bluntly and honestly, as one professional soldier to another, and the men were impressed with his confidence and sincerity.[82]

Pétain's speeches varied, but generally the major themes were repeated at every stop. He told the men that he understood their frustration at the length and cost of the war but that the army and the nation desperately needed them at this grave hour. The enemy still held the sacred soil of France, and hundreds of thousands of French people lived under the iron-handed rule of the invader. The government and the people depended on them; the safety and security of France for generations to come rested on their shoulders. Pétain also told them that there would not be any major offensives until their strength had been rebuilt. He gave them a vision "of innumerable American troopships looming up on the horizon and making for the coast of France" and spoke of the hundreds of tanks and heavy artillery pieces rolling off the assembly lines.[83] "We shall wait for the Americans and the tanks," he told the *poilus*, and everywhere in the army this statement was received with enthusiasm.[84]

Pétain concluded his inspection of the division by distributing large numbers of decorations for gallantry to the men. The Légion d'honneur, Medaille Militaire, and even the Croix de Guerre had previously been awarded predominantly, if not exclusively, to officers. Pétain determined that it was high time that the bravery of the ordinary soldier was recognized as well, and he distributed these decorations lavishly on the troops. He personally pinned the decorations to the men's chests and then distributed small gifts of tobacco, pipes, and other personal tokens of appreciation to the decorated soldiers. The personal visits of the commanding general of the army to the troops in the field had an enormous impact on the men and vividly demonstrated that Pétain was a very different man from his predecessors. Throughout the French army the acts of collective indiscipline, after a final flurry in mid-June, subsided, and the morale and determination of the French soldier to see the war through to victory returned. As the British observer Sir Edward Spears later noted, "rested, well looked after, confident in the leadership, the French soldier was transformed."[85]

Recent studies by social and cultural historians have rejected the centrality of Pétain's role in suppressing the mutinies and in rallying the French army. They argue instead that French soldiers decided to return to the fight after having negotiated the terms by which they would continue faithfully to serve their military commanders. These scholars assert that the mutinies reached their zenith after Pétain had assumed command and that his leadership was not the essential dynamic in resolving them. They contend that there was instead a dialogue transpiring between the soldiers and the high command, with the soldiers being the driving force, dictating the new terms of their service.[86]

There is no question that Pétain was far more attuned to the needs of the common soldier than any of his predecessors had been and indeed solicited input from the men on the needed improvements at the front. However, since 1915, when Joffre had given him command of the French Second Army, he had already been working toward many of the reforms he enacted as commander in 1917. In autumn 1915 Pétain's army was the only one that achieved any noteworthy successes in the French offensive in Champagne, mainly because of his abilities to coordinate artillery fire with infantry assaults and his realistic attitude about what could be accomplished, given the tactical situation on the western front. At Verdun in 1916, as commander of the Second Army and later of Central Army Group, he enforced his style of tactics, emphasizing that massive concentrations of artillery fire were necessary in order to allow the infantry to advance. He fought and beat the Germans at their own game by gradually winning artillery superiority over the battlefield, achieving victory with shells rather than with bayonets. It was also at Verdun that he began making a serious effort to ease the burden of the common soldier's life through such measures as improving rations and rotating units out of the line and into rest areas on a regularly scheduled basis.

Thus, to say that the soldiers were making their voice heard would be correct, but it should be emphasized that at last they had found a sympathetic ear. The soldiers were no longer willing to follow Nivelle, but they would follow Pétain because of his tremendous reputation for battlefield skill and his genuine compassion for the common soldier.

Pétain's critics have made much of the fact that the mutinies reached their apex after he had assumed command. Yet he took charge while the mutiny was in full swing, and there was a time lag involved in implementing his reforms. Clearly, the entire French army could not be placed on leave at the same time; a rotation schedule had to be worked out. It was quite natural for soldiers whose unit was not in the first cycle to become disgruntled and to express doubts that any change at all had been made in the system. The leave camps and rest areas did not spring up overnight but took several weeks to establish. The same could be said for improvements in food, changes in tactics, and issuance of awards for valor to enlisted men. Pétain began his series of visits to the front in early June 1917, but it took several months to complete this tour; thus, not every unit was immediately exposed to his new brand of leadership and his personal assurances regarding the changes he was implementing. Talk was cheap to the veteran *poilus,* and it was not until they had been personally affected by the reforms and the new commanding general had visited their units that their attitudes began to change.

When these factors are considered, it is remarkable how swiftly discipline and fighting spirit were restored after Pétain's reforms went into effect. Given their recent betrayal by Nivelle's formula for victory, the fact that the average French soldiers were willing to listen to Pétain and believe in his promises, especially in terms of new tactics, speaks volumes to the faith and confidence that they had in their new commanding general. Here was a man who knew his business, a true professional who would not waste their lives through carelessness or sheer stupidity; hence, he was a general they were willing to follow. Through his reforms, his speeches, and his actions, Pétain gradually brought an end to the in-discipline within the army and rallied its battered ranks to the defense of the Republic. It was a most extraordinary display of personal leadership and indeed represented the essence of what true military leadership is. "In war," Napoleon once said, "men are nothing; one man is every-thing."[87] In France during the terrible year of 1917, Pétain was that man.

Pétain's promotion occurred just weeks before Pershing's arrival in France. Therefore, throughout America's involvement in the war he was the main French officer in charge of the maintenance of the Franco-American military relationship and was greatly responsible for its ultimate suc-cess. Indeed, from the very beginning of Pétain's assumption of command, he was convinced that the United States would play a critical role in the war and would prove to be France's greatest friend and ally in the final struggle. He proved to be an extremely valuable friend to the United States during the war, and, along with Marshal Joffre, continually supported the development of an autonomous American military pres-ence on the western front, even when his views clashed with those of his military and civilian superiors.[88]

The news of America's entry into the war had initially been over-shadowed by the events of the Nivelle offensive, but as the French army attempted to recover in the aftermath of its defeat, U.S. intervention was seen as tremendously important to the outcome of the war. Pétain espe-cially viewed intervention as a great turning point and believed that the U.S. Army, if properly trained and equipped by the French, could become a powerful military ally on the western front. Like Joffre, he wanted America's burgeoning military power to be harnessed to the French war effort, not the British, and he took immediate steps to begin forming a close relationship between the U.S. and the French armies.

Shortly after America's entry into the war, Pétain stated that the cre-ation of a great American army "is a moral necessity. . . . This Great Peo-ple must fight under its own colors and its cooperation will thus be more appreciable in the eyes of the Allies as well as in the eyes of the enemy." He conceded that the American forces needed a tremendous amount of assistance, especially in regard to instruction in modern warfare. Thus, it was vital "to entrust to France the instruction and training of the Ameri-can Army. For France, as a matter of fact, is the best qualified nation to at-tend to this and America has closer relations with her than with England."[89]

Just days before Pétain's official assumption of overall command of the French army, he contacted Colonel James A. Logan Jr., the head of the American military mission in Paris. Pétain insisted that Logan move into an office at Pétain's headquarters because, as Logan reported, "he wished to have a representative of our mission near at hand so as to consult with in the preparation of the different propositions [regarding Franco-American military cooperation] to be submitted to our Government." Logan informed Major General Joseph Kuhn, chief of the U.S. Army War College, that Pétain was "extremely kind in all his relations with us."[90]

Despite his early support for American military autonomy by June 1917, at the very height of the French army mutinies Pétain suddenly reconsidered his position, fearing that given the current conditions, it would take too long to implement Joffre's plan to build an autonomous American army. He abruptly reversed his stance and announced that he favored the earlier Nivelle plan for incorporating companies or battalions of Americans directly into the shattered divisions of the French army, at least initially, while the process of building an autonomous American army went on apace. He did not believe the two concepts were mutually exclusive and thought that this method would not only rebuild the French army but also reinvigorate it by allowing the positive impact of fresh American troops to affect as many French units as possible.

Marshal Joffre, just back from his tour of the United States, learned of Pétain's sudden change of heart and immediately moved to bring him back in line. He wrote to Pétain on 9 June to explain in detail the agreement he had concluded with the Americans and to emphasize the importance of Franco-American military cooperation. Joffre was especially anxious to ensure that, unlike Nivelle, Pétain understood that the Americans wished to have an autonomous military force on the western front. Joffre stated that it was essential for the French high command to accept this condition since it was vital for the future of Franco-American military relations. He said that Pershing should be allowed to "retain control over all of his units" and be allowed to have input in how the French trained the American forces.[91] Joffre followed this letter up with a personal visit to Pétain's headquarters, where, after some tense moments and strong debate, he succeeded in once more bringing Pétain around to supporting American military autonomy.[92]

It could be argued that Pétain was somewhat duplicitous in his dealings with the Americans on the issue of autonomy. Although this may have been the case, it came from no sinister motive; rather, it was reflective of his personality. His personal outlook on the war could swing from optimism to an exceedingly pessimistic view of events, depending on the current military situation facing France. He was intimately aware of the brittle nature of the sword he wielded, the state of the French army in 1917, and unlike most World War I commanders he had a genuine compassion for the trials of his men and knew they had reached the limits of their endurance. Thus, although in principle he agreed with American military autonomy, he would change that position when he believed it jeopardized his primary responsibility, the French army and the nation it defended.

Pétain was hardly alone in his pessimistic view of the war. On the eve of Pershing's arrival in France, Joffre wrote to Painlevé once more to stress the importance of developing an autonomous American military force. The marshal reminded the minister of war that the British were still anxious to secure U.S. soldiers for their army and that if Painlevé did not support American autonomy, then "we would risk losing the benefits of the exceptional position of France on this question." The "exceptional benefits" would of course be a powerful American army serving side by side with the French on the western front and France consequently receiving the lion's share of U.S. military and economic support. Joffre pointed out that opposition to American military autonomy would strengthen British arguments for amalgamation of those troops into the British army since they spoke the same language.[93]

Joffre's forceful arguments had a tremendous impact. When he met with Pershing in Paris on 16 June 1917, he was able to inform the general that the French government and high command were in complete agreement on the issue of American autonomy and that "all of the elements of the American Army would be under the overall direction of General Pershing." With this clearly understood, Joffre then informed Pershing that the French believed the Americans should eventually occupy their own sector of the western front, preferably in the region of Lorraine.[94]

The French marshal also informed Pershing that he had been designated as the official liaison between the French army and the Americans and that he would always be available for consultation on military matters: "In the course of these talks we can . . . examine together all questions relative to the organization, training and employment of the American Army." Pershing was pleased with this news, as he had the utmost respect for Joffre and knew of the marshal's firm support for autonomy. He later reported to the War Department: "Marshal Joffre insisted that his mission be carried out in accordance with the wishes of the American High Command, and from our earliest arrival we have looked upon him as our great friend and adviser."[95]

Although Joffre had been important in founding and guiding the Franco-American military relationship, once in France, Pershing would have to deal with the new commander, Pétain. The two commanders first met at Pétain's headquarters in Compiègne on 16 June. Unbeknownst to Pershing, the French army mutinies had only begun to subside just days before his arrival, and some members of the French high command were even concerned that his arrival would exacerbate the mutinous troops rather than quiet them since U.S. intervention promised that the war would continue.[96] Thus, Pétain was serious and formal at first, as there was much on his mind in those dark days, but he soon lightened a bit and even revealed his sarcastic sense of humor. The two men took an instant liking to each other, and their relationship, paramount to the establishment of the Franco-American military alliance, remained strong throughout the war. Pershing later recalled their first encounter:

> [Pétain] has a kindly expression, is most agreeable, but not especially talkative. His keen sense of humor became apparent from the jokes he told at the expense of some of his staff. . . . My impression of Pétain was favorable and it remained unchanged throughout the war. Our friendship, which I highly treasure, had its beginning at this meeting. Complete cooperation is difficult even under the most favorable conditions and is rarely attained between men or peoples of different nationalities, but it seemed probable that Pétain's breadth of vision, his common sense and his sound judgment would make for understanding, and this proved to be the case.[97]

Harbord, who was also present at this first meeting, wrote, "Pétain, who commands the armies and the military zone of a certain width behind the actual lines, is the strong man of the hour, feared by the politicians, the idol of the soldiers. He scarcely conceals his contempt for the civil powers."[98]

In an attempt to make conversation, Pershing remarked to Pétain that he had recently visited the Chamber of Deputies and was most struck by the beautiful architecture and the many moving speeches that were made in honor of their arrival and of America. Pétain replied laconically that he had never been inside the building. Pershing, flustered and perhaps fearing that his story had appeared boastful, hastened to explain that he had only gone there at the invitation of the French government. Pétain gave a wry smile and said, "Well, they would never invite me."[99]

As the two generals and their staffs settled down to lunch, conversation flowed, but Pétain retreated into one of the brooding silences for which he was sometimes known. As the talk swirled about the history of France, wine, the surrounding countryside, and other mundane matters, Pétain suddenly looked up from his meal and interrupted the flow of chatter: "I hope it is not too late." The words brought conversation to a halt; an air of reflective contemplation settled over the table. Pétain knew better than anyone the desperate nature of the situation in France at that moment, and Pershing realized how much the French needed American assistance.

France was indeed in the midst of a national crisis, and Pétain and the French government decided that it would be an excellent idea to employ Pershing as a morale booster. The French viewed Pershing as the representative of the armed might of America on its way to France; Pétain and others reasoned that perhaps because the American promise had arrived, if not the actual army, that that would be enough to provide at least a marginal boost to French morale. The real boost would come in the future, but Pétain believed it was essential to sow the seeds of Franco-American military cooperation so that by 1918 the harvest would be ready.

After their meeting at Compiègne, Pershing and his staff were whisked off by the French government to the first of many public displays celebrating the new military relationship designed to help boost morale. French music halls had added pro-American songs such as "Vive l'Oncle Sam" and "Le Drapeau américain" (The American Flag) to their repertoire, and a special performance was held in honor of Pershing and his officers at Paris's famous Opéra Comique.[100] The Americans arrived at yet another scene of patriotic pandemonium and to the general acclaim of the crowd gathered outside the theater and the sold-out audience within, who rose to their feet and delivered a thunderous ovation as Pershing and his officers were ushered into the presidential box. Onstage was a backdrop depicting ships flying the American flag, and in front of this stood an honor guard of French soldiers, along with crippled French veterans in their wheelchairs. Two beautiful young ladies, an American woman dressed in white and carrying an American flag and a French girl wearing a chiton with the tricolor draped over her shoulders and the little "mourning bonnet" of Alsace on her head, stood in front of the soldiers.

As the crowd settled into their seats, the American, Mrs. Abby Richardson, began to sing the "Star-Spangled Banner" with a "superb voice," as Harbord recalled. When she finished, the crowd roared its approval as thunderous applause echoed through the hall and cries of "Encore!" erupted. Even the hard-bitten old cavalryman Harbord, so often sarcastically witty about such affairs during his first days in France, remarked, "It made tears come to your eyes and the little chills run up and down your spine." As the applause subsided, the lighting faded and then focused on the young Frenchwoman, Mlle. Arthe Chenal. Her voice began softly yet clearly to cut through the noise of the crowd as she began to sing "La Marseillaise": *"Allons enfants de la patrie, le jour de gloire est arrivé!"* As she continued, many in the audience began openly to weep, and as she drew a sword and waved it over her head, the crowd boisterously joined in the final stanza: *"Aux armes citoyens! Formez vos bataillons! Marchons, marchons! Q'un sang impur, abreuve nos sillons."*[101]

Like so many of the morale-building functions that Pershing and his staff attended during their first days in France, this ceremony was rife with symbolism. The backdrop of ships flying the U.S. flag represented the American assistance on its way across the sea to France; the French honor guard the strength and the suffering of the French army and nation; the soldiers standing at attention the French nation armed, defiant, and ready to welcome its new American comrades-in-arms; the contingent of disabled veterans the gloriously terrible sacrifice that France had already made to the cause. The American singer dressed in white signified the purity of America in terms of its noble and virtuous ideals as well as virginity, given the conflict that the Americans were about to enter and the losses they would suffer. The young Frenchwoman was a living embodiment of "Marianne," the symbol of the French Republic. Her mourning cap for the lost province of Alsace had been a patriotic fashion for Frenchwomen since 1871, when the German Empire had stripped that territory from France; thus, the cap stood for one of the major goals the nation was fighting for.[102]

For all of the warmth and fanfare that had greeted Pershing, he was still a general without an army, although that was soon to change. Fourteen thousand U.S. soldiers and marines began arriving at St. Nazaire, France, on 28 June 1917. They were the first contingent of a vast host of American soldiers who would fight in France and who eventually would number approximately 2 million men before the war ended. Arriving with this first group was Captain George C. Marshall, the future chief of staff of the U.S. Army in World War II, who was serving as operations officer for the U.S. First Division.

Marshall had made a vow to attempt to communicate with the French in their native tongue, a language he was struggling to master, and while taking a brisk stroll around the docks to help recover from the long voyage he encountered a French stevedore hard at work. Excitedly, Marshall approached the longshoreman to comment on the lovely weather. *"Je suis très beau aujourd'hui!"* Marshall announced to the Frenchman, who looked up at the American officer, shook his head, and muttered something in French as he went back to work. Confused, Marshall quickly translated his remark in his mind and suddenly realized how horribly he had botched his first attempt to communicate. "During the ensuing twenty-six months," Marshall later recalled, "I never spoke French again except when forced to."[103]

Pershing and his staff viewed the first American soldiers to arrive with a critical eye since the vast majority were raw recruits who had received only minimal training before being shipped overseas. The veteran regulars of the U.S. Army had been scattered for use as NCOs and trainers for the vast host that was in the process of forming in the United States. Pershing wanted to cloister these men immediately in a training depot where they could be given proper instruction in soldiering before the French army and people glimpsed them, but neither the French government nor the army was willing to wait for such niceties. The Fourth of July was rapidly approaching, and Pershing was informed that the French wanted to stage a massive celebration in honor of American independence and the great Franco-American military alliance of the American Revolution. The Fourth of July was proclaimed a French national holiday by the Ribot government, and Pershing was invited to have a battalion from his newly arrived forces take part in a great parade in honor of the event.

In honor of the occasion, Pétain issued a general order to the French army announcing the planned festivities and once again proclaiming to the French soldiers that help was indeed on the way:

> Tomorrow—being the celebration of the Independence of the United States—the first American troops landed in France will parade in Paris. Later they will join us on the front. Let us hail these new comrades in arms who, without any after-thought of gain or conquest, actuated simply by the wish to defend the cause of Right and Liberty, have ranged themselves alongside of us! Others are preparing to follow them, and soon they will be on our soil. The United States means to put at our disposal, without reckoning, their soldiers, their gold, their manufacturing plants, their ships, their whole country. They wish to repay a hundredfold the debt of gratitude contracted formerly by them to La Fayette and his companions. Let there be but one single shout heard from all parts of the front on this 4th of July: "Honor to our great Sister Republic! Long live the United States!"[104]

The festivities began with a moving, martial ceremony at the Invalides, where the American battalion stood facing a French battalion in the Cour d'Honneur of the Hôtel des Invalides, the sacred courtyard of the French army. With the mammoth statue of Napoleon mounted on the balcony of the courtyard and the golden dome of the chapel of St. Louis in the background, the French and American armies were linked together for the first time since the American Revolution. Pershing recalled: "There in this national shrine, sacred to the memory of the glorious past of the French people . . . and where Napoleon himself lies buried, an official welcome was extended on Independence Day to America's first contingent of troops. No other occasion that I recall was more significant or more clearly indicated the depth of French sentiment and affection for their old ally."[105]

As a French military band played, Marshal Joffre entered the courtyard, followed by General Pershing and then the president of the French Republic, Raymond Poincaré. Pershing was presented with an embroidered American flag from the city of Puy, the birthplace of Lafayette. Then the American flag, which had been carried through the streets of Paris by the American volunteers who had enlisted in the Légion étrangère in 1914, was presented to the elderly French veterans who served as the curators of the Invalides so that it would be enshrined beside the other great banners from French military history. As Harbord recorded in his diary:

> It was a tremendously moving scene. Perhaps twice in her history foreign troops have entered that old Cour d'Honneur; once in 1815, after Waterloo; again in 1870 after Sedan, and violated that inner shrine of French history; but never before has an ally penetrated with its armed men that holy of French holies. It certainly meant much for France, much for Germany, and I believe a new era for America; and no American could look on it without a thrill and the tears starting to his eyes.[106]

Harbord observed that the American soldiers "looked very tall" next to the Frenchmen but noted that the latter had a fire in their eyes and a firmness in their jaw that reflected the intrepidity of men who had been under fire before. The raw Americans were exuberant and full of wild-eyed optimism, and if their marching lacked the measured cadence of the veteran French troops, they made up for it with an enthusiastic swing in their stride that spoke of confidence.

With the ceremonies concluded, the French band played a series of ruffles and flourishes, and then American musicians broke into a John Philip Sousa march; the U.S. Army moved out from the courtyard and into the bright summer sunshine of Paris. The new chief of staff of the French army and the future supreme Allied commander, the fiery and flamboyant General Ferdinand Foch, later recalled his first glimpse of American soldiers at this parade: "They made an excellent impression. We were impressed in general by the height of the men, by their well-fitting uniforms, by their physical development and poise, by their splendid health and vigor."[107]

It seemed to many of the Americans that the whole city of Paris had turned out to greet them, and for five miles they passed through a cheering throng lined up along both sides of the broad avenues. Some women and girls pelted the soldiers with flowers and rushed into the procession, linking arms with the soldiers, kissing them, and joining in the parade. Other women, dressed in mourning black, were seen sitting at the side of the street weeping uncontrollably, while some dropped to their knees and crossed themselves as the Americans went by. Pershing later recalled, "These stirring scenes conveyed vividly the emotions of a people to whom the outcome of the war had seemed all but hopeless."[108] French correspondents witnessing the parade concluded that the arrival of the Americans marked a major turning point in the war and ensured the ultimate "triumph of justice and the right against the barbarous force of our enemies."[109]

It was indeed a day of joy and deliverance for a nation that only weeks earlier had been on the brink of despair, perched precariously on the edge of disastrous defeat. But the Americans had arrived, and victory could not be far behind. The professional soldier in Pershing frowned somewhat at the parade, which he thought "looked like a moving flower garden" and possessed "only a semblance of military formation," but there was no doubt of the electrical effect the troops had on the French people. "The troops," he later reported with much pride, "were greeted with an enthusiasm that defies description."[110]

At last the procession reached Picpus Cemetery and the grave of the Marquis de Lafayette. The gathered French dignitaries included President Poincaré, Premier Ribot, Marshal Joffre, and General Foch. The American contingent consisted of Ambassador Sharp and Pershing and his staff officers. After a series of eloquent speeches, the French invited Pershing to say a few words. Uncomfortable with his French, Pershing turned to his aide, Colonel Charles E. Stanton, who was fluent in the language, and asked him to deliver some appropriate remarks. Stanton gave a fire and brimstone speech regarding what the Americans would do to the Germans and then held forth on the historic relationship between the U.S. Army and the French army, which the tomb before them symbolized. Stanton announced that America had incurred a great debt to Lafayette and the French people for helping the United States win its independence and that it was now time for America to repay that debt. Then Stanton turned and faced the tomb, and in a grandiloquent gesture that brought forth uproarious applause from the crowd, he announced, *"Lafayette, nous voici!"*[111]

Although the Americans were enthusiastic, the stark realities of war that confronted them in France and the suffering of the French people brought home to them the sobering realization that the task they were undertaking would be an arduous one. Quentin Roosevelt, youngest son of former president Theodore Roosevelt, was one of the first American pilots to arrive in France. Quentin had a great love for France and its people and was deeply disturbed by what he saw upon his arrival in Paris. He wrote to his family in summer 1917 that the great French city was no longer the exuberant place they remembered from past vacations but was the war capital of a grievously stricken nation, where the strain of war was starkly evident: "Everywhere you see women in black, and there is no more cheerful shouting and laughing. Many, many of the women have a haunted look in their eyes, as if they had seen something too terrible for forgetfulness. They make one realize the weight that lies on all alike now."[112]

After the flurry of celebrations commemorating the Fourth of July, Pershing found time to tell Secretary of War Newton D. Baker about the situation in France. He wrote that the French "were very tired of this war" and that Pétain had warned him of the possibility of a revolution if the morale of the nation did not revive soon. Pershing declared that he would do everything in his power to help revive French morale by giving speeches and appearing at various events to help restore the faith of the French in their government, their army, and the promise of American support. He was pleased to report that the Fourth of July celebration had "stirred all of France" and that Pétain had informed him that the morale of the French army had dramatically improved with news of the arrival of American soldiers. As Pershing concluded, "So for the present things look better. I shall do everything consistent with my position to encourage and hearten both people and soldiery."[113]

Aside from morale building, Pershing realized that in the months to come the United States would have to provide substantial military power to the Allied cause if victory was to be achieved. He informed Baker that he would need at least 1 million men by May 1918 and that this force would be the foundation for a U.S. Army that would "strike the decisive blow" and win the war.[114]

After the disastrous Nivelle offensive, the morale of the French nation and army had reached its lowest point of the war. The French soldiers lost their sense of trust in their military and political leaders and lost hope that the war could ever be won. It was Pétain who restored the morale of the army, through his series of sweeping reforms and by the sheer force of his personality. He was recognized throughout the army for his clearheaded tactical ideas and his sense of compassion for the man in the trenches. He could not conjure up France's long-lost legions, but he could and did restore the army's pride, sense of duty, and willingness to fight.

The morale of the French people had also reached its nadir in spring 1917. The workers had gone on strike in record numbers during May, and the French Socialists and various pacifist organizations seemed to have gained the upper hand in French popular opinion as late as June. Indeed, in June, France, in the opinion of Pétain and others, seemed on the verge of revolution and collapse. Yet the same crowds who had hurled paving stones at gendarmes and shouted *"Vive la paix!"* and *"A bas la guerre!"* had only weeks later greeted the newly arrived Americans with hysterical displays of patriotism and affection that defied description. Food prices remained astronomically high, wages abysmally low, the widows and orphans still wept, but the French people had rallied at the sight of the American soldiers, determined that with this new assistance the Republic would not fall and the invaders would be driven from the sacred soil of France.

Even after the first contingent of Americans had arrived, Pershing and the AEF numbered barely one division of raw recruits. But the electrical effect this handful of troops had on French morale was immeasurable. A nation that had lost hope found it once more, and for the first time in years dared to dream that tomorrow would not bring just a better day but could, and would, bring victory. Such was the priceless gift that Pershing and the Americans brought to France in 1917, and an entire country rallied to them, embraced them, and welcomed them as brothers in the common struggle against the common foe. There were still many obstacles to overcome and many battles to fight, but the French people now knew that with their ally they could yet emerge triumphant from the terrible struggle and drive the enemy from their soil. But in order to accomplish this, the Americans would have to be equipped and trained for modern warfare. As the fanfare surrounding their arrival settled down, the French army prepared to undertake this daunting task.

CHAPTER 4

● ● ● ● ● ● ● ● ● ● ● ● ● ● ●

The Role of France in Arming and Training the American Expeditionary Forces

In 1917 the United States was faced with the daunting task of raising, equipping, and training the largest army in American history. In the twenty years preceding the nation's entrance into World War I, the U.S. Army had fought two wars and conducted numerous small military operations in Asia, Central America, the Caribbean, and Mexico. Although these campaigns were comparable with the European experience during the same time period, warfare had undergone a massive transformation since the outbreak of the Great War, and American officers and military planners were only beginning to grasp this in 1917.[1]

The U.S. Army emerged from its wars of empire as a small, lightly armed force, well prepared for fighting a low-intensity conflict. In fairness, this was in keeping with the traditional role of the army throughout the history of the Republic, with the notable exception of the American Civil War. The challenge the nation now faced, however, was unprecedented in its history. The army of 1917 simply did not have the manpower, training, or equipment to wage war against the Imperial German Army. To accomplish its mission, the U.S. Army would have to be vastly expanded and almost completely reequipped and retrained for modern war.

Since America lacked the qualified instructors and modern weapons required for this monumental task, it looked to France for assistance.

On the day the United States declared war on Germany, the U.S. Army was composed of approximately 133,000 men and 5,800 officers; the National Guard numbered 67,000 men and 3,200 officers.[2] Though this force was adequate to police America's frontiers and empire, it was hopelessly small in terms of what would be required on the battlefields of Europe, where the major combatants fielded armies numbering in the millions. Thus, the first issue the Wilson administration addressed in preparing the United States to play a part in World War I was the mobilization of American manpower. The nation had to create a massive ground force capable of fulfilling the role and expectations of a great power entering into the conflict that became the largest and bloodiest the world had yet known.

The United States had traditionally relied on volunteers to fill the ranks of its armed forces in times of war. In the face of the mobilization requirements for mustering an army large enough to fight on the Continent, however, military professionals as well as President Wilson and Secretary of War Newton D. Baker favored a national conscription act over forming the traditional volunteer regiments. This decision was based on several factors, not the least of which was that during the nation's largest war prior to this one, the American Civil War, many of the volunteer units had been commanded by "political generals."[3] These men had earned their posts because of their prowess in mustering votes for the Republican Party rather than for their military abilities. The fact that Wilson's archrival Theodore Roosevelt was already clamoring to raise his own volunteer division, which he intended to be an updated and expanded version of his Rough Riders regiment, further added impetus to the administration's drive for conscription. Marshal Joffre had proven instrumental during his visit to the United States in lending his considerable military reputation to the idea, informing recalcitrant congressman that such a measure was absolutely necessary in modern war. Although a conscription act was indeed passed, it nevertheless took time to set up the machinery of a national draft. Meanwhile, thousands of young American men had begun flocking to recruiting offices to volunteer from the moment the declaration of war was issued. The Wilson administration was thus in a bit of a quandary over how to proceed with its plan for conscription while still taking advantage of the exuberant patriotism these volunteers exhibited.[4]

In the end, a compromise solution was reached whereby the army essentially was split into three separate but mutually supporting branches: the regular army and the National Guard, whose ranks already had been swelled by the initial wave of volunteers, and the national army, which would be composed of those men drafted into service under the Selective Service Act. Although this scheme suffered from some early teething problems, the system worked remarkably well in mobilizing manpower for the war effort. By November 1918 there were 527,000 men in the regular army; 382,000 in the National Guard; and over 3 million in the draftee national army, representing the largest U.S. Army in the history of the nation. Of this total, approximately 2 million men reached France before the war ended.[5]

In order to train this massive body, General Pershing and the U.S. War Department worked out a plan whereby the men would be organized into divisions in the United States and receive basic instruction in soldiering, with an emphasis on rifle training, drill, and physical exercise. The divisions would then be shipped to France, where they would undergo advanced training in modern warfare at the hands of French instructors. By 1918 more advanced courses were added to the curriculum in the U.S. training facilities on gas warfare, artillery, grenades, and various officer training courses as well, although even divisions that completed these more thorough programs were still sent to advanced training facilities in France before actually going to the front.[6]

Although the U.S. Army provided the bulk of basic instruction to these recruits in the United States, both France and Great Britain also sent over instructors to help advise the army in its training process. France sent 286 officers as training advisers, all specialists in particular aspects of modern warfare. By far the most predominant specialty among the French advisers was artillery; these instructors comprised approximately one-fourth of the French advisers sent to America. After completing the basic course, the division was shipped as a complete unit to France, where the men entered advanced schools for infantry, artillery, and other disciplines to learn the art and science of modern warfare.[7]

The exceptions to this arrangement were the first four divisions (the First, Second, Twenty-sixth, and Forty-second) sent to France in 1917; these essentially underwent all their training at the hands of the French army in order to facilitate the rapid establishment of an American military presence on the western front. Technically speaking, the first two divisions of the AEF were part of the regular army, but the men were regulars in name only. The army had scattered its experienced men throughout the United States to serve as instructors for the new recruits and as cadres for the newly forming divisions. As a result, the regular divisions, as well as those of the Twenty-sixth and Forty-second National Guard divisions, were overwhelmingly composed of raw volunteers.[8]

Although the lack of trained manpower posed major problems for the U.S. Army in the early stages of American involvement in the war, perhaps the most severe obstacle it faced during its expansion was the almost complete lack of weapons in its inventory for waging modern warfare. With the exception of small arms, such as the excellent Springfield M1903 rifle, the army's weaponry in 1917 was either obsolescent or nonexistent.

Among its shortcomings, the army most keenly felt the shortage of artillery, the penultimate weapon of the Great War. The U.S. Army in 1917 possessed only a relatively small number of light field-artillery pieces and none of the modern heavy guns and heavy howitzers that had become such essential weapons in the arsenals of the Great Powers during World War I. Pershing freely admitted the army's deficiencies in this vital arm, calling it "one of the greatest handicaps of the United States" in the war.[9]

Pershing planned to have an army of 1 million men in France by June 1918 who were capable of functioning as an autonomous force, one that could conduct its own operations. He envisioned that this initial force, which he planned eventually to expand to 2 million men, would require 2,524 guns and howitzers of all types. The War Department informed him, however, that only 80 light-artillery pieces, the U.S. M1902 3-inch gun, could be sent to France in September 1917, with 40 more arriving the following month. After those shipments, which represented emergency orders to American armaments manufacturers, there would be no future shipments of artillery pieces until June, due to the time lag involved in gearing up U.S. industry to a war footing. In point of fact, due to myriad difficulties, even the small number of guns promised to Pershing never reached him.[10]

The first major problem arose when the U.S. Army's chief of ordnance, Major General William Crozier, insisted that major modifications needed to be made to the existing M1902 3-inch guns before they could be shipped overseas. Crozier had helped develop a new version, the M1916 3-inch gun, which he believed was markedly superior to the older model. Further, he ordered the new M1916 to be modified so that it could fire the French 75mm shell, in order to make it easier to supply artillery ammunition to the American forces. Unfortunately, the new gun suffered from teething problems, which Crozier's mandated modifications only made worse, and in field tests it was revealed to be both fragile and inaccurate. As it became apparent that the M1916 needed a major overhaul, the United States grew increasingly desperate to produce artillery pieces. Various American armament manufacturers then purchased the rights to make the French 75mm gun and a modified version of the British 18-pounder (the

M1917), which could fire the French 75mm ammunition. Yet this new solution took a great deal of time to reach, and even more time was wasted
as U.S. factories had to retool their machinery and train their workers to
manufacture the foreign artillery pieces.[11]

In the end, the whole effort turned out to be a frenzied waste of time,
effort, and money. Hardly any American-manufactured artillery pieces of
any type were ever actually used in combat. After the war, the U.S. Army
chief of artillery, Major General William J. Snow, bitterly observed, "It
may be said, then, that we could not and did not equip our Army with artillery during the War."[12]

Marshal Joffre had offered to provide all the artillery and machine
guns required by the first American division to be sent to France. By May
1917, following Joffre's initial reports on the horrendous state of American preparedness for war, the French government expanded this initial
offer into a formal proposal to provide vast amounts of artillery, machine
guns, and ammunition to the United States in order to hasten the mobilization and deployment of its divisions to France. From these negotia-
tions arose an arrangement whereby the French armaments industry
would almost single-handedly provide the modern weaponry that the
U.S. Army desperately lacked.

On 22 May 1917 the French minister of armaments, Albert Thomas, cabled the special French mission on industrial cooperation in the United
States, headed by André Tardieu, instructing him to offer artillery pieces
and ammunition to the Americans. Basing his numbers on Pétain's estimates of the French army's own needs and the production capacity of the
French armaments industry, Thomas personally contacted the War Department on 25 May and offered to provide the AEF with five 75mm guns
a day, beginning on 1 August, and two 155mm howitzers a day, beginning on 1 October. He also offered initial allotments of 1 million rounds
of ammunition for the 75mm guns and 100,000 shells for the 155mm
howitzers. He explained that these initial ammunition supplies would be
further augmented by daily allotments of 30,000 75mm shells and 6,000
155mm shells.[13]

With this firm offer of assistance in hand and dismal reports of the
prospects for U.S. industry to begin mass producing American-designed
artillery and shells, the War Department and the Government Accounting Office (GAO) informed General Crozier on 9 June that the army
would adopt the French 75mm gun to replace the U.S. 3-inch gun and the
French 155mm howitzer to replace the U.S. 6-inch howitzer and that
modifications would be made to all existing artillery pieces so that they
could fire French ammunition. The War Department explained that

"there was no prospect otherwise of obtaining the number of cannon required for the successful prosecution of the war." Although this meant that the U.S. Army's field artillery would be equipped with foreign ordnance, it was later noted that the decision "seemed to be in harmony with the traditional American respect for French military institutions and thought." Thus the army formally adopted the French 75mm gun and 155mm howitzer as its standard field artillery in the Great War. Licenses were granted to various American armament manufacturers to begin building the weapons; however, since it would take a long time for production to begin, the weapons would be supplied by French industry. Pershing later wrote, "The wisdom of this action is shown by the fact that when the Armistice went into effect on November 11 not a single American made gun of these types had reached the front."[14]

The decision was widely celebrated by the French government as it further bound the AEF to the French army. Significantly, the government decided to announce the agreement on Bastille Day, 1917, as part of the general morale-building effort of tangible evidence that the Americans would fight side by side with the French.[15]

One of the more surprising shortages the U.S. Army faced in 1917 was its lack of modern machine guns. The American inventor Hiram Maxim had developed the first true machine gun in 1885 but had been unable to sell his invention to the government. Maxim took his deadly weapon overseas and rapidly found a booming market for it among the Great Powers of Europe. Another American inventor, John M. Browning, developed his machine gun in 1900 but despite his best efforts failed to win a contract with the U.S. government for his weapon. Browning was later vindicated when the army adopted his gun soon after war was declared in 1917.[16]

The Lewis light machine gun, designed and developed by two Americans, had been tested for the American Ordnance Department in 1913, but the board turned it down. The Lewis gun became one of the standard automatic weapons of the British army in the Great War, serving both as an infantry weapon and as the main armament on various types of British aircraft. The Ordnance Department did decide to adopt the Vickers machine gun in 1913, but Congress refused to provide funding for its procurement. This weapon also saw service with the British army in the war. The U.S. Army labored on with its obsolescent Colt-Marlin machine guns, which had become so outdated by the time of America's entrance into the war as to be virtually useless. Indeed, although the weapon was standard issue in 1917, none of the U.S. Army divisions that saw combat in Europe were equipped with it.[17] As the historian James Huston wrote in regard to weapons procurement for the army in the decade just prior to World War I, "Apparently the War Department was waiting for the best [and was] confronted by the eternal dilemma of whether to standardize production or wait for a better model. In this case it waited, and the Army probably had the best machine guns and automatic rifles in the world—after World War I was over."[18]

As with the shortage of artillery pieces, Pershing later lamented the army's dearth of automatic weapons:

Our earlier divisions were seriously handicapped in their preparation at home by lack of machine guns for training, many units not receiving this arm until after their arrival in France. When it is recalled that each division at the beginning of the war was allowed only 92 machine guns and no automatic rifles, and that under our war organization 260 machine guns and 768 automatic rifles were required, the result of delay in providing these guns needs no further comment.[19]

As a consequence of this combination of shortsightedness and an unwillingness to provide adequate funding for the U.S. Army, the nation that was the home of some of the greatest inventors of automatic weapons in history possessed only a small number of outdated machine guns when it entered World War I.

These shortcomings in the army were due to two separate but integrally related issues. First, America's political leadership, and many of its military leaders as well, thought that military power meant sea power. Presidential administrations from Cleveland to Wilson had drawn on the teachings of A. T. Mahan and provided funding for a powerful and modern fleet but failed to pay much attention to the needs of the army. It was deemed secondary to the navy in terms of its importance to national defense, and the minuscule funding it received in the years prior to World War I reflected this thinking.

The decision to focus military spending on the navy meant that the army lacked not only the funds to maintain a large force but also the financial resources to equip itself with the latest weaponry. The army simply could not continually upgrade to the latest weaponry available and thus had to be cautious in terms of purchasing a piece of equipment that might be made obsolete within a few years.

The French having agreed to supply the artillery for the AEF, on 21 June 1917 Pershing inquired if they could expand their offer of armaments to include the modern automatic weapons that the U.S. Army desperately needed. The French were quick to respond, and by July, as the first American soldiers were arriving, French Minister of War Painlevé informed Pershing that France was prepared to issue machine guns and automatic rifles to them. Painlevé offered to provide 168 Hotchkiss machine guns, with 20,000 rounds of ammunition for each gun, and 444 Chauchat automatic rifles, with 3,000 rounds of ammunition for each weapon, for this initial contingent of American troops, promising further aid in the future.[20]

Another disturbing shortage, especially for a nation that had produced the inventors of heavier-than-air flight, was the complete lack of modern airplanes. Indeed, when the United States declared war on 6 April 1917 it possessed only fifty-five training aircraft, and as Pershing remarked, "51 were obsolete and the other 4 were obsolescent." Even more troubling, the U.S. Air Service had no combat aircraft whatsoever at a time when Germany, France, and Great Britain each possessed well over 1,000 combat planes. Again, France assisted the United States in this area. Some American-manufactured aircraft reached Europe, and the British also provided aircraft, but the overwhelming majority of planes flown by the U.S. Air Service in the war were French. In fact, of the forty-three American air squadrons in operation on 31 October 1918, thirty were equipped with French planes, ten with American aircraft, and three with British.[21]

Great Britain also provided some weapons to the American Expeditionary Forces, but France supplied the majority of heavy weapons, artillery, equipment, and aircraft (see Table 1).[22]

These figures are even more impressive when one considers that virtually no American-manufactured artillery pieces ever saw service on the western front, almost all the shells fired in combat by U.S. artillery were manufactured in France, and no American-made tanks ever reached the front. Pershing lauded the French for their efforts to supply weapons and ammunition for the AEF and later reported, "It should be fully realized that the French government has always taken a most liberal attitude, and has been most anxious to give us every possible assistance in meeting our deficiencies."[23]

The only major piece of heavy ordnance that the British supplied in large numbers to the AEF was the trench mortar, perhaps because of an accident that befell Major General Leonard Wood and a team of U.S. officers. A French trench mortar that they were inspecting exploded, killing its crew and severely injuring Wood and others. Although not specifically stated, this incident may have led to a general belief among the AEF high command that the French trench mortars were unsafe.[24]

Some of the French weaponry was supplied at no charge, but the majority of the artillery pieces and other weapons and materiel of war

Table 1. Equipment Furnished to the AEF, 6 April 1917–11 November 1918

Equipment	France	Britain
Field artillery	3,532	160
Railroad artillery	140	0
Caissons	2,658	0
Trench mortars	237	1,427
Automatic weapons	40,884	0
Tanks	227	26
Aircraft	4,874	258

Source: Marcel Vigneras, *Rearming the French* (Washington, DC: CMH, 1957), 3–4.

France provided was not free; rather, it was exchanged for American raw materials. This was a marriage of convenience that turned out to be a mutually beneficial arrangement for both countries.

The United States had vast amounts of raw materials for use in making weapons, but its armaments industry was incapable of producing the prodigious number of guns necessary to equip the AEF and was unable to meet those needs in the immediate future. In contrast, the French armaments industry was one of the world's largest when war broke out in 1914, and after nearly three years of total war the French had tremendously expanded their capacity for production of guns and ammunition. Thus, French armaments manufacturers could accommodate the needs of the AEF, provided enough money and raw materials were made available to produce the weapons. This meant, however, that the French army would have to allow weaponry and ammunition earmarked for its own stockpiles to be diverted to the nascent AEF. Pétain and others were willing to make this sacrifice because they believed that this long-term investment in the AEF would reap handsome dividends in the form of a powerful American army fighting with of them on the western front.

The major limitations the French faced in terms of armaments production were a shortage of capital and raw materials. The government essentially had no foreign debt prior to 1914, securing what funds it might need through its own private banks. Indeed, France possessed large reserves of capital and was a lending nation, not a borrower, before the Great War. However, the enormous expenditures necessitated by the largest conflict in history, and the decrease in trade and production of goods for overseas export that the war caused, drastically reduced the government's capital reserves. American financiers had been quick to provide assistance to France, but they were at first limited by the Wilson administration's initial decision in 1914 to prohibit American banks and financiers from making loans to nations at war. Wilson changed his mind on this issue in 1915, and from that point America became the leading foreign financier of France's war effort. The House of Morgan in particular soon became a major creditor for the French government, but other American financial firms also joined in.[25]

After America entered the war, the U.S. government also began to provide financial assistance to France in the form of outright cash subsidies and low-interest loans. The United States also reimbursed France for the expenses incurred in establishing training facilities for the AEF there. American government purchases of weapons generated another source of capital for the French, but generally the French exchanged big ticket weaponry such as heavy artillery for desperately needed American raw materials instead of cash.[26]

Even though the influx of American capital eased some of the problems of French war production, France suffered from a critical shortage of raw materials. This was especially severe because the Germans had captured areas of northern and eastern France during the 1914 campaign that were vital to the French war effort. Indeed, the zone occupied by the German army for virtually the entire war was responsible for 14 percent of all prewar French industrial production. Moreover, the occupied region had been a major prewar source of raw materials. Before the war, France had obtained 75 percent of its coal, 81 percent of its cast iron, 63 percent of its steel, 85 percent of its cloth, and 94 percent of its wool from the area the German army occupied from 1914 to 1918.[27]

It is truly astounding how well French industry was able to cope with this dire emergency in finding alternate sources, both in metropolitan France and throughout its empire, for these materials. However, French steel production, perhaps the most vital raw material of modern war, never quite recovered from the blow, and even by 1917 steel was being produced at only half its prewar levels.[28] Thus, it came as no surprise when the French requested this commodity from the Americans in exchange for weapons. Tardieu's mission in the United States worked out a formula whereby America would provide France with six tons of steel for each 75mm gun, forty tons of steel for each 155mm howitzer, and sixty tons of steel for each 155mm gun. Since the U.S. Army had adopted these French weapons as their standard field artillery pieces, this exchange system allowed the AEF to equip itself fully with the artillery it desperately needed in the shortest amount of time.[29]

Securing sufficient amounts of ammunition for the large number of guns also proved to be a daunting but surmountable obstacle, albeit again with tremendous assistance from France. By 1917 American manufacturers were already producing and selling to France and Britain large amounts of smokeless powder, brass, and other materials for use in the making of artillery shells. But the United States did not possess the capacity to manufacture large numbers of the shells themselves and thus once more relied on the remarkable French armaments industry, which provided virtually every shell fired by the AEF in combat. Nevertheless, from 6 April 1917 to 11 November 1918, the United States produced more smokeless powder than France and Britain put together, and both of these nations relied heavily on American supplies of this valuable commodity. In addition, American production of TNT, ammonium nitrate, and other high explosives was roughly double that of France. Thus, America provided the raw materials, France provided the finished product, and the two nations were codependent in this regard.[30]

Even as officials of the two governments were still hammering out details on financial and industrial cooperation, the U.S. Army was engaged in planning the largest overseas deployment of soldiers in the nation's history. In fulfillment of the agreement reached between Secretary of War Baker and Marshal Joffre, the army was sending over a half-trained and almost totally unequipped division to be issued French weapons and to undergo French training and instruction. The U.S. First Division became the model for all future American units shipped to France, and its experiences are worth examining in close detail since they reveal both the benefits and the conflicts that arose once French and American soldiers actually began to serve together.

On 28 May 1917, Colonel Frank Parker, the chief of Liaison Group for American General Headquarters wrote to the chief of the American military mission in France concerning proposed plans for training the U.S. First Division. Parker advised that the training camps of the U.S. soldiers should be as close to the front as was prudently possible so as to immerse the soldiers in "the atmosphere of war." As Parker pointed out, "If the French army is to be our model and if the American is to fight beside the Frenchmen according to the latter's methods, then the training of the American troops should be done in as close contact as possible with the French troops, not only from the technical point of view but from that of mutual acquaintance, mutual understanding, and mutual respect."[31]

Parker wrote that the French had formulated a plan for training the Americans. It involved taking one of their divisions, which was staying at a rest camp, according to Pétain's principle of rotating a division out of the line after it had spent several weeks at the front, and teaming it up with a newly arrived American division. As Parker explained it, "The French divisions, while in these camps, are constantly in training and bring with them the latest methods from the front. Our officers and men can see each day the practical work of the French, can talk freely with their French comrades, can get French experts to come over, assist and advise and in general live in the midst of the French veteran troops while these latter are in training. The French are only too anxious to assist us in every way."[32]

The exact location of the first training facility for the U.S. soldiers was vitally important because it was generally accepted that it should be in close proximity to the future American sector of the western front. This sector was to be in the French province of Lorraine, a position that placed the AEF in the midst of the French army rather than alongside it or between the French and British armies. This positioning would not only provide a heavy French influence on the training of the AEF but also would virtually ensure that the combat actions of the Americans would be intimately associated with those of the French army and thus make paramount the military relationship these two armies shared.

Placing the AEF in Lorraine has long been thought to have been Pershing's decision, based upon his own perceptions of the logistical and strategic situation on the western front and the recommendations of his staff. As Pershing wrote in his memoirs, "Although we were generally committed to operate with or near the French when our army should be ready, it was necessary to consider the different possibilities of the problem [of deployment] as a whole before making the final decision."[33] His statement intimates that although "generally committed" to serving in the French sector of the lines, he had still not firmly committed to this decision. Pershing records in considerable detail in his memoirs the myriad logistical and operational reasons for his careful selection of the French province of Lorraine as the sector where the AEF should be deployed. His biographers and other historians of the AEF have echoed the idea that it was Pershing who chose to place his forces in Lorraine with the French. However, this notion is false.[34]

The decision to place the AEF with the French had already been made by President Wilson and Secretary of War Baker two months earlier. From that moment, there was never any reconsideration of the question by anyone in the administration. Although Wilson and Baker gave Pershing a tremendous amount of authority over military matters, the decision to place the AEF with the French army was intimately tied up in a political and economic decision-making process that was far beyond the realm of Pershing's authority. Indeed, the French high command also had an important role in the choice, although this previously has been ignored.

On 20 May 1917, over a month before Pershing officially requested the sector of Lorraine and four days before he had even been named commander of the AEF, the French army chief of staff General Foch wrote to General Eugène Debeney, commander of the French Central Army Group, to request that he locate a good site within his zone of operations for use in training American soldiers. On 22 May Debeney replied, recommending the use of the French army camp at Gondrecourt, in Lorraine. Debeney asserted that Gondrecourt was a good choice since it was located in close proximity to the sector that the Americans would in all likelihood take over, once they were built up to full strength. He also explained that during the previous winter the camp had been used for the simultaneous training of two French divisions, and so the facilities would be adequate to handle Pétain's plan for placing a French division with the Americans to serve as instructors.[35]

Based on this evidence, it would appear that the French had already selected Lorraine as the American sector as early as May 1917, during Marshal Joffre's initial meetings with Secretary of War Baker when the subject of the possible use of American soldiers on the western front was first seriously discussed. Since Debeney's letter is marked "Secret," in all likelihood this information was not shared with the Americans themselves, and therefore Pershing may have believed that he had chosen Lorraine based on all the factors he wrote about in his memoirs. It is also definitely possible, indeed probable, that the French provided subtle direction in steering Pershing and his staff to select Lorraine. Joffre had broached the idea to Pershing of deploying the American forces there shortly after the AEF commander's arrival in France and noted with satisfaction Pershing's "decision" to do so. This placement firmly ensured that the Americans would operate in the midst of the French forces and would thus provide their future combat strength, in the form of an autonomous army, to support French, not British, military operations.[36]

In mid-July Pershing ordered Major General William L. Sibert, commanding general of the U.S. First Division, to move his infantry brigades to Gondrecourt and to send his artillery brigade to the French artillery school at Valdahon to commence training. Captain George C. Marshall was the operations officer for the First Division in 1917. Marshall and the other staff officers arrived in Gondrecourt to discover that although the training areas were more than adequate, there was a serious shortage of space and housing for barracks. Consequently, the enlisted men of the First Division were housed in the numerous large barns in the rural village, and officers such as Marshall were placed in the homes of local French families. Marshall was billeted with the Jouatte family, which consisted of M. and Mme. Jouatte, as well as a woman and her daughter who were refugees from northern France. As with most French households in

1917, there were no young men in the Jouatte home. Their only son was a soldier in the French army and had been captured by the Germans at Verdun the year before; the refugee's husband was also serving in the French army.[37]

Marshall was given a small room on the second floor of the house that "contained a little bed of the Napoleonic type, a washstand, two chairs, and a fireplace." Marshall recalled that "at first it seemed very small, but later with the cold, dreary weather, it proved to be an ideal billet." He became very close to the Jouatte family during his six-month stay with them. He grew especially fond of the matronly Mme. Jouatte, who "was in no small measure responsible for my being able to keep a stiff upper lip and wear an optimistic smile" during the trying days spent attempting to train and field a combat-ready division.[38]

One of Marshall's early trials was the food that the U.S. Army's hastily trained cooks dished out at the division mess hall. He described it as "soldier chow slung at you and on themselves by casual soldier waiters, plenty of grease in the food, on the table, and frequently on the guests—quantity and not quality being the standard of the cook."[39] Dissatisfied with this arrangement, he approached Madame Jouatte with the possibility of running a private mess at her home for himself and selected officers.

Marshall reached an arrangement whereby Madame Jouatte would do the cooking and run the mess while he supplied sugar, white flour, canned milk, and other items that were desperately scarce in France but that he could obtain through the U.S. Army commissary. Marshall's messmates included Colonel Hamilton A. Smith, Major Lesley McNair, Captain Paul H. Clark, and one of the French trainers assigned to the First Division, Lieutenant Jean Hugo, the great-grandson of the celebrated French author Victor Hugo. Marshall recalled: "The arrangement proved a unique success; the meals were delicious, Madame Jouatte was '*très gentille*' and eccentrically amusing, and the atmosphere was very cozy and homelike—in decided contrast to everything else in Gondrecourt."[40]

Marshall also noted that Mme. Jouatte became the target of some good-natured, and wholly platonic, flirtation from the officers. But on one occasion a particular exchange was perhaps a tad more suggestive than was intended, and she appeared greatly disturbed by the daring remark addressed to her. Concerned, Marshall and the other Americans quickly asked Hugo if they had offended her and Hugo replied, "I think Madame is alarmed, but pleased!"[41]

Major General Joseph T. Dickman, commanding the U.S. Third Division, was billeted in the house of Madame Frossard and recalled the "cordial relations [that] were established with the French people." He later wrote, "It was gratifying to receive from all parts of the area reports of the friendly relations existing between our officers and soldiers and the French people. It is certain that we left behind us an enduring and favorable impression of the young American soldier from beyond the seas."[42] Even though Dickman's Third Division arrived in France in spring 1918, some eight months after the First Division and after the novelty of having American soldiers around had worn off, relations between them and the French civilians still remained very warm.

Since Marshall and Dickman were officers, it could be argued that they received preferential treatment from the French civilians. Yet the testimonies of American enlisted men billeted with French families reveal that they too established wonderful relationships with the people, who welcomed them with open arms. The American soldiers in general had a great respect and sympathy for the ordeals that three years of total war had forced upon the people of France.

Private Lloyd C. Short of the U.S. Second Division wrote to his family: "Our camp here is in a little village and we are sleeping overhead in their houses at present. The people are real good to us and try to learn us how to talk French." Short wrote of his affection for the French and how "pretty" everything was, with the farms well maintained even though the only males around were either young boys or old men. He wrote that if one made a little effort to speak French it was warmly received, and in general, "the French people over here are very nice to us and try to make it as comfortable as possible for us." Short believed in the cause he was fighting for, had a strong affection for France and its people, and indeed believed that this nation that had suffered so grievously at the hands of the Germans epitomized what the war was all about. He was killed in action at the Second Battle of the Marne.[43]

While recuperating from wounds, Sergeant Lloyd Norris wrote home, "I am having a very pleasant time here, have become acquainted with a very nice [French] family who had me to their home for dinner and supper. . . . They are very good to me . . . and will do most anything for me to make me feel at home." The family took Norris under their wing, and Madame Abray, the matron of the household, wrote to Norris's mother to inform her that her son was doing well. Mme. Abray hastened to add, "I would not have you ignorant of the fact that he is wounded in the thigh, though not seriously; and with all the good care by which he is surrounded, and a little time of rest he will be able to run again." Mme. Abray wrote Mrs. Norris that her letter carried with it "the best kisses of your son."[44]

Placing American soldiers with French families turned out to be an astonishing success from the point of view of building up comradeship between the soldiers and the people. Yet it could easily have had the opposite effect. Colonel Robert Lee Bullard commanded the First Brigade of the First Division in July 1917, later rising to the rank of lieutenant general and commander of the U.S. Second Army in late 1918. He noted the remarkable success of the billeting program, even though historically Americans had always been opposed to such a system, and pointed out that such practices indeed had even been one of the main causes for the American Revolution. As he recalled, "To this condition, however, in the course of time, our soldiers became used, and when at last we were leaving France [after the war], revisiting some of the old regions that had been occupied by troops under my command, I found individual American soldiers back there on furlough, visiting French friends with whom they had established close relations when in their former billets. The billeting accounted for many French brides upon our return to the United States."[45]

Not everything went smoothly, of course, during this initial contact between the French populace and the American soldiers, as both attempted to adjust to the customs and ways of the other while adapting as best they could. One practice that the Americans were never quite able to understand or adjust to was the custom in rural communities of collecting a *fumier* (large manure pile) from animal droppings in the streets to use as fertilizer in their fields. The pile was added to daily and was placed prominently next to the front door of most rural dwellings. Bullard recalled that a *fumier* was "a disagreeable thing, irritating and dangerous in the dark, and a kind of front yard ornamentation to which our soldiers could never grow accustomed." American soldiers in Gondrecourt also repeatedly ran afoul of French authorities because of their extravagant use of wood from precious local forests and their occasional use of fences and even sideboards of homes for firewood. [46]

The soldiers resented the fact that the shopkeepers consistently raised their prices in accordance with the sudden influx of American money into the community. Many soldiers voiced complaints both during and after the war regarding these French war profiteers, as they believed that the very people they were coming to save were taking advantage of them to make a tidy profit off the free-spending Americans. There was resentment and acrimony over this issue, and much of it has crept into historical accounts of the AEF, where it is often held up as evidence of a mutual dislike between the Americans and the French.

Without question, French shopkeepers and merchants did take full advantage of the free-spending Americans, yet it should be recalled that these individuals also took advantage of their own nation's soldiers. Indeed, French soldiers had complained bitterly of these war profiteers since the earliest days of the war, and they were, arguably, the most hated of all civilians, occupying an even lower place than the *embusqués* (slackers) who managed to stay in the rear or who avoided military service by holding a job in a war-related industry. A French trench newspaper, written, edited, and published by the *poilus* themselves, complained with biting sarcasm: "And then there is the sad category of profiteers. They do not sound gloomy, and they are certainly smiling, I can assure you. They willingly adopt a heroic stance as craftsmen of the nation's defense, selling [items] for fabulous prices . . . manufactured under conditions very little different from those of normal times. This is the class of the new rich. . . . It is wise to observe the movements of these vampires carefully and the 'high cost of living' can only be avoided by rigorous sanctions."[47] Americans who believed they were being singled out for exploitation by war profiteers because of their nationality were actually being singled out because of their class; they were soldiers and thus the natural prey of war profiteers.

Not every American was blind to this. Bullard recalled that while the obvious profiteering angered him, too, he realized that the high prices hurt the French civilians and soldiers far more than they affected the relatively affluent American troops. He also later stated that American shopkeepers had engaged in the same activity when the U.S. Army had deployed to Texas during the 1916 crisis with Mexico. Thus, while this problem of French profiteering remained a cause of complaint among some American soldiers, others realized that war profiteers come in many different national varieties, as do the targets of their exploitative practices.[48]

Pershing always insisted that the American soldiers conduct themselves as gentlemen among the French populace and went to great lengths to ensure the good behavior of his men. In many ways the success of the training program for the AEF depended on the goodwill of the French people themselves, who played a valuable role in the process by providing housing and food for the soldiers. Shortly after the U.S. First Division arrived at Gondrecourt, Pershing issued a general order to all the American troops in France:

> It is of the greatest importance that the soldiers of the American Army shall at all times treat the people of France, especially the women, with the greatest courtesy and consideration. The valiant deeds of the French Armies and those of their Allies by which they have together successfully maintained their common cause for three years, and the

sacrifices of the civil population of France in support of their armies command our profound respect. This can best be expressed on the part of our forces by uniform courtesy to all the French people and by faithful consideration of their laws and customs. . . . The intense cultivation of the soil in France and the conditions caused by the war make it necessary that extreme care be taken to do no damage to private property. The entire French manhood capable of bearing arms is in the field fighting the enemy. Only old men, women and children remain to cultivate the soil. It should therefore be a point of honor with each member of the American Army to avoid doing the least damage to any property in France.[49]

Most American soldiers felt a great deal of sympathy for the ordeal that the French people had endured during the course of the war and believed that the French in turn showed them much affection and held them in high esteem. Typical was Sergeant Major Vernon Mossman, Eighteenth Infantry Regiment, U.S. First Division, who later recalled, "The French were very nice and congenial. Having been through three years of war, suffering great loss of life and damages to their cities and communities, they treated us with great respect as we came to their aid as an ally."[50]

On the whole, the personal behavior of U.S. troops in France during the course of the war was exemplary, and without question this helped the Americans establish a sincere bond of friendship with the French people. The soldiers especially endeared themselves to the French through the kindness they showed French children, whom they showered with candy and small gifts. Indeed, most American soldiers quickly warmed to the French people, a response that was not surprising at the time. As Bullard recalled:

Americans carried with them to France a great affection for the French. There can be no doubt of it. Its causes are found in the beginnings of our history and in the sympathy of our people for the weaker people whom Germany was "bleeding white," deliberately assassinating, when we decided to enter the war. This [affection for France] helped to keep Franco-American relations smooth. Good relations were also helped by the lively gratitude on the part of the French for our having come to their assistance in the war. They often expressed it.[51]

The establishment of an excellent rapport between the American soldiers and the French populace was extremely important. The French people were in many ways seriously inconvenienced by the arrival of the

American soldiers. Their homes and barns were turned into barracks, their fields converted into training areas, and prices were driven up by the free-spending American troops. These circumstances could have produced such resentment among the ordinary citizens that the entire training program could have broken down before it got off the ground. Instead, the American soldiers managed to ingratiate themselves with the French people and went out of their way to behave more like guests than saviors. The French appreciated this and reciprocated with friendship and hospitality. Yet as important as this initial relationship was, the real test of camaraderie between France and America came when the raw American soldiers began their training with the veteran French troops assigned to be their instructors and mentors.

General Pétain handpicked the Forty-seventh *Chasseurs Alpin* Division to be paired with the U.S. First Division at Gondrecourt and to serve as their instructors in modern warfare. The *Chasseurs Alpin* was an elite infantry division trained in mountain warfare but used during the Great War as special assault troops in French offensives. The *Chasseurs* were nicknamed the Blue Devils because of the oversized dark-blue beret and dark-blue tunic they wore to mark their status as an elite unit. Their regimental flags were bedecked with croix de guerre ribbons and bore battle streamers from virtually every major engagement the French army had fought in the war. General d'Armand de Poudrygain commanded the division. Marshall described him as "a little, wiry man, with one eye, which shot sparks every time he talked." De Poudrygain was considered by his peers to be a tough and effective commander, and it was for this reason, as well as for his division's impeccable record, that he was chosen to lead this important training mission.[52]

Although at first glance it would appear that many difficulties would have to be overcome in terms of the different traditions and historical experiences of the U.S. Army and the French army, in reality they had much in common. Although the United States did not maintain a large standing army in peacetime, as France and the other Great Powers did, the U.S. Army nevertheless had always been organized and trained according to the western European style of warfare. Indeed, the French in particular had traditionally had a major influence on the U.S. Army since the founding of the nation.

French intervention in the American Revolution had been the decisive factor in enabling the colonies to win their independence from Great Britain, and the French had exerted an influence on the Continental army, from 1778 on, in terms of equipment, organization, training, and operations. During the conflict, the young French nobleman the Marquis de

Lafayette, who was virtually a son to George Washington, had commanded an entire division of the Continental army. American and French soldiers had served side by side in various battles but most importantly during the Yorktown campaign, where French assistance had proven to be critical. At Yorktown the French forces under Rochambeau had constituted approximately half of George Washington's army, and French heavy artillery and siege engineers, along with the brilliant handling of a French naval squadron under Admiral de Grasse, had proven to be the decisive factors in this monumental Franco-American victory that led directly to American independence.

After the Revolution, French influence became even more marked and direct. During the years of the early Republic, Sylvanus Thayer emerged as one of the greatest American military intellectuals of the time. Thayer was a U.S. Army officer who served as an instructor at West Point and was superintendent there from 1817 to 1833, where he is still revered today as the "father of the Military Academy."[53] Thayer was fascinated by the campaigns of Napoleon and idolized the French emperor as the greatest commander in all of history. Angry over the generally poor showing of the U.S. Army in the War of 1812, Thayer decided that the United States needed to learn the art of war from the French army, which he believed to be the finest in the world. He journeyed to France in 1815, shortly after Napoleon's final defeat and exile, where he inspected the École polytechnique and purchased over 1,000 French books on military theory, military history, and military engineering. These books became the foundation for the library at West Point, the first genuine military library in the United States. As superintendent, Thayer inculcated the U.S. Military Academy with French instructional methods and unabashedly copied their system of military instruction for officers.[54]

Dennis Hart Mahan, another distinguished faculty member at West Point, reinforced Thayer's tradition of following the French example. Mahan made the study of the French language and the French army a compulsory subject at the academy. He is best known for his introduction of the study of military history into West Point's curriculum and for his strong belief in the practical uses of the subject for serving officers. In this regard, the Napoleonic Wars were by far the most strongly emphasized area of historical study there. Mahan founded the Napoleon Club as a form of postgraduate study at West Point that in many ways was the precursor of the U.S. Army War College and U.S. Army Command and General Staff College of today.[55]

Furthermore, many of America's greatest military commanders were pronounced Francophiles. Winfield Scott, one of the most significant figures in the development of the U.S. Army in the early Republic, was an ardent admirer of the French. He was an enthusiastic scholar of the campaigns of Napoleon and, like most of his contemporaries, believed the French emperor to be a military genius and the French army to be the finest in the world. Scott read French fluently (something he took great pride in), and with the encouragement of his commanding officer Major General Jacob Brown, he headed a board of officers who undertook an extensive study of French infantry tactics in 1814. This led to the formal codification of a slightly modified version of the French system as the standard infantry doctrine of the U.S. Army for the next forty years.[56]

The French influence can be seen at many levels in both the Union and Confederate armies during the American Civil War. In terms of ordnance, the standard field-artillery piece on both sides was the 12-pound Napoleon, an American copy of the French weapon named for Emperor Napoleon III.[57] Although rifles were mainly of American or British design, they all fired the French designed minié ball, an expanding soft-lead bullet that had revolutionized the battlefield by enabling rifles to have the same rate of fire and ease of handling as muskets.[58] Both sides wore French-style kepis as headgear, and both the Union and Confederate armies contained volunteer regiments that outfitted themselves in the gaudy uniform of the famous French Zouaves of the Second Empire. The irony of Confederate soldiers openly imitating the dress of North African troops was apparently lost at the time but says a great deal about the high regard that soldiers of both the North and the South held for the French army.

Virtually all the major commanders of the American Civil War were heavily influenced by the French through their training at West Point and through their own study of the campaigns of Napoleon. General Thomas J. (Stonewall) Jackson was an ardent admirer of the French emperor and enjoyed reading histories of Napoleon's campaigns. He always carried a copy of Napoleon's "Maxims" in his saddlebags while on campaign. George B. McClellan was an active member of the Napoleon Club at West Point, frequently quoted the emperor in his dispatches during the Civil War, and emulated Napoleon in everything, from how he posed for photographers to his Orders of the Day for the Army of the Potomac. Although this affinity for the French army suffered somewhat after the defeat of France by the Germans in 1871, its reputation as one of the world's historically preeminent fighting forces remained strong among Americans at the time of the Great War. Hence, they willingly accepted instruction from a foreign army that had such a formidable reputation and that traditionally had always had a major influence on their own armed forces.[59]

The first thing the neophyte infantrymen of the U.S. Army learned from the French in 1917 was that in modern warfare weapon systems were so diverse and the tactics so complex that specialists were needed. In the U.S. Army before the war, an infantryman was first, last, and always a rifleman. In the infantry of the French army of 1917, in addition to riflemen, there were grenadiers, rifle grenadiers, automatic riflemen, mortar men, and 37mm trench gunners. Each of these specialists had a role to play in battle and each was a master of his own particular weapon. Not only did the U.S. Army not have specialists such as these, they did not have any of the weapons, either. These weapons, with the exception of the automatic rifle, which was unique to the French army at this time, had become commonplace on the modern battlefield, but the American infantryman was woefully ignorant of their use in battle.[60]

Modern warfare, to the French in 1917 and to the British and Germans as well, meant combat in the maze of trench systems that made up the western front. Horrific casualties inflicted by machine guns and heavy artillery had forced both sides in the conflict to go to ground during late fall 1914. French, British, and German soldiers had dug increasingly elaborate defensive positions that transformed warfare on the western front from a war of maneuver into a titanic siege. The opposing armies were locked into a labyrinth of fortifications that stretched from the English Channel to the Swiss Alps. On the western front gains were measured in yards and casualties in the tens of thousands. An entire generation of European manhood had already been destroyed on these battlefields, and yet no tangible gain had been achieved by either side. The French explained to their American trainees that warfare had thus changed dramatically in 1914. They would teach the Americans not only how to fight this modern war on the western front, but also how to survive it.

The instructors explained that in modern trench warfare the grenade was a far more valuable weapon than the rifle and bayonet. The grenade was a sort of "poor man's artillery," a way for the infantryman to discharge his own small version of the high explosives that dominated the battlefields of the Great War. In order to fire a rifle or use a bayonet an infantryman had to expose himself to the enemy's fire, and in World War I this meant almost certain death. On the other hand, a soldier could use a hand grenade from the safety of his trenches, lobbing it in a high arc so that he could strike at enemies in their trenches in a form of indirect fire. A rifle grenade worked on much the same principle, but with a greater range for the explosive.

American soldiers who had been trained to engage targets with their Springfield rifles at distances of up to 500 yards on firing ranges were astounded when their French instructors placed targets only 50 to 100 yards down range for rifle practice. The French calmly explained to their bewildered trainees that in the trenches of the western front a soldier would never see a target beyond that range anyway, so why bother trying to perfect long-range marksmanship? It was better to spend the time working on mastering weapons such as the grenade, automatic rifle, mortar, or trench gun, which could deliver far more killing power than a single .30-caliber bullet.

Although it might appear that language would have posed a major difficulty in the training process, it is rarely mentioned as a problem either in training or in later combat operations. Indeed, a staggering 94 percent of U.S. brigade, division, and corps commanders surveyed after the war reported either "no difficulty" or only "slight" difficulties arising from language problems, with only a paltry 1 percent indicating "numerous" problems.[61]

There are several reasons for this, including a rather intensive effort by the AEF to train their officers in French. Primarily, the French made sure that the officers they assigned to training duties with the Americans spoke English. The French noncommissioned officers and enlisted men who assisted used a mixture of broken English and impromptu sign language to communicate verbally and emphasized a hands-on approach that ensured the instruction went smoothly. Moreover, interpreters supplied by the French army were scattered liberally among the various training camps to assist in solving any language problems. At each camp an American officer, chosen by the AEF staff from the trainees assigned to the facility, was designated to be the primary liaison with the French commanding officer. Thus, the French instructors had ready access to an interpreter should the need arise, and language difficulties were rarely a problem.[62]

Generally, the French instructors had a favorable impression of American soldiers and noted that they exhibited a tremendous fighting spirit and eagerly expressed their desire to go into battle as soon as possible. Unfortunately, the instructors reported that these positive attributes were also a problem, as the trainees quickly grew restless with the training process in their impatience to get to the front. Nevertheless, the French noted that the American soldiers exhibited great respect and deference for their "professors" and expressed a great love for France. The general conclusion was that the greatest fault of the trainees was their overeagerness for action. The French instructors hardly considered this a real problem, provided that the restless energy of the Americans was properly channeled.[63]

General de Poudrygain, the commander of the Forty-seventh *Chasseurs Alpin,* was the first French general to work closely with the American soldiers, and the French army relied on him heavily to supply observations concerning the general demeanor, attitude, professionalism, and fighting spirit of these newcomers. Shortly after the training program began, Poudrygain reported on its progress to General Pétain and to General Nöel de Castelnau, commanding general of the French Eastern Army Group, in whose sector the training was being conducted. Reporting that during this early period of training the Americans had made an excellent impression on his officers and men, he observed, "All in all, [American] Officers and men display a great fondness and admiration for France, have a great esteem for our army and are making a full effort with an eager desire to become familiar with the conduct of actual war. In these first days a confident camaraderie has been established between the staffs and the troops of the two divisions, American and French."[64]

Poudrygain described the average American soldier as "in general young, not trained (4 recruits for every 1 veteran soldier) ardent and confident of his strength and desiring to fight as soon as possible, very docile [toward officers] and disciplined." He also observed that most of the Americans demonstrated considerable skills in sports and noted that this was already proving particularly useful in grenade training. Apparently, he was referring to their skill in throwing a baseball, which could easily translate into throwing a grenade. He also reported that they had a great desire for instruction in warfare and learned their lessons quickly and well.[65]

American soldiers were in turn impressed with the experience, professionalism, and knowledge of their French instructors. Sergeant Major Vernon C. Mossman later recalled, "We were trained by their most seasoned fighters. We had great respect and admiration of them." Corporal Frederick Shaw rated French soldiers as "excellent" and stated, "I feel our [U.S. First Division] was fortunate in that we received the bulk of our training overseas, enabling us to become acclimated and train on the terrain. Also [we received] more special instruction by [French] veterans in various areas of combat."[66]

Other American units who followed the First Division also had a positive relationship with their French instructors. Lieutenant General Edward M. Almond, then a fresh-faced Second Lieutenant, served with the U.S. Fourth Division and commented, "In general we thought that the French officer we came in contact with in a training way was an alert, educated, but sometimes emotional type." Almond commanded a machine gun company, equipped with French Hotchkiss machine guns, and believed that the training he received was "very useful. Particularly in the teaching of our men through French training teams . . . how to operate the equipment with which they were armed. . . . [The French instructors] were considered by our men to be hard task masters in teaching the successful operation of the gun and in target practice."[67]

The individual American soldiers, most of whom were completely raw trainees anyway, and the junior officers of the First Division accepted the French training methods without question and eagerly adopted French tactical methods as their own, much to Pershing's dismay. He was concerned that the soldiers and junior officers of the AEF, whom he deemed inexperienced and impressionable, were far too infatuated with their veteran instructors and hence gave French views on warfare too much credit. Pershing and other senior AEF officers considered this to be dangerous because they increasingly believed that French and British tactical doctrine was not aggressive enough. Colonel Harold B. Fiske, who later became head of the AEF training section, summed up the general impression that Pershing and the AEF high command had:

> The offensive spirit of the French and British Armies has largely disappeared as a result of their severe losses. . . . Our young officers and men are prone to take the tone and tactics of those with whom they are associated, and whatever they are now learning that is false or unsuited for us will be hard to eradicate later. In many respects, the tactics and technique of our Allies are not suited to American characteristics or the American mission in this war. The French do not like the rifle, do not know how to use it, and their infantry is consequently too entirely dependent upon a powerful artillery support. Their infantry lacks aggressiveness and discipline. The British infantry lacks initiative and resource.[68]

Thus, the senior officers of the AEF, from the staff of the U.S. First Division to Pershing himself, who together represented the professional element of the U.S. Army, were quite upset by French methods of infantry training. They were dismayed by what they saw as an excessive reliance on artillery fire and "trench weapons" (as Pershing described grenades, mortars, and other special weapons of the French infantry) to support their attacks. Pershing was particularly concerned about the French belief that the rifle was not an especially useful weapon. He was further troubled when the instructors focused their infantry training exclusively on preparing American soldiers for a war waged in the trenches of the western front. He firmly believed that trench warfare was a temporary state of affairs and that he must ready the American soldier to participate in great battles of movement fought in the open, to be led by the AEF, that would break the war out of the stalemate. He thought the American infantry should focus at least half, if not more, of their training time on "open warfare." This dispute caused a serious rift to develop between senior American officers and their French counterparts.

Although the Americans gave various reasons as evidence of this perceived lack of aggressiveness in the French, the main point they constantly referred to was the utter disdain that most French infantry in 1917 held for the rifle and bayonet as a useful weapon. French infantry had learned that rifle fire was an ineffective method for attaining the kind of fire superiority required to support an advance against an entrenched enemy; their experience on the western front from 1914 to 1917 had taught them that artillery and machine guns were better. Even during trench raids, when the fighting was waged at close quarters, grenades and pistols were far more useful than rifles and bayonets. If the fighting became hand-to-hand, which it often did on a trench raid, a soldier armed with a long bayonet-tipped rifle was at a severe disadvantage in the close confines of a trench, compared to a soldier armed with a pistol, knife, or homemade club.

The American infantryman traditionally had been trained to rely on the rifle and bayonet as his main, indeed sole, weapons. Both in the pre-war U.S. Army and in the initial training the soldiers received in 1917 before they were sent overseas, these two arms were stressed to the exclusion of virtually all others. This was in keeping with an American tradition of arms that stretched back to the founding days of the Republic. The image of the rugged frontiersman and his Kentucky long rifle was firmly ingrained not only in the popular imagination but also in American military doctrine. Riflemen had won American independence, conquered the wilderness, and expanded and defended the frontiers of the Republic from its founding. Whether it was Andrew Jackson's men devastating British assault columns at New Orleans, Davy Crockett's boys from Tennessee mowing down waves of attacking Mexicans at the Alamo, or James Longstreet's men turning back a dozen Union assaults at Fredericksburg, the American military tradition was founded on the concept that the American soldier with his rifle was the weapon of decision on the battlefield.

In defense of Pershing, this belief in the power of rifle fire was more than just a romantic myth. Indeed, from their widespread introduction as the main weapon of European and American infantry in the 1850s, rifles had dominated the battlefields of the second half of the nineteenth century. In the American Civil War , from 1861 to 1865, rifles had been the de-

cisive weapons in the conflict. Although artillery had played an important role, rifle fire accounted for approximately 75 percent of the battlefield casualties. Rifles had also been effective in the Plains Indians Wars,
the Spanish-American War, the Philippine Insurrection, and various low-
intensity conflicts waged by the United States. In virtually every battle
fought by the U.S. Army from 1866 to 1916, artillery, and even automatic
weapons, had played a distinctly supportive role; the main fighting was
done by rifle-wielding infantry or cavalry.

In the U.S. Army, marksmanship was prized, and proper enthusiasm
on the bayonet course was looked upon as a strong indicator of individual aggressiveness. Pershing often waxed poetic during the Great War on
the wonders of the rifle and bayonet, writing in October 1917: "Close ad-
herence is urged to the central idea that the essential principles of war
have not changed, that the rifle and the bayonet remain the supreme
weapons of the infantry soldier and that the ultimate success of the army
depends upon their proper use in open warfare."[69] He scoffed at the
elaborate schemes for employing the wide variety of weapons that
French infantry used on the battlefield, later writing, "Machine guns,
grenades, Stokes mortars, and one-pounders [37mm trench guns] had become the main reliance of the average Allied soldier. These were all valuable weapons for specific purposes but they could not replace the
combination of an efficient soldier and his rifle."[70]

In many ways the French army had entered the Great War with a similar philosophy. After their disastrous defeat in the Franco-Prussian War
(1870–1871), the French had conducted a thorough examination of their
army and its doctrine. Led by military theorists such as Louis Loyzeaux
de Grandmaison and Ferdinand Foch and inspired by the writings of the
late Charles Ardant du Picq, the French conducted a sweeping examination of the victorious battles and campaigns of Napoleon and compared
these to the defeats of 1870 and 1871. They concluded that the secret to
Napoleon's success was his audacity and his insistence on always being
the attacker on the battlefield, regardless of the overall strategic situation.
In stark contrast, the French army of the Franco-Prussian War was seen
as passive, relying on defensive firepower rather than on the bayonet to
fight its battles. Herein, argued the adherents of the so-called "cult of the
offensive," lay the reasons for French defeat. Thus, the path to success
was aggressive offensive action spearheaded by bayonet-wielding French
infantry, whose naturally superior élan would carry the day, regardless of
the odds. By 1911 the cult of the offensive held sway in French military
circles, and the theories of its leading advocates had become official
French army doctrine.[71]

When the Great War began in 1914 French infantry had surged forward in wild infantry charges, with little to no artillery support, in a desperate attempt to close with the bayonet on the Germans. It was not until hecatombs of French dead had been piled high by German machine-gun and artillery fire that the French realized the folly of blind valor in the face of modern weaponry. They suffered catastrophic casualties in the opening campaigns of the war and came close to being completely defeated before Joffre began to implement changes in their tactical doctrine that emphasized closer coordination between infantry and artillery and de-emphasized shock action by the infantry.

Pétain had never been enamored of the cult of the offensive. Rather, he had spent virtually his entire career stressing the role of firepower on the modern battlefield and the need to develop superiority of fire over the enemy before the infantry could move forward. Pershing's brash statements about spirited charges by bayonet-wielding American soldiers carrying the day must have been a source of great consternation to Pétain. The grim death tolls in the French army of 1914 and 1915 had convinced his own countrymen of the folly of this tactical approach. Yet now Pétain had to face an American who, although he had never read Grandmaison's works, nevertheless appeared to be as dedicated an adherent of the *offensive à outrance* as he himself had been.

Significantly, statements Pershing made both during and after the war indicate that apparently he was completely unaware of prewar French army doctrine. Even more important, he seems to have had only the most rudimentary knowledge of the operations of the French army, or of any other European army for that matter, during the war. He upbraided the British and French for "allowing" their armies to become mired in trench warfare. He apparently believed the stalemate on the western front represented a character flaw in Europeans instead of a new set of conditions imposed by the deadly effects of modern weaponry on the battlefield. He particularly assailed the French for being "defensive minded":

It was, perhaps, logical to expect that the French should take this view as, nationally, unlike the Germans, they had been on the defensive, at least in thought, during the previous half century. It is true that on occasions the French assumed the offensive, but the defensive idea was ever in mind. In the situation that followed the first battle of the Marne, the great armies on the western front were entrenched against each other and neither had been able to make more than local gains. The long period during which this condition had prevailed, with its resultant psychological effect, together with the natural leaning of the

French toward the defensive, to which should be added the adverse effect of their recent spring experience [the Nivelle offensive], had apparently combined to obscure the principles of open warfare.[72]

Peyton C. March, who commanded the artillery brigade of the First Division in 1917 but quickly rose to the rank of general and became chief of staff of the U.S. Army in 1918, was astonished in the postwar years when he read Pershing's remarks concerning the nature of the French army. In commenting on Pershing's clashes with the French army and its leadership, both in 1917 and later in 1918, March wrote that these differences "were accentuated by [Pershing's] profound ignorance of the French military policy, curious in a regular officer of such high rank." March challenged, and rightfully so, Pershing's characterization of French military doctrine as being traditionally defensive-minded during the fifty years leading up to the Great War:

The fact is precisely the opposite of this statement. The entire French military policy has for years been founded on the attack; always the attack. As a matter of fact, they carried out this policy in the early days of the World War to an extent which caused disaster to them. This fundamental error of General Pershing's was not known to me, nor to Secretary Baker, during the war. It never occurred to either of us that such an entire misconception of the genius of the French army was possible.[73]

Although Pershing's biographers and supporters have always been quick to defend his tactical philosophy and to scoff at the French as lacking aggressiveness, Pershing's tactical philosophy has been severely criticized by less biased military authorities who are by no means Francophiles. The British historian and strategist B. H. Liddell-Hart was an admirer and staunch supporter of Pershing, but he did not hesitate to criticize the AEF commander's tactical doctrine. Liddell-Hart believed that Pershing's tactical philosophy was seriously flawed because it failed to appreciate the developments that had occurred in warfare since 1914:

Pershing, and most of his officers, bred on open fighting, were aghast at the way in which the other armies, especially the French, had become immersed in trench warfare. Bred also on the rifle, they ascribed this immersion not to its true cause, the battlefield mastery of the machine gun, but to the excessive use of grenades and other trench weapons. . . . Further they connected the loss of offensive spirit, which they found so marked among the French, with the prevalence of trench warfare and trench weapons. Both assumptions were true in part, but only the lesser part. For trench warfare and trench weapons had arisen because riflemen could no longer make headway against machine guns. Inspired by the right idea, but based on false premises, Pershing established the cult of the rifle in the new American army. And believing that it was possible to break through the trench front, given troops full of the offensive spirit, he trained his men for open warfare and attack with all the fervor which the French had shown before 1914.[74]

More recently James W. Rainey has taken Pershing to task for supporting a contradictory tactical doctrine for the U.S. Army. Rainey notes that Pershing espoused an ill-defined doctrine of "open warfare" (indeed, Rainey charges that Pershing never truly defined this term) that was hopelessly at odds with the tactical realities of the western front. Yet at the same time he constructed and equipped the AEF as a heavily armed, monolithic, and inflexible structure that was far more suited for a grinding war of attrition in the trenches than a war of maneuver. This would suggest that Pershing recognized that the AEF would be involved in heavy trench fighting instead of engaged in the open warfare that he so often spoke of. What was the reason for this seeming contradiction? As Rainey argues:

A partial answer may be that Pershing's hidebound insistence on preparing his Army for open warfare had something to do with the "amalgamation controversy," that political-military debate in which he strenuously fought off repeated Allied requests to employ AEF soldiers as individual fillers for their own depleted units. One of the arguments Pershing employed to keep these wolves at bay was his claim that the AEF must remain intact so as to be able to employ its unique tactical solution to the stalemate of the trenches.[75]

Although Rainey's argument certainly has merit, I believe that it overlooks a major factor in the Franco-American dispute over training. Significantly, neither Pershing nor any of his subordinates ever murmured a word of dissent regarding how the French trained American artillerymen at Valdahon, or later how they instructed American tank crews or pilots. Nowhere in their discussion of these forms of training did the Americans say that the French were not aggressive, their methods unsound, or that they were in any other way lacking in professionalism and ability. It was only in the matter of training infantrymen that the officers of the two armies were at odds. Why would Pershing and his officer corps choose the infantry as a place where they could, and should, make a stand for a uniquely American approach to modern warfare?

No conclusive answer can be given, but it could be argued that although Pershing was willing to admit that his army of raw recruits was in need of instruction in weapons that the U.S. Army did not possess, he refused to accept that American doctrine regarding the weapons that it did possess (i.e., rifles) could possibly be flawed. Being a professional soldier, he had a tremendous amount of pride in his army and in his own abilities. He repeatedly commented in his memoirs and other writings that the principles of warfare had not been changed by the Great War, even though it was readily apparent that many of those principles indeed had been changed. Perhaps to say otherwise would have been tantamount to an admission that he needed as much training in modern warfare as his soldiers did.

In 1917 Pershing was in the awkward position of being a commanding general in charge of the smallest force on the western front. Unquestionably, no matter how much the French tried to make him feel welcome, they also acted from a position of superiority that apparently, and unintentionally, rankled Pershing. It was one thing to say that his recruits needed French instruction but quite another to intimate that the professional officer corps of the U.S. Army, including himself, also required French instruction in modern battlefield tactics. In point of fact, American officers did need tactical instruction, and some quickly recognized the worth of French infantry tactics in the training camps and again when they had actually gone into the front lines in late 1917. But as the historian Allan Millett has observed, "For an officer to insist that the French infantry had some tactics worth copying was to risk being labeled a defeatist of the 'trench warfare' school by the AEF general staff."[76]

Pershing truly believed that his own limited combat and command experience was the equal of any of his French counterparts and thus considered himself as knowledgeable as they were on military matters. Although his prewar experiences were certainly comparable to that of the senior commanders of the French army, or for that matter of the British army, the science and art of warfare had undergone a fundamental transformation in 1914. The French officer corps had been forced to learn difficult lessons regarding prewar theoretical concepts of battle and the folly of attempting to apply colonial experiences to the battlefields of the western front. While Pershing was leading a small cavalry expedition in search of Mexican bandits in 1916, Pétain had led the French Second Army at Verdun during one of the longest, largest, and bloodiest battles in history. Thus, one can only imagine the thoughts French officers must have had as they listened to Pershing explain in excruciating detail how he knew all about machine guns and how to attack them because of his experience in the Punitive Expedition against Mexico. The tremendous difference between a handful of Mexican bandits with a Gatling gun in a rundown hacienda and an Imperial German Army machine-gun platoon inside concrete bunkers on the Hindenburg Line was either lost on Pershing or it was a reality he simply refused to accept.

Pershing's great fault as a commander was his belief that he knew everything there was to know about modern warfare, even though he had not studied the 1914–1917 campaigns and had no experience in the present conflict. His insistence that trench warfare was a state of mind rather than a physical reality reveals a serious flaw in his approach to the battlefield, for he offered no real solution to the deadlock. In 1917 the French and British were developing armored warfare and a new artillery doctrine to attempt to break through the German defenses. The German army was undergoing a massive doctrinal transformation emphasizing the use of specially trained and specially equipped storm troops combined with new methods of artillery fire to achieve the same result. Pershing, however, repeated over and over again that American ardor and dash, exemplified in mass infantry assaults, would suffice to break the enemy defenses. Prior to the Great War such opinions could have been excused on the basis of ignorance, but by 1917 it was a horribly simplistic view of the modern battlefield that was completely divorced from the tactical reality of the western front.[77]

The net result of this dispute between the French army and Pershing over infantry tactics and training was a somewhat schizophrenic experience for the American infantrymen of the First Division. During the mornings, the *Chasseurs Alpin* trained the Americans for warfare in the trenches, endlessly drilling them on the use of grenade and mortar and conducting mock trench raids. In the afternoon, American officers took the soldiers and ran them through battlefield exercises in the countryside, where they practiced Pershing's open warfare, maneuvering and advancing through fields, woods, and villages in a style of fighting that had not been seen on the western front since 1914.

The men of the First Division were on constant display during their time in training at Gondrecourt. Marshall later noted that the division was "Exhibit 'A' of the AEF" and lamented that "there was no 'B,' 'C,' and 'D.' Review followed review in rapid succession; first for General Pershing, and then for Marshal Joffre, President Poincaré, General Pétain and many others."[78]

By and large, the Americans made an excellent impression on their visitors, but not always. On one occasion General de Castelnau paid a visit to the Americans at Gondrecourt.[79] The occasion of his visit prompted General Poudrygain to place a French chef as an adviser to the American cooks, for as Marshall recalled, "The First Division seemed devoid of any talent of this nature."[80] Under the direction of the French chef, exquisite food with fine champagne was served as the officers of the First Division and Forty-seventh *Chasseurs Alpin* dined with their distinguished guest. The waiters were Americans, and one of these men apparently discovered the joys of champagne shortly before going on duty. The meal had scarcely begun when the drunken American waiter promptly dumped a large bowl of creamed fish sauce down the front of Castelnau's uniform, "more or less completely obliterating his decorations," as Marshall recalled. Castelnau remained unperturbed and carried on his conversation as if nothing had occurred. A horrified General Sibert rushed to clean off the French general while one of his aides chased the waiter through the kitchen and out into the street.[81] This humorous incident illustrates that the problem of inexperienced and inadequately trained personnel was not limited to American soldiers serving in the combat branches but also extended to the support personnel of the AEF.

While the infantry brigades of the First Division trained at Gondrecourt, the artillery brigade underwent its training at the French artillery school at Valdahon. General Pétain was a strong advocate of the importance of firepower on the modern battlefield, and he took a particular interest in ensuring that the Americans understood modern (i.e., French) artillery tactics and theory. He believed that since they would be using French guns and howitzers, and since the military efforts of the two armies would be inextricably linked during the war, it was particularly important for the Americans "to adopt our methods and our procedures" for artillery fire.[82]

By 1917 the French army had developed a tactical concept of artillery use that involved massing a large number of guns and placing overwhelming amounts of artillery fire on enemy positions as a prerequisite for any successful infantry advance. The French attacked at Verdun on 20 August 1917, and utilizing massive firepower from heavy artillery, blasted their way northward for several miles along both banks of the Meuse River, inflicting heavy casualties on the Germans while keeping their own losses light. The operation was a brilliant tactical success and had an immediately positive impact on the morale of the French army.[83]

On 23 October the French struck again, with a surprise offensive against the dreaded Chemin des Dames, the same location where Nivelle had shattered the French army's morale only six months earlier. But Pétain was not attempting to rupture the entire German defense system; he was only after the infamous ridge itself, which had come to symbolize futility to many French soldiers. After a week of heavy fighting, the Germans were driven from the ridge with heavy losses and Pétain was content to take the position and consolidate his defenses rather than attempt to follow up the success in the face of stiffening German resistance. Once again, a limited attack with a limited objective had proven successful. In terms of French morale, the seizure of the Chemin des Dames had inestimable value.[84]

These tactical victories had tremendous importance from the standpoint of restoring French morale; however, the French were still faced with a serious problem that could not be easily addressed: a dire shortage of manpower. By December 1917 this shortage had become so acute that Pétain was forced to make plans to reduce the number of battalions in French divisions and had to consider the possibility that entire divisions would have to be disbanded, due to a lack of replacements.[85]

Indeed, during his command of the Second Army at the Battle of Verdun, Pétain had experimented with what he called "artillery offensives," whereby his guns would unleash massive barrages on German positions with no thought to an infantry assault to follow, thus waging an entire battle with artillery alone. The catch phrase, "artillery conquers, infantry occupies," epitomized French doctrine by this time, an approach taken as a result of the astronomically high casualties of the previous three years. Pétain utilized overwhelming firepower, indeed American observers thought excessive firepower, against an enemy as a means to keep his own casualties low, even if this meant accepting only small tactical gains on the battlefield instead of the illusory breakthrough that had long been sought by both sides.

American military observers had viewed the developments in European artillery practice from afar during the years of American neutrality. Report after report piled up regarding the massive revolution in artillery tactics, but virtually nothing was done to act on the recommendations of these observers. Operating under President Wilson's strict guidelines for American neutrality, whereby even planning for possible participation in the war was seen to be in violation of the neutrality principle, and given U.S. budget constraints, the army's artillery branch slipped quietly into obsolescence. Indeed, the historian Mark Grotelueschen has observed that American artillery doctrine in 1917 "consistently minimized the importance of artillery to combat operations" by emphasizing mobility over firepower and stressing that the decisive force on the battlefield was the infantry, with the guns playing only a subsidiary, and very minor, role.[86]

Such an approach was hopelessly outdated and completely unsuited for the tactical realities of the western front, where firepower, not mobility, reigned supreme. Thus, the tactical instruction in artillery use the French army provided proved to be absolutely essential to the development of the AEF. Brigadier General March commanded the First Division's artillery brigade in summer 1917. In contrast to Pershing's conflicts with French trainers and their methods, March enjoyed an excellent rapport with his instructors. He recalled that the French officers assigned to train the artillery brigade were "officers of ability and long experience . . . who were of great assistance in the early stages of our training, when none of us had yet seen the French field guns."[87]

March's men drilled relentlessly on the famous *soixante-quinze* (M1897 75mm gun), the pride of the French army. Although heavier guns and howitzers had supplanted it in some ways, it was still their standard field gun during the war and by 1917 had been adopted as the standard field gun of the U.S. army as well. Pershing in particular was enthralled with the weapon; like pre-1914 French commanders, he was enamored of its rate of fire and mobility. March remarked that he and his men learned how to fire the French gun quickly because it was similar in many ways to the U.S. Army's 3-inch gun.[88]

American gunners were trained to employ artillery in modern trench warfare, with the guns sited in semipermanent positions. They were taught to place destructive fire on fixed targets such as wire entanglements and machine-gun positions and to use counterbattery fire against similarly emplaced enemy artillery. This was practical training for the siegelike conditions that had prevailed on the western front for the past three years, which the Americans would in all likelihood face themselves, but it was a direct contradiction to Pershing's expressed desire to ready his troops for mobile open warfare operations, free of the trenches. Nevertheless, the AEF high command acquiesced in this issue, partly out of a deep respect for the French army's methods and partly for the simple reason that it took a very long time for the American artillery batteries to receive their proper allotment of horses, which were used to move most guns during the war.[89]

Another branch of American service that was heavily influenced by the French was the nascent U.S. Tank Corps. The British had first introduced the tank as a weapon of war near the end of their grinding offensive at the Somme in September 1916. Although its debut had not been decisive, due mainly to mechanical problems and the small number of machines actually engaged, the local tactical successes that had been achieved were spectacular. The tank held out the promise that it could be the key to breaking the deadlock of the trenches. The French had rapidly followed the British in developing and fielding armored units, and the few successes they achieved during their ill-fated offensive at the Chemin des Dames in April 1917 largely had been due to their armored forces.

The U.S. Army had no tanks and no tank development program when war was declared. However, Pershing and other American officers were quite interested in the possibilities the new weapon offered. The problem was that the Americans were completely unschooled on the subject. Nevertheless, Pershing let it be known soon after his arrival that he was looking for a bright young officer to learn about tanks and possibly head a future U.S. Tank Corps.

In October 1917 Captain George S. Patton Jr., then serving as an aide on Pershing's staff, wrote to him formally to request the position of command of the yet unborn U.S. Tank Corps: "I speak and read French better than 95 percent of American officers so could get information from the French direct. I have also been to school in France and have always gotten on well with Frenchmen."[90]

Patton's letter of application is important from the standpoint of the history of the U.S. Army, as he would later be known as the father of American armor and became one of the greatest battlefield tacticians and military strategists the United States ever produced. Significantly, among his other qualifications for the post, he wrote that he spoke and read French quite well and that he had "always gotten on well with Frenchmen." Indeed, he wrote to his wife Beatrice: "The French are certainly nice and do everything they can to help us. They are some soldiers too. Personally I like them much better than the British possibly because they do not drink tea. Which to my mind is a most hellish and wasteful practice."[91]

Patton was no doubt being facetious about his reason for preferring the French. Certainly one of his main reasons was that the French officers with whom he dealt in 1917 and 1918 treated him with courtesy and respect. The British officers routinely adopted an attitude of condescension when interacting with Americans, a complaint that many French officers had also made about their British allies during the war.

Patton's affection for the French was also rooted in his deep interest in military history and philosophy. His studies revolved around land warfare and the writings of men such as Guibert, Napoleon, Jomini, and others, who, Patton thought, provided an essential intellectual foundation for its study.[92] Historically, Britain's strength had always been the Royal Navy; the might of France had always been based on its army. For a career U.S. Army officer with a strong interest in military history, like Patton, it would have been natural to believe that the French were far more accomplished in land warfare than were the British and thus more worthy of study and emulation.

Despite the reputation that the British army enjoys with historians of World War I concerning their advanced theories of armored warfare, Patton himself went to the French army to learn about tanks. Although the French provided virtually all the American tanks that were used in the war, at the time of Patton's decision, Pershing and Baker thought that at least half the tanks the AEF would use would be purchased from the British. Therefore, one cannot ascribe Patton's decision to seek French advice on armored warfare as being based solely on the assumption that French tanks would be used.

On a personal level, Patton possessed a strong belief in reincarnation. Significantly, during the dozen or so past lives he thought he had led, he was never an English soldier, though he believed that on at least three occasions he had fought against the English. During one of his past lives he believed he had been an officer in the Napoleonic Wars serving with the famed French cavalryman Marshal Joachim Murat in Napoleon's Grande Armée. In another, he had been a French knight who died under a hail of English arrows at Crécy. And in yet another life, he believed he had been a Scottish Highlander during the 1745–1746 Jacobite uprising against English rule, which might further explain his animosity toward the English. Patton certainly believed that the experiences he had gone through in these past lives were a vital part of his makeup as an individual and as a soldier. Given this belief, he had a natural inclination for his personal rapport with the French and his enmity toward the English.[93]

Pershing gave Patton the job of organizing the U.S. Tank Corps in autumn 1917 and charged him with establishing a center for training American tankers as well. Initially, however, the corps was composed of Lieutenant Colonel George S. Patton Jr. and an aide. At the time of Patton's appointment, Pershing and Baker were negotiating with both the French and the British governments for the purchase of tanks, and Pershing was especially enamored with the British heavy tanks. Since the British had been the first to use tanks on the battlefield, they are often incorrectly attributed with being the first to invent them. In fact, the French developed tanks at approximately the same time as the British and were quite angered when the latter jumped the gun and revealed to the Germans the existence of the machines in 1916. The French subsequently had used tanks in their offensives of spring and late summer 1917 with mixed but generally favorable results and had enthusiastically embraced this new weapon.

Given that the French and British were more or less on a par with one another in regard to theories of armored warfare, Patton apparently made his decision to seek out advice and training from the French because of his professional admiration and personal affection for the French army. He truly believed he could learn more effective tactics from the French, based on his historical perceptions of the two countries. He also thought that the French would treat him with the professional respect and courtesy appropriate to his rank and station.

Patton went to the French training center for armored warfare at Chamlieu to begin his study. The French exceeded his expectations in helpfulness and courtesy. He was tireless, inspecting the different varieties of French tanks before deciding that the Renault was the best model. He fired the machine gun and light cannon used in the different models of the Renault, inspected the tank repair facilities, and had long conversations with the French officers on their theories of armored warfare. Patton and his aide also put a Renault tank through its paces on the training course. He immensely enjoyed this aspect of the assignment and noted what great fun it was "to hit small trees and watch them go down." Putting his fluency in French to work, he grilled the instructors with questions about the Renault, even to the point that the officers had to bring in an expert mechanic to answer some of his questions.[94]

While at Chamlieu, Patton dined nearly every evening with General Jean Estienne, a former artillery officer who had become the driving force in the development of French armored forces. It was Estienne who had succeeded in convincing General Joseph Joffre to support the development of tanks in the French army as early as 1915, and he had led the first French tanks into combat in 1917. Patton and Estienne would sometimes talk for hours after the meal was over, about tanks, armored tactics, and the tactical problems of the western front. After their conversations, Patton would retire to his quarters, where he would work into the early morning hours translating French training manuals into English for use at the American Tank Corps training center he would eventually head.[95]

During Patton's time at Chamlieu, the British army launched their celebrated tank attack at Cambrai on 20 November 1917. Their initial breakthrough was so spectacular that even after a German counterattack completely wiped out their gains, the battle captured the imagination of tankers everywhere on the western front. Patton took leave to visit the site of the battle and spoke with J. F. C. Fuller, the driving force behind the British Tank Corps, later famous as one of the foremost military strategists and historians of the twentieth century. Because of both Fuller's and Patton's later careers, some authors have tried to make much of this first meeting between the two men. Yet apparently Patton was not especially impressed with either Fuller or the British Tank Corps; after a visit of only a few hours, he returned to Chamlieu to resume his studies with the French and made virtually no comment on what he had seen with the British.

While the Americans trained throughout summer and early fall, the French government anxiously watched and waited for the moment when these new soldiers would enter the front lines alongside their own tattered legions. One of the most frequent visitors to the various American training facilities was the redoubtable Georges Clemenceau, whose nickname "the Tiger" had been well earned in the numerous political battles and personal duels he fought during the course of his long public life.[96]

Clemenceau was known to have but one great love and passion in his life: the Third Republic of France. From an early age his heroes and idols were the great figures of the First French Republic, especially the radical Jacobins, and there is no question that this heavily influenced his own approach to politics. As a young man he became a devout believer in a republican form of government at a time when such views were dangerous, and he hated all forms of nobility as well as the power of the Roman Catholic Church. In 1865, chafing under the imperial political atmosphere of Napoleon III's Second Empire, Clemenceau went to America to immerse himself in a democratic culture and society. He lived in New York City and taught French at a girl's school, eventually marrying one of his students, before returning to France in 1869. In 1870 the Second Empire fell in the opening weeks of the Franco-Prussian War, when Napoleon III was defeated at the Battle of Sedan and captured. In the turbulent weeks that followed, Clemenceau took part in the establishment of the Third Republic. The new government named the ambitious young republican as mayor of Montmartre, his first political office, and he was given political authority over the Eighteenth District of Paris during the siege of Paris and the Commune, managing to survive both events.[97]

After the Franco-Prussian War Clemenceau rapidly became a force in French politics. An accomplished writer, speaker, and duelist, he used these three attributes to carve out a reputation as a man who could, and did, make or break governments. Although he had begun his political career firmly aligned with the Left, by the time of the Great War he occupied a unique place in the French political scene. He had few political allies and had made enemies in every party of the wide political spectrum that was the Third Republic. As his biographer David Newhall notes, "The Moderates quailed before his immoderacy, the Right gagged on his unrepentant anti-clericalism, while the Socialists and left-wing Radicals shuddered at memories of his [former] ministry."[98]

Yet despite his seeming lack of support, Clemenceau enjoyed a large popular following among the French people and was a senior member of the Senate and the editor of an influential newspaper. As the revolving door of French politics swept one ministry after another from power during the war, his star began to rise. Whatever faults he might have had, even his most bitter enemies admitted that no one was more determined to bring victory to France. He never doubted or wavered in his support for the war, although he freely criticized how it was being run. He was an unrelenting champion of the necessity not only to drive the Germans from French soil but also to liberate the lost provinces of Alsace and Lorraine and to erase the stain of 1871 from the honor of France. His editorials were required reading in the halls of power in Paris, and each one concluded with the same terse statement: "The Germans are seventy miles from Paris."[99]

By autumn 1917, President Poincaré, desperate for a man who could form a government, provide the stern wartime leadership that France so desperately needed, and still guard against a military dictatorship, turned to his old antagonist Clemenceau. Thus in November, at the age of seventy-six, Clemenceau became premier of France, and shortly after, in an unprecedented move, also minister of war, holding both posts simultaneously until the end of the war and in the process becoming the most powerful man in the history of the Third Republic. Shortly after assuming his post Clemenceau made it perfectly clear where his priorities lay in this time of dire crisis. In his first speech as premier he announced, "My formula is the same in every respect. Domestic policy? I wage war. Foreign policy? I wage war. I always wage war."[100]

Even in the months prior to his assumption of power, Clemenceau determined to let the soldiers of the French army know that the government supported them and that he would not waver in the pursuit of victory. He often went out to the front lines, sometimes as much as three times a week, to visit French (and later American) units in order to encourage the men and to let them know their efforts and sacrifices were appreciated and that they were not forgotten. During these tours he often put on displays of bravado, heedlessly exposing himself to enemy fire in order to encourage the soldiers. On one occasion while touring a frontline position of the French army, he suddenly jumped up onto the firing step of the trench he was in and shook his fist at startled German sentries only a few hundred feet away, shouting, "*Cochons! Salauds!* We'll get you in the end!"[101] The hip waders, old felt hat, and shabby tweed overcoat that he wore on these tours of the trenches became legendary and added to his mystique.[102]

Because of the time he had spent in America, Clemenceau had a deeper understanding of and appreciation for the United States than virtually any other French political or military figure. He realized America's strengths and its weaknesses, and he also realized how much France needed American military assistance. After General March's artillery brigade had been training at Valdahon for several weeks, the instructors there sent back glowing reports to French army GQG and the government on the excellent progress the Americans were making in learning the ways of modern artillery fire. After receiving these reports, Clemenceau decided to visit the training facility and see for himself how they were getting along. March recalled, "On [Clemenceau's] arrival I put at his disposal an automobile to take him to the firing grounds so he could see the actual firing by the American command, but he declined any such luxury, as he also later declined a horse. Equipped with long hip boots, he trudged out on foot to the firing point, regardless of rain or weather."[103]

March recalled Clemenceau's first inspection tour of Valdahon in late summer of 1917:

> Clemenceau sat next to me at . . . meals, and his comments on events and things in general were a source of unceasing delight to me. He spoke perfect English; in fact, he told me, apropos of this, that he had read "every substantial book in the English language during the preceding twenty years." I replied that I doubted if there were very many Americans who could say the same thing. He asked me when he first came if I would have any objection to his bringing to the mess table with him some special food which he always ate, and appeared at dinner with a little black bag in which were bread and water and other things of a particular kind which he found healthful for him, so I said to him, "I presume you owe your extraordinary vitality at your present age to the good care you have taken of yourself in eating and drinking." I saw the French Mission sitting around the table chuckling when I said this to the "Tiger," and when he replied, "My boy, there is no folly I haven't committed," the entire French delegation, who knew him much better than I did, burst into unanimous applause.[104]

March was not alone in his admiration. Robert L. Bullard also fondly recalled the lively conversations he enjoyed with Clemenceau during the French premier's visits to the American troops training at Gondrecourt:

> [Clemenceau] told me that he had once lived in the United States. His talk of America and Americans, his manner with me and his treatment

of members of my staff, all indicated a very thorough understanding of us. At dinner he discussed with me some of our great Americans, and he spoke with the utmost admiration of Andrew Jackson. The mention of the name brought to me a realization of what seemed to me a quite remarkable resemblance between the characters of the two men—fierce, fighting determination. "Mr. Clemenceau," I said, "you are like Andrew Jackson, very like him." "Ah yes, perhaps," he laughed, with evident pleasure, "but I never fought a duel on horse-back"—a little envy in his tone.[105]

Bullard did not fully understand the premier's remark until a French aide informed him later that Clemenceau had been a notorious duelist in his younger days. Bullard also noted the great respect that the French officers showed for Clemenceau: "They felt that after the weak-kneed governments that had preceded, they had a man who was going to fight."[106]

Clemenceau was indeed a fighter, and he was most impressed with the fighting characteristics of the American troops he encountered in their training facilities. He was anxious to begin moving the First Division into the front lines as soon as possible in order to show the weary French soldiers that the Americans were in France in body as well as spirit. Yet by September, five months after America's declaration of war, not a single American soldier had gone to the front lines. Marshal Joffre had promised Secretary of War Baker that General Pershing would have the final say on when his men were ready to enter the front line, and Pershing held the French to that promise.

Nevertheless, both Clemenceau and the French high command soon put tremendous pressure on Pershing, at least to give the U.S. First Division some practical experience by placing it in the front lines for a brief period of time. Pershing at first resisted and pointed out to Clemenceau and Pétain that it was very important for the morale of the Allied armies that the Americans make a good showing in their first battle. Yet at the moment, Pershing argued, the American troops were so raw that they could easily step into a disaster. Pétain asserted that the French would never allow that to happen. Individual American battalions would be placed into the line as part of French regiments, and the First Division's artillery batteries would be placed with experienced French artillery batteries. Thus, the French would take every precaution to ensure that the Americans would not be on their own in their first appearance on the western front. After considerable prodding from the French, Pershing at last gave in and issued orders to move the U.S. First Division into a "quiet" sector of the French front line to give the American soldiers their first combat experience of the war.

On 20 October the men of the U.S. First Division boarded trucks at Gondrecourt to begin their journey to the western front and into the maelstrom of World War I. In spite of the best efforts of both the War Department and General Pershing, the men were still not properly outfitted. Among other problems, the campaign hat they wore was useless; soldiers would have to wear helmets in the combat zone, and the large hats could not be stored properly in a trench. A design for a new field cap was in the works, modeled after the French design, but had yet to be produced. So the American soldiers, George C. Marshall recalled, "presented a curious spectacle" as they headed off to war:

> The overseas caps had not yet been issued and the stiff-brimmed campaign hat was out of the question; consequently each soldier had met the situation as best suited his fancy. Many had purchased olive drab kepis of the Belgian type, with a gold tassle hanging from the front lip; a large number had cut off the brim of the campaign hat and wore the close-fitting skull piece; a few had fashioned for themselves headgear from bath towels; and some wore the dark blue Alpine caps, evidently procured from their Chasseur friends. Aware of the reason for this array, we were all much amused, but the staff officers from GHQ [Pershing's headquarters] were scandalized and registered a very poor opinion of the division.[107]

The First Division entered the front lines in the Einville sector, a scene of heavy fighting in 1914 but since then one of the quieter places along the western front, a *bon secteur*, where both the French and German armies sent units worn out in the fighting to the north to recover and to recoup their losses. Life here was good for both sides, with very little activity. The infantry battalions of the First Division were assigned to regiments of the French Eighteenth Infantry Division, commanded by General Paul E. Bordeaux, and were slowly and cautiously inserted into the front lines "to learn their trade of trench war," as the soldier-historian Laurence Stallings wrote, "for it was not an art."[108]

The American soldiers going into the trenches of the western front for the first time were grateful for the training they had received from the French in this type of war, for there were none of the rolling wheatfields and villages that Pershing had been training them to maneuver across and through. Both sides hunkered down in bunkers and trenches, and both sides endeavored to keep the quiet sector quiet. However, "quiet" was not on the agenda of the Americans. After months of training they were finally being given a chance to go into action, and they wanted to make the most of it. Historian Laurence Stallings wrote, "The arrival of *les américaines* was like a sudden burst of noisy roisterers into the truce of a family fireside. Every man in the 1st Division wanted to go on a patrol, and then a raid; each wanted to kill a German, to capture one, to be the first."[109]

The general enthusiasm and exuberance of the First Division was not unique to their particular unit but was characteristic of the average American soldier's reaction on entering the front lines. General Eugène Savatier, who commanded the French Thirty-fourth Infantry Division in 1917 and 1918, remembered the meticulous care he took to safeguard the American soldiers assigned to him in winter 1917 and how he endeavored to ensure that everything went off without a hitch:

> I took all these precautions not because of distrust, but as a matter of simple prudence, as is done with all troops entering a sector and also out of courtesy, because I was anxious to prevent our friends from falling victims at the start of a sally by the enemy. But they were irrepressible! They did all they could to bring this very thing about! If the night relief took place without a hitch and in the deepest silence, as soon as the sun was high enough some of the doughboys, who had no place in the frontline, wanted absolutely to "see the Boche" and "kill the Boche." They climbed, like cats, into the highest trees (the sector . . . was in the woods), and began to fire on the enemy sentries or on the platoons, which from the height of their observation post they could see running between the first and second line trenches.[110]

Such youthful enthusiasm soon brought on the consequences the French expected, as the Germans were both angered and curious at the sudden upsurge of activity in their quiet sector and decided to have a look at the newcomers. The Germans brought in an elite assault company that specialized in trench raids to welcome the Americans to the western front.

On the night of 2 November the American soldiers of the Second Battalion, Sixteenth Infantry Regiment, the same battalion that had marched through Paris on the Fourth of July, moved into the trenches for the first time. The men quietly established themselves in their fighting positions and anxiously peered out into the darkness. At exactly 0300 hours on 3 November, a massive German artillery barrage burst upon the Americans. Within minutes the artillery fire concentrated itself into a "box barrage," isolating a single platoon of F Company, Second Battalion, with a curtain of fire and steel, through which nothing could get through. The open end of the box faced the Germans. Suddenly, there was a roar as bangalore torpedoes were detonated, blowing gaps through the barbed wire in front of the Americans. Seconds later, a shower of hand grenades exploded in their position, as the German assault troops leaped down into the trench with pistols and knives.[111]

It was all over in three minutes. The veteran German troops, operating along a rigidly timed schedule, pulled back, taking their own wounded and dragging off eleven American soldiers as prisoners. The German artillery fire swiftly sealed off the open end of the box, preventing any American pursuit. An eerie quiet descended once more over the battlefield. As Stallings wrote, it had been "a formal exercise along established principles, as clever and as dull as a number from a corny ballet." And when it was done, three American soldiers lay dead.[112]

The surprise and swiftness of the raid stunned the inexperienced Americans. At dawn on 3 November, Captain George C. Marshall left his billet to go up to the front on a routine inspection, oblivious of the earlier events. As he entered his car, General Bordeaux hurried to catch him and somberly reported, "The first Americans have been killed." Marshall and Bordeaux rushed off to the Sixteenth Infantry Regiment's headquarters and learned that there had been some sort of attack and that several American soldiers were dead and perhaps as many as a dozen more missing. They also learned that Berlin radio was reporting fourteen Americans had been captured during a trench raid. They drove as far as they could toward the front before getting out and proceeding on foot to the scene of the attack.

Marshall and Bordeaux worked their way forward along a section of trench flattened by the German bombardment and saw an unexploded bangalore torpedo in the American wire entanglements, close to a shallow furrow and a gap in the wire, evidence of how the Germans had penetrated the American defensive position. Marshall also saw strands of white tape in No Man's Land marking lanes of attack for the German raiders. Then he saw the bloody evidence of a desperate struggle that had evidently been waged hand to hand. He recalled, "The bodies of the first three Americans who fell in the war—Corporal Gresham, Private Enright, and Private Hay—were just being removed from the ground where they had fallen. One of the three had had his throat cut and this was seized upon by some as evidence of German brutality."[113]

On 4 November the French army buried these American soldiers with much ceremony. The French constructed an elaborately decorated altar at the nearby village of Barthelmont, where honor guards representing the different branches of the French army and an honor guard from the Sixteenth U.S. Infantry Regiment stood watch over the three caskets draped by a large American flag. A French army chaplain performed the religious

ceremony in the village, and then the caskets were brought to a field ad-
jacent to the town and placed next to the open graves. General Bordeaux,
accompanied by his entire staff as well as the French corps commander
and his staff, took position with the honor guards, who had formed a
square about the bodies. A French army band played a funeral march,
and then Bordeaux advanced to the center of the assembled soldiers. As
French artillery pieces began methodically to fire a gun every minute at
the German lines, he addressed the gathered guards of honor and the
slain soldiers themselves:

> Men! These graves, the first to be dug in our national soil, at but a short
> distance from the enemy, are as a mark of the mighty hand of our Al-
> lies, firmly clinging to the common task, confirming the will of the
> people and Army of the United States to fight with us to a finish; ready
> to sacrifice as long as it will be necessary, until final victory for the no-
> blest of all causes; that of the liberty of nations, of the weak as well as
> the mighty. Thus the death of this humble Corporal and of these two
> Private soldiers appears to us with extraordinary grandeur. We will,
> therefore, ask that the mortal remains of these young men be left here,
> be left to us forever. We will inscribe on their tombs: "Here lie the first
> soldiers of the famous Republic of the United States to fall on the soil
> of France, for justice and liberty." The passerby will stop and uncover
> his head. The travelers of France, of the Allied countries, of America,
> the men of heart, who will come to visit our battlefield of Lorraine, will
> go out of the way to come here, to bring to these graves the tribute of
> their respect and of their gratefulness. Corporal Gresham, Private En-
> right, Private Hay, in the name of France I thank you. God receive your
> souls. Farewell![114]

Almost seven months after President Wilson's declaration of hostilities,
the United States of America had at last truly entered the Great War.

By January 1918, three more divisions had joined the First Division in
France. Although the pace of American deployment overseas seemed
painfully slow at times, Pershing and his staff succeeded in using the first
four American divisions to set the precedent for training and equipping
all future American divisions. Thus, the groundwork was laid to ensure
that the flow of American troops and materiel of war would change from
a trickle in 1917 to a mighty torrent of men and supplies in 1918.

In April 1917 the U.S. Army had been little more than a small frontier
constabulary, neither armed nor trained for modern warfare against the
most formidable military power in the world. Capable of raising a large

army, but unable to arm or to train it, the United States turned to the Allies and especially to France for assistance. The French provided the overwhelming majority of weapons used by the AEF in the Great War and most of the training that the U.S. Army needed before it could enter the battle.

Meanwhile, France, battered almost to the point of exhaustion by the bloodiest war in its history, had found new life and hope for victory in the supplies of capital and natural resources that America sent, enabling them to fulfill the tremendous potential of their massive armaments industry. Moreover, the French army had succeeded in beginning the daunting but essential task of training the brash young Americans for the deadly trade of modern warfare, a task they were honored and happy to carry out. They were pleased not only because of the special bond of affection that was visibly present between the two republics but also because they knew that the AEF would be fighting with them and adding their potentially enormous combat power to the French sector of the front.

The biggest obstacle the French army faced in its task of preparing the U.S. Army for modern war was the commander of the AEF, General John J. Pershing. Pershing insisted on preparing his soldiers for a type of open warfare that had not been seen on the western front since 1914 and that few French officers thought would ever return. While Pershing attempted to accept the best that the French army had to offer in terms of weapons and training so as to prepare his soldiers for modern warfare, at the same time he in many ways undermined the process. He insisted on a flawed tactical doctrine that was not applicable to the trenches of the western front where his forces would first see combat, and he risked compromising the combat efficiency of his army and his own reputation with his French allies.

Yet the French succeeded, in spite of Pershing, in teaching the American soldiers the fundamental lessons of how to live and fight in the trenches. They also instructed the Americans in other aspects of modern combat, such as armored warfare, and in all cases attempted to treat the officers and men with the utmost respect while politely pointing out the shortcomings of U.S. doctrine. This policy not only provided for a more effective learning environment, but it further strengthened professional and personal ties between the two armies and reaffirmed their military relationship. This relationship was severely challenged in the months ahead. Yet the strong foundation of professional respect and personal friendship that the soldiers of the two republics enjoyed, established in these opening months of America's involvement in the Great War, proved strong enough to endure that challenge.

CHAPTER 5

• • • • • • • • • • • • • •

The Amalgamation Controversy, December 1917–February 1918

In the waning days of 1917 the Allies looked back in bitter disappointment at the year gone by and viewed the coming year with an increasing sense of dread. They had suffered serious defeats on virtually every front of the war that year, beginning with the failed French offensive at the Chemin des Dames in April and culminating in the disastrous month of November. In that month the great British offensive at Passchendaele had finally ground to a halt, ending in a stalemate that had gained but five miles at a cost of approximately 270,000 British casualties and had failed, again, to provide a breakthrough of the German lines. A surprise British attack at Cambrai on 20 November, using over 300 of the new tanks, had broken through the German trenches and made spectacular gains; but within a week the Germans had launched a counterattack, and the British were quickly pushed back to their original starting point. November also witnessed the conclusion of the Battle of Caporetto, where the Italian army had been routed in a defeat so serious that Italy itself had almost collapsed before British and French reinforcements, and the failure of the Central Powers to provide adequate reserves to exploit their unanticipated success, had staved off complete disaster.[1]

The most dire news that month, however, came from the eastern front, where on 7 November the Bolshevik Revolution swept aside the pro-Allied provisional government of Alexander Kerensky and brought V. I. Lenin's Communists to power, with the promise of ending Russian involvement in the war. In the wake of Lenin's seizure of power, Russian resistance to the Central Powers collapsed, and by December the new Bolshevik government had signed an armistice ending Russian involvement in the conflict as Russia sank into civil war.[2]

Within weeks of the armistice, the German high command of Field Marshal Paul von Hindenburg and General Erich Ludendorff began the process of shifting hundreds of thousands of soldiers from Russia to the western front. The unstable political situation in Russia and the need to keep pressure on the Bolsheviks to sign a formal peace treaty forced the Germans to keep some divisions tied down there. Nevertheless, hundreds of thousands of combat-hardened German troops were soon being transferred to the western front for what everyone knew would be the greatest German offensive in the west since the beginning of the war.[3]

For the first time in the war, Germany would be able to focus its massive military might on one front, and neither the British nor the French were confident that they would be able to hold when the blow fell. The Allies' main concern was manpower, since the great bloodletting of the previous three years had left their nations desperately short of men. As German troop trains steamed westward, swelling the ranks of their forces already on the western front, neither the British nor the French were capable of matching them. Indeed, there were serious concerns that the Allies would be unable to maintain their existing force structure, due to the lack of replacements available. As the Germans grew stronger with reinforcements, the French and British had tapped the last of their manpower reserves, and all signs pointed to an impending disaster in the spring, when the weather cleared and the Germans launched their anticipated offensive.[4]

On 28 December Premier Clemenceau acted to rectify the manpower shortage in the French army by demanding, and receiving, permission from the Chamber of Deputies to call up the draft class of 1919 a year early and to enact new legislation giving police additional authority to scour the countryside for *embusqués* who had heretofore managed to escape the draft. Unfortunately for France, even these measures were not enough. By January 1918 Pétain was forced to reduce the number of battalions in each French division from twelve to nine, informing Clemenceau that with this measure he could maintain the French army at its current organizational size. Pétain cautioned that reduced battalion strength or no, if French losses were only "moderate" in 1918, and in no year of the Great War could French casualties be so classified, he would still have to break up perhaps as many as twenty divisions by January 1919.[5]

The wild card in this contest of numbers was the United States. The vast and heretofore untapped manpower reserves of America were viewed by both Britain and France as the key to victory, but how these men should be used became a major cause of disagreement among the Americans, British and French. As the months ticked by after the U.S. declaration of war in April 1917, the leaders of both Great Britain and France grew increasingly impatient with the slow progress of American deployment. Both nations determined that a major reason for the delay was General Pershing's insistence on building an autonomous American military force on the western front. Thus in December 1917, in a rare joint move, the French and the British approached first Pershing and then the Wilson administration with alternative plans for American deployment that involved the amalgamation of small American units, companies, and battalions into the armies of the Allies.

President Wilson, Secretary of War Baker, and General Pershing had been steadfastly against such an amalgamation. Wilson and Baker objected because they believed that the United States would never be an equal partner with the British and the French in the political realm if they were not viewed as such on the battlefield. As early as June 1917 Wilson was already looking ahead to the eventual postwar peace conference, and he wrote to his adviser Edward M. House, "England and France have not the same views with regard to peace that we have by any means." Wilson firmly believed that one of the best ways for him to play a leading role in the political settlement after the war was to have an autonomous American military force that was recognized by France and Britain as having provided a valuable contribution to the victory.[6]

Pershing's objections to amalgamation were both professional and, arguably, personal. As a military professional he believed that the British and French armies had been so thoroughly damaged by three years of war that they were institutionally incapable of prosecuting the war to a successful conclusion. He thought that only a powerful and autonomous American army would be capable of carrying the burden of the Allied war effort and of bringing the conflict to a victorious end sometime in 1919. On a personal level, he had no intention of being a general without an army, even though the circumstances he found himself in, with the United States attempting to raise a European–sized army from scratch, forced him to wait for many months while he oversaw the raising, training, development, and deployment of the AEF.

In December 1917, however, Pershing was faced with the fact that although American military mobilization was beginning to pick up the pace, he still had only four divisions plus support troops in France, totaling roughly 200,000 men, and a large number of these were still in training. Although many factors were involved in accounting for this delay, the major reason was the lack of an adequate number of vessels for transporting the men to Europe. It was partly to meet this shipping problem that in February 1918 the Wilson administration selected a new chief of staff for the U.S. Army, General Peyton C. March.[7]

March turned all his energies to solving the shipping problem and made dramatic progress. He confiscated ships for the war effort from civilian shipping firms as well as from organizations such as Herbert Hoover's Belgian War Relief program. He crowded more men into ships than it was theoretically possible to do by having the soldiers sleep in shifts, so that several men used the same bunk. March also streamlined the procedure for loading and unloading men and supplies and greatly lowered the turnaround time for ships in port. These draconian measures eventually resulted in a significant increase in the number of American soldiers being shipped overseas. However, it took time to implement these schemes, and in early 1918 it was difficult to forecast with any certainty how effective the United States would be in solving the problem.[8]

It appeared to Allied planners that the AEF would be hard-pressed to take the field as an autonomous force by summer 1918, and winter 1918 was looking more like a realistic estimate. With the Germans set to attack in spring, neither the French nor the British thought they could afford to wait for the Americans to build an autonomous army of their own in Europe. In December 1917 the Allies began to make subtle, and not so subtle, suggestions to Pershing that he might want to rethink the original arrangements for training and deployment of the AEF and consider the possibility of amalgamating small American units into the British or French armies.

As far as Pershing was concerned, amalgamation was not an issue for discussion, in spite of the apparent shortcomings of the present mode of deployment. Since the original Baker-Joffre agreement of May 1917, the U.S. Army had categorically rejected the concept of amalgamation, and Pershing had made an autonomous American presence on the western front his top priority as commander of the AEF. Indeed, one of the main reasons why the United States had decided to place the AEF with the French army rather than with the British had been the willingness of the French to accept American military autonomy when the British adhered steadfastly to amalgamation.[9] That the British would renew their efforts to obtain American soldiers and revive their proposal to amalgamate them into the British army is not surprising. Yet now the French, too, were pushing for amalgamation, even at the risk of jeopardizing the special relationship they had established with the AEF.

In assessing this change in French policy, one must consider that the circumstances in France had changed dramatically between the time of the original Franco-American agreement on military cooperation in May and the reopening of the discussion on amalgamation in December. The severe shortage in manpower was in itself enough reason for the French to consider a change in their policy, but other factors provided further impetus.

It is fair to say that when the French had agreed to support the concept of an autonomous American military presence on the western front they did not think that more than a year would pass before this force could be established. Indeed, in his original message to the French government announcing Franco-American military cooperation, Joffre had stated his belief that the Americans would play a decisive role in the 1918 campaign.[10] Yet by January, with the Germans massing for an offensive in early spring, only four American divisions stood on French soil. As the decisive moment of the war rapidly approached, the Americans were still not ready for battle and did not appear likely to be so in time to render any assistance during the imminent campaign unless drastic measures were taken.[11]

During a routine visit to Pétain's headquarters in December 1917, Pershing was informed of French concerns about the impending German offensive and their dissatisfaction with the slow pace of training and deploying AEF divisions. Pétain told Pershing that he wanted immediately to transfer the regiments of the AEF currently in Europe to French divisions for active service on the front. The French commander said that he would like to modify the existing plan for bringing American soldiers over by divisions and instead bring them over by regiments, then incorporate these new regiments into French divisions. Pétain hastened to inform Pershing that after two or three months of service, the regiments would be returned to the AEF commander and allowed to reconstitute themselves into American divisions for the purpose of establishing Pershing's autonomous American sector. He argued that under this new arrangement, the Americans would gain valuable experience at the front while also rendering immediate assistance to the French army during the present critical situation.[12]

Pershing was surprised by the proposed changes and immediately voiced his opposition to a plan that he believed "virtually meant the building up of French divisions by American regiments." He expressed his concern that American staff officers would never be sufficiently trained under such a system and that it would be virtually impossible to withdraw American regiments from French divisions without rendering the French division understrength and unfit for frontline service. Pershing recalled, "[I] also mentioned the difference in language as being an insuperable barrier to any idea of active service under an assignment that might become permanent. . . . I told the French that it seemed to me better, if such a course became necessary, that we should amalgamate with the British, who were still making overtures for our troops."[13]

Pershing's objections to the French proposal are curious, especially his comment that language would pose "an insuperable barrier." Indeed, 94 percent of senior American officers had reported that language differences posed either no difficulty or only minor difficulties in relations between American and French forces. All the American soldiers in France at that time had been trained by French instructors, and the limited amount of combat the Americans had seen had come in the French sector of the line, where they operated in much the same fashion that Pétain proposed, i.e., as regiments of French divisions. The successful fulfillment of both training and combat duty seemed to provide ample evidence that language differences between the soldiers were simply not a problem.[14]

Pershing apparently used the issue of language to support his thinly veiled threat that if he was forced to amalgamate his forces he would choose to be with the British, a possibility the French had apparently either discounted or completely neglected to consider when they reopened discussion on the issue. Pershing himself wrote that Pétain gave no reply and made no countersuggestion to his threat and thus concluded, "It looked as though there was an understanding between [the British and French]" on this issue. It could be argued, however, that Pétain's silence was more from shocked surprise than from any collusion with the British.

It is indeed a possibility that the French had failed carefully to think through the possible ramifications of their new amalgamation proposal. Perhaps Clemenceau and Pétain had reckoned that the Americans were by that time so committed to serving with the French army that they could push the matter of amalgamation without fear of this relationship changing. The complete lack of French support for American service in the British sector of the western front in the months to come further suggests that the French were not in collusion with the British but on the contrary were still very much in competition with them. Indeed, later events indicated that the French did not want the Americans to amalgamate at all if it meant they would be with the British army rather than with their own.

Unknown to the French, Pershing was bluffing. Indeed, he was staunchly opposed to amalgamation with either of the armies. Under pressure from Pétain, Pershing more than likely simply lashed out and struck where he believed the French were most vulnerable by pointing out that he could place the AEF with the British if the issue were forced. The simple truth was that Pershing wanted, and believed the United States needed, an autonomous American army under its own officers and with its own sector of the western front. Issues of personal, professional, and national pride were enmeshed in his thinking on this subject, as was his sincere belief that the U.S. Army was the only force capable of securing victory for the Allied cause. With his mind firmly set on these issues, he was willing to go to whatever lengths he believed he needed to secure American military autonomy.

When Pétain's overtures for amalgamation were rejected, Clemenceau supported his army commander, pressing Pershing on the issue. The French premier and minister of war wrote that it was "heart-rending" to see excellent American troops remain idle "while my country's fate was every moment at stake on the battlefields, which had already drunk the best blood of France." Clemenceau attempted to pressure Pershing directly on the issue, but to no avail, and later he recalled that Pershing "owed it to the romantic side of America's intervention to form a self-contained American Army, a duty I never failed to acknowledge." Clemenceau wanted to see an American army in the field as soon as possible, but if that was not going to happen then he wanted at least to see American soldiers in the field and was increasingly frustrated by Pershing's obstinacy on this issue.[15]

The British also chose this time to press hard on the amalgamation question. Quite possibly they sensed a rift in the Franco-American military relationship and hoped to make the most of it. On 17 December the British envoy Sir Cecil Arthur Spring Rice wrote to Wilson's close adviser, Edward M. House: "The advisers here suggest that possibly a suitable arrangement would be for one American Regiment to be attached to each [British] division and for one of each of the 3 battalions to be attached to each of the 3 brigades in the division."[16]

British Prime Minister David Lloyd George followed up this opening with a "personal message" for House to communicate to the president, in which he stressed the impending crisis on the western front and urged Wilson to reconsider his stance on amalgamation: "It would appear that the Germans are calculating on delivering a knockout blow to the Allies before a fully trained American army is fit to take its part in the fighting." Consequently, speed was essential, and the quickest way to put American forces into the field was to amalgamate them with existing British and

French divisions, by companies, battalions, or both (even the British had abandoned the idea of individual amalgamation).[17]

Foreign pressure began to escalate repidly, and on 18 December Secretary of War Baker cabled General Pershing that "both English and French are pressing upon the President their desires to have your forces amalgamated with theirs by regiments and companies. . . . We do not desire loss of identity of our forces but regard that as secondary to the meeting of any critical situation by the most helpful use possible of the troops at your command." Baker assured Pershing that he would have "full authority" over his forces, but it was apparent that the entreaties of the French and British to the administration were beginning to have an impact on Washington.[18]

Baker's message to Pershing triggered the AEF commander's greatest fear: that the amalgamation issue would begin to involve the Wilson administration, and thus his authority over whether it should take place would be circumvented. Indeed, this was the case, as both Wilson and Baker believed that meeting the present crisis on the western front was more important than American military autonomy, at least in the short term. Pershing, however, still thought that autonomy was an essential part of the overall plan for victory. He believed that given the battered condition of the British and French armies, an Allied victory would be impossible without the assistance of a fresh, powerful, and autonomous American army. He therefore continued to drag his feet on implementation of any form of amalgamation, although he avoided any direct clash with Wilson or Baker on the subject.

Frustrated by Pershing's continuing intransigence, President Raymond Poincaré wrote to Wilson: "The fate of the war may depend on the conditions in which your valiant troops will be engaged on the battle front." Poincaré declared that the formation of an autonomous American Army would not be abandoned, merely postponed. He expressed his confidence that the Americans would never wish "to stand mere spectators of the battles which will be fought and in which our common hope will be at stake." The French president stressed that the "historical role" that the United States has been called to in this conflict would be compromised if Americans were not engaged on the battlefield. This was a less than subtle hint that if Wilson wished to have a role in the peacemaking process after the war, then American soldiers needed to participate in the fighting. Poincaré discussed Pershing's intransigence on the matter and then added, "I doubt not that, under your high inspiration, the valorous American army will contribute to the victory, heartily conforming itself, like the French troops, to the necessities of the struggle."[19]

Pershing's intransigence, and perhaps his threat of a change in American policy regarding deployment of the Americans with the French army, also prompted Clemenceau to go over the AEF commander's head and to take the issue directly to the Wilson administration itself. He instructed the French ambassador to reiterate to Secretary of War Baker that the French government believed it was vital to amalgamate American troops by regiments into French divisions and that the disagreements between Pétain and Pershing needed to be settled immediately.[20]

Pershing was furious when he learned that Clemenceau had side-stepped him and communicated directly with Washington about an alleged disagreement between himself and Pétain. He was incensed that a politician was meddling in what he viewed as a purely military question. Apparently he was unaware of Clemenceau's famous quip, "War is too important to be left to the generals." Major Harbord, Pershing's chief of staff, recorded in his diary, "After the most frank and open conference with General Pershing, [Clemenceau] listened to General Pétain's accounts of their differing opinions [on amalgamation], and with no warrant of military knowledge to justify him in taking sides, he sent a cablegram to Ambassador Jusserand in Washington to the effect that Pershing and Pétain could not get along."[21]

It is clear from accounts of the conversations between Pershing and Pétain at this time that both Harbord and Clemenceau overstated their positions for effect. Most certainly there was a serious disagreement between the two men over the issue, but Clemenceau's assertion that they did not have a good working relationship was blatantly false. By the same token, Harbord underestimated the seriousness of the dispute, perhaps because the American high command did not see this issue as a major cause for dissension. He failed to consider that the French viewed the issue as critical.

Pershing decided to take on the Tiger and wrote a letter to him, enclosing copies of the cables he had received from the War Department regarding Clemenceau's allegations of major disputes between him and Pétain on various military issues: "May I not suggest to you, my dear Mr. President, the inexpediency of communicating such matters to Washington by cable? These questions must all be settled here, eventually, on their merits, through friendly conference between General Pétain and myself, and cables of this sort are very likely, I fear to convey the impression in Washington of serious disagreement between us when such is not the case."[22]

Clemenceau wasted little time in firing back. The following day he wrote Pershing, defending his actions by saying that he had not written to the American president or the secretary of war but to his own ambassador with instructions for his conversations with those two men. To Clemenceau, this was an important, albeit subtle, distinction. He concluded, "I shall exercise all the patience of which I am capable in awaiting the good news that the American Commander and the French Commander have finally agreed on a question which may be vital to the outcome of the war."[23]

This exchange of letters indicates the increasingly strained relationship between the commander of the AEF and the French government and also reveals that Pershing had, or at least wanted to have, a simplistic view of the Franco-American military relationship. At no point should Pershing have assumed that amalgamation was a purely military issue that he and Pétain would decide, without what Pershing viewed as outside political interference. Although he prided himself on staying out of political issues, his position as commander in chief was rife with political dimensions that had to be handled successfully if he were to wage a military campaign effectively. Meanwhile, the pressure the French were placing on the Wilson administration began to take effect.

After his meeting with Jusserand, Secretary of War Baker informed President Wilson of the French insistence on the matter of amalgamation and noted that he was concerned enough about the alleged disagreement between Pershing and Pétain to cable the AEF commander, asking him to clarify the situation. But Baker told Wilson that he was less than confident regarding French motives for amalgamation: "The disinterested ground urged by the French Ambassador, to the effect that it was for our good and was merely an accommodation on the part of the French, seems hardly to cover the whole case." Baker urged Wilson to follow Pershing's lead on the matter and to rely on his judgment.[24]

Baker's questioning of French motives reveals that just as the French seemed to have won over the Wilson administration to their position, they overplayed their hand by placing unwanted, and perhaps unnecessary, pressure in order to force the issue. In all fairness to the French, the critical military situation they faced in winter of 1917–1918 was the driving force behind their policies; they were grasping for American soldiers like a drowning man for a raft. Nevertheless, they most certainly blundered badly at this stage of the negotiations.

Pershing became increasingly angry at both the French and the British governments, and he forcefully replied to Baker's inquiries on the subject of amalgamation. In the event of a major crisis on the western front he was willing to take extraordinary measures, he said, including amalgamation of American battalions into French or British divisions. However, he did not believe that the present situation qualified as such a crisis. He reiterated his two major objections to amalgamation, both of which were equally important in his mind. First, he believed that American soldiers would lose their national identity if forced to serve in French and British units. This rationale had political overtones in terms of the importance of the United States as an equal partner in the coalition. Second, there were practical military reasons in terms of morale.[25] Pershing had serious concerns about the combat effectiveness of American units fighting and serving under a foreign flag and believed that serious problems in morale would result in an overall decrease in combat efficiency. He also noted that at a later date these American battalions or regiments could not be easily pulled from the Allied divisions without risking serious disruption. He conceded that there could be short-term benefits to a policy of amalgamation, by strengthening French and British divisions with American manpower. Yet he believed that these benefits would be far outweighed by the long-term negative effects in terms of morale, fighting effectiveness, and the future disruption of the British and French armies when the autonomous American army was formed.[26]

Pershing further pointed out to Baker that a serious rift existed between the British and French, a matter he had commented on before, and that the AEF could become a political football tossed between the two allies: "Attention should be called to prejudices existing between French and British Governments and armies, and the desire of each to have American units assigned to them to the exclusion of similar assignments to the other."[27]

As Pershing fought hard to hold the line with the Wilson administration on the amalgamation issue, the French and British suddenly received support for it from an unlikely source, General Leonard Wood. After losing out to Pershing in the competition for command of the AEF, Wood had accepted command of what Secretary Baker referred to as a tactical division being organized at Camp Funston, Kansas. Wood hoped that this command would guarantee him overseas service, but in reality Baker had sent Wood to Kansas to keep the politically unreliable general as far from the national and international scene as possible. Wood contented himself with the thought that he would eventually command at least a corps in the AEF, or perhaps even become the new U.S. Army chief of staff.[28]

Yet as the months went by with no word of any future assignment, Wood slowly realized that his fate was permanent banishment from both the halls of power in Washington and the scene of action in Europe. An aggressive letter-writing campaign to his Republican friends in Washington stirred up some discontent over the administration's treatment of him, but not enough to force Secretary Baker's hand on the matter. To every Republican entreaty as to why Wood's talents were not being put to better use, Baker simply explained that it was Pershing's decision as to which officers would serve in the AEF, not his.[29]

Wood's dismay over his inability to take a more active part in the war was compounded by what he viewed as the abysmal performance of both the War Department and Pershing in getting the U.S. Army ready for war. The soldiers at Camp Funston lacked blankets and clothing as well as weapons, shortages Wood believed he could have handled had he been in a position of higher authority. He bombarded numerous newspapers throughout the Midwest with scathing articles on America's lack of preparation for war and its ineptitude at mobilization once it had begun, blaming all of it, of course, on the Wilson administration.[30]

In late 1917 Wood saw a golden opportunity to communicate his opinions on how the war was being mishandled by the government and the army. The War Department ordered all generals currently training National Guard divisions, which included Wood, to go to Europe to tour the front in order to get a better idea of the actual battlefield conditions they were readying their men for. He decided to use the trip as a means to grab the limelight and perhaps to talk his way into a significant position of command in the AEF.

Wood arrived in Paris on 31 December and was greeted by Colonel Frank McCoy, a former aide who now worked on Pershing's staff. McCoy carried with him a message from General Pershing that promised Wood a command in the AEF if he would keep his mouth shut and avoid controversy during his visit. Wood replied that he had no intention of causing controversy; he merely wanted to become better acquainted with the overall military situation on the western front. However, he soon found his part of the deal too difficult to keep.[31]

Wood was wined and dined by the French high command and French government during his stay in Paris, and they quickly began to press upon him the necessity of amalgamation. The French flattered Wood by telling him how famous he was in France and how they had been surprised that Pershing had been selected instead to command the AEF. The Paris Mail ran a full-page story on Wood's visit and included a picture of him under the banner headline, "America's Greatest Fighter," an appellation the French began routinely to use in reference to him during his visit and one that, by insinuation, placed Pershing in a poor light.[32] The French government did not completely control the French press per se during the war, focusing more on censoring rather than on running stories, so it can be inferred that the press and by extension possibly the French people were growing impatient to see American soldiers at the front.

Apparently the praise went to Wood's head. Within days of his arrival in Paris, in the midst of Pershing's swirling debates over amalgamation, Wood came down firmly on the side of the French and British in the dispute. In Paris, as well as in London, he took full advantage of the international attention he was receiving to fire off one scathing remark after another, both in public and private conversations. He attacked in no particular order the Wilson administration, the failures of American military mobilization, and Pershing's poor performance as commander of the AEF. He also told the French and the British that if he were in command of the AEF, he would have no major objections at least to some form of amalgamation of American soldiers into their armies. Indeed, his statements were so blatantly prejudiced and visceral (at a major meeting with British officers he referred to President Wilson as "that rabbit") that both his friends and foes began openly to wonder if his previous head injury had caused mental damage as well as physical.[33]

Clemenceau was quick to capitalize on this new ally in the cause of amalgamation. A rumor even developed in certain political circles that he had approached the Wilson administration with the possibility of replacing Pershing with Wood as commander of the AEF. There is no direct evidence that this occurred, and Clemenceau was certainly knowledgeable enough about the American political scene in 1918 that he had to have known this was not a feasible suggestion. The Wilson administration would never have placed Wood in such a position of authority, especially since his political unreliability had been demonstrated yet again by his latest outbursts to the foreign press.[34]

True or not, the fact that such a rumor could circulate is highly indicative of the increasingly deteriorating relationship between the French and Pershing. Without question, Clemenceau saw Wood as infinitely more amenable to French interests and desires regarding amalgamation than Pershing was, and he certainly would have looked with favor upon an American change in command at this time. In all likelihood, Wood did not really believe that amalgamation was the best course to take. He was probably advocating such a policy in order to garner French support in his quest to receive a significant position of command in Europe.

Wood was scheduled to return to America in January, but he was in no hurry to leave the halls of power in Paris for the plains of Kansas and was attempting to find a way to extend his stay when fate found one for him. While touring the front line, the French army put on a firing display of trench mortars for their distinguished visitor. Wood was standing only ten yards away from one of the mortars when it misfired, causing a massive explosion that instantly killed the crew, decapitated a French officer standing next to Wood, and mortally wounded four other French officers standing nearby. Wood survived the blast, but his arm was severely lacerated and he was hospitalized in Paris just days before he was supposed to return to America. Pershing swallowed his pride and visited him in the hospital, but despite this generous gesture, Wood continued his bombastic outbursts to reporters gathered at his bedside.[35]

Wood spent three weeks recuperating from his wound and then began once more to make the rounds of the French high command and to tour American training facilities. During these tours he upbraided Pershing for not making better use of French instructors and for not adopting the French art of war more closely for the American army. Although this further endeared Wood to the French high command and government, it was the final straw for Pershing.

On 18 February 1918, Pershing informed Secretary of War Baker that he believed Wood was physically unfit for a command in the AEF. Pershing wrote that as a result of the head injury Wood had suffered in Cuba, he was "seriously and permanently crippled and it is with difficulty that he can use his left leg. As far as observed he did not spend much time actually in the trenches [during his tours of the front]. In any event, I consider him quite incapacitated for the difficult work he would be called upon to perform as a division commander." Pershing followed this letter up on 24 February with a scathing note to the new chief of staff, General March, informing him that Wood was "the same insubordinate man he has always been." Pershing was furious at the attention that the British and French had given Wood and with the banner headlines that proclaimed him as "America's Greatest Soldier." Pershing rather cruelly noted that "[Wood] drags his left leg worse than ever and the sight of a lame man going about our allied armies posing as 'America's Greatest' must have been anything but inspiring to our Allies."[36]

In late February 1918, Pershing sent his chief of staff, Major Harbord, to inform Wood that his tour of Europe was over and that he must return to Camp Funston and resume his duties there. Wood protested, but Pershing's orders stood, and although he managed to delay his departure until March, he was finally sent home. Pershing took steps to ensure that he remained there. Wood returned to the United States, apparently blissfully unaware that he had said or done anything out of line. He even expected to receive command of at least a division in the AEF. However, the Wilson administration acted on Pershing's recommendation and its own good judgment and kept Wood in an administrative post in the United States for the remainder of the war. The impact of his whirlwind tour of Europe and his conversations with the French government and high command on the amalgamation dispute were exceedingly detrimental. As Pershing's biographer Donald Smythe wrote, "Wood's talk reinforced European fears about the competency of a separate American Army, strengthened the movement for amalgamation, weakened Pershing's prestige, and raised the question whether he was the best man to command in Europe."[37]

Wood's visit and the attention it generated from the French government, military, and press represented the nadir of the Franco-American military relationship in the Great War. Pershing personified the U.S. Army in Europe, and whether the French liked it or not, Pershing was and would remain the Wilson administration's choice for command of the AEF. The actions of Clemenceau and other members of the French government and military to court favor with Wood had the effect of greatly antagonizing Pershing, and by extension, of damaging their relationship with the AEF.

As the Franco-American military relationship rapidly cooled, the British sought to take advantage of the dispute to drive a wedge between the two allies by once more proposing that American soldiers be trained, equipped, and placed with the British army. On 9 January General Sir William Robertson, the chief of the British General Staff, and Field Marshal Sir Douglas Haig, the commander in chief of the BEF, paid a visit to Pershing's headquarters at Chaumont. Robertson and Haig outlined the critical situation on the western front regarding the buildup of German forces and discussed Pershing's proposed timetable for the arrival of American soldiers in Europe. Robertson stated correctly that although Pershing hoped to have forty-five American divisions in Europe by the end of 1918, currently there were only four in France and part of a fifth. According to current shipping schedules based on available British and American tonnage, there would be fifteen American divisions in France by summer and thirty by December, but that would leave fifteen divisions still waiting to be transported to Europe.[38]

Robertson said that a careful study of British shipping needs revealed that on a temporary emergency basis only, they would be able to divert enough ships from their normal food transport duties to move these extra American divisions to Europe by summer. Thus Pershing's program for the buildup of an American army would be placed back on schedule. Pershing was grateful for the offer of extra shipping, since that shortage was severely hamstringing the establishment of the AEF, but he sensed there was a catch to the plan. Indeed there was.

Robertson informed Pershing that the British wished to transport to Europe only the combat elements of the extra divisions, specifically the infantry battalions, that would be placed directly into existing British divisions and serve in the British army sector rather than in the French. Robertson envisioned that 150,000 American soldiers, organized into 150 battalions, would arrive in Europe in time to lend real assistance to the British army during the coming German offensive. He explained that he and Haig hoped to establish British divisions that would contain 9 British battalions and 3 American battalions. As the American troops gained combat experience, Haig assured Pershing, these battalions would be gradually placed together into American brigades within the British division, and eventually these brigades would be joined together to form American divisions. No mention was made of when, or if, these soldiers would ever be returned to Pershing for use in his AEF.[39]

Pershing was torn by Robertson's proposal. On the one hand, he desperately needed shipping, and any plan that promised to bring over 150,000 American soldiers had to receive serious consideration. On the other hand, the whole scheme smacked of amalgamation and a complete repudiation of everything he had stood for in the months during his time as commander of the AEF. Nevertheless, the Wilson administration tacitly supported some form of amalgamation, even if they resented being pushed into it; and Pershing realized that the only course open to him was to make the best of a bad situation. He knew that extra shipping meant extra American soldiers and any agreement promising that had to be worth pursuing. He could deal with the consequences later.

On 17 January Pershing wrote to Secretary of War Baker recommending that the Robertson plan be accepted, although he also took the occasion to outline his concerns and reservations. He argued that the plan be accepted only as a "temporary measure to meet a probable emergency" and that it must not interfere with the regular shipment of American troops. He also stated that the amalgamated American troops must be made available to him when he requested it, an important stipulation that would have significant ramifications later.[40]

Pershing met with Pétain a few days later and informed him that he had accepted a British proposal to place American soldiers with the British army. Pershing hastened to add that it was only because the British were providing the shipping to transport the men, a commodity the French simply did not have in enough numbers to offer, and that he had agreed to break with the heretofore uniquely Franco-American military relationship on the western front. Pétain received the news calmly and said that it was a shame that a similar arrangement could not have been worked out with the French army.[41]

Pétain's calmness was probably due to two reasons. First, as much as he disapproved of the method, the net result of the British proposal would be more American soldiers in Europe and in a shorter span of time. Given the exigencies of the dire situation on the western front, this would still have tangible even though indirect benefits for the French. A second real possibility for Pétain's restraint was his realization that this amalgamation plan had yet to be implemented; there was still time to win the Americans back to the original policy of cooperating directly with the French army rather than with the British. To have become demonstratively angry at this point would have jeopardized future plans for Franco-American military cooperation and turned a tactical setback into a strategic defeat. Pétain believed that the relationship between the French army and the AEF was a strong one, and his own personal and working relationship with Pershing had also grown tremendously during the months since the arrival of the Americans in France. Thus, a strong foundation of professional respect and personal friendship remained between the French and American forces that would enable the relationship to continue to flourish, despite recent setbacks like this one.

Even with their differences over amalgamation, training methods, and other professional issues, a strong bond of genuine friendship had developed between Pétain and Pershing over the past six months.[42] The two men had great respect for each other, even if they disagreed, and Pershing perhaps felt sorry about his decision to place American soldiers into British divisions without also extending the same gesture to the French. He hastened to tell Pétain that regardless of where the American divisions were initially trained, all of them would undergo advanced training with the French army. He also stipulated that the original agreement for Franco-American military cooperation was still in effect and that he had no objection to placing American regiments with French divisions for training purposes. As far as amalgamation went, Pershing recalled later:

> To meet the need for replacements in their units, I consented to send temporarily to the French four colored Infantry regiments of the 93d Division. Some of the units had arrived, and others were expected soon to be en route, but they did not have in France even the beginning of a brigade or divisional organization. One regiment was to go to each of four [French] divisions, with the provision that they were to be returned for the formation of the 93d Division when called for.[43]

Pétain readily agreed to Pershing's plan and accepted his offer of the four black regiments for service with the French army. On hearing the news, Clemenceau immediately cabled Pershing to inform him both of his approval of the plan and his joy that an agreement had been reached. Pershing replied, "I appreciate your message and am happy to confirm the very satisfactory understanding that exists. Permit me to assure you Mr. President that my sole aim is to assist you by the most complete cooperation between our armies to the end that victory may come to the allied cause."[44]

Shortly afterward, Pershing reported to Baker that he had reached a "very satisfactory understanding with Clemenceau and Petain." The training of American soldiers would go on as before, with French instructors and with American regiments undergoing advanced training in the trenches as part of French divisions and corps, but Pershing emphasized that this was for "training duty" only. Pershing informed Baker: "The French seem equally satisfied. A few days ago I had a very cordial telegram from M. Clemenceau expressing his gratification that an agreement had been reached."[45]

The agreement that Pershing reached with the French is significant at several levels. Primarily, it reestablished harmony in the Franco-American military relationship and reaffirmed the American commitment to place the bulk of the AEF with the French army. The offer of four American regiments for use as reinforcements for French divisions is also significant; unlike the arrangement with the British, the French were not offering anything extra in exchange for these troops. While the British were going to the extraordinary length of diverting shipping from their civilian food needs to bring over American soldiers, Pétain had nothing to give other than the original arrangement by which American soldiers had been serving with the French. The French were certainly offering and delivering a great deal under the terms of the original and subsequent agreements, but the point is that nothing extra was offered in exchange for these American regiments.

The motives for Pershing's decision to allow these four regiments to amalgamate with the French army are certainly varied and debatable. Some historians have asserted that Pershing offered black regiments for service with the French as evidence of his racism. Yet given that "Black Jack" Pershing had served with and commanded black soldiers earlier in his career and had been a staunch defender of their use in combat at that time, it would be erroneous to conclude that his decision was based solely on racism. To illustrate, when Pétain asked for eight more black regiments in June, Pershing refused him, saying, "The colored regiments are composed of American citizens and I do not feel warranted in employing them on any basis other than that followed in the case of white regiments." He believed that black soldiers could perform well as combat troops and thus, unlike many of his contemporaries, did not believe that they should be restricted to noncombat support roles.[46]

Nevertheless, Pershing did not have a high opinion of black officers and believed that the Old Army system of having white officers command black regiments was the best. Indeed, his earliest command and combat experiences had been under these very circumstances, and his success apparently reaffirmed his belief in the merits of this system. Although he did not believe that blacks should be given positions of authority, he did believe that they could fight well under "proper" (i.e., white) leadership. By modern standards this was a racist attitude, but it was actually somewhat progressive for the time. One must look beyond the racial issue as a criterion for assigning these regiments to the French army and examine other possible factors that may have influenced his decision.

First, Pershing realized that although some American soldiers would be serving in the British sector, the vast majority would still be with the French, and the future American sector of the western front lay in the midst of the French army's zone of operations. Thus, there was every reason to defuse the current dispute between him and Pétain. What better way to do that than to offer at least a token gesture of amalgamation? Second, it could be argued that Pershing was genuinely interested in preserving his friendship with Pétain and the special relationship between the two armies that they had worked so hard to establish during the past seven months. This understanding would have been impossible had he offered Pétain troops that he considered to be of inferior quality. Therefore, any suggestion of racial stereotyping must be seen as a secondary consideration to his primary motivation of reestablishing Franco-American rapport.

Soon after having agreed to Robertson and Haig's proposal to amalgamate 150 American battalions into the British army in exchange for extra British shipping, Pershing began to have second thoughts on the matter. The truth was that both he and the Wilson administration had grave misgivings about placing the AEF with the British army, however handsome their offer of extra shipping might be. Secretary of War Baker had noted as early as May 1917 that the American people were more supportive of placing the AEF with the French army, and indeed this was one of the major reasons behind the Joffre-Baker agreement on Franco-American military cooperation.[47]

Pershing noted the difficulties that attended even simple matters involving American interaction with the British. For example, during winter 1917–1918 the AEF had difficulty in securing enough shipments of winter clothing from the United States and in order to alleviate the problem purchased British army overcoats. This caused a great hue and outcry among the Irish-Americans, who refused to don the coats because the British coat of arms was emblazoned on the buttons. Due to the cold, they compromised and wore the overcoats, but only after first clipping off the British buttons. Pershing had to rush a shipment of U.S. Army buttons to the rebellious regiment. Their pride assuaged, the Irish-Americans calmed down, and Pershing recalled, "The regiment then turned out looking both smart and serene" wearing their U.S. Army buttons.[48]

Pershing had grave reservations about the feasibility of placing American units into the British army, but he needed their shipping to transport his men to Europe, and he had already given at least a verbal assurance to the British endorsing their proposal. Moreover, he was unsure of exactly what options might be available to him to protest at this late stage, given that seemingly everyone, including Baker and Wilson, supported at least some form of temporary emergency amalgamation. Puzzling over his dilemma, he decided to go to Paris to pay a visit to Marshal Joffre.

Shortly after his triumphal trip to the United States in April and May 1917, Joffre had been named Inspector General of American Troops by Minister of War Paul Painlevé. Joffre's title was as impressive as it was powerless, for he had no official authority within the French army or government to implement or carry out policy. The new government of Georges Clemenceau, long a critic of Joffre during the marshal's tenure as commander in chief of the French army, had made no effort to make use of his services or even to include him in their discussions of military affairs. Joffre essentially served as an adviser to Pershing and the Americans on military matters, but only when they sought him out for advice, which thus far had not been very often. Yet as Pershing began to feel increasingly isolated in his position against amalgamation with the British, it was Joffre to whom he turned for advice and support.[49]

Pershing visited Joffre on 26 January and began by apologizing for how long it had been since his last visit, explaining that his duties with the AEF had kept him extremely busy in recent months. Joffre inquired as to the current status of the AEF; Pershing said that training was progressing very well, but the problem remained of getting more American soldiers to Europe. He then informed Joffre of the British shipping proposal and his agreement to place American battalions into their divisions in exchange for transport.[50]

Joffre had championed American military autonomy during his visit to the United States, and it now appeared that the work he and the French mission had accomplished in establishing a special military relationship between the AEF and the French army was about to be swept away, simply because of British offers of sea transport. Joffre politely heard Pershing out and then asked to speak to the him in an unofficial capacity, as a friend and as one brother officer to another.[51]

Joffre told Pershing that he had grave reservations about this scheme to amalgamate Americans into the British army. He argued that British and French military intelligence had overestimated the number of new German divisions that were being sent to the western front for their spring offensive. He personally believed that the German attack could be stopped without having to resort to emergency measures such as amalgamation. The French marshal told Pershing that the real motivation for the British scheme was simply a desire to rebuild their army, which had suffered grievous losses and was indeed in bad shape.[52]

Joffre declared that amalgamation was a poor way to rebuild the British divisions. He pointed out that from a military standpoint, a division composed of nine British and three American battalions would never be as effective in combat as a division composed entirely of the battalions of one nation or the other. He told Pershing that the British had to know this, as they had never mixed their colonial battalions with regular British divisions and did not place even Scottish or Irish battalions in divisions with English battalions.[53]

Joffre further argued that American soldiers would not react well to being ordered into battle by foreign officers and that if one of these mixed divisions suffered a reverse, the English officers would be quick to blame the Americans for the failure, adding, "You must consider the American people at home and their interest in and their support of the war, which could be adversely affected by amalgamation." Joffre's arguments resonated with Pershing because so many of them expressed his own and the Wilson administration's, not only on amalgamation but also on the placement of American soldiers with the British army. Pershing was elated at Joffre's support for his position and after their meeting wrote, "Here, then, was a distinguished French soldier who could see these questions in their true perspective without prejudice or bias."[54]

Gaining the support of Joffre's prestigious military opinion, which was still respected if not feared, provided Pershing with the help he believed he needed to pursue his struggle against amalgamation. The British might not care for Joffre, or the current French government for that matter, but his name still carried great weight with both Baker and Wilson. Once more Joffre had proven instrumental in upholding a policy supporting an autonomous American military presence on the western front, and once more he had done so at the expense of the British.

On 29 January, on the eve of a major meeting of the Allied Supreme War Council, Pershing conferred with General Sir William Robertson and his staff to discuss final details on the proposed amalgamation of the 150 American battalions into the British army. Pershing stunned the British by informing Robertson that while he would accept the British offer to ship 150,000 American soldiers to Europe to serve in the British sector, he had to insist that these men be brought over as six complete divisions, not as 150 individual battalions.

Robertson was shocked and said he would have to confer with the British prime minister on the subject before agreeing to it. Pershing waited and the following day met an angry David Lloyd George, who informed him that he thought the matter of amalgamation had already been decided. Pershing suggested that the prime minister was in error and that the only agreement he would sign would be one that brought American soldiers over as complete divisions. Lloyd George was furious but also realized that the issue had boiled down either to no American troops or some, under Pershing's conditions. Deciding that the latter course was more prudent, he agreed to it.[55]

On 31 January Pershing wrote to Undersecretary of War Henry P. McCain: "Your conclusion that the proposition to send Infantry battalions for service with British Divisions was recommended by me was erroneous. Have had matter under consideration for some time and am convinced that the plan would be grave mistake. Stated my views fully to Sir William Robertson which resulted in delay until arrival of British Prime Minister yesterday." Pershing restated the reasons for his opposition, carefully pointing out that one of his major objections was "the probability that [amalgamation] would excite serious political opposition to the administration in the *conduct* of the war."[56]

Despite Pershing's protestations, it is clear that he had originally agreed to Robertson's plan, albeit reluctantly, and then changed his mind. He asserted that his decision was founded on the military grounds of increasing the overall combat effectiveness of American divisions and of following a course that would establish an autonomous American military presence on the western front in the shortest possible time. He happily informed the War Department that the British had accepted his terms and agreed to ship over six complete American divisions for training and service in their sector of the front.

President Wilson liked the new plan and was quick to support the AEF commander on his decision. Wilson wrote to Baker outlining his endorsement of Pershing's agreement with the British and again firmly supporting the general's stand against amalgamation. He instructed Baker to inform Pershing "that we consider the objections to the plan just those which he states in the enclosed despatch and that in our judgment those objections are final. That we have no objection to the programme which he here suggests by way of substitute." Wilson expressed his pleasure with the offer of extra shipping from the British but stressed that only the most dire emergency could be allowed "to interfere with the building up of a great distinct American force at the front, acting under its own flag and its own officers.[57]

Over the course of the war the British provided shipping for the AEF and transported approximately half the American soldiers who served in Europe. The irony, however, was that the vast majority of them marched off the British transports and into the French sector of the western front. Although under the agreement signed by Pershing and Robertson ten American divisions were trained by the British, at least partially, only two (the Twenty-seventh and Thirtieth) actively served with the BEF. The others were transferred to French or American command for active combat duty. The American forces with the BEF were dubbed the U.S. II Corps, but in reality this formation was essentially four infantry brigades, as there was no American corps artillery assigned to the force. The divisional artillery brigades were trained by the French and attached to Franco-American forces rather than to their parent divisions serving with the BEF. Thus from first to last, America's primary military relationship during the war was with France, not Britain.[58]

The experiences of the officers and men of the ten U.S. divisions assigned for training and service in the British sector, despite their small numbers, provide a glimpse into the important differences between American service with the French army and with the British army. These differences are highly significant in understanding the importance of the Wilson administration's decision to place the bulk of the AEF under the tutelage of the French army and also in envisioning how the American military experience in the war might have differed had this policy not been followed.

From the outset of their deployment to the British sector of the front, American soldiers had difficulties with their new trainers and especially with the English officers and men they were assigned to serve with. The worst case of Anglo-American relations was found in the U.S. Thirty-fifth Division, which had a terrible relationship with the British forces. A U.S. Army study conducted shortly after the war concluded, "The 35th Division did not get along very well with the British. They did not like the British noncoms, or the British soldiers, or the British officers. . . . There were occasional fights between our men and theirs. This did not aid in cementing the entente."[59] Thankfully for all concerned, the Thirty-fifth Division was transferred to the French zone of operations, after only three weeks with the British, to complete its training under French supervision. In sharp contrast to the serious problems it had experienced with the British, it reported that its relations with its French instructors were "very cordial."[60]

The Thirty-fifth Division was in some ways an exception, as the Americans generally tended to establish good relationships with Scottish, Irish, and Welsh soldiers as well as with the British Commonwealth forces from Canada, Australia, and New Zealand. However, virtually all the American units reported varying degrees of difficulty with the English, and especially with English officers. American soldiers of the Twenty-seventh Division reported that the average English officer was incredibly overbearing and that this quality extended down into the ranks. A survey of soldiers in the U.S. Sixtieth Infantry Brigade found that "Tommy considered himself a superior soldier to the American and took no pains to conceal it . . . in fact he took every opportunity to impress upon the mind of the American soldier that such was the case. Our soldiers resented any such attitude and denied that it was based upon fact." The U.S. Army's postwar study on relations between the AEF and the British concluded, "In general, the American soldier considered the English enlisted man as difficult to make friends with. . . . He was inclined to be condescending toward his American cousins, but [the Americans] were fully prepared to take this out of him by whatever means necessary; after which perfect harmony prevailed."[61]

Major General Joseph Dickman, commanding the U.S. Third Division, landed briefly in England in spring 1918, before continuing to his division's training camp in France. He noted that there was a high degree of animosity between the British colonials and the English soldiers and that American troops passing through England en route to France did not get along with the Tommies either. Dickman later recalled: "Friction was also reported between the Americans and the English, the latter stating that the Americans had delayed coming across for fear of being licked, to which the Americans retorted that the British were already whipped, and that they had hurried over to help them out."[62]

Certainly there were many instances of positive relations between the British and American forces; however, animosity toward English officers, in particular, was a major feature of Anglo-American military relations while such occurrences were extremely rare in Franco-American military relations. Why was this the case? The historian Edward M. Coffman has suggested that "it was difficult to forget what every schoolboy learned about the king, the embattled farmers, redcoats, and all the rest. Of course many overcame the stereotype and the suspicion to respect and to like the British; but apparently most soldiers disliked the 'Limeys' and never let anything change the situation. Australians and Canadians seemed to share this feeling and, on occasion, in barroom brawls in the French villages behind the lines, they would join with the Yanks against the English."[63]

In understanding Coffman's allusion to the American Revolution, it is important to acknowledge the tremendous use of imagery and personalities from that war that both France and the United States employed to celebrate and affirm the tradition of their historical relationship as military allies. Certainly the average American soldier, and by extension the American public as well, could not help but recall that the enemy against whom France and the United States had first allied was Britain.

How widespread and common was the American soldier's animosity toward the English? So much so that even the Germans noticed it. According to General Erich Ludendorff, first quartermaster general of the German Empire and its virtual military dictator throughout most of America's involvement in the war,

> As far as the relations of the American soldier to his allies were concerned, there was a decided difference between the sentiments he harbored for the French and those he manifested for the English. The latter were not considered good "pals" and usually were not much liked. It was charged against them that they preferred to let others do their fighting. There were cases where American prisoners of war earnestly requested not to be sent to the same concentration camp as the English. "Right from the start, there will be fights! They are too obnoxious to us!" On the other hand, the French were looked upon with sympathy, in spite of being criticized as "none too clean," and although the shopkeepers overcharged American doughboys outrageously. Inasmuch as the French greeted the sons of the new world with enthusiasm, as their savior in time of need, friendly relations were quickly established. Frequently, the memory of General Lafayette was invoked.[64]

Many Americans did have ambivalent feelings toward the British, and although all British soldiers did not necessarily harbor feelings of animosity toward the Americans, they did adopt a certain attitude of superiority over their allies that both exacerbated and confirmed the Americans' hostility to them. The actions and attitudes of the British toward the Americans throughout 1918 revealed a prevalent feeling of superiority over a former subject people. In contrast, the historical relationship between the United States and France was one of alliance between sovereign nations, not one of mother country to former colony. To have placed the AEF under the direction of the British army during America's first venture into the maelstrom of European conflict would have been to assign the United States to the same subservient position held by the empire's dominions and colonies. America would not have ranked as an equal partner within an international military coalition. The importance of the Franco-American military relationship is thus heightened by the knowledge of what the alternative situation might have been had America's primary military relationship been with Britain.

At the meeting of the Allied Supreme War Council on 1 February the issue of amalgamation was again raised by the Allies. Pershing motioned to General Tasker H. Bliss, the American representative on the council, to make the formal reply to the Allied request. Bliss informed the council of the decision to accept the British offer to transport six American divisions to Europe and conceded that "if the German attack finds these battalions on the British front they will fight to the extent of their capacity wherever the attack finds them." Bliss also noted that Pershing and Pétain had reached agreement on the training to be given American divisions by placing them with the French army in the front lines for advanced instruction and to gain combat experience. He emphasized that although these arrangements for training were welcomed by the United States, they were merely a "stepping-stone" toward the ultimate goal of the formation of an autonomous American army.[65]

Bliss stressed that the limited amalgamation of American regiments was a temporary measure taken only to meet the needs of the present emergency and concluded his report: "Such a thing as permanent amalgamation of our units with British and French units would be intolerable to American sentiment." When he had finished speaking, Clemenceau rose "and declared that this point was settled."[66]

After two months of bitter debate and controversy, the issue of amalgamation was essentially laid to rest. During the crisis that followed the launching of the German offensive in March 1918 the subject would be raised again, but there was never any real chance that it would occur, given the agreement hammered out during winter 1917–1918. In many ways, like most good agreements, the arrangement represented a compromise by both sides. The British would provide extra shipping to move more American soldiers to Europe at an accelerated pace. The French and British both agreed to end their calls for amalgamation of small American units into their armies. In exchange, Pershing would continue to allow

American battalions and regiments to be placed temporarily with French divisions for training purposes and would extend that same arrangement in a limited fashion to the British. The Americans also agreed to move all their divisions into the French sector for their final training, including the ones brought over and given initial instruction by the British.

The placement of all American divisions with the French for their final phase of training could be interpreted as a move to placate wounded French pride over the termination of their exclusive arrangement for training American soldiers. On the other hand, there were sound practical reasons for Pershing to insist on this. First, the French would train the bulk of the AEF combat divisions during the war. In order to get everyone on the same page concerning methods of fighting and mode of operation at the front, it was important not to have any soldiers unfamiliar with the system used by the rest of the AEF. Second, the chosen, if not yet occupied, American sector of the western front had already been designated as Lorraine, a zone in the midst of the French army sector and not in contact with the British sector at all. Virtually all units of the AEF, however they arrived in Europe and whoever gave them their initial military training, would be most closely associated with the French army in active operations, and thus it was vital that they be exposed to the French method of war.

The dispute over amalgamation disclosed both the strengths and the weaknesses of the Franco-American military relationship in World War I. Certainly the great weakness revealed was that although the two nations had a common goal and purpose, to defeat Germany and win the war, they also had national interests that were peculiar to each nation and that could at times diverge from the interests of the other. This was amply demonstrated when the drastic manpower shortages confronting France forced them to change their stance on American military autonomy. Yet ultimately this difference was worked out, to the satisfaction of both sides. The episode demonstrates that the military relationship between France and the United States was strong and flexible enough to accommodate disputes without breaking apart.

"Exhibit 'A' of the AEF." Officers of the U.S. First Division being addressed by French president Raymond Poincaré in August 1917 as General John J. Pershing and General Philippe Pétain look on.

U.S. Marines roll into a French village in May 1918. Note the enthusiasm of the crowd greeting them and that the crowd is composed exclusively of women and children. By the final year of the Great War the manpower of France had been destroyed on the battlefields of the western front.

French refugees fleeing from advancing Germans northeast of Paris in May 1918. Such scenes were all too common to the American soldiers moving toward the battle zone and inspired both sympathy for the plight of the French and a hatred for the Germans.

Center, in uniform, Marshal Joseph Joffre listens attentively while an American sings "La Marseillaise" at the dedication of a memorial to Lafayette in New York City during the visit of the French mission in May 1917. *Far left,* former premier René Viviani is overshadowed, as always, by the victor of the Marne.

Marshal Joseph Joffre and General John J. Pershing in the courtyard of the Hôtel des Invalides, Paris, 4 July 1917. The Americans are welcomed with open arms to the holy ground that houses the tomb of Napoleon and the trophies and mementos of the glorious military past of the French army.

"We will wait for the Americans and the tanks." In autumn 1917 an eager Pétain looks over the first elements of an American army that will eventually number over 2 million men and provide immense physical aid, lifting the morale of his battered French army.

From the beginning of America's involvement in the war to the end, the French and American armies remained inextricably linked. Pictured is, *right,* Major General Joseph Kuhn, U.S. Seventy-ninth Division, with his immediate superior, Général de Division Claudel, French XVII Corps, *center,* and his staff, during the final stages of the Meuse-Argonne campaign in November 1918. The French XVII Corps was part of the U.S. First Army and included American divisions.

General Philippe Pétain, commanding general of the French
Armies of the North and Northeast from 15 May 1917 through
the end of the war. Pétain also served as commander of the
ad hoc Franco-American Army Group in autumn 1918. He was
a great friend to Pershing and sincerely admired the American
army. He was a staunch supporter of the AEF and was
instrumental in the development and maturation of the U.S.
First Army into a viable combat force.

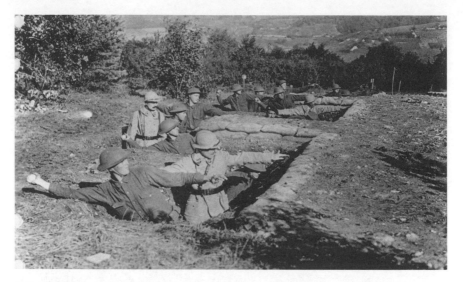

Learning the tools of the trade. U.S. Marines being taught the fine art of grenade throwing by their French instructors. The U.S. Army and Marines were hopelessly lacking in even the most basic modern weapons, including grenades, which were supplied to them by the French, who also trained them in their use. The French trained, in part or in whole, approximately 80 percent of the American divisions that served in combat during World War I.

18 July 1918. The Second Battle of the Marne is under way, and the great Franco-American counteroffensive has begun. Here French infantry rest in defilade beside French Renault tanks.

The mind and soul of the AEF, General John J. Pershing. A West Point graduate and career soldier, Pershing was a strong-willed man with a highly developed sense of honor and an easily offended pride. Although he had no great knowledge of or appreciation for the French army, he worked closely with the French high command to ensure the closest possible military cooperation between the two republics while still maintaining at least the aura, if not the reality, of American autonomy.

U.S. Army Chief of Staff Peyton C. March, Secretary of War
Newton D. Baker, and Major General Omar Bundy, U.S. Second
Division, in early 1918.

The Americans have arrived, and Paris goes wild. The first contingent of U.S. troops to arrive in France parades through the streets of the capital on the Fourth of July 1917.

The "Blue Devils," officers and men of the elite French Forty-seventh *Chasseurs Alpin* Division assigned to train the U.S. First Division at Gondrecourt, France. American soldiers were impressed with the experience, professionalism, and knowledge of modern warfare that their French instructors possessed, and the French were struck by the physical strength and eagerness for combat the Americans displayed.

Right, Brigadier General James G. Harbord interrogating German prisoners captured during the Battle of Belleau Wood. Note that he is wearing a French helmet, even though when he initially landed in France he thought it looked "silly." Service with the French changed his attitude toward them considerably during the course of the war.

Premier Georges Clemenceau visits the command post of the U.S. Second Division shortly after the final clearing of Belleau Wood in late June 1918. To his immediate left is the Second Division commander Major General Omar Bundy, and to Bundy's left is Général de Division Degoutte, Commanding General of the French VI Army, which the Second Division was assigned to during the battle.

An American artillery battery of the U.S. First Division, equipped with the famous French *soixante-quinze (*75mm gun), prepares for action during the Second Battle of the Marne in July 1918. Almost every gun and virtually every round of artillery ammunition the Americans used during the Great War was manufactured by the French.

A Franco-American color guard in Paris at a ceremony in which the French army awarded Major General James G. Harbord the Légion d'honneur, France's highest award for bravery and service.

The French army honors an American soldier of the U.S. Forty-second Division killed in action in early 1918. The French were very proud of the service of the American soldiers assigned to their armies and took extraordinary measures to recognize the sacrifice these men from across the sea made who had died for France. Note that both a French and an American flag are draped over the casket.

(Right, top) Battle-hardened French troops leading Americans on a trench raid in early 1918. French soldiers not only assisted in the instruction of U.S. troops at training centers but also gave advanced instruction in the trenches to U.S. regiments that were attached directly to French divisions for this purpose.

(Right, bottom) African-American soldiers of the U.S. 369th Infantry Regiment, assigned to the French 157th Infantry Division, the famous Red Hand Division. Note that the African Americans are armed with French rifles, bayonets, and automatic rifles and are wearing French helmets. Although African-American soldiers were not well liked by the American high command, the French were happy to have the support and were especially enamored of the 369th Regiment, which they showered with decorations for valor.

Texans of the U.S. Thirty-sixth Division making friends with a
French youngster by discussing the finer points of a cross-
cultural passion: fishing. American soldiers were often billeted
in French villages and even with French families, especially
during the first year of the war. The natural tendency of the
young Americans to befriend the children greatly assisted in
winning the affection of the French people.

Desperate German defenders in the Meuse-Argonne cootor under attack by American troops, late October 1918. The Franco-American forces had little room for maneuver, and the Germans, defending one of the most important sectors of the entire defensive system, could not withdraw. The result was a bloody and exhausting battle of attrition that nevertheless resulted in a critical victory.

Raoul Lufberry, the dark, moody loner who was the highest scoring ace of the elite French pursuit squadron N-124, the Escadrille Lafayette. Lufberry and his fellow pilots of the Escadrille Lafayette became international celebrities and encouraged American sympathy for France during the period of U.S. neutrality. The squadron's exemplary combat record resulted in the French army's high opinion of their capabilities at a time when most Europeans regarded the Americans with disdain.

(Right, top) A gathering of some of the American and French dignitaries who helped to create the Escadrille Lafayette and later the Lafayette Flying Corps, which encouraged American volunteers to come overseas and fight for France. Paul Rockwell, a former member of the French Foreign Legion and a volunteer ambulance driver whose brother Kiffin was killed in action with the Escadrille Lafayette, is standing in the center, his head slightly cocked to his left. Former French premier René Viviani, who accompanied Joffre on the French mission to the United States in April and May 1917, is seated at the far left.

French infantry holding a trench near Verdun in autumn 1916. Americans greatly respected French soldiers and held their battle-experienced trainers in awe.

"A fraternity of arms." French and American soldiers manning a machine-gun position in summer 1918. Virtually every major engagement the United States fought during the Great War was a Franco-American battle. French soldiers fought beside U.S. troops and in support of every major American operation. On the day the war ended, the number of French soldiers serving in the U.S. First Army was greater than the number of soldiers in the entire U.S. army when America first entered the war.

CHAPTER 6

• • • • • • • • • • • • • •

Springtime of War: The First Franco-American Battles, May–June 1918

The long anticipated German offensive in the west began with Operation Michael, which burst across the front of the British Fifth Army on 21 March 1918.[1] This attack was the first of a series of blows carefully prepared and orchestrated by General Erich Ludendorff and designed to bring Germany victory in the war before American reinforcements could arrive to tip the scales against them. Through the skilled use of the new stormtroop tactics, which involved surprise and the careful coordination of elite infantry battalions, or Stürmtruppen, with massive well-orchestrated artillery barrages, the Germans soon gained tremendous success. The British front was ripped apart, and the Germans were soon advancing farther and faster than in any previous offensive, German or Allied, on the western front since 1914. Apparently, the Germans were well on their way to achieving a great victory.[2]

The German high command certainly believed this to be the case. Admiral Georg von Müller, a member of the kaiser's staff, recorded in his diary that the kaiser visited Field Marshal von Hindenburg and General Ludendorff in their headquarters at Avesnes and returned, "bursting with news of our success." The kaiser even shouted to a train station guard, "The battle is won, the English have been utterly defeated." Schools and businesses were closed throughout Germany as a national holiday was proclaimed in honor of the victory. The kaiser addressed a gathering of his sycophantic followers and informed them that if a peace delegation from the Allies arrived at that moment, then "it must kneel before the German standard, for it was a question here of a victory of the monarchy over democracy."[3]

The situation grew increasingly grim as dire reports from the British front seemed to signal that the Germans had scored a triumph of such monumental proportions that the entire western front might have come unhinged. As the British were driven back, the French high command scrambled to shift troops northward to plug the widening gap between the two Allied armies while still maintaining a strong force before Paris. On 23 March, with his front spread ever thinner to try to maintain contact with the retreating British, Pétain decided to request that Pershing relinquish his best-trained American divisions for service in a quiet sector of the front. This action would enable Pétain to strip French divisions from that sector and send them north into the battle. It would also scatter Pershing's divisions into French corps and French armies, a move that Pershing had vigorously opposed in the past. Although Pétain fully realized the possible dangers of reopening the debate over the use of American troops, he believed that Pershing would recognize the dire situation on the western front and want to help.[4]

Pershing closely followed the dramatic events that unfolded during the first days of the great German offensive and carefully considered how he could lend assistance to the Allies. As a consequence, he was receptive to Pétain's request for use of American divisions and reacted quickly to his appeal for aid. Pershing recalled, "The reports from the front gave an extremely dark picture of disaster and I felt that we should do everything possible to render assistance. It was to offer General Pétain such of our troops as could be used that I went to Compiègne on the 25th [of March]." When he arrived, Pershing was surprised to find Pétain's headquarters in a state of gloom and depression that he had not seen the French army exhibit during his entire time in Europe. Even the normally calm Pétain was visibly upset by the recent developments along the front.[5]

Pétain showed Pershing the latest situational maps that revealed the seriousness of the German breakthrough. Pétain indicated where he believed the line could be held but expressed concern that this might not be possible, given the lack of reserves available for his army or the British. Pershing realized that he did not have enough men to form an American army, but he still wanted to assist in whatever way he could. Assessing the gravity of the situation, he offered to take all the trained American divisions, form them into the U.S. Army I Corps, and then place this new corps at the disposal of the French commander. This action would also allow him to group all the trained American divisions together in their own sector, under their own senior officers, and thus be better prepared for the eventual establishment of an autonomous American army with its own sector of the western front.[6]

Pétain stated that he appreciated the gesture and understood Pershing's desire for an American command, but unfortunately he did not believe American staff officers were sufficiently trained at that time to handle duties at the corps level and to take responsibility for their own sector of the front. He also pointed out that although the infantry was available for this task, the Americans lacked sufficient numbers of artillery batteries and support troops to establish a viable corps. Pershing reluctantly admitted that this was true and that given the dire emergency they now faced, he would temporarily suspend his demands for an autonomous American sector. He qualified this by adding that he wanted Pétain's support for the establishment of an autonomous American army at the earliest possible date after the present crisis had subsided. Pétain agreed but refused to set a date for such an event. Pershing accepted Pétain's conditions and at that point offered him all the trained American divisions currently in Europe.[7]

Pershing's meeting with Pétain on 25 March is significant on two levels. First, as hard-pressed as the French were, it was the British sector that was bearing the brunt of the German attack and was indeed the main target of the enemy offensive. Yet Pershing made no attempt to offer Haig any form of assistance to help alleviate his dire situation; instead, Pershing went to Pétain. Pershing's action again demonstrates that although it was part of a multinational military coalition, America's primary military relationship was with France. Second, Pershing offered to sacrifice his long-cherished plan to establish an autonomous American presence on the western front, at least temporarily, in order to meet the needs of the present crisis. His gesture was most magnanimous and indeed reflected just how serious he believed the situation to be. It also clearly demonstrates that amalgamation of American forces with the French did in fact take place, although by divisions rather than by individuals or small units.

Pétain accepted Pershing's offer, but even at this moment of crisis the French commander did not want to see the inexperienced divisions of the AEF thrown into the furnace of the battlefront just yet. He explained to Pershing that the best way to employ American troops, for the moment at least, was for them to replace the French divisions in the quiet sectors of the south. This would allow those experienced French divisions to shift north into the battle. Pershing readily agreed and immediately placed the four trained AEF divisions (First, Second, Twenty-sixth, and Forty-second) on full alert, with orders to move to whichever part of the western front Pétain directed them.[8]

The following day, 26 March, one of the most important Allied military conferences of the war was held at Doullens, France; there the foundation was laid for the establishment of a unified Allied military command. Because the original purpose of this meeting was to establish a better method for coordinating military operations between the British and French armies, no Americans were present. Yet the Doullens Conference was to have far-reaching effects on the future employment of the AEF and indeed in many ways it took place because of the early and persistent demands by the United States for a unified Allied military command, which the Americans believed was essential to securing victory. It is important to understand at least the essentials of the conference and the issue of a supreme Allied commander in order to grasp the structure of the Allied high command that would oversee the military operations of the AEF during the battles of 1918.

As early as May 1917 Pershing had noted that the British and French lacked "real teamwork":

> It had been apparent for some time that there was a lack of cooperation between their armies. Their efforts were often separate and distinct. First one and then the other would attack, each apparently without reference to the other. Generally speaking, such methods could not seriously affect the enemy, who would thus be at liberty to utilize his reserves against them in turn. I had often remarked that the Allies would never win the war until they secured unity of action under some form of coordinated control.[9]

The first steps toward a form of interallied command were taken at the Rapallo Conference in November 1917 when the Supreme War Council was established. At that time Pershing had informed both the British and the French that there was a strong need for a supreme Allied commander who would act without national bias to oversee the "conduct of operations by the combined armies." Thus, American support for a supreme Allied commander was well known and well established when the Doullens Conference was held to address the problem of the individual national prerogatives that were guiding French and British military strategy.[10]

Since 1914 the primary focus of British defensive strategy had been aimed at protecting their lines of communication and supply to the sea by defending the channel ports; the French were primarily concerned with defending Paris. As a result of these differing priorities, the two armies had begun to separate under the strain of the German attack. Indeed, the German high command was counting on this very reaction, which was one of the major reasons that Michael had been directed against the juncture of the two armies in the Somme River Valley. By late March there was a danger that the two major Allied military forces on the western front would be isolated from each other by the Germans and defeated in detail.[11]

In order to prevent this separation and a subsequent permanent rupturing of the front, both the British and the French decided that the time had come for the appointment of a supreme Allied commander who would coordinate and direct the Allied armies according to the best military strategy for the alliance as a whole. Since the French army was the largest of the Allied forces and held the longest section of the front and because the BEF commander Field Marshal Sir Douglas Haig lacked the confidence of his own prime minister, David Lloyd George, it was quickly determined that a French general should assume the post.

Pétain seemed like the logical choice for the position, but Haig believed that he had not been forthcoming in providing French support to the threatened British front during the German offensive. Moreover, during the conference, Pétain slipped into one of his infamously pessimistic moods and expressed doubts as to whether the offensive could be stopped. At one point Pétain pointed to Haig while saying to Clemenceau, "There is a man who will be obliged to capitulate in [the] open field within a fortnight, and [we will be] very lucky if we are not obliged to do the same." As Clemenceau later wrote, "This speech was by no means calculated to confirm the confidence we wanted to hold on at all costs."[12]

Shortly after this incident, the discussion returned to the dire situation on the front, and especially to the latest German drive toward the city of Amiens. The British admitted that if the battle continued at its present pace, this vital northern French city would fall to the Germans sometime in the next twenty-four hours. This analysis made even the optimists in the crowd bleak with despair when suddenly, as Clemenceau later recalled,

there was a bustle, and Foch arrived, surrounded by officers, and dominating everything with his cutting voice. "You aren't fighting? I would fight without a break. I would fight in front of Amiens. I would fight in Amiens. I would fight behind Amiens. I would fight all the time." No commentary is needed on that speech. I confess for my own part I could hardly refrain from throwing myself into the arms of this admirable chief in the name of France in deadly peril.[13]

The British were also impressed and quickly suggested that Foch should assume the duties of supreme Allied commander, and the French delegation agreed. Clemenceau personally disliked Foch, but he respected him and saw in this general a kindred spirit who would continue the battle no matter what the odds or how desperate the situation.[14]

Foch's precise duties were somewhat unclear at first, so another conference was held at Beauvais, with Pershing present, a few days later, and Foch was clearly designated as the supreme Allied commander. His position was unique at the time, for although there had been international military coalitions and alliances before, they had never placed themselves under the guidance of one man. In many ways Foch laid the groundwork for the duties and responsibilities of a supreme commander of an international military force, a role that became increasingly common during the wars of the twentieth century, especially for the United States. Yet at the same time, his powers were limited to providing direction and offering suggestions to the army commanders rather than actually exercising command over the various Allied armies. Pétain, Haig, and later Pershing had considerable autonomy in the planning and conduct of their military operations, albeit Foch did harness these operations to an overall strategic plan; he was an integral part of the Allied victories in the final year of the war.[15]

With the creation of his new position, Foch, along with Pétain, became one of the principal French officers with whom Pershing and the senior officers of the AEF dealt throughout the battles of 1918. It is important to know something of the man and his methods in order to understand how he affected the military relationship between France and the United States.

Foch's most outstanding characteristic was his aggressive approach to warfare. His prewar military writings emphasized the importance of the attack and that "the will to conquer sweeps all before it."[16] Typical of his approach to war was the famous communiqué that he allegedly wired to GQG at the most desperate stage of the Battle of the Marne in 1914. Then in command of the French Ninth Army, he supposedly cabled to Joffre's headquarters: "My center yields, my right retreats, situation excellent, I attack." Although the story is probably apocryphal, all authorities agree that the message captures his spirit and typifies his incredibly optimistic and intensely aggressive approach to warfare.[17]

Foch was a volatile and colorful man who in the heat of explaining his theories of warfare would often seize his listener by the shoulder with one hand while jabbing him in the ribs with his fist to emphasize a point. His eccentricities were the subject of good-natured joking among the junior officers at GQG. French staff officer Jean de Pierrefeu witnessed this during a particularly jovial meal in the officer's mess at GQG in 1915:

A liaison officer had returned that very evening from Foch's headquarters, and mimicked the general. With his left hand in the opening of his jacket, he sawed the air with his right. "You understand, I attack here, I attack there, I break through, I tumble them head over heels." His hand indicated his dispositions, seemed to feel its way among the troops; and then his closed fist struck at the routed enemy. His incisive voice, at one moment jerky, became explosive. He raised his chin, flicked up the peak of his *képi*. Then, throwing himself back in his chair, he drew out an imaginary cigar, and held it under his nose to enjoy the aroma. . . . Shouts of laughter greeted this performance; all were delighted with the fidelity of voice and gesture. "He is an amazing character," remarked an officer. . . . Everybody had an anecdote to tell of General Foch, whose absence of mind, fits of rage, and original ways were celebrated throughout the army.[18]

On learning of the Doullens Conference and the selection of a supreme Allied commander, Pershing immediately motored to Foch's headquarters at Clermont-sur-Oise to inform him, as he had already informed Pétain, that the AEF was willing and eager to participate in the fight. Pershing arrived at a somber scene, as he found Foch, Pétain, and Clemenceau intently studying the current situation map when he entered the room. Pershing motioned to Clemenceau and Pétain that he wished to speak with Foch in private. As Pershing later recalled, "Under the inspiration of the moment, my French was spoken with a fluency that I could not have mustered ten minutes before or after." Pershing informed Foch, in words that were soon to be reprinted on the front page of virtually every newspaper in France and America:

I have come to tell you that the American people would consider it a great honor for our troops to be engaged in the present battle. I ask you for this in their name and my own. At this moment there are no other questions but of fighting. Infantry, artillery, aviation, all that we have are yours; use them as you wish. More will come, in numbers equal to

requirements. I have come especially to tell you that the American people will be proud to take part in the greatest battle of history.[19]

Foch was visibly moved by the American's remarks, so much so that he
seized Pershing by the arm and rushed him out into the courtyard where
Clemenceau and Pétain stood and asked him to repeat to them what he
had just said. Pershing did so and noted, "They, of course, showed keen
interest, especially M. Clemenceau." Pétain, who was not particularly
pleased to find himself under Foch's orders, simply remarked that he was
already aware of this and had previously discussed with Pershing the
employment of American soldiers at the front.[20]

Pershing's unpublicized conference with Pétain on 25 March had been
far more important than this encounter with Foch, since it was there that
the offer of American assistance was initially made and the details for
participation in the campaign worked out. Nevertheless, it was at the
meeting with Foch where the offer was made public, and the publicity
generated by the event provided a tremendous morale boost to France
and America at a time of grave crisis. The meeting and Pershing's dramatic offer were viewed on both sides of the Atlantic as a formal announcement that the AEF was going to enter the fight.

The French army, government, and press seized on Pershing's statement for use as a propaganda tool to help inspire the French soldiers and
people with the news that at long last the American soldiers were actually entering the front lines. Postcards were printed up both by the French
government and private dealers, with a photograph of Pershing surrounded by victor's laurels atop the words DISPOSEZ DE NOUS COMME IL
VOUS PLAIRA (use us as you wish), with the complete text of his message
to Foch printed below the title. The American press also gave full play to
Pershing's announcement, and the American war artist G. P. Hoskins me-
morialized the meeting in an oil painting, *America's Greatest Moment*.[21]

As American divisions prepared to enter the front lines, General Pétain was determined that in the crucible of the battlefield the Franco-
American military relationship would grow stronger. To this end he
immediately issued instructions to the French officers and instructors
who would be working closely with the Americans in the months to
come. He told his men that "the military assistance of our American Allies assumes an importance which will make it one of the decisive factors
in the happy issue of the war."[22]

Pétain continued, "In April of 1917, at the moment of their entrance
into the war, the United States did not have, properly speaking, an army,"
and he recounted the tremendous efforts that it had made to raise an

army and ship it to France. He also spoke of the "works of enormous importance" carried out by Americans in improving French harbors and French railways, works that would continue to benefit France long after the war was over. And he cited the humanitarian efforts of the American Red Cross that had placed "at our disposition considerable sums to relieve people who have met with all kinds of misfortunes."[23]

Pétain told his officers that the Americans respected the military experience of the French army but cautioned them to remember that America was "a great nation" and that their ability to handle tasks and understand modern war should not be underestimated. He added:

French officers should endeavor to be personal friends with American officers. Between people who are living constantly side by side, official relations are necessarily very much influenced by personal relations. The French officers should, therefore, always endeavor to live with their American comrades under the best terms of friendship, and to gain their confidence by demonstrating to them that the advice which they give, and the criticisms which they make, have no other object than the general interest. Such relations are easily realized for the American is by nature cordial and generous. It is important to ensure in the future, as has been the case in the past, close collaboration between the two Allied armies, a collaboration which constitutes the most certain guarantee of the final success of our common efforts.[24]

Pershing noted on his copy of Pétain's order that "this is truly a letter that signifies true cooperation in a spirit of trust and confidence."[25]

Indeed, the cornerstone of the Franco-American military relationship was the development and maintenance of a mutual friendship between American and French soldiers, encouraged by the high command of both armies. Nevertheless, these relationships, both personal and professional, had to be founded on a mutual respect and affection that no official policy could truly establish. French soldiers at many levels of command and even among the rank and file repeatedly demonstrated an open affection and respect for their American allies as the two armies went into battle together in 1918.

American divisions began to move into the trenches of the French army sector in April, and as they entered the front lines they began to take casualties. Just as the French army had given a hero's burial to the first Americans killed in action in 1917, so the first American soldiers to fall in the new sectors were also recognized by the French forces serving with them. Although by 1918 one would think that the French soldiers had become calloused toward death, they greatly cherished the memory of their fellow soldiers who had fallen in battle. Indeed, they took on an almost mythical importance, and preserving the memory of their sacrifice was extremely important to the average French soldier.

The French also extended this reverence to those Americans who fell in battle. General Eugène Savatier, commander of the French Thirty-fourth Infantry Division during the 1918 campaign, recalled the death of the first American soldier who fell in his sector during the course of repulsing a German trench raid:

> The affair had been all to the honor of the American battalion, and my men were delighted. One fact, however, saddened our hearts. A fragment of a shell killed one of the American soldiers. I quickly went with two of my officers to salute the remains of this first victim on the very spot where he had fallen, and placed the French *Croix de Guerre* on the breast of this brave fellow, whose heart after beating for us ceased beating far from his parents and his fatherland. I wanted to prove to him that in us he had found a new family, and we insisted on attending his funeral in great numbers.[26]

Savatier's account of this incident is quite moving. He and other French soldiers had grown fond of their American allies to the point that he wanted to express to the fallen soldier that "he had found a new family" among the French soldiers with whom he had fought. A nation will be grateful for financial or political support given to it by another country during a time of crisis. Yet what Savatier, and by extension the entire French army, was expressing through these ceremonies was gratitude for the ultimate form of support. An American soldier far from home had spilled out his lifeblood in the defense of France, and in doing so he had become more than an ally—he had become a brother.

This affection of French soldiers for the Americans was dramatically reflected in the letters that French soldiers sent home. As early as January and February 1918, when American soldiers were still rarely seen at the front line, French military censors noted that approximately 20 percent of the letters they had surveyed not only mentioned Americans but gave glowing appraisals of their military capabilities, even though hardly any had been in action yet. French postal censors noticed that when writing to their families, ordinary French soldiers "manifested their appreciation of the importance of the American intervention" and expressed "great confidence" in the Americans and their impact on the future outcome of the war. None of the surveyed letters expressed any disparaging remarks about them.[27]

The actual participation of American units in the fighting further cemented the bonds between the two armies. Douglas MacArthur, then a thirty-eight-year-old staff officer with the U.S. Forty-second Division, went to the front in early spring 1918 as part of the division's final training course with the French army. Soon after arriving, MacArthur accompanied a group of French soldiers on that most detested and terrifying of assignments in the Great War, a trench raid. He recalled:

> Just short of the trench [the French] intended to raid, a German guard heard them. His gun flashed in the night. The alarm spread through the trench, across the front. Flares soared and machine guns rattled. Enemy artillery lay down a barrage in front of the lines trapping the party. But the raid went on. They leaped into the trenches, and the fight was savage and merciless. Finally, a grenade, tossed into a dugout where the surviving Germans had fled, ended it. When we returned with our prisoners those veteran Frenchmen crowded around me, shaking my hand, slapping me on the back, and offering me cognac and absinthe. I was probably the first American soldier they had seen. General [Georges] de Bazelaire [commanding the French VII Corps] pinned a Croix de Guerre on my tunic and kissed me on both cheeks. I was now one of them.[28]

In mid-April Foch ordered the U.S. First Division to move from its quiet sector in Lorraine north to Picardy to join the French X Corps of General Eugène Debeney's French First Army. The U.S. First Division's new position was opposite a small salient in the newly established front line, opposite the village of Cantigny. The Germans had occupied this sector during their offensive the previous month, and although their new trench system was not as formidable as their original positions, they had managed to fortify heavily the abandoned village of Cantigny and to transform it into an unyielding defensive position. By May, with the front relatively stabilized, Pershing and the French high command decided that an American offensive would provide a great morale boost for both the French and American forces, and plans were laid for the First Division to execute an assault and to seize Cantigny from the Germans.[29]

Some contemporary writers and later historians have characterized Cantigny as the "first American battle" of World War I. The official U.S. Army records state with great pride that the attack on Cantigny was conducted "without the assistance of French infantry."[30] George C. Marshall, then a colonel and chief of staff of the U.S. First Division, wrote that the attack was launched "without the assistance of any French divisions."[31]

In the interests of self-promotion, whether individual or institutional, these statements have served to create the illusion that the Battle of Cantigny was a purely American operation. In fact, the American attack on Cantigny was a joint Franco-American operation from start to finish, as the First Division operated under French corps and army command throughout the course of the battle, and French artillery, armor, and aircraft provided overwhelming support for the operation as well.

On 12 May French General Charles Vandenberg, commanding the French X Corps, notified his superiors that the commander of the U.S. First Division, Major General Robert L. Bullard, wanted to stage a surprise attack against the fortified village of Cantigny. Vandenberg reported that the Americans were eager to launch the assault, which he described as being essentially a large trench raid. He expressed his belief that with surprise "and counting upon the enthusiasm of the executants we have the right to count on a complete and easy success, susceptible of having great moral effect." General Eugène Debeney, commanding the French First Army, was delighted with the proposal and quickly gave his approval to the operation.[32]

Bullard chose the U.S. Twenty-eighth Infantry Regiment to execute the assault, and Debeney ordered the French First Army and French X Corps to provide artillery support for the attack. The French artillery designated for support fire included massive 240mm and 280mm guns and howitzers designed to smash the more heavily fortified sectors of Cantigny, and 155mm GPF guns to provide counterbattery fire to knock out the German artillery.[33] Allan R. Millett has observed, "French reinforcements were critical. . . . Because the 1st Division's artillery brigade numbered only nineteen firing batteries, the French contribution was almost double the American, and the heavier French guns, howitzers and mortars provided the margin of fire superiority."[34]

In addition, Debeney placed a French *lance-flamme* (flamethrower) company and a French heavy tank company composed of twelve St. Chamonds with the U.S. Twenty-eighth Infantry regiment in order to provide direct support for the American attack. The French Air Service maintained air superiority over the area of the attack and with aerial reconnaissance provided vital intelligence information regarding German positions and troop movements. "America's first battle" of the war was clearly a Franco-American operation.[35]

U.S. Army First Lieutenant Daniel Sargent, Fifth Field Artillery, U.S. First Division, was assigned by his commanding officer to the French artillery batteries as a liaison officer. Sargent drew the assignment because he could speak French and had some knowledge of French artillery. He was assigned to an advanced observation post where, accompanied by a French officer, Lieutenant Gouin, he would observe the attack and direct French artillery fire to support the American infantry. Sargent recalled that Gouin "spoke English better than I did" and was a very capable officer.[36]

Sargent noted that the French officers attached to the American division for the operation were highly experienced and, perhaps because they were veterans, much more casual than the American officers were. He noticed, for example, that many of the French officers' jackets were unbuttoned, a habit that would have brought swift and severe rebuke from the Pershing-trained staff of the U.S. First Division.[37]

The French had assigned some of their best men to the task of supporting the Americans in their first major battle of the war and wanted it to be a success. The overwhelming number of guns, tanks, and special units assigned to the already oversized American division also speaks for the determination of the French to ensure that the Americans succeeded. The French wanted to turn an otherwise minor military operation into a significant morale boost for the Allies and did everything in their power to bring that about. Interestingly, Colonel Marshall was always extremely critical of the lavish artillery support that the French used to support their infantry. However, he made no comment whatsoever on the large number of French batteries assigned to support his division's attack at Cantigny, other than to complain later when the guns were withdrawn.[38]

After three days of preparatory fire by the big French guns and the First's own artillery batteries, which were equipped with French guns and ammunition, the U.S. Twenty-eighth Infantry Regiment went over the top on 28 May and stormed the fortified village of Cantigny in a few hours of savage fighting. The assault was brilliantly staged, and effective liaison between the French and American units participating in the attack was superbly maintained throughout the first day of battle. The Germans attempted to stage a large counterattack that afternoon, but French aircraft alerted the Americans to the German troop concentrations and directed devastating artillery fire on the German assault battalions, effectively breaking up the counterattack before it could ever get started.[39]

Lieutenant Sargent played a valuable role throughout the battle as the liaison officer. Even though many of the French batteries were withdrawn early because of a serious German breakthrough far to the south, a large number of them stayed to support the Americans. At one point in the fighting, Sargent received a telephone call in his observation post, which he shared with French forward observers, from an American artillery battery commander. The American wanted to know if Sargent could hear German shells coming over Cantigny en route to the American rear area. He replied that he could and was then asked if he would calculate the angle of the fire and give an approximate location as to the whereabouts of the German batteries. He hesitated at first since this was his first battle and he had received only a little bit of training (from the French) on counterbattery fire. Nevertheless, he put up a brave front and said he would do his best.[40]

Sargent worked intently with only his ear and a compass to assist him as the next salvo of German shells sailed over. The French liaison officers watched him intently to see how he would do. He made his estimates and then telephoned them in, using, as he later recalled, "the most scientific terms I could think up, and with a tone of absolute certainty." American and French guns soon unleashed a counterbattery barrage at the coordinates Sargent had supplied, and the German artillery fell silent. Sargent admitted he did not know if the enemy guns had been destroyed or had merely ceased firing, but his performance greatly impressed the French officers, who smiled and nodded to one another. Then a French artillery officer looked at Sargent approvingly, gestured toward him and "to my astonishment (and satisfaction), muttered: 'This officer knows his business.'" From that point on his fellow Americans treated him deferentially, due to the praise he had elicited from the French officers and the obvious high regard they had for him.[41]

For the next three days the fight for Cantigny raged, as the entire U.S. First Division was eventually brought into the battle to hold the village. After the initial American capture of the town, the Germans launched a total of six major counterattacks in the span of just forty-eight hours. The Germans directed every gun and heavy mortar they could muster and pounded the Americans with powerful artillery barrages. But after the debacle of the first counterattack, shattered by French guns, the German infantry assaults were uncoordinated, and American officers noted that the German infantry appeared demoralized by the destruction of their first attempt to retake the town. The raw Americans managed to fend off every assault, and by 1 June the Germans had abandoned Cantigny.[42]

In their first major battle of the war the Franco-American military team had acquitted themselves well. French support for the attack and subsequent defense of Cantigny was critical, and General Debeney was pleased by the performance of the American infantry under his overall command, particularly singling out the U.S. Twenty-eighth Infantry Regiment for praise in his General Orders: "Regiment animated by a magnificent offensive spirit. On May 28, 1918, under the orders of Colonel H. E. Ely, darted forth with irresistible impetus to attack a strongly fortified village. Attained all of its objectives and held the conquered ground despite repeated counter attacks."[43]

General Savatier spoke with many French officers who had witnessed the operation and later recalled the general impression of the Americans' performance in their first major battle. French officers told Savatier that General Robert L. Bullard had performed magnificently during the battle, and they especially praised the tactical finesse he displayed in maneuvering his reserves and utilizing his artillery support to its fullest advantage.[44] Accolades for the U.S. First Division's performance did not pour in from either Foch or Pétain, however, because the day before the Cantigny operation began, a disaster befell the French forces defending the Chemin des Dames ridge, and both men had to focus their energies to meet this new threat.

The French had secured the Chemin des Dames in a series of attacks, beginning with the failed offensive of April–May 1917 and continuing with a second much more successful, albeit limited, attack in October; the sector had been quiet since then. At 0200 hours on 27 May 1918 the German Army Group Crown Prince began Operation Blücher, a massive surprise assault against General Duchêne's French Sixth Army, which also contained five British divisions sent there to rest and recover from Operation Michael. The attack opened with a murderous concentration of artillery fire ably directed by Colonel Georg Bruchmüller, the artillery genius of the German army. The barrage inflicted grievous casualties among the tightly packed Allied infantry that Duchêne had deployed in a dense formation on his front line, against Pétain's orders, instead of establishing a defense in depth. The Sixth Army's artillery batteries were also hard hit with gas and high-explosive shells. The French artillery was outnumbered by the German guns by a ratio of approximately 3 to 1 and was also poorly concealed, several not having changed their locations since the limited French offensive the previous autumn. Consequently, the German counterbattery fire was particularly lethal, and within hours most of the French guns had been either knocked out or forced to withdraw, leaving their infantry to the mercy of the German assault forces.[45]

At 0445 hours the elite German Stürmtruppen battalions swiftly moved forward and were in the Allied trenches before the French and British could even react. In a few desperate hours of fighting, all the Allied divisions holding the ridge had been annihilated. This new German offensive had ripped a huge hole in the front line of the French Sixth Army. As the attack rapidly progressed, a panic ensued among the French troops as Duchêne's position collapsed, and the Germans were soon advancing farther than they had previously imagined possible. Ludendorff had originally planned Blücher as a diversionary attack to force the French to move their divisions away from the British sector of the front so that he could resume his offensive in the north. However, as reports flooded in of huge gains and the collapse of French resistance, it seemed that perhaps this attack could be converted into a decisive blow, if given enough support. Ludendorff immediately ordered the offensive to be reinforced and expanded.[46]

As the German offensive rolled forward, Pétain took charge and desperately committed individual battalions to the battle as soon as they came on line, hoping to slow the attack until he could muster his reserves. Although this purchased Pétain a little time, French staff officer Jean de Pierrefeu recalled that these small French units were "like drops of rain on white hot iron"; they were soon destroyed. The Germans crossed the Aisne River, seven miles behind the French front line, on the first day of the battle, and within forty-eight hours Army Group German Crown Prince had crossed the Ourcq. Two days later, the Germans reached the Marne at Château-Thierry, just fifty miles east of Paris, and France faced its greatest peril since the beginning of the war.[47]

The German breakthrough along the Chemin des Dames threw the Chamber of Deputies and the population of Paris into a panic and rumors were rife regarding the very real possibility of the government abandoning the capital. Alarmed, the American general Francis J. Kernan, working with the Services of Supply, urgently cabled Pershing, requesting instructions "in case an emergency may arise necessitating removal [of French government] from Paris." Pershing urged Kernan to remain calm, but he ordered a fleet of trucks to be assembled and stationed outside the American embassy in Paris in case evacuation became necessary.[48]

The defeatist politicians of the French Left, especially the Socialists who were openly espousing a policy of peace at any price, and even some conservative members of the chamber who had lost faith in the French high command, heaped recriminations on Foch and Pétain. Clemenceau, however, refused to heed the calls for their dismissal. When a delegation of Socialists showed up in his office to demand that at least Pétain should be relieved of command, Clemenceau exploded, rushed at them, and physically threw them out. Even at seventy-six the Tiger still had plenty of roar. Nevertheless, the danger to the capital forced an emergency session of the Chamber of Deputies to convene on 4 June, and Clemenceau had to defend his government as well as his generals while German armies pushed deeper into the heart of France.[49]

In one of his finest performances Clemenceau rose to the occasion in this moment of crisis and once more rallied the French nation to fight. He denounced defeatists and all those who questioned the leadership of Foch and Pétain during this dire emergency. Defending both, he told the

Chamber, "These men at this very moment wage the hardest battle of the war, and they wage it with a heroism which I am incapable of describing." He announced that no matter how grave the situation became, he would never abandon the capital of France to the enemy. Glaring at the defeatists, he boldly announced, "I will fight in front of Paris, I will fight in Paris, I will fight behind Paris."[50] He told the chamber that the German reserves were being used up in these battles while American reinforcements arrived in large numbers to reinforce the French front and to play their "decisive part" in the war. He reminded them that from the very first day of America's declaration of war he had told them the verdict of the Commission of the Army and would repeat it: "American cooperation will decide the end of the war."[51]

Clemenceau's ministry survived the Leftist assault by a vote of 377 to 110. Yet even though the political crisis subsided, at least for the time being, the military crisis was still very real. Everything depended on the generals whom Clemenceau had so vigorously defended and on the Americans whom he had touted to win on the battlefield a victory that would save not only Clemenceau's government but also France itself from defeat.

As political turmoil seethed in Paris, Supreme Allied Commander General Foch moved to support General Pétain's forces by ordering French divisions, which had previously been sent north to aid the British, to the French sector in the south. Foch also ordered, with Pershing's permission, five of the American divisions currently in training with the British to move south to Lorraine and the Vosges for active service near Paris in order to relieve French divisions serving there.[52]

These movements would help alleviate the crisis, but with the Germans already at the Marne and threatening to advance on Paris at any moment, more immediate action would have to be taken. The only available reserves were the American divisions, which, with the exception of the U.S. First Division, had been used only in quiet sectors of the front. Pershing had offered all the American soldiers and quickly agreed in this present crisis to release two more divisions, the U.S. Second and the partially trained U.S. Third, for active service on the threatened French front along the Marne River.[53]

Due to the incomplete training of the U.S. Third Division, General Pétain issued specific orders for it to be placed in a purely defensive role to protect the Marne crossings and gave explicit orders for the unit not to become involved in offensive operations until further notice was provided by his headquarters. The Seventh machine gun battalion of the Third Division did play an important, albeit small, role in the defense of the Marne crossings from 31 May to 1 June. But the remainder of the U.S.

Third Division essentially remained unengaged until the Second Battle of the Marne erupted on 15 July.[54]

Meanwhile, the U.S. Second Division, which Pétain did consider to be ready for action, was thrown into the furnace at its hottest point. Pétain rushed trucks from the French Service Automobile to the sector where the division had been training in order to move it to the front with the greatest possible speed. At 0400 hours on 31 May, French truck convoys, consisting of from sixty to seventy-five *camions* each, began arriving to transport the American infantry to the scene of action; the artillery followed later, transported in French trains.[55]

The French had pioneered the use of motorized vehicles for transportation of troops and movement of supplies on the battlefield. Indeed, during the Battle of Verdun in 1916 the French Service Automobile had rushed reinforcements to the battlefield and provided virtually all the supplies for the entire French Second Army during the first critical weeks. In 1918 the Americans were duly impressed with the speed and efficiency that the Service Automobile displayed in moving large numbers of troops to the front in a short period of time.[56]

Although movement was rapid, traveling by truck in 1918 was not necessarily a pleasant experience, as French colonials from Indochina drove the *camions* full of American soldiers at breakneck speeds along the narrow dirt roads of the French countryside. The seats inside the *camions* were narrow wooden boards, and the trucks were outfitted with hard-rubber wheels guaranteed to allow the riders to feel every bump in the road. The colonial drivers hated to get caught behind another truck column because of the great clouds of dust they created; the dust blinded the drivers and swirled into the open backs of the trucks, choking the passengers and covering everything in fine layers.

When different truck convoys approached the same intersection, the wide-eyed American passengers would hold on tightly as each group floored their accelerators and roared forward at breakneck speed in an attempt to outrace the other column and get ahead. Rushing toward the intersection and only barely avoiding a horrendous collision, one column would pull ahead of the other, followed by a cavalcade of obscene gestures and cursing from the losing convoy and much celebration by the victorious drivers.[57]

The Americans were dropped off just short of their area of deployment, and as they began their march to the scene of action they encountered a throng of French refugees fleeing the scene of battle. James Harbord, now commanding the Fourth (Marine) Brigade of the U.S. Second Division, was greatly disturbed by what he saw:

Everything that a frightened peasantry fleeing before a barbarian invader would be likely to think of bringing from among their little treasures was to be seen on that congested highway. I have never seen a more pathetic sight. Probably the flight of Evangeline and the Acadians immortalized by Longfellow may have equaled it, but I doubt that even they carried in their faces the terror shown by these victims flying before the Hun advance.[58]

Private Leo Bailey, a marine, remembered the scenes of human misery the Americans passed as they rushed forward to the front:

There were people of all ages, except men of military ages; there were children riding on the creaking wagons, held in place by their feeble grandparents; everyone who was able to do so was compelled to walk. There were carts drawn by every conceivable animal: cows, oxen, dogs, horses. The other cattle were driven along by the side of the wagons. The procession was noiseless, for the marchers were too miserable to more than glance at us as we passed and probably thought: a few more for the *Boches* to devour . . . each procession occupied half of the hot, white road from which there rose a cloud of bitter dust—the young going up to slaughter and be slaughtered; the old and their youth fleeing from the *furor Teutonicus*. Each half pitied the other, and the fresher half swore to avenge the feebler.[59]

Bailey's comment that the Americans "swore to avenge" the refugees was typical of the American attitude toward the French population and of the average soldier's view of his general role and purpose in the war. The French army and government had already noticed these attitudes as early as 1917. A confidential report from the Deuxieme Bureau of the French army noted that the American soldiers arriving in France "expressed a sincere friendship for us and a profound pity for our sufferings" and that they "desired to have the glory of being the saviors of France and of humanity." Once more we can see that aside from the strong official military relationships, the average American soldier had an affinity for France and its people and a real desire to fight to save them both.[60]

The French had suffered a serious defeat, and the fragile morale of their army dropped precipitously as the Germans advanced to the Marne. The arrival of the U.S. Second and Third Divisions at the most threatened section of the broken front, however, provided extremely valuable and much needed support. These oversized divisions, each the size of a French corps, added tremendous fighting power to the battered

French Sixth Army and played a vital role in restoring the integrity of the French lines and halting the German advance.[61]

The arrival of the Americans at the front also gave a tremendous morale boost to the battered soldiers of the French army. Frederick Palmer, an American journalist, traveled with the U.S. Second Division as it moved toward the front on the night of 31 May, and he recalled passing the demoralized French soldiers who had been in heavy combat for five days and had had little time for sleep or food. Suddenly, the retreating French recognized that the troops moving up through the darkness to relieve them were Americans, and a murmur went through the once-silent columns of soldiers and refugees. The murmur suddenly became a chorus of voices shouting *"Les Américains!"* At last, at long last, the Americans were moving into the battle.[62]

The French staff officer Jean de Pierrefeu wrote that the sight of these "magnificent youths from overseas" moving forward into the fight encouraged every French soldier and civilian who saw them. He noted that the fresh and exuberant Americans stood in sharp contrast to the battle-weary French troops, who had been "wasted by so many years of war . . . their sunken eyes shining with a dull fire." The Americans represented a fresh transfusion of blood "coming in floods to reanimate the dying body of France." Pierrefeu believed that these American soldiers moving toward the front signified the future of France:

> We looked upon them as an inexhaustible source of strength, carrying everything before it, and so, in those critical days, although the enemy had once more reached the Marne, and might well believe us to be disheartened, the hearts of French men were filled with a new courage. Our soldiers coming out of the trenches, stern and savage, were suddenly reassured and cheered by the sight of their brothers in arms.[63]

Pierrefeu's image of the Americans providing a transfusion of blood to "reanimate the dying body of France" provides striking testimony to the moral and physical impact that their arrival at the moment of crisis had on the French army. Still, arriving at the front was one thing; fighting was something very different.

On 1 June the U.S. Second Division moved forward, taking up defensive positions in the open fields north of the Marne astride the main highway to Paris and opposite a small forest, the Bois de Belleau, and the village of Vaux. Pétain assigned the division to General Duchêne's French Sixth Army, who in turn placed the Americans at the disposal of General Degoutte, commanding the French XXI Corps.[64]

Degoutte, who until this time had yet to work with American troops, informed the Second Division's commander, Major General Omar Bundy, that the Americans were to plug a yawning gap in the French line and take up defensive positions astride the main road to Paris. After informing them of their assignment, an anxious Degoutte inquired of Bundy and his staff if they thought their division could hold. Colonel Preston Brown, the division chief of staff, looked sternly at Degoutte and replied, "General, these are American regulars. In a hundred and fifty years they have never been beaten. They will hold." Degoutte was at first taken aback by this display of American bravado, then nodded affirmatively and appeared reassured. He informed Bundy and his staff that as soon as the German advance was halted, the French XXI Corps intended to counterattack, and the Americans would take part in the assault.[65]

Thus, the U.S. Second Division fought at Belleau Wood and Vaux under French corps and French army command. They fought alongside French divisions operating on each flank and were supported throughout the operation by French artillery, far more French guns than American, and French aviation. Despite Pershing's earlier struggles to resist amalgamation, the crisis of 1918 had caused him completely to abandon, if only for the moment, his commitment to it. From the moment Pershing gave Pétain permission to use these American forces in battle, he relinquished all tactical control over them, a great sacrifice on his part but one that enabled the Americans to make a major contribution.

Some American historians have written with disdain of the French army during this engagement and have stated that the American soldiers themselves expressed similar contempt for the French troops they encountered.[66] Although in some cases this may have been true, many American soldiers possessed a far greater depth of understanding for the actual situation confronting the French in 1918 in general, and this battle in particular, than many historians have given them credit for. Brigadier General A. W. Catlin, at the time a colonel commanding the Sixth U.S. Marine Regiment of the Second Division, admitted that the French were "thoroughly demoralized" but hastened to add, "And they had good reason to be. They had been fighting interminably, pounded by guns, poisoned with gas, and borne back and broken by superior numbers."[67] The Americans soon had their chance to experience what the French had been going through.

The arrival of the U.S. Second Division on 1 June significantly stabilized the situation along the entire front of the French XXI Corps. Indeed, General Degoutte made the American division the lynchpin of his defensive positions, placing them directly across the Paris road and moving up a French infantry division on either flank. Degoutte issued orders to General Omar Bundy, informing him, "The American regiments should fully understand that they are to hold in place and that French elements driven back by hostile attack are to be allowed to pass through the American lines, in order that they may be reorganized under the protection of their American comrades."[68]

With the French Sixth Army still trying to regain its feet from the pounding they had been taking from the Germans since 27 May, Degoutte intended to use the big American division assigned to him as a shield behind which he could rally his corps. From 1 to 5 June the U.S. Second Division was struck by several German assaults, but the Americans repulsed each one, inflicting heavy loss on the attackers. Bundy's division held and served as an inspiration to tired and demoralized French units, which did indeed begin to rally behind the Americans. As the German offensive ran out of steam, the French rapidly recovered from their earlier defeats and soon were eager to counter-attack.[69]

On 5 June General Degoutte ordered the Second Division to attack the following morning and to capture the Bois de Belleau and the village of Vaux, which lay directly opposite the American position. This attack would be part of a local counteroffensive by the French XXI Corps designed to push the Germans back from their advanced positions near the Marne. Degoutte also ordered the French 167th Infantry Division to attack alongside the Second Division and to seize critical objectives on the western flank of the American advance. American and French artillery and French aircraft would support the combined operation.[70]

American writers have often overlooked or denigrated the French role in the fighting at Belleau Wood and Vaux, but the attack by the U.S. Second Division was part of a general French counteroffensive involving Degoutte's French XXI Corps. The American attack on Belleau Wood was an important part of this operation, but it was only one portion of the overall battle; and in actuality, this engagement, like virtually all American engagements in the war, was a Franco-American effort. The French 167th Infantry Division and French Tenth Colonial Division operated on either flank and attacked in conjunction with the U.S. Second Division while the French 164th Division also operated in support of the Americans throughout the course of the battle. French artillery batteries were directly attached to the Second Division to provide fire support, and French corps and army artillery also provided support. French aviation units kept the skies clear of German planes, provided intelligence on German troop movements, and directed both French and American artillery fire throughout the course of the battle.[71]

Brigadier General James Harbord's Fourth Marine Brigade was assigned the task of seizing a small knoll, Hill 142, to the west of the Bois
de Belleau, as well as the wood itself. The U.S. Marine Corps regiments
that fought in the war were integrated into the army as the Fourth
Brigade of the Second Division. This brigade, consisting of the Fifth and
Sixth USMC Regiments and the soldiers of the U.S. Army Third Brigade
(Ninth Infantry Regiment and Twenty-third Infantry Regiment), cooperated marvelously during this battle, and indeed throughout the war, and
together made the U.S. Second Division one of the elite units of the AEF.[72]

Although the Germans were well established on Hill 142, French intelligence believed that only a small force held the wood. On 6 June the
American marines advanced smartly behind a heavy artillery barrage
laid down by French and American guns.[73] The infantry showed good
discipline as they swept up and over Hill 142, clearing it of German resistance after a few hours of sharp fighting. Harbord then wheeled his
brigade to the east, intent on following up his success by swiftly occupying the supposedly lightly defended Bois de Belleau and then consoli-
dating his position for the day. However, the marines quickly discovered
that the Germans held the wood in force.[74]

Since the last French reconnaissance of the German position on 3 June,
the entire 461st Infantry Regiment of the German 237th Division had
moved in and fortified itself in the thick forest. As the marines moved
against the wood at 1700 hours, they encountered unexpectedly heavy resistance, and the attack faltered. The marines took frightful losses from
well-concealed German machine gunners who raked the inexperienced
troops as they attempted to advance over open ground. With a supreme
effort of courage and determination, the marines gathered themselves
and charged forward into a hail of German fire. The American infantry
seized the German machine gun nests along the edge of the wood at bayonet point, and few prisoners were taken. After several hours of heavy
fighting, the marines managed to claw out a toehold in the Bois de Belleau as night fell. It became apparent that this would be a long and difficult struggle.[75]

On 7 June, Harbord's Fourth Brigade renewed the fight for the wood
and began a vicious yard-by-yard struggle against a tenacious defender
who made the marines pay heavily for each advance, counterattacking at
every opportunity in the rugged terrain. Nevertheless, by 12 June the
marines had pushed the Germans to the extreme northeast corner of the
wood; but exhausted and suffering from their heavy casualties, their advance faltered. On 25 June they made one final push, backed by a massive French artillery barrage, and stormed the German's final defensive

positions. That same day, the Third Brigade of the U.S. Second Division finally stormed the fortified village of Vaux as well as Hill 204 on the eastern flank of the Bois de Belleau, further solidifying the line and establishing complete control over the entire sector by 2 July. The German breakthrough had been cauterized and the road to Paris barred.

The valor and rugged determination the Americans exhibited throughout this engagement made a profound impression on the French units operating on their flanks and in support of the operation. Throughout the course of the fighting at Belleau Wood, reports flooded into Pétain and Foch's headquarters regarding the valor of these Americans and the skill and tenacity they were demonstrating in the fighting. During the height of the battle, an ecstatic Foch used the occasion of the first anniversary of Pershing's arrival in France to send a congratulatory telegram: "One year ago you brought to us the American sword. Today we have seen it strike. It is the certain pledge of victory. By it our hearts are more closely united than ever." An equally thrilled Pershing replied, "No higher mission could be given an army than to draw its sword side by side of the splendid French army in the great cause. We shall strike with all the power in us."[76]

Other French dignitaries were also quick to commend Pershing on the happy coincidence of this American battlefield success coinciding with the one-year anniversary of his arrival in France. As Clemenceau wrote:

On the anniversary of your arrival in France to take command of the American troops I wish, my dear General, to express to you once more the greatest admiration for the powerful aid brought by your army to the cause of the Allies. With ever increasing numbers, the American troops cover themselves with glory under your orders in barring the route of the invader. The day is coming when, thanks to the superb effort of your country and the valor of her sons, the enemy, losing the initiative of operations, will be forced to incline before the triumph of our ideal of justice and civilization.[77]

General Pétain also wrote to Pershing:

Your coming to French soil a year ago filled our country with enthusiasm and hope. Accept today the grateful homage of our soldiers for the daily increasing aid on the battlefield brought by their American brothers-in-arms. The last battles where the magnificent qualities of courage and military virtue of your troops were demonstrated in so brilliant a manner, are a sure guarantee of the future. The day is not far off when the great American Army will play the decisive role, to which History calls this army on the battlefields of Europe. Permit me, my dear General, to express to you on this anniversary day, my entire confidence and assure you of my feelings of affectionate comradeship.[78]

Pétain's language reveals both his affection and respect for the Americans. He refers to the Americans as "brothers-in-arms" rather than as allies. Such language recalls General Eugène Savatier's thoughts on the first American to fall in his sector and his hope that the soldier had realized that although far from his home, he had found a new family in the French army. Pétain also addresses more practical matters when he writes that it will not be long before a "great American Army" will fulfill its destiny on the battlefields of Europe. Moreover, his statement reaffirms French support for the creation of an autonomous American army at a time when U.S. divisions were still serving under French command because of the emergency brought on by the German offensives.

Pershing's reply to Pétain suggests the nature of their personal relationship, and by extension, the relationship between the AEF and the French army:

Your letter of June 13th written on the anniversary of my arrival in France has touched me deeply. I am convinced that the work done in the past year has been alone made possible by the sympathy and cordial cooperation of yourself and the Army of France. As you say, we have but begun our work and I hope and believe that with your cooperation the American Expeditionary Forces will play the role assigned to them in a manner worthy of the traditions of the United States of America and of the French Republic.[79]

Pershing gives extraordinary credit to Pétain and the French when he states that all the work done from June 1917 to June 1918 to create a modern American army had been made possible by their "sympathy and cordial cooperation." Pershing's use of language also evokes emotions rather than thoughts or specific actions. Perhaps he is revealing his own belief in the emotional ties of friendship between himself and Pétain and the AEF and the French army. Noting the strong bond between the two nations, and indeed the mutual responsibility of both countries in their creation of this new American military force, he hopes and believes that the AEF will be "worthy of the traditions of the United States of America and the French Republic."

Pétain and Pershing had become friends by 1918, despite and perhaps even because of their disagreements over issues such as training and amalgamation. The two men shared a mutual respect and admiration that transcended national and cultural boundaries and that was founded on a deep appreciation of the other's military abilities and a certain fondness for the way the other handled affairs. The two men simply enjoyed each other's company. The French staff officer Jean de Pierrefeu commented, "General Pershing delighted Pétain. He was the only man who succeeded in astonishing him."[80] Pershing's biographer Donald Smythe noted that Pershing had "the deepest respect and admiration for Pétain" and cited one of Pershing's aides as saying that the general loved Pétain.[81] James G. Harbord summed up their relationship:

> Their relations had to be close to be effective. Both were strong men, they were nearly of an age, neither of them was averse to power, and both were direct in their methods of attaining an end. No doubt there were many frank conversations between them. General Pershing well knew how to show the deference due to Pétain's superior experience and then much larger command, without making it an invitation to patronage, or an appeal for official guidance. . . . They had to meet as equals, and the watchword had to be Co-operation. They became great friends.[82]

Harbord's marine brigade was given the lion's share of the credit for the American victory, much to the consternation of the Second Division's U.S. Army Brigade, and shortly after the battle he assessed the impact the victory had on the war and on the French army:

> The effect on the French has been many times out of all proportion to the size of our brigade or the front on which it has operated. Its firm stand brought the Germans to a halt in their farther advance on Meaux, which was the road to Paris from the northeast. It heartened up the French immensely. They say a Marine can't venture down the boulevards of Paris without risk of being kissed by some casual passerby or *boulevardière*. Frenchmen say that the stand of the Marine Brigade in its far-reaching effects marks one of the great crises of history, and there is no doubt they feel it. In another way it has given their High Command a confidence in American troops that will contribute powerfully to the early establishment of an American sector in the Western front.[83]

First Lieutenant John W. Thomason, Jr., USMC, fought at Belleau Wood and was equally proud of his unit's accomplishments there. He later wrote home, "When the Boche spear drove . . . towards the heart of France and the world—Paris—it was the honor of our division in general and of the Marines in particular to be flung upon the point of that spearhead."[84]

Given the heat of the moment, both Harbord and Thomason somewhat exaggerated the importance of their brigade's contribution. Three French army corps contributed artillery, infantry, and aviation support to the operation; without it, the battle the Americans waged, though undeniably impressive, would nevertheless have been impossible to carry out. Yet the impact on morale, as Harbord notes, was greatly disproportionate to the actual number of American troops involved. The battle of Cantigny had proven that the Americans could carry out a small and carefully planned operation, when properly supported and under French guidance. But the fighting at Belleau Wood and Vaux demonstrated that the Americans were capable of entering the chaos of a swirling melee and had the skill and tenacity to engage in an extended and determined battle with the best the Germans had to offer and still emerge victorious.

By the end of June Americans were arriving in ever larger numbers, and it was now apparent that they had become excellent soldiers, an outcome the French liked to take at least some credit for while at the same time acknowledging that the Americans "were natural fighters."[85] Pierrefeu noted the sudden upswing in morale at French GQG in the wake of the American success:

This state of mind had at its origin, I think, the sight of the Americans, of whom every one had doubted whether they would ever arrive in time, and the excellent impression they produced, although it had been prophesied that they could not be turned into soldiers for six [more] months. Then their coming into action at Belleau Wood, where they showed themselves full of courage and dash, delighted the Third Bureau. Colonel Dufieux frequently said to me: "Do not forget the Americans in the communiqué; they are admirable."[86]

The French were quick to heap accolades and awards on the U.S. Second Division and especially on Harbord's marine brigade. Harbord and his two regimental commanders were awarded the Croix de Guerre, and the marine brigade and its component regiments were cited in the Orders of the Day of General Degoutte's French Sixth Army.[87]

In addition to the individual and unit awards liberally handed out by the French high command, General Degoutte (recently promoted to command of the French Sixth Army) issued a proclamation: "In view of the brilliant conduct of the 4th Brigade of the 2d U.S. Division, which in a spirited fight took Bouresches and the important strongpoint Bois de Belleau, stubbornly defended by a large enemy force, the general commanding the Sixth Army orders that henceforth, in all official papers, the Bois de Belleau shall be named 'Bois de la Brigade de Marine.' "[88]

The marines were and indeed still are proud of this commendation. Lieutenant Thomason believed it not only reflected well on the marines but also spoke highly of the positive relationship between the Americans and the French. In his view, Degoutte's action was typical of an army that appreciated his own concepts of glory and honor, and it strongly reinforced his romantic opinion of France. Shortly after the battle he wrote to his parents, announcing the name change of the wood and pointing out that "it takes the French to do a graceful thing like that."[89]

As American regiments, brigades, and divisions went into battle during spring and summer 1918 under French corps and army command, the French were quick to show their admiration and respect for the deeds of bravery Americans performed by issuing medals and citations to individuals and units. By the end of the war the French army had awarded American soldiers with 11,687 decorations for valor in combat and other services rendered to France, including 719 individuals who received France's highest honor, the Légion d'honneur.[90]

In a somewhat puzzling reaction, this French practice angered Pershing. He requested of Pétain that in the future all "propositions for bestowing French decorations on American officers and soldiers [would] be, before being put into effect, transmitted to the American General Headquarters in order to obtain the opinion of these Headquarters." To Pétain's credit, this was one agreement he made with Pershing that he did not make any real effort to enforce. Although Pershing's motives are not entirely clear on this issue, apparently he viewed foreign decorations as an indirect threat to his hopes for an autonomous American force. He reasoned that an American army should be the equal of the French and British, not only in numbers and modern weaponry but also in tradition.[91]

Harbord, himself a recipient of several French awards for bravery, did not agree with Pershing on this matter:

The position of General Pershing on decorations was probably not understood by the French below the level of their G.Q.G. or was considered by veteran French Generals as a vagary of those amusing Americans now so newly in the War. At any rate French Corps and Division commanders stirred by American gallantry—something they could well understand—did for our men and officers what they would have wished us to do for theirs, and awarded the Legion of Honor, the Croix de Guerre, and Medaille Militaire, all of which were put on the official ice at the [U.S. Army] Personnel Bureau, G.H.Q., until after the Armistice had been signed. Scores of those who had descended into the Valley of the Shadow and won them died without them in later engagements, and unconscious of more than that the French had tried to reward them and our G.H.Q. had prevented it. With apparently a psychological blind spot for the sentiment and moral value of bits of ribbon or a cross, General Pershing could be moved by neither appeal nor argument.[92]

Even after Pershing had placed a stop order on the awarding of foreign decorations in early 1918, and despite official protestations, the French continued to award citations for bravery in battle to American officers and men until the final day of the war.

After the Armistice was signed, and against Pershing's wishes, the U.S. Army's adjutant general developed a new method for handling the numerous foreign awards, mainly from the French, given to Americans for gallantry in action. Under this new system, past French awards were recognized and the medals were allowed on the U.S. Army uniform. Pershing did support the creation of more American citations for bravery, since the Medal of Honor was the only such award possible when the United States entered the war, but even then he was notoriously chary about awarding such citations. His intransigence on this issue left bitter feelings among many AEF veterans. Harbord wrote in 1936: "Nearly twenty years after the World War General Pershing is not quite forgiven for the lack of sympathy with which this matter was handled in the A.E.F. prior to the Armistice."[93]

French commanders had nothing but praise for the battlefield performance of the American soldiers in May and June 1918. Pétain was particularly thrilled by their achievements in their initial battles with the Germans. Officers on his staff noted that his whole demeanor, extremely pessimistic throughout the spring battles of 1918, began to change dramatically with each new report of the successes of the American forces serving under French command. According to Pierrefeu: "General Pétain was particularly struck by the sight of the Americans whom he met wherever he went. His mind, naturally inclined to see the significance of facts, showed him clearly the life-giving power they represented. At this time the name of the Americans was always on his lips, and he spoke like a builder of imperishable monuments would speak of an inexhaustible material which would allow him to build without fear of shortage."[94]

As the German offensive spent itself and the Franco-American counterattacks drove them away from Paris, Pétain announced to his staff, "The weld will be made, and then we have nothing to fear. If we can hold on till the end of June, our situation will be excellent. In July we can resume the offensive; after that, victory is ours." His prophecy proved to be remarkably accurate.[95]

The performance of the Americans in their first major battles of the war was a resounding success, and the French recognized it as such. There had been no question about how many American soldiers could eventually be put into the field, but there had remained doubt as to their fighting abilities. After the victories at Cantigny, Belleau Wood, and Vaux, those doubts no longer existed in anyone's mind, friend or foe. Yet as encouraging as those results were, they were still small-scale affairs by the standards of World War I, and it remained to be seen how the Americans would perform in a major battle. Until that test could be passed, the French would balk at the formation of an autonomous American force because the U.S. soldiers still lacked the experience of participating in large-scale operations on the western front. Yet as Allied intelligence began to detect the ominous signs of a major German buildup for another offensive in July 1918, it became increasingly apparent that the great test for the AEF was rapidly approaching.

CHAPTER 7

● ● ● ● ● ● ● ● ● ● ● ● ● ●

The Second Battle of the Marne: The Franco-American Battle That Turned the Tide

The critical moment of the 1918 campaign, and indeed of the Great War itself, came in summer. The great German offensives that had begun in March and continued throughout spring had gained a tremendous amount of ground and had dealt serious blows to the armies of France and Britain. The attacks, however, had been costly for Germany as well, and their front line was dangerously overextended by the size of their gains. Despite the tactical successes the offensives had clearly been, they had failed to destroy the Allied armies completely. Ludendorff, the architect of the offensives, later recalled, "It was certainly discouraging that our two great attacks [Michael and Blücher] had not forced a decision." He still thought that Germany could win the war and that those two offensives had placed the German army in a favorable position to do just that.[1]

Ludendorff believed that in modern war the military resources of nations were so vast that it was impossible to produce a tactical situation whereby all the military power of a nation could be destroyed in a single engagement. In his view, such a great Napoleonic-style victory was possible only as the culminating battle in a series of massive engagements in which the enemy's forces had been so severely damaged that they would be vulnerable to the final masterstroke. By July 1918 Ludendorff believed that the situation created along the western front by his offensives had indeed produced just such an opportunity. He thought that with one final push the French and British armies would begin to fall apart and their governments would lose the will to continue the war. Germany would thereby achieve victory before the arrival of American soldiers could tip the balance in favor of the Allies.

Ludendorff, however, was running out of time in his race to end the war before the Americans could arrive on the western front in strength. When the first German offensive of 1918 had burst across the British lines along the Somme in March, there were 300,000 inexperienced American soldiers scattered throughout France. Yet just four months later, that number had quadrupled to 1.2 million soldiers, and American forces had made their successful debut in battle at Cantigny, Belleau Wood, and Vaux. More troops were arriving every day, and during this pivotal month of July an additional 313,410 arrived in France.[2]

Ludendorff later recalled, "I did not delude myself at this time as to the imminence or the strength of the American forces then coming into action." He was not convinced, however, that the new divisions being deployed would prove to be equal in combat capability to the regulars of the U.S. First and Second Divisions, whom the Germans had encountered in their initial engagements against American forces. He also doubted that American officers had the experience or skill to conduct large-scale operations at the corps or army level. Nevertheless, the sheer numbers of American troops arriving on the western front did give Ludendorff reason for concern. Yet to him that concern was a catalyst for bold action, not caution, as every day that passed brought more American soldiers into the battle. Thus, the need to undertake another offensive and secure a decisive victory immediately was made even more acute by their rapidly increasing presence.[3]

Furthermore, Ludendorff realized that by summer 1918 the morale of both the German army and people was beginning to waver. The civilian leadership was especially disappointed by Ludendorff's failure to deliver his promised victory on the battlefield. Hopes had run high indeed after the brilliant opening of Operation Michael and had been briefly rekindled by the breakthrough along the Chemin des Dames. Yet as the weeks wore on and the German offensives ran out of steam without achieving the elusive knockout blow to the Allied armies, political pressure began to mount on the German high command to end the war with a negotiated settlement. On 24 June the German foreign minister Richard Kühlmann addressed the Reichstag and advocated the opening of political negotia-tions with the Allies in the hope of securing a satisfactory diplomatic so-lution to the war while Germany was still capable of negotiating from a position of strength. The speech caused a tremendous stir, both in the Reichstag and among the German press. Hindenburg and Ludendorff re-acted strongly to this challenge and condemned Kühlmann as a defeatist who would throw away all that German arms had achieved when they were on the very brink of victory. Kühlmann, however, was not alone, and the speech reflected a growing disillusionment with the war among certain elements of the civilian leadership and a significant segment of the German people themselves.[4]

By summer the morale of the long-suffering German population was beginning to break down under the strain of four years of total war. Everywhere that summer there were signs of discontent, as a food short-age, combined with general war weariness, produced an environment ripe for antiwar agitators and Communist revolutionaries. In June the Berlin police warned the government that support for peace at any price was growing, as the population began to dread the possibility of another winter with no coal and no food.[5] The soldiers of the German army were tired, and their ranks had been heavily depleted by the casualties they had suffered during their series of tactically brilliant, but strategically in-decisive, offensives of 1918. They were also suffering from food short-ages, and influenza was rapidly spreading through the army. Although the Allied armies on the western front were also beginning to suffer from the influenza epidemic, it struck harder among the German soldiers, who were malnourished and weak because of the inability of the high com-mand to provide them with sufficient rations.[6]

Determined to press the war to a military victory, Hindenburg and Lu-dendorff moved swiftly to suppress the growing air of defeatism spread-ing through the army and the home front. They demanded the resignation of Kühlmann, long an antagonist of the two, deeming the ac-tion necessary to improve morale at home and in the trenches. The kaiser listened to his military chiefs and forced Kühlmann to resign on 8 July. His resignation ended any real hope for a diplomatic solution to the war and reaffirmed the government's commitment to a policy of achieving a final military victory on the battlefield as the only possible solution to the problems the country now faced.[7]

With his domestic political opposition successfully suppressed, at least for the moment, Ludendorff threw himself into planning his next major offensive, one he hoped would destroy enough Allied military forces that their will to continue the war would be broken and they would be forced to sue for peace. He was encouraged because the previous offensives of 1918 had been tactical victories, and he believed that Germany still possessed the military power to decide the war on the battlefield. Nevertheless, he knew that its military resources were finite and that civilian morale was fragile; therefore, a failure on the battlefield at this late stage would not only expend the army's final offensive capability but also probably resurrect civilian opposition to the war.

In early June, Ludendorff began planning two major offensives to be undertaken in July, one against the French in Champagne and the other against the British in Flanders. The first would be launched against the Reims salient in Champagne by the army group of German Crown Prince Wilhelm, composed of the German First, Third, Seventh, and Ninth Armies. The German Seventh Army would strike the western flank of the Reims salient in Champagne while the First and Third launched attacks against its eastern flank. Ludendorff envisioned that the three armies would penetrate the French lines and then rapidly push south of the Marne River, simultaneously launching converging attacks intended to link the armies near the town of Epernay. The German Ninth Army, newly arrived from the eastern front, was ordered to assume defensive positions in the Marne salient to protect the vulnerable western flank of the advance.[8]

If successful, the offensive in Champagne would isolate and destroy the French forces in the Reims salient, shorten the German front line, free vital rail networks, and secure a bridgehead south of the Marne River that could be used as a base for a future advance on Paris. Ludendorff also apparently believed that the shock of losing a large number of troops and the great city of Reims might be enough either to knock France out of the war or at least to cripple its army's offensive capability permanently. He further hoped that the attack would force the Allies to strip reserves from the British front in Flanders, allowing him to deliver a coup de grâce to the British, once the French had been defeated, and thus complete Germany's victory in the Great War.[9]

By July, as Army Group Crown Prince began to mass for the offensive against Reims, it was clear to most Germans on the front and at home that the decisive moment had arrived. The impending offensive in Champagne was a badly kept secret, and the German press impulsively christened the operation as the culminating battle of Ludendorff's *Friedenstürm* (Peace Offensive). The thought that this would be the final battle of the war and that a victorious peace would follow its inevitable success served to inspire the soldiers assembling for the offensive and boosted the morale of civilians on the home front. Ludendorff made no attempt to discourage the rampant speculation that the climactic battle of the war was at hand, perhaps because he himself believed it to be so. He was certainly confident of the impending operation's success, although he recognized it would be difficult and would place heavy demands on his soldiers.[10]

Although Ludendorff was optimistic, there were other members of the German army high command who were growing increasingly uneasy about the overall military situation on the western front. Colonel Mertz von Quirnheim, one of Ludendorff's staff officers, went so far as to advise him to abandon all offensive operations because he believed the army was reaching its breaking point. Ludendorff shrugged off Mertz's suggestion and replied that there was no other way to secure victory and that he had to risk it. Crown Prince Wilhelm was also concerned and believed the Reims attack was a gamble, but he reasoned that there was no other choice except to run such risks, given the increasingly critical situation at the front. American soldiers and resources, arriving in ever increasing numbers, would soon swing the balance of power on the western front irrevocably in favor of the Allies; then it would be only a matter of time. Thus, the German high command, the common German soldier, the civilian leadership, and the people themselves increasingly viewed the coming battle before Reims as the decisive moment of the war. Imperial Germany would either win or lose the greatest war in history on Ludendorff's next throw of the iron dice.[11]

The Allies also believed that a critical juncture had been reached, and Supreme Allied Commander General Foch yearned to retake the initiative by launching a powerful Franco-American offensive against the German forces occupying the Marne salient. Foch and General Pétain had begun the initial planning for the operation at a meeting held at Foch's headquarters on 14 June.[12] In the weeks that followed, Foch began to gather every available French and American division, shifting them into position around the German salient in preparation for the attack that GQG believed would turn the tide of the war.[13]

With Pershing's consent all the trained American divisions (First, Second, Third, Fourth, Twenty-sixth, Twenty-eighth, and Forty-second) were used to reinforce the French Fourth, Sixth, and Tenth Armies in order to bolster the French positions in Champagne and along the Marne River. Foch also moved five semitrained American divisions from their French training areas to a quiet sector of the line in Alsace, effectively freeing up ten French divisions for service in the coming battle. Then Foch stripped the British sector of five American divisions, brought over as a result of the shipping agreement signed by Robertson and Pershing earlier in the year, and transferred these troops to the French army's strategic reserve.[14]

The move clearly violated the terms of the Anglo-American shipping agreement, which had stipulated that the Americans brought over would serve with the British. Haig and Lloyd George protested the move, but Foch insisted that these American troops were subject to his command and that as supreme Allied commander he had the prerogative to move them as he saw fit. Significantly, especially in light of his future stormy relations with Foch, Pershing did not utter a single word of protest. To the contrary, he was delighted to have these American forces assigned to the French sector, where the bulk of his forces were already operating. Such a move, in Pershing's eyes, made it much more feasible to establish an autonomous American army at an early date. With the transference of these five divisions from the BEF to the French army, Foch firmly reestablished the unique bilateral military relationship between France and America that had been so severely challenged by the U.S. shipping agreement with the British. Thus, in the long run, it was the French army that reaped the benefit from the work of the British in bringing additional American forces to Europe.

Aside from such political considerations, Foch's moves were firmly connected to military events on the field. Always the military theorist, he was clearly following Napoleon's maxim, "When you have resolved to fight a battle, collect your whole force. Dispense with nothing. A single battalion sometimes decides the day."[15] In the process of concentrating every available French and American unit he could lay his hands on, Foch created a composite Franco-American military force that would be fighting together as a team in the most critical battle of the war. The time had come to see if the months the French army had spent arming and training the AEF would now reap dividends on the battlefield.

On 4 July, the French army and the government proclaimed America's Independence Day a national holiday, and many festivities were held throughout the front lines and training areas. Pétain marked the occasion by ordering an emotionally charged martial ceremony in which the French 167th Infantry Division was assigned to the U.S. I Corps commanded by General Hunter Liggett; this Franco-American corps was then attached to General Degoutte's French Sixth Army. Liggett noted that the occasion marked "the first time that an American Command had foreign troops under its control since our War of Independence."[16]

The French 167th Division had fought side by side with the U.S. Second Division the previous month during the Battles of Belleau Wood and Vaux, but at that time both divisions were part of the French XXI Corps. Now an American army corps had been formed and a French division placed under the overall corps command of a U.S. officer. Liggett later expressed his belief that the formation of the U.S. I Corps marked a significant change in the Allied attitude toward American officers commanding large formations of men. Although by summer 1918 the French had indeed developed a positive opinion of American officers and their capabilities in commanding large formations, as evidenced in their willingness to place French soldiers under American command, the same cannot be said for the British. The British high command maintained a negative opinion of American officers throughout the war and never considered placing its divisions under American command. As late as October 1918, when the U.S. First Army held its own sector of the front and was heavily engaged in the Meuse-Argonne, the BEF commander Field Marshal Haig bemoaned the "ignorance" of American officers and equated their professional abilities with those of the Belgian army, a comparison intended as an insult to both parties.[17]

In sharp contrast to the British, the French officers and men assigned to Liggett's corps were "good comrades and good soldiers," and he was delighted to find that the commanding general of the 167th Infantry Division, General Schmidt, had no qualms whatsoever about serving under his command. Liggett recalled that Schmidt informed him "that he preferred to serve under American command; that his own corps commanders were too inclined to annoy him with petty details."[18] Pétain's placement of a French division under American corps command on 4 July marked a major stage in the maturation of the leadership role of the AEF, and by extension the United States itself, within the Allied coalition and signaled another stride forward in the ever-strengthening bond between the U.S. and French armies, forged on the battlefields of the Great War.

By early July Foch was ready to launch his offensive; but before the attack could go forward, American and French military intelligence learned that the Germans were preparing to mount a major offensive near the French city of Reims, on the eastern flank of the salient Foch intended to strike.[19] Foch wanted to preempt this expected German drive with his own offensive, but Pétain argued against it. He pointed out that if the Germans struck in Champagne, then they would be even more vulnerable to Foch's blow against their Marne salient. Pétain therefore advised Foch to conduct a counteroffensive that would catch the Germans off balance and at their most vulnerable, having already committed themselves to the attack. Foch reluctantly agreed, and ordered Pétain to prepare for two battles, a defensive battle followed by a massive counteroffensive.

The Second Battle of the Marne was thus fought in two stages, the first a defensive struggle to halt the German offensive and the second a decisive counterattack designed to eliminate the German salient along the

Marne, cut off and annihilate the German forces in the region, and seize the initiative on the western front for the first time since the great German offensives had begun in March. This would mark the first major offensive by the French since the Chemin des Dames debacle in spring 1917, but there were several pertinent features that reassured the French that this battle would be different.[20]

The French this time had gathered approximately 500 tanks to spearhead the counteroffensive, the largest employment of armor yet seen in military history. In contrast, only 132 tanks had been used in the Nivelle offensive of April 1917. At the time of Nivelle's attack, there had been no real tactical doctrine in the French army for employing this new weapon system; thus, the relatively few tanks available had not been properly utilized on the battlefield. And the weather had been abysmal during Nivelle's offensive as rain, mixed with sleet and snow, had turned the battlefield into a quagmire. Moreover, the French had confronted the most formidable system of defensive works on the western front.[21]

Although not every problem in the employment of armor had been eliminated in the past year (mechanical breakdowns continued to be the bane of both British and French tanks), new models of tanks, and improved versions of older models, had been introduced that were more reliable and effective. A general French armored doctrine had also been formalized, beginning with Pétain's issuance of several notes and instructions to his army and corps commanders in spring 1918 regarding the proper employment of armor and culminating with Pétain's Directive number 5, issued 12 July, which specifically addressed how offensive operations should be conducted and the role of armor in such operations.[22]

The target of the impending French attack was much more vulnerable this time, as the Germans, having only recently won the ground and still primarily focused on offensive operations, had not adequately prepared for the defense of their position. The hastily dug trenches they occupied bore no resemblance to the concrete bunkers and multilayered defensive network of the Hindenburg Line. And the clear summer weather and relatively open terrain of the planned area of attack was more promising.

Another major advantage Pétain had was the powerful American forces that Foch placed at his disposal. Five fresh American divisions, each the size of a French or German corps, would be available to assist in defending against the German attack, and four more would be held in reserve (including the only veteran AEF units, the U.S. First and Second Divisions) for use in the counteroffensive. These divisions provided a tremendous augmentation to French fighting power. The Americans' eagerness and enthusiasm for battle were contagious and would provide a significant morale boost to the tired French units serving with them. Pétain intended to use the Americans not only as the backbone of his defensive action but also as the spearhead for his counteroffensive; indeed, he placed these divisions in the most critical sectors of the line and gave them some of the most important and difficult objectives for the battle.

The final factor that set this operation apart from the failed attack of the previous year was that Foch, ever the advocate of the audacious offensive, and Pétain, the brilliant defensive strategist and proponent of the use of crushing firepower, would be in command of the battle. In the coming engagement, each of these commanders, among the finest ever produced in the Allied camp, would be able to fight his style of battle in conjunction with the other and in the process deliver a crippling blow to the German army.

As Pétain arranged the forces that Foch provided to him, he purposely scattered the American divisions in order to stiffen the defenses of as many sectors of the French lines as possible. He did so as much for the effect on morale as for reasons of military necessity. He reasoned that the more French soldiers saw Americans in the battle, the more the overall morale of the French army would be buoyed by their presence. The Americans would be fighting with the French in the coming engagement, and Pétain wanted to make sure that as many French soldiers as possible saw that this was the case. The American contribution to the battle indeed was both physical and moral, and each was equally important to the overall success of the operation.[23]

Pétain assigned the U.S. Forty-second Division, commanded by Major General Charles T. Menoher, to General Henri Gouraud's French Fourth Army in order to bolster the French defenses east of Reims, an area that French military intelligence believed to be one of the main targets of the impending German offensive. Gouraud had already heard wonderful things about the Americans' fighting abilities from French officers who had witnessed them in action at Cantigny, Belleau Wood, or Vaux and was ecstatic to have them assigned to his command. For his part, Gouraud's dash and command presence enthralled the Americans who came in contact with him, and he became an instant celebrity with the officers and men of the AEF.

Douglas MacArthur, who served as chief of staff of the U.S. Forty-second Division in July 1918, later wrote of Gouraud:

With one arm gone, and half a leg missing, with his red beard glittering in the sunlight, the jaunty rake of his cocked hat and the oratorical brilliance of his resonant voice, his impact was overwhelming. He seemed almost to be the reincarnation of that legendary figure of battle and romance, Henry of Navarre. And he was just as good as he looked. I have known all of the modern French commanders, and many were great measured by any standards, but he was the greatest of them all. . . . Gouraud was without a weakness.[24]

James G. Harbord also met Gouraud and recalled, "His manner, his bearing and address more nearly satisfied my conception of the great soldiers of the First Empire than any other commander I met in France."[25]

To many Americans, Gouraud seemed to embody the glorious history of the French army. As one examines the reasons why the officers and men of the U.S. Army so readily accepted French leadership on the battlefield, it is well to remember that the French army exuded a certain mystique to many Americans serving in the Great War. Whether it was a vision of Napoleon's Grande Armée conquering Europe, or sunburned Legionnaires subduing the Arabs of North Africa, for many American soldiers a romantic vision of *la gloire* surrounded the French army, an image that the French themselves actively cultivated. Gouraud's indomitable spirit and his excellent capabilities as a commander soon made him a legend among the Americans.

Of course, as Napoleon once observed, there is but a short step from the sublime to the ridiculous. As an artillery brigade of the U.S. Forty-second Division moved toward the front in July, they passed in review before their commander Colonel Henry J. Reilly and a host of French officers. As the guns rolled by, Reilly was horrified to see a drunken American artilleryman strapped to one of the guns and belting out American marching songs at the top of his voice. Reilly ordered the review halted and the man brought before him, whereupon, in front of the gathered French officers, he delivered a blistering tirade that soon reduced the man to tears. When Reilly demanded an explanation, the drunkard, with tears streaming down his face, launched into a rambling speech about his eternal commitment to Franco-American friendship, saying that his greatest ambition was to enter the battle and die for France. At this point a French officer, deeply moved and on the verge of crying himself, rushed forward, kissed the man on both cheeks, and implored for Reilly to act with leniency and allow the man to die nobly for France. Reilly recalled suppressing a smile as he turned the drunkard over to his officers and ordered them to sober him up and send him forward to the front.[26]

General Pershing was somewhat apprehensive over the employment of the Forty-second Division in the coming battle, as he believed that it was neither adequately trained nor experienced enough to participate in active operations. Gouraud, on the other hand, harbored no such reservations and had the utmost confidence in his new American troops. He placed the division in the very center of his position and assigned them the task of holding perhaps the most critical section of his entire defensive line astride the road to Châlons-sur-Marne. He believed, correctly as events turned out, that this road would be the main axis of advance for the Germans, and he wanted it held by the best soldiers he had. The historian James J. Cooke wrote of Gouraud's deployment: "Here was a general who meant business and who appeared to have more confidence in his Americans than did AEF Headquarters."[27]

This was the first glimpse of Americans for many French soldiers, and they were thrilled to have such formidable allies. They remarked on the size and physical strength of the average American soldier and the fighting spirit, indeed exuberance, that many expressed as they headed toward the front line. Word of American fighting prowess had already swept through the ranks of the French army, and French soldiers looked upon these new arrivals with great admiration and an expectation of even greater things to come. They remarked that the Americans had *cran* (guts), and it was widely rumored in the French ranks that the Germans were deathly afraid of Americans because they did not take prisoners.[28] French troops also commented on the generosity of the Americans, who were always willing to share any extras they might have in the way of food or tobacco with their French allies. Indeed, as American soldiers moved into position in preparation for the desperate battle that lay ahead, the soldiers of the two republics got along exceedingly well.[29]

Gouraud's deployment of his Fourth Army in Champagne was modeled on Pétain's tactical doctrine, as he expressed it in December 1917 in his Directive number 4 to the French army. It urged the French army to abandon its practice of meeting an enemy offensive by crowding as many men into the front line as possible. Pétain advocated a thinly held front line manned almost exclusively by small teams of machine gunners. These men, virtually suicide units, would be used to delay the enemy's advance but were not intended to stop it. Rather, the main line of resistance was to be established behind the front line and echeloned in depth, with the artillery moved farther back as well so as to be within reach of their front lines but out of range of the German batteries. These tactics would ensure that the massive artillery barrage and especially the crushing fire of the powerful but short-ranged heavy *Minenwerfers* (trench mortars), which preceded the German Stürmtruppen battalions, would strike a lightly held front line instead of a densely packed one. Thus, far fewer French soldiers would be exposed to the fury of the barrage, and the second line of defense, relatively unscathed by the initial bombardment and beyond the range of the trench mortars, would become the main line of resistance.[30]

On 6 July, with the German attack expected at any moment, Gouraud deployed his Fourth Army for defense, according to Pétain's system. In particular, the French front line in the Fourth Army's sector was all but abandoned. The first trench was manned exclusively by small observation detachments and machine-gun teams in fortified strongpoints. These positions were known as "islands of resistance," and the teams of soldiers holding them were assigned to alert the main French defensive position one and one-half miles to their rear of the approach of the German infantry through the use of telephone, signal rockets, and carrier pigeons. These teams would remain in position, calling in artillery fire on the German infantry and holding out in their strongpoints, desperately trying to slow the enemy advance, until they were overwhelmed by artillery fire or the Stürmtruppen.[31]

Clemenceau toured Gouraud's front line and was greatly moved by the stoical courage displayed by the men manning these suicide positions, whose discipline belied the commonly held assumption that the French soldier of 1918 was a dispirited, dejected, and near-mutinous soldier. Clemenceau recalled that these soldiers greeted him with eyes that "burned with an invincible resolution," even though they "had abandoned all chance of surviving to the triumph for which they offered their life." Clemenceau, who had made many such trips to the front, never forgot this particular tour of the French Fourth Army's front line on the eve of the great battle before Reims and told a postwar audience, "He who has not lived through such moments does not know what life can give."[32]

Thanks to the excellent work of French and American intelligence, as well as the clumsiness of the Germans in failing to conceal their extensive preparations, Gouraud was convinced that the expected offensive would strike his sector of the line.[33] He therefore ordered a series of aggressive trench raids against the German positions in Champagne in order to obtain prisoners, ascertain enemy strength, and maintain the most current information possible on their order of battle. With the German attack apparently imminent, the French IV Corps launched a large raid on the evening of 14 July that succeeded in capturing twenty-seven German soldiers. One of the prisoners divulged that the long-awaited attack was to start between 0300 and 0500 hours on 15 July, with the supporting barrage scheduled to begin at midnight 14 July.[34]

Gouraud gambled that the prisoner's information was correct, and at

2330 hours on 14 July, just before the scheduled German bombardment was to begin, he unmasked his carefully concealed artillery batteries and unleashed a massive barrage of his own. The French artillery pounded the German frontline trenches and likely assembly areas, focusing their fire on the infantry and thus inflicting heavy casualties on the tightly packed assault formations waiting for the word to advance. Shortly after midnight, the German artillery answered, and the night became like day as the crashing and booming of almost 4,000 French and German guns lit the sky and shook the very earth. The Second Battle of the Marne had begun.[35]

The battle started badly for the Germans, as the preemptive French bombardment inflicted heavy casualties on the assault divisions of the German First and Third Armies and wreaked havoc among the German high command, who now knew that the secrecy of their operation had been hopelessly compromised. Some German battalions were so heavily damaged by the bombardment that they had to be rotated out and reserve battalions brought forward before they could even begin their attack, causing massive confusion and delays in launching the main infantry assault.[36]

When the offensive by the German First and Third Armies finally did go forward, they encountered unexpectedly stiff resistance from the French machine-gun teams whose islands of resistance proved to be more difficult to overcome than expected. Indeed, one of these small teams held out for over ten hours, refusing to surrender and inflicting heavy casualties on the Germans until they were finally overwhelmed.[37]

After penetrating the French front line position, the German infantry was surprised to see how few French soldiers had actually been involved in holding up their advance and were concerned by the apparent lack of casualties caused by their preparatory bombardment. As the German assault battalions quickly consolidated and prepared to press forward, they were dismayed to see looming before them an extremely formidable defensive system; Gouraud's main line of defense had been virtually untouched by their massive artillery barrage. The Germans realized that this new system could never be carried without considerable artillery support, but the line was beyond the range of most of their batteries.[38]

During the afternoon of 15 July, the Germans attempted to displace their artillery batteries and move them forward to place them within range of this newly discovered defense system. But the progress of the German guns was slowed by the cratered front line positions, caused by their own barrage. As they slowly attempted to work their way forward, they came under increasingly heavy counterbattery fire from long-range French 155mm GPF guns, which inflicted enormous casualties on the

German gunners and their pieces. The German infantry gallantly attempted to press the attack, even without adequate artillery support, but they were met with withering rifle and machine-gun fire from the well-entrenched French and American forces. Moreover, French and American gunners delivered deadly accurate artillery fire from well-placed batteries already ranged in on all likely avenues of attack against the main defensive system.[39]

As the day wore on, the Germans became increasingly desperate to open up the old Roman road as a means of advancing toward Châlons-sur-Marne, their main objective for this stage of the offensive. During the course of the day they launched seven separate assaults against Gouraud's positions here, taking heavy casualties in each attack. By sheer force of will, small groups of German Stürmtruppen battled their way through the hail of fire that met their advance and forced their way into the main defensive system, where the fighting became hand to hand. Most Germans never reached the main defense line, however, as the fire from French and American machine guns and small arms inflicted severe casualties. Sergeant Norman Summers served with the 167th Infantry Regiment of the U.S. Forty-second Division during the battle and recorded in his journal: "One of our gunners in the machine gun company is credited with killing a whole company of Germans. He was so sick of the slaughter he had to be carried from his gun."[40]

In the heat of battle, American regiments and companies from the Forty-second Division became intermingled with units from the French Thirteenth and 170th Infantry Divisions holding Gouraud's main defense line. Although utter confusion could have resulted, instead the French and Americans fought well together, even as mixed small units. These ad hoc Franco-American combat teams launched impromptu counterattacks that successfully forced the Germans from their hard-won gains and drove them back to the abandoned front line position, which was then subjected to murderous American and French artillery fire. Colonel Douglas MacArthur recalled that by the early afternoon the German assault battalions had become "exhausted, uncoordinated and scattered, incapable of going further without being reorganized and reinforced."[41]

As darkness fell over the battlefield, the attack by the German First and Third Armies, Operation Reims, had ground to a halt in front of Gouraud's positions. They had made no appreciable gains whatsoever in this sector on a day when, according to the German plan, they were supposed to have advanced over twenty kilometers. Instead, Gouraud's Franco-American forces had inflicted massive casualties on the Germans while utterly denying the attackers even the most modest of their first-day objectives. Indeed, it was the quickest and most decisive defeat the Germans had suffered since their adoption of infiltration tactics in late 1917 and revealed for the first time that their offensive system could be defeated.

The French were particularly thrilled by the performance of the American troops during the battle east of Reims. Gouraud praised the division and remarked that the Americans had fought magnificently. He reported to Pétain that he had heard nothing but praise from the officers and men of the Fourth Army regarding their American brothers in arms, and their conduct boded well for the future.[42]

Major J. Corbabon, head of the French military mission attached to the U.S. Forty-second Division, reported that French soldiers greatly admired the conduct of the American troops. He described the Americans in the battle: "Calm and perfect bearing under artillery fire, endurance of fatigue and privations, tenacity in defense, eagerness in counterattack, willingness to engage in hand-to-hand fighting—such are the qualities that have been reported to me by all the French officers I have seen." Corbabon added that the Americans admired the French performance in this battle as well and that the esteem the Americans held for the French army had been made "all the greater by this common victory."[43]

Sergeant Norman Summers noted that "the French were very proud of the way we stood up under fire and a French general said we were as good as any of his storm troops." The French *poilus* expressed not only their pride in the American soldiers but also a genuine affection for their brothers in arms. Summers wrote, "After the battle the French would put their arms around our men and say *'bon camarades.'*"[44]

The German Seventh Army's attack against the western face of the Reims salient was more successful than the attacks by the German First and Third to the east. The Seventh Army was faced with the daunting task of forcing a crossing of the Marne and establishing a bridgehead on the south bank of the river as its initial objective. French artillery once more wreaked havoc with the initial attack as, being forewarned of the timing of the offensive, thanks to Gouraud, the artillery of the French Fifth and Sixth Armies also opened fire at 2330 hours on 14 July, catching the Germans off guard. As in Gouraud's sector, the French artillery inflicted terrific punishment on the troops massing for the assault along the north bank of the Marne. Nevertheless, shortly after midnight, the German's own barrage started and the Stürmtruppen battalions swept forward, accompanied by engineers loaded with boats and bridging equipment.

The German attack along the French Fifth Army's front went particularly well, despite the heavy losses suffered by the French guns, as the elite German divisions struck understrength French divisions that had been poorly deployed by the Fifth's commander General Berthelot. For various reasons, including Berthelot's disdain for Pétain's defensive concepts, the Fifth Army was not deployed according to the precepts called for in Directive number 4 and consequently suffered heavy casualties during the initial German barrage and assault. Moreover, it was the only French army to participate in the Second Battle of the Marne that did not include any American formations in its order of battle. Foch had sent Berthelot a small Italian corps, recently stripped from the Alpine front, as his only reinforcements. The Italians proved no match for the German Stürmtruppen, and in a matter of hours they had been virtually annihilated. Berthelot's French divisions had suffered heavy losses in the battles of May and June and were still somewhat understrength and demoralized. The French Fifth Army was knocked back over five kilometers before managing to regain its balance and slow the advance, but not before the German assault divisions had made a serious penetration of its front.[45]

The only serious reverse the German Seventh Army suffered on 15 July occurred near Château-Thierry, where the assault struck the right of General Degoutte's French Sixth Army. The right-center was held by General Mondesir's XXXVIII Corps, to which the U.S. Third Division was attached, commanded by Major General Joseph T. Dickman. This division, and in particular Colonel Ulysses Grant McAlexander's Thirty-eighth Infantry Regiment, caught the brunt of the assault by the Seventh's right flank.

As in Gouraud's sector, the preemptive French and American artillery bombardment pounded the German Stürmtruppen and caused heavy casualties as they waited for the signal to attack. The artillery fire also took a heavy toll on the German engineers, who were struggling to bring up bridging equipment and boats. Despite their heavy casualties, the German *pionieres* managed to throw several pontoon bridges across the Marne and also ferried infantry across in small boats, using ropes that had been secretly put in place the previous night.[46]

As part of their supporting artillery fire for the attack across the Marne, the Germans focused a particularly heavy gas attack on the U.S. Third Division, perhaps believing that the inexperienced Americans would be more vulnerable to the physical and psychological effects of the weapon. The Americans were indeed unnerved by the massive gas barrage on their positions, but proper discipline was maintained and surprisingly few casualties were suffered by the bombardment. Nevertheless, the barrage did succeed in severely discomfiting the Americans, forcing them to wear their gas masks for seven hours straight at one point in the battle under the blazing July sun as they fought in a cloud of poison that blanketed their positions like a dense fog.[47]

One of the German units to cross the Marne successfully was the German Tenth Division, a formation rated by Allied intelligence as a first class division and one of the best in the Imperial German army.[48] This crack division slammed headlong into Colonel McAlexander's Thirty-eighth Infantry Regiment, which was fighting in only its second engagement of the war. Although heavily outnumbered by a battle-hardened foe, McAlexander's infantry refused to yield their ground and engaged the Germans along the banks of the Marne. Several American platoons fought literally to the last man in a desperate attempt to halt the German advance at the water's edge. These men sold their lives dearly and delayed and frustrated German attempts to establish bridgeheads over the Marne for many hours.[49]

As the Germans forced their way across the river, the French divisions on the right of the Thirty-eighth Infantry Regiment received orders to withdraw to the secondary (i.e., main) line of resistance. Four companies from the U.S. Twenty-eighth Division had also been assigned to this sector, but due to a breakdown in communication these men failed to receive the orders to withdraw when their French allies did. Slow to realize that their position was hopelessly compromised, these companies suffered heavy casualties before fighting their way back to friendly lines. Some continued the battle as part of the U.S. Third Division, and others rejoined the French divisions they were assigned to along the main defensive line.[50]

Despite the precarious situation his regiment was in, McAlexander did not receive orders to withdraw. He redeployed his regiment so as to refuse his exposed right flank and ordered his men to hold their ground. However, he did not remain passively in his defensive positions while the Germans consolidated their foothold on the south bank. To their shock, he delivered a brilliant counterattack with elements of his regiment against the exposed flank of the elite Sixth Grenadier Regiment of the German Tenth Division.

The suddenness and fury of the American attack surprised the grenadiers, who gave way before the fierce bayonet charge. In a few minutes of desperate combat, the Sixth was hurled back across the river, suffering so many casualties in the process that it was effectively knocked out of the battle, and the advance of the German Tenth Division was brought to an abrupt halt. The German Thirty-sixth Division attempted to help out their comrades in the Tenth by shifting the axis of their attack to place pressure on the Americans, but they too were repulsed by McAlexander's regiment, with the help of rapidly arriving French reinforcements.[51]

The U.S. Thirtieth Infantry Regiment, Third Division (operating on the left of McAlexander) was also heavily engaged by no fewer than three different German regiments on the first day of the offensive. Lieutenant Marchand, a French infantry instructor attached to the Thirtieth, reported to his superiors that "the young soldiers of the 30th are admirable. They have a valor equal to that of the best French soldiers." Noting that the American infantry fought with skill and determination, he wrote, "It was the rifle, hand-to-hand fighting and often the revolver which stopped the enemy." Although casualties among both the Thirtieth and the Thirty-eighth were high, the losses they inflicted were grievous; the three German regiments that struck them were essentially hors de combat by the end of the day.[52]

As Major General Dickman's Third Division continued to hold its ground, the French divisions of the XXXVIII Corps also fought back stubbornly. On the evening of 15 July the French Seventy-third Division launched a counterattack against the Germans, which successfully restored the integrity of the U.S. Thirty-eighth's exposed right flank, although it failed to dislodge the Germans from their bridgeheads. French and American artillery batteries also performed magnificently in supporting the infantry and wreaking havoc as they repeatedly blasted the German pontoon bridges out of existence and kept the small bridgeheads under a withering fire throughout the battle. French aircraft launched attacks on the bridgeheads and inflicted heavy losses on the densely packed German troops attempting to cross the Marne or caught on the bridges.[53]

As before Reims, the French and Americans made a formidable team along the Marne, and where they stood and fought together, the line held. General Mondesir, commander of the French XXXVIII Corps, said after the battle, "If we succeeded in keeping our front line intact and repelling all attacks, we owe it to the very effective fire of the Franco-American artillery, and to the magnificent resistance of the infantry of General Dickman."[54]

In assessing why the German attack of 15 July was far more successful against Berthelot's French Fifth Army than against Gouraud's Fourth Army or Degoutte's Sixth Army, many historians have pointed out that Berthelot had not pursued Pétain's policy of defense. Rather, he had placed too many of his men in the front line, where they were far more exposed to the initial German barrage. Without questioning this assessment, I believe it is also important to recognize that Berthelot's Fifth

Army did not possess any American troops. I would argue that, aside from the considerable fighting power provided by one of these oversized American divisions, the effect of the Americans in their midst served to strengthen the French troops' resolve to fight. Certainly, the Germans who took part in the battle believed this to be the case, as they reported that each new American success served to bolster French morale and encourage their resistance. Significantly, no Americans were present in the one French army that suffered a reverse on the opening day of the battle.[55]

By nightfall 15 July it had become painfully apparent to Crown Prince Wilhelm and his staff and to the ordinary German soldiers serving under them that the great offensive against Reims had failed miserably. The only success had been the crossing of the Marne, but they had suffered tremendous casualties in the effort, and those still alive huddling in shallow bridgeheads were exposed to constant shelling from French and American artillery. As sporadic fighting continued through the night, Crown Prince Wilhelm was dismayed when he received news of the disastrous defeat suffered by the First and Third Armies before Reims. Although encouraged by the tactical success achieved by the Seventh Army, he believed that the complete and utter defeat suffered in the east severely compromised the overall chances for the success of the operation. With the eastern pincer of the offensive destroyed, there was now no hope of carrying out the double envelopment of the Reims salient that the Germans had originally envisaged. Late that evening Crown Prince Wilhelm met with his father, Kaiser Wilhelm II, who had received nothing but wildly optimistic reports to that time. The crown prince quickly dampened his father's spirits, informing a disappointed kaiser that he regarded the situation as "unpromising."[56]

Throughout the German high command that night, a mood of gloom and pessimism began to settle in as it became apparent from their intelligence reports that the offensive had essentially failed. The massive artillery barrage that had preceded their assault had succeeded only in destroying unoccupied trenches; the main French defense system remained intact. Yet despite these setbacks, the crown prince determined to renew the offensive the following day, if for no other reason than it seemed too early to cancel such an important operation. He later recalled, "We gave orders that [the main French defensive system] should be prepared for assault by fresh bombardment, but in my heart of hearts I had to admit the bitter truth that the offensive had failed."[57]

The crown prince held out hope that the Seventh Army could exploit its small success and perhaps make a serious enough penetration that the French high command would panic and abandon the exposed Reims salient. With this in mind, Crown Prince Wilhelm ordered the Seventh Army to resume the offensive the next day and the First and Third Armies essentially to launch only holding attacks to their front to prevent the French from shifting forces from Gouraud to Berthelot.

Pétain was swift to react to the results of the first day's battle. He rushed his carefully hoarded reserve divisions to Berthelot's front to help cauterize the German breakthrough and also moved the French Ninth Army from reserve to a position opposite the German bridgeheads along the Marne. The German crossing of the Marne and their success gained along the western face of the Reims salient so concerned Pétain that he ordered reserve divisions designated for the long awaited counteroffensive to reinforce Berthelot's battered forces as well. He also ordered preparations for the counteroffensive to be suspended until he could better contain the German advance against the Fifth Army and so that he might reinforce the eastern sector of the planned attack. Pétain realized that Berthelot's army was in no shape to go on the offensive, and until it was brought up to strength there would be no hope of making the planned counteroffensive the truly decisive double envelopment that Pétain and Foch envisaged.[58]

General Mangin's Tenth Army was designated to lead the attack against the western face of the Marne salient, and he was particularly upset by the postponement of the counteroffensive and by the stripping of his reserves for defensive assignments elsewhere. Mangin, aggressive to a fault, attributed Pétain's decision to caution and indecisiveness. When informed by Reserve Army Group commander General Fayolle of Pétain's decision, Mangin exploded with fury and proclaimed that Pétain and his staff were a "pack of grocers." Mangin shouted at Fayolle, "Give me all the divisions of the French army and you will see! I will do it all!"[59]

On the afternoon of 15 July, Foch stopped by General Fayolle's headquarters en route to a meeting in Flanders with Field Marshal Sir Douglas Haig and was informed of Pétain's decision to postpone Mangin's attack. Foch, who was just as aggressive as Mangin, was irritated by the decision. Foch believed Pétain was being far too cautious, given the great victory Gouraud had won. In a rare move, Foch intervened and countermanded Pétain's order, one of the few occasions when Foch used his authority as supreme Allied commander to overrule the French commander in chief. Foch telephoned Pétain: "It must be understood that until there are new developments that you will communicate to me, there can be no question at all of slowing up and less so of stopping the Mangin preparations. In case of absolute and imperative necessity you will employ such troops as are absolutely indispensable to meet the situation, informing me of it at once."[60]

Pétain, chagrined, backed down. Although he disapproved of Foch's decision, he agreed to renew preparations for the counteroffensive, make do with the forces he currently had at his disposal, and vowed not to touch Mangin's reserves. The attack date was set for 18 July; nothing could stop it now. Although Pétain followed Foch's orders, he nevertheless retained doubts about the timing of the counteroffensive and believed that an attack on 18 July would be premature.[61]

Pétain has been severely criticized for his hesitancy to launch the counteroffensive at an early date. Some critics have even gone so far as to charge that one can see the roots of the disaster of 1940 in Pétain's hesitancy and emphasis on the defensive at this critical stage of the Second Battle of the Marne.[62] Yet this is a patently unfair criticism, especially when one considers that Pétain was already preparing local counteroffensives to place pressure on the German bridgehead south of the Marne, as well as reinforcing Berthelot's Fifth Army for its role in the general counteroffensive against the eastern face of the Marne salient. It was not a matter of if the counteroffensive should be launched but when, and Pétain believed that Foch and Mangin's eagerness to attack could result in an ill-timed assault that would not produce the decisive victory he wanted. As events turned out, this was precisely what happened.[63]

With the back of the German offensive broken, Foch decided to launch his counteroffensive at the earliest possible moment in order to strike before the Germans had time to recover from their defeat and before they had a chance to dig in. The main blow would strike the western face of the German's Marne salient where the Sixth Army, under Degoutte, and the Tenth Army, under Mangin, had been concentrating their forces for over a week. Of the two armies, Mangin's held the greater responsibility, for a rapid breakthrough in his sector could capture the critical rail center at Soissons and thus cut off the German Seventh and Ninth Armies in their salient before they could disengage from their offensive operations and withdraw. Foch knew his generals well, and in placing Mangin in this role he had chosen a commander who possessed an audacity rivaled only by Foch himself and an aggressive fighting spirit that bordered on recklessness.

Mangin had made his reputation as a colonial officer serving in West Africa, Indochina, and North Africa. He had a colorful persona, accentuated by his habit of traveling in a bright red Opel, which he had captured from the Germans early in the war, and by having a Senegalese warrior as his personal aide. Personally, he was recklessly courageous and showed a stubborn determination in the attack that often resulted in heavy casualties for his forces, but he achieved results. It had been Mangin who, with a combination of innovative tactics and audacity, had retaken legendary Ft. Douaumont on 24 October 1916 during the Battle of Verdun and thus forever secured for himself a place of glory in the annals of the French army. His enemies dubbed him *le boucher* (the butcher), but his men followed where he led. He was notorious for situating his command post well forward in the zone of battle and exposing himself to enemy fire in a reckless and off-hand fashion. With his tactical skills, his courage, and his audacity, he was the perfect man to lead the great Franco-American counteroffensive.[64]

Mangin chose the elite French XX Corps, a legendary formation in World War I, to spearhead his assault. Foch had commanded the corps in 1914 and led it during a heroic defensive that had saved the city of Nancy from the German invaders in the opening weeks of the war. In 1915 the XX Corps had added further battle honors to its credit during the great French offensive in Champagne and was already known in the French army as the Iron Corps when in 1916 it was hurled into the inferno of Verdun. Under the command of General Balfourier, it force-marched through a driving snowstorm to the scene of action in a desperate bid to plug a yawning gap in the French front line torn by the advancing Germans in the opening hours of their offensive. This famous corps fought itself to pieces holding the critical ridgeline east of Verdun, where it played a major role in halting the German drive on the sacred French city and thus added even more luster to its already formidable reputation. It was no surprise that in July, GQG assigned the corps to the "post of honor" in what the French believed would be the decisive battle of the war.[65]

Given the importance of the XX Corps's mission, Pétain decided to assign the best units he had to it and accordingly added the First Moroccan Division, widely recognized as one of the finest in the French army. While this was an obvious first choice, Pétain's other choices were somewhat more controversial. The French Tenth Army's chief of staff, General Joseph Hellé, recalled, "Pétain wanted [American divisions] associated with the great offensive. He wanted to put them, if only for a few days, in the 'most visible' place of this great offensive action which was the beginning of our victory. Quickly, he moved the two divisions [U.S. First and Second], which were the best American troops, to the left of Mangin, joining them to the Moroccan division—one of our best divisions."[66] On the eve of the battle, Hellé reported to Foch's headquarters and informed the Allied high command of Pétain's decision to place the Americans in the XX Corps. He noted that General Eugène Savatier, one of Foch's staff members, "was visibly surprised" when informed of this assignment.[67]

Interestingly, Foch incorrectly states in his memoirs that the U.S. First and Second Divisions were part of the U.S. III Corps during the Second Battle of the Marne. In actuality, although originally assigned to it, by 18 July both divisions had been transferred to the French XX Corps and were part of it throughout their participation in the Second Battle of the Marne. The U.S. III Corps, lacking corps artillery and essential support units, existed only on paper, and the French exercised tactical and operational control over the U.S. First and Second Divisions throughout the battle.[68] Foch's oversight leads one to believe that either he disapproved of Pétain's decision to place the U.S. divisions in the Iron Corps, or in his later years was hesitant to credit the Americans with spearheading the critical assault in an otherwise French battle. Unlike Pétain, Gouraud, Degoutte, and other high-ranking French officers, Foch was still skeptical of American military capabilities during summer 1918.[69]

Mangin himself was pleased to have American divisions assigned to his Tenth Army for the coming battle. As General Hellé recalled,

My late chief, General Mangin, was delighted to receive American divisions to cooperate in his offensive. He wished to see all the units before they entered into line. An American general presented his troops, and proved to him the marked enthusiasm of each of his regiments for the impending attack. General Mangin congratulated his American ally, expressing his satisfaction at the fine troops, whose courage was already famous with the French.[70]

The significance of their assignment to the elite French XX Corps was lost on the American soldiers themselves, who were rushed forward to the battle zone on short notice and learned of their corps assignment only right before the attack began. General James G. Harbord, recently promoted to the post of commanding general of the U.S. Second Division, never mentions the honor of the assignment but does complain of the short notice he was given regarding his division's participation in the great attack. French army trucks moved his division through the night of 17–18 July, and he was not informed of the final destination or of his exact orders. Harbord, exhausted and hungry after a long and arduous night march with his division to reach the jump-off point for the attack, was furious with the French staff officers who had kept from him the information on the exact role his division would play in the forthcoming operation. He demanded an explanation, but, as he later recalled, the French officers merely shrugged their shoulders and with a battlewise look in their eyes, said simply, "*C'est la guerre.*"[71]

Although Harbord ascribed this lack of forewarning to the French staff officers' inefficiency, in reality it was due mainly to the inordinately tight security that Mangin had drawn about his impending offensive that left even division commanders uninformed until the last moment.[72] Furthermore, Foch and Pétain disputed the exact role for the division until the last moment, as Pétain had wanted the unit to bolster his defenses along the Marne. Foch at length overruled him, but the dispute unquestionably added to the delay in deploying the division.[73]

Whatever the precise reason, the result was that Harbord's assignment was incredibly difficult. After an all-night truck ride, he had only a few hours to grope his way through the darkness and move his men into attack positions just before dawn. Given these circumstances, his division's superb performance in combat over the next two days is even more impressive.

On 0435 hours 18 July, Mangin's Tenth Army and Degoutte's Sixth Army attacked the western flank of the German salient along the Marne. First Lieutenant Ladislav Janda served in the U.S. Ninth Infantry Regiment, Second Division, and reported, "At 4:35 to the dot a livid flame seemed to shoot up out of the forest [Foret de Viller-Cotterets] behind us and seemed to hang there as our guns opened up one continuous roar of bombardment that was deafening."[74]

The XX Corps spearheaded the Tenth Army's assault, supported by a massive artillery barrage and approximately 320 French tanks that provided excellent support to the advancing infantry. The Franco-American forces surged forward, breaking the thinly held German front line, and pushed ahead as far as eight kilometers in the first day of fighting. Mangin later noted with pleasure that "the results were particularly brilliant in the center, where the 1st and 2nd American divisions [were] organized with the Moroccan division of [General] Daugan [and] were excellent assault troops."[75]

The German Ninth Army, charged with defending this sector of the line, was expecting some sort of a localized attack to be launched against them but was unprepared for the massive assault that actually struck their lines. The ferocity of the Americans and their French allies astounded the Germans, who did not believe that their enemies could recover so quickly from the fighting that had been raging since the opening of their offensive three days earlier. The German 241st Division and the Eleventh Bavarian Division were completely annihilated during the first day's fighting, as the Franco-American Tenth Army captured approximately 7,200 prisoners and twenty-one guns. By nightfall the entire front of the German Ninth Army was in danger of collapse.[76]

First Lieutenant John W. Thomason Jr. served with the Fifth USMC

Regiment, Second Division, during the battle, and his company was charged with maintaining liaison with the Moroccan division on their flank. Since his company and the French occasionally became entwined in the confusion of battle, Thomason often found himself fighting side by side with them, later writing his parents, "I had a wonderful opportunity to see the very Past Masters of the old game of war at work."[77]

The French army regiment that Thomason saw most often that first day was a Senegalese regiment from French West Africa. Describing them as "the chosen shock troops of France," he added, "Long rangy men they are, strong and wiry with fine aquiline features and the regal carriage of kings. And they love to fight. They love it! For fighting and nothing else they are on this earth. In their hands the long French bayonet is a fearful thing and they have a very wicked knife for close quarters. The Boche seems to fear them more than anything on earth for they take no prisoners."[78]

That Thomason, a native Texan whose grandfather had been a Confederate officer, could overcome his racial prejudice and express such glowing admiration for black soldiers speaks volumes regarding the respect that American soldiers and marines had for the French army. The fierce Senegalese equally impressed other Americans involved in the Second Battle of the Marne, and these first meetings between French colonial troops and American soldiers produced some interesting cross-cultural encounters.

On one occasion, Corporal Frederick Shaw of the Eighteenth Infantry Regiment, First Division, found his unit resting beside some Senegalese troops. Shaw took out a fresh pack of cigarettes, lit one, and then offered the pack around to his friends. He "noticed a longing" in one of the Senegalese soldier's eyes, so Shaw generously tossed him the remainder of the pack of smokes. The Senegalese soldier was delighted by the gesture and immediately offered in exchange a necklace made from the dried ears of dead Germans, whom the warrior had killed in battle. Shaw recoiled in horror, to the dismay of the Senegalese. A nearby French Foreign Legionnaire quickly intervened and explained to Shaw that the Senegalese felt he owed Shaw a gift in exchange for the cigarettes. The Legionnaire informed Shaw that the ear necklace was the most prized possession of a Senegalese warrior and "if you refuse, he's insulted and just might pull his knife on you." Shaw wisely took the necklace.[79]

General Berdoulat, commanding the XX Corps, and his staff observed the attack of the Franco-American force from a nearby hill, where they anxiously awaited word on the progress of the offensive. Suddenly, signal rockets rose from the American sector of the XX Corps's lines, requesting the French artillery to shift its rolling barrage forward as the first objectives had already been taken. As Berdoulat later recalled, "Ha! I could not resist an expression of my delight. That meant the infantry were on the go. The Americans!" Mangin's chief of staff, Hellé, remarked, "Familiar as I was with the swiftness of the Americans by this time, the persistence of their rush and 'go' later on in the course of this same advance again took me by surprise. . . . I do not wonder they got out of touch with the Moroccans. We were quite unprepared for such fury in an attack."[80]

For two days Mangin's Tenth Army and Degoutte's Sixth Army, each boasting a complement of two oversized American divisions and supported by armor, drove relentlessly forward against the western face of the Marne salient as German resistance continued to stiffen instead of collapsing. The American divisions proved to be the spearheads of the advance. They were eager for combat, aggressive to a fault in their desire to attack, and showed great dash and courage as they set a frenzied pace for the advance. These rapid advances often resulted in American units getting far in front of the French units they were cooperating with, causing some historians to charge that the French army of 1918 contained dispirited troops who repeatedly failed in their assignments and were constantly outperformed by the American units.

Although there is some validity to this argument, many AEF officers did not share this low opinion of the French army, when memories were still fresh and postwar political differences and national rivalries had not yet emerged. A study compiled immediately after the war by the U.S. Army polled senior AEF officers on the subject of the overall efficiency of the French army in comparison to the U.S. Army. It found that 44 percent of the respondents believed that the French army was either superior to the U.S. Army in terms of efficiency or the equal of it, and 34 percent believed that the U.S. Army was more efficient. Even among the respondents who believed the American army was more efficient, it was still generally conceded that the French possessed "greater experience and superior training" but that "the American gains the desired end more quickly." One U.S. corps commander offered an interesting take on the superior speed of American divisions in the attack. He "expressed the opinion that although the Americans made faster progress toward their objectives, by the same token they became exhausted more quickly, and were sooner in need of relief and replacement [than the French were]." Given the natural pride of U.S. Army officers for their organization and the patriotism that can sometimes color judgments involving such comparisons, these statistics are amazing and reveal the high opinion of the French army that many Americans held during the Great War.[81]

The XX Corps had made excellent progress but at a heavy cost in lives. On 20 July General Mangin ordered the French Fifty-eighth Division to relieve the exhausted and bloodied U.S. Second after that formidable unit had suffered over 4,000 casualties in just forty-eight hours of battle. The following day Mangin ordered his Tenth Army to continue to execute its attacks with an aggressive spirit as he was eager to exploit the breakthrough that had been achieved. The U.S. First Division was played out by the end of 21 July, and it too had to be relieved, but not before the Franco-American XX Corps had made a serious penetration of the German positions and in the process inflicted terrible losses. Moreover, the Franco-American attack threatened to completely collapse the right flank of the German Ninth Army and brought the vital road and rail line connecting Soissons to Château-Thierry, which the Germans in the south of the Marne salient depended on for their supplies, under the fire of their guns.[82]

Faced with a possible disaster, the German crown prince ordered an abandonment of the Marne bridgeheads and a general withdrawal from the Marne salient. The Germans displayed amazing discipline during this delicate maneuver. After the initial shock of 18 July they recovered, kept their heads during the crisis, and performed a marvelous fighting withdrawal rather than allowing themselves to be routed. This was partly because General Berthelot's Fifth Army, as Pétain had feared, had not been ready for its role in the attack on 18 July.

The Fifth Army, reinforced by French divisions and two British divisions drawn from the Allied strategic reserve, finally went into action on 20 July, but the moment had passed. Determined German resistance slowed the Anglo-French advance, but liaison between the British and French troops was absolutely abysmal and resulted in needless casualties. Indeed, cooperation between the British and French in Berthelot's Fifth Army was virtually nonexistent, and both the Allies suffered from their mutual prejudices. The lack of Anglo-French cooperation during the Second Battle of the Marne stands in marked contrast to the tremendously successful combined operations mounted by the Franco-American forces during the engagement. This contrast bears testament to the wonderful achievement of Pétain and Pershing in establishing such a close personal and professional relationship between the French and American soldiers.[83]

The Germans moved with great speed and skill to disengage from their precarious position astride the Marne before the second wing of the French advance began. Once again, the Germans proved themselves to be tenacious defenders, as small groups fought determined rearguard actions that cost the Allies many casualties. Although they were forced to abandon their positions along the Marne completely and lost much heavy equipment and some guns, they managed to extricate the bulk of their forces from the salient before it collapsed.

Thus, the strategic objective for the offensive—rapidly cutting off the Germans in the Marne salient—was not realized. Nevertheless, their withdrawal from the Marne marked the end of Germany's bid for victory in the war and the beginning of a terrible and hopeless struggle for survival by a battered and demoralized Imperial German army that would drag into autumn 1918. Although the Franco-American counteroffensive was perhaps launched too early, thus allowing the Germans to disengage and avert a complete disaster, the Second Battle of the Marne was the heaviest defeat the German army had yet suffered in 1918.

It was along the Marne in that hot summer that Germany's hopes for a military victory in the war were forever destroyed. Although British historians laud the accomplishments of Haig's offensive at Amiens on 8 August as the moment when Germany's leaders realized they were beaten, the Franco-American victory at the Second Battle of the Marne was the real turning point. The war diary of the German Seventh Army recorded on 18 July that in the wake of the Franco-American counteroffensive, "the Army Group German Crown Prince was forced to give up all intentions of continuing our offensive for some time to come. And here, we at once see an undoubtedly great strategic success for Marshal Foch and, based on this viewpoint, July 18, 1918, marks a turning-point in the history of the World War."[84]

The impact of the Second Battle of the Marne on the morale of the German military and political leadership as well as on the common soldiers and the German people themselves was nothing short of catastrophic. Imperial German Chancellor Georg Graf von Hertling recalled, "We expected grave events in Paris before the 15th of July. But on the 18th, even the most optimistic among us knew that all was lost. The history of the world was played out in those three days."[85]

Crown Prince Wilhelm described the Franco-American offensive of 18 July as "the decisive turning point of the war" and recalled that the German defeat at the Second Battle of the Marne was the saddest moment of his life. He later wrote, "When this move upon Reims failed, I no longer entertained any doubt that matters at the front as well as affairs at home were drifting towards the final catastrophe—a catastrophe which was inevitable."[86] Field Marshal Paul von Hindenburg later lamented the German defeat at the Second Battle of the Marne: "How many hopes, cherished during the last few months, had probably collapsed at one blow! How many calculations had been scattered to the winds!"[87]

Ludendorff was thrown into a state of confusion and depression by the Franco-American success, perhaps made doubly disconcerting since he had considered the French army incapable of offensive action and the American army as nonexistent. These two forces fighting as a combined team had destroyed his carefully laid schemes and turned the tide of the war. His staff noticed that his great mind had seemingly broken down under the strain, and modern scholars have concluded that he suffered a nervous breakdown in the wake of his defeat along the Marne.[88]

On 22 July Kaiser Wilhelm II traveled to Avesnes to meet with Field Marshal Hindenburg and First Quartermaster General Ludendorff. The kaiser was provided with a report on the unsuccessful outcome of *Frieden-stürm,* and Hindenburg candidly admitted that the great offensive in Champagne had been a "total failure." Admiral Georg Alexander von Müller recalled that the conference greatly disturbed and depressed Kaiser Wilhelm II, who, after the meeting, "spoke of himself . . . as a defeated War Lord for whom we must show consideration." The next day at lunch, the kaiser informed his inner circle that he had not been able to sleep at all after his meeting with the high command, due to nightmares in which he saw "visions of all the English and Russian relatives and all the ministers and generals of his own reign marching past and mocking him."[89]

As the Germans fell into an increasingly darker mood of despair, an atmosphere of joy and confidence permeated the ranks of the French and American armies. At Pétain's headquarters the mood had changed dramatically from the somber scene in the days before the great German assault on Reims to an atmosphere of ebullient joy in the wake of the great victory that had unfolded before them on the battlefield. French staff officers took turns mimicking the reactions of various German leaders to the news of the Franco-American offensive. Pershing's liaison officer Major Paul Clark reported, "And in between laughs they would read the latest message, mark it on the map, shake my hand and utter eulogies about the Americans. . . . Several have said 'Without the Americans this would never have been possible.'"[90]

In the flush of victory, General Mangin was ecstatic over the success of the offensive and described the advance of the American divisions of the XX Corps as being "particularly brilliant."[91] He issued a General Order for the French Tenth Army, which, considering the critical role played by the French themselves in the battle, was most magnanimous in singling out the Americans for praise:

Shoulder to shoulder with your French comrades you were thrown into the counteroffensive battle that commenced on the 18th of July.

You rushed into the fight as though to a party. Your magnificent courage completely routed a surprised enemy and your indomitable tenacity checked the counter-attacks of his fresh divisions. You have shown yourselves worthy sons of your great country and you were admired by your brothers in arms. 91 guns, 7,200 prisoners, immense booty, 10 kilometers of country re-conquered; this is your portion of the spoil of this victory. Furthermore, you have really felt your superiority over the barbarous enemy of the whole human race, against whom the children of liberty are striving. To attack him is to vanquish him. American comrades, I am grateful to you for the blood you have so generously spilled on the soil of my country. I am proud to have commanded you during such days and to have fought with you for the deliverance of the world.[92]

After the fighting, French liaison officers and advisers who had served with the American divisions in the battle offered professional critiques on their performance, universally praising their morale and fighting spirit. Lieutenant Marchand, serving with the U.S. Thirtieth Infantry Regiment, Third Division, reported that the Americans "are controlled by two main ideas, the spirit of sacrifice and a hatred of the Boches. I saw hundreds of men set out on the most dangerous missions with a dash which approached fanaticism."[93]

Some French officers, however, believed that the American troops were perhaps a little too aggressive. They reported that these troops had a tendency to charge headlong over open fields instead of working their way forward slowly and taking advantage of the available terrain to cover their advance. American attacks on German machine-gun nests were particularly criticized, as these small German teams had inflicted inordinately high casualties on the eager Americans, who tended to hit them head on, without waiting for armor or artillery support, during the pursuit phase of the battle.[94]

General Daugan, commanding the French Moroccan Division, reported to Pétain that the Americans "fought remarkably with a bravery beyond all praise." However, Daugan also said that they still "had a great deal to learn," reporting that their attack formations were too dense and criticizing their tendency to "execute massed movements under fire and undergo unnecessary casualties." Nevertheless, on the whole, he was impressed, informing Pétain that not only did the Americans show much promise as troops but that they also were "'Good Comrades' and freely offer[ed] their help to their neighbors."[95]

Pétain, and indeed the whole French army, was pleased with the performance of the Americans. As word of their contributions to the victory quickly spread through the ranks, French military censors noted a sudden upsurge in positive comments about the Americans in letters that French soldiers sent home from the front. During summer 1918 the Americans became a favorite topic in those letters. The postal control authorities estimated that each month perhaps as many as 30 percent of these letters referred to the Americans, making them by far the most-mentioned French ally. The censors reported an overall feeling among the French army that the Americans would prove to be the decisive factor in defeating the Germans.[96]

After the battle, French soldiers described the Americans as "splendid," "marvelous," and "having great enthusiasm." One French *poilu* wrote, "Our new allies have comported themselves magnificently on the field of battle" and another that honor should be given to them as "the lion of the battle." The French high command noted with great pleasure that "the Americans are everywhere the object of warm praise [from the French soldiers]: they are praised for their organization, their ardor in combat and their good comradeship." The French soldiers were especially impressed with the prowess of the Americans in the attack and held them in much higher esteem than they felt for their British allies.[97]

The American participants in the battle were equally impressed by their French comrades' performance, describing them as "excellent" and "very good soldiers." Others remarked that the "French soldiers were very brave." Sergeant Major Vernon T. Mossman, First Division, recalled, "We had great respect and admiration of them"; Pfc James Shuff, First Division, stated, "The French were best; next to us."[98] First Lieutenant John W. Thomason Jr. spoke for many American soldiers when he wrote, "I have a very profound admiration for the French. They are the greatest fighting nation in history and in this war they have vindicated and freshened the laurels that the ages have placed upon the brows of the French soldier."[99]

Without question, the Americans and French had performed well as a military team, and the many months of training and working together had paid off handsomely on the battlefield. The bonds that tied American and French soldiers together were cemented by shared combat experience, but grew from a solid and genuine affection for one another based on mutual admiration. As one French soldier wrote, "The English are our allies, but the Americans are our friends."[100]

It was in the crucible of the Second Battle of the Marne that the American Expeditionary Forces came of age. A host of high-ranking French officers, including Pétain, Mangin, Gouraud, and Degoutte, were completely convinced by the Americans' performance there that they were ready to assume responsibility for their own sector of the western front. General John J. Pershing recalled, "With every new demonstration of the efficiency of Americans in battle, the French became louder in their praise, and it looked as though they were ready to welcome the formation of an American army as soon as the various elements could be assembled. In talking it over with Pétain, I proposed anew that we should now take positive steps to plan for a sector for the American Army."[101]

There was no reference to a British or for that matter a U.S. government opinion on whether the time had come to establish an autonomous American army. Rather, the decision would be made by supreme Allied commander General Foch in consultation with the commander in chief of the French army General Pétain, again demonstrating the mentor relationship that the French had with the AEF. As far as Pétain was concerned, he needed no further convincing and believed that the time had indeed come for the American army to be formed at the front. He suggested to his friend General Pershing that the two of them should approach General Foch on the matter and press for the formation of the American First Army at the earliest possible moment. Thus, as the war entered its final climactic stage, the AEF prepared to take on its greatest role of the conflict. Yet this role was played out as part of a Franco-American military force that had matured on the battlefield into a potent combined military force.[102]

The Second Battle of the Marne was the turning point of World War I. Its impact on the morale of the leadership of Imperial Germany was devastating, and it was equally damaging to the morale of German soldiers in the trenches and to the civilians at home. All hope for victory vanished, and for the first time in the war Germans had to begin considering the grim prospect that they would lose the most titanic struggle in world history. B. H. Liddell-Hart has written, "How apt, if how strange, the historical coincidence by which as the Marne had been the first high water-mark and witnessed the first ebb of the invasion in 1914, so four years later it was destined to be the final high-water mark from which the decisive ebb began."[103]

Although the French army played the dominant role in the battle, and Italy and Britain made minor contributions, the French singled out the large American contingent for special praise in honor of their contributions to victory in the Second Battle of the Marne. Colonel Jean de Pierrefeu wrote that the importance of the American forces to the victory could not be ignored. He argued that these divisions proved vital in stopping the German offensive, stiffening French morale and resistance, and spearheading the counteroffensive. He pointed out that Pershing's willingness to move semitrained American divisions into the quiet sectors of Alsace also proved to be a tremendous help, for this released many French divisions to participate in the battle. Pierrefeu believed that the Americans provided the decisive advantage to the French during the battle, later writing, "Not to perceive [this] fact is to confuse matters of primary and secondary importance."[104]

The battle demonstrated that after long months of training, the Franco-American military team had matured into a powerful force on the western front, capable of defeating the Germans on the offensive as well as on the defensive. The soldiers cooperated magnificently, and their unique skills and attributes were superbly complementary on the battlefield. This cooperation continued as the Franco-American forces entered into their final and largest military operation during the great Allied offensives in autumn 1918.

CHAPTER 8

● ● ● ● ● ● ● ● ● ● ● ● ●

The Franco-American Armies in the Autumn Campaigns, 1918

On 21 July 1918, General Pershing, commander in chief of the AEF, and General Pétain, commander in chief of the French army, journeyed together to the headquarters of General Foch, supreme Allied commander. With a major Allied conference scheduled for 24 July, Pershing had decided to visit Foch beforehand to press his position for the formation of the American First Army. Pétain, who wholeheartedly supported the scheme, decided to accompany his American friend and lend his considerable influence to support Pershing's position that the time was right for the Americans to take their place in the field. Pétain was convinced of their capability to form an autonomous army and to assume responsibility for their own sector of the western front, as were most members of the French high command, including Joffre, Mangin, Gouraud, and others. General Foch, however, still retained doubts.

Foch believed that the Americans should continue to function as they had in the highly successful operations during the Second Battle of the Marne, where they had fought as part of the French army. Most of the French high command viewed their outstanding performance in that battle as firm evidence of their ability to assume a greater responsibility in the war. But Foch believed that the battle demonstrated how well American soldiers could fight under overall French command and saw no reason to ruin an excellent military team that had just produced one of the greatest French victories of the war. He wanted to maintain the Franco-American military relationship at this stage at least a little longer before allowing it to progress toward American autonomy.

Although Foch was virtually alone among the French high command in his views, as supreme Allied commander he had enough power to prevent such autonomy. Pershing put forth his plan for the assembly of six American divisions to be organized into two corps that together would be the nucleus of the First Army, which would assume responsibility for its own sector of the western front in Lorraine. He conceded that it would require French artillery, armor, and aviation units to be attached to it and would also require tremendous French logistical support. Although he would take personal command of this new army, he pointed out that it would be placed in a French army group and that he would agree to be under the overall authority of its commander. He stressed that the operations of the U.S. First Army would require "the most intimate coordination between the French and ourselves." Even on the brink of American military autonomy, Pershing still recognized and accepted the special Franco-American military relationship that had existed since America's entry into the war.[1]

Pétain asserted that this arrangement was most acceptable to him and complimented Pershing on his choice of sectors. Since it was the same one the French had chosen for the Americans in May 1917 it is no surprise that Pétain saw it as a wise choice. It also ensured that the Americans would be operating as part of a French army group, lending its considerable fighting power to French operations and subject to overall French direction, exactly what they had envisioned since Marshal Joffre had broached the first proposals for Franco-American military cooperation the previous year.[2]

Foch agreed that the plan had merit but wanted a little more time to consider the proposal. The following day, he relented, informing Pershing, "I have the honor to confirm to you my entire adhesion to the project of uniting in an Army under American command those of your divisions whose state of instruction permits them to engage in the battle." Foch instructed Pershing to work out with Pétain the details regarding the American occupation of the previously French-controlled sector.[3]

What caused Foch's change of heart? He later said that the major problems with the American army "were rooted in its youth and inexperience of war." In all likelihood, he relented because his major objection—that the Americans lacked experience—could be overcome only through a trial by fire. The Americans were eager and confident and had demonstrated their combat capabilities. At last he agreed that the time had come to allow them a greater degree of autonomy, with command of their own army with their own sector. Pétain's position as army group commander, with the Americans somewhat under French supervision, probably helped to ease his mind.[4]

The decision to form an autonomous American army on the western front was not an American one, although it was certainly an American aspiration. Nor was it an Allied decision, as the British had no input whatsoever on this issue. Rather, it was the French high command, which had developed, trained, and led American forces into battle, that now decided that the U.S. Army was ready to take its place as an equal partner on the western front. The French had prepared the Americans for this moment, and it was the French who gave their final approval to the implementation of Pershing's plan.

On 24 July General Pershing, General Pétain, Field Marshal Haig, and General Foch met at Foch's headquarters to discuss the ongoing campaign and the preparations for a general Allied offensive in the near future. Foch boldly informed the Allied commanders that "the moment has come to abandon the general defensive attitude forced upon us until now by numerical inferiority and to pass to the offensive." He stressed the importance of armor in the coming operations, and Pétain lamented that the French army was "very short of tanks." Field Marshal Haig reported that the British army was well equipped with tanks and by the end of summer would have all that they could possibly need. This is curious because the British had previously refused to provide tanks to the Americans, citing shortages of this weapon, yet he now said that they had them in abundance. Meanwhile, the French, though desperately short of tanks, were taking great pains to equip the AEF with as much armor as they possibly could.[5]

Foch sketched out in rough detail a general plan for simultaneous offensive operations by the Allied armies. The most important part for the Americans in the plan was the portion calling for "the clearing of the Paris-Avricourt railroad in the region around Commercy, by reducing the Saint-Mihiel salient. This operation should be prepared without delay and executed by the American army as soon as it has the necessary means." Pershing now not only had an army, but he also had a mission for it.[6]

An ecstatic Pershing left the meeting and immediately issued the formal order for the creation of the American First Army, to be officially effective on 10 August 1918. After hearing the news of Foch's decision, Premier

Georges Clemenceau was quick to cable Pershing, "Cordial congratulations for the creation of the American First Army. History awaits you."[7]

With the full support and cooperation of the French, an autonomous American presence on the western front was about to become a reality. Yet at this moment, unexpected trouble arose from the ally not consulted in this decision, the nation that had been the odd man out since the foundation of the bilateral Franco-American military relationship, Great Britain.

In order to form the U.S. First Army, Pershing began to gather the scattered units of the AEF together, including the American divisions assigned to training in the British sector of the front.[8] Foch immediately agreed that Pershing should have these divisions but hesitated to give a direct order to Haig. Instead, he urged Pershing to go in person to visit the BEF commander to request that the American divisions be released and sent south to join the American First Army.

In August Pershing inspected the American divisions training in the British sector, and during his tour, Britain's King George V visited the general. The British monarch "was anxious to have as many [American troops] as possible serve with the British army, . . . their presence had an excellent effect in stimulating the morale of [the] men." The king remarked on how much he liked America and how wonderful it would be to say after the war "that the two English-speaking peoples had fought side by side in this great struggle." Pershing thanked him but replied that the United States was forming an army of its own and would require virtually all its troops for that purpose.[9]

The British clearly knew the reason for Pershing's visit, and Pershing himself probably suspected that they knew. Given this mutual, if unstated, understanding of the purposes of each party, George V's heavy-handed rhetoric about English-speaking peoples can be seen as rather hypocritical. The British attitude of superiority toward the Americans during the war alienated Pershing as well as most other officers and enlisted men of the AEF and was indeed a major reason for the almost complete lack of military cooperation between the British and the Americans.

Soon after this meeting, Pershing went to Haig's headquarters to request that the American divisions be released from their current assignment and sent south to join the American First Army. Haig was understandably furious when he heard Pershing's request but contained himself. He protested that he was intending to use those divisions, which the British had shipped over and trained, as he pointed out, in support of his own offensive. Pershing explained that he could understand Haig's position but that the terms of the shipping agreement clearly stipulated that the AEF commander retained complete control over all American divisions in Europe and that he was now exercising that authority. After some haggling, a furious Haig curtly informed Pershing that the American divisions would be released.[10] As Haig recorded in his diary:

> [Pershing] stated that he might have to withdraw the five American Divisions which are training with British Divisions. I pointed out to him that I had done everything to equip and help these units of the American Army, and to provide them with horses. So far I have had no help from these troops. . . . If he now withdraws the five American Divisions, he must expect some criticism of his action not only from the British troops in the field but also from the British Government. All I wanted to know was *definitely* whether I could prepare to use the American troops for an attack [along with the British] at the end of September against Kemmel. Now I know I cannot do so.[11]

The following day Pershing called on Clemenceau and told him of his meeting, and at times heated exchange, with Haig. Clemenceau quickly made political hay of the dispute by informing Pershing that although he might have once had doubts regarding the feasibility of fielding an autonomous American army, he now clearly saw the wisdom of the general's position and promised to provide his full support to him in his endeavors.[12]

Clemenceau then produced a pair of telegrams that he had recently received from Prime Minister David Lloyd George, protesting that too many American divisions were serving in the French sector of the line. The prime minister had added, "It must not be forgotten that the greater part of the American troops were brought to France by British shipping and that because of the sacrifices made to furnish this shipping our people have the right to expect that more than five divisions of the twenty-eight now in France should be put in training behind our lines."[13]

After showing Pershing the telegrams, Clemenceau also informed him that Lloyd George had been holding meetings with the Italian ambassador to Britain over the disposition of American forces and that the two had decided to place pressure on Foch and Pershing to send American divisions to Italy, where they would be grouped under British command. Certainly Clemenceau gave this information to Pershing in order to strengthen Franco-American relations at the expense of the British, but in this regard the British were their own worst enemy.

Pershing had no trouble believing that Clemenceau's information was true because the British had just begun pressuring him to send American divisions to Italy, although they had refrained from stating that they would be placed under British command. Pershing's visit to Haig's head-quarters and his demand for the return of the American divisions stationed in the British sector set in motion a series of British moves to obtain American troops that succeeded only in further alienating Pershing and the Americans. Pershing recalled that in August 1918, "The British clung to the use of Dunkirk as the supply port for an American army which they hoped would be sent to their front for service under their control." Even more infuriating to Pershing, the British at this time also attempted to resurrect the issue of amalgamation by proposing to Foch that American battalions and regiments should be placed into Allied divisions. However, the French gave no support whatsoever to this plan and told the British that it was unacceptable to both the French and the American armies.[14]

The British obviously were desperate for American support, but perhaps something else was at work. Pershing later wrote, "The impression left on our minds was, first, that the British desired to discourage the concentration of our forces into one army, and, second, that perhaps there was a desire to check the growth of too friendly relations between Americans and French."[15] In Pershing's opinion, the British had actually become so fearful and suspicious of the special relationship that existed between the AEF and the French army that they were taking desperate measures in summer 1918 to try to disrupt the close military association between the two. If this were indeed the case, and there is certainly strong evidence to support it, then the British approach to the issue was a poor choice. By protesting over the transference of American divisions to Pershing and dragging their feet on the establishment of an autonomous American military presence on the western front, not to mention bringing up amalgamation again, the British succeeded in driving the Americans completely into the arms of the French.

In early August Pershing began to form the U.S. First Army in Lorraine in preparation for the long-anticipated attack against the St. Mihiel salient. Its reduction had been on both Pershing's and Pétain's minds since June 1917 and had been included in Foch's memorandum of 24 July 1918 as an objective for the general Allied offensive, which had begun in other sectors of the front. Although the French had already demonstrated their confidence in the combat abilities of American soldiers, that August they took the step of assigning large numbers of French troops to the new American First Army.

On 20 August Ferdinand Foch, recently promoted to marshal, wrote to Pershing: "I have the honor of asking you to take command of the French troops which are to cooperate in the attack of the American army in the Woëvre, . . . in order to make certain that by single command the best possible results will be obtained from the Allied forces."[16] On the same day, Pétain also wrote to him:

> With a view to securing the best coordination of efforts in the offensive action in the Woëvre, I propose to place under your orders, insofar as concerns tactical matters and for the duration of the operation: The II Colonial Army Corps which will hold the front between your two masses of attack. The French forces (2 army corps, 6 divisions) which will attack on your left up to Bezonvaux. General Hirschauer, commanding the Second Army will be charged, under your direction, with the preparation and execution of this attack. I believe you will fully agree to these dispositions which give a better guarantee of the success of the projected operation.[17]

Pétain's assignment of large numbers of French soldiers to American command provides concrete evidence of the vast faith he had in the military abilities of the AEF and in the leadership capabilities of Pershing and his corps commanders. Again, such faith and confidence stands in marked contrast to the British attitude toward American military capabilities. The British high command looked upon American soldiers as being of excellent quality but believed that their officers were incompetent and unqualified to command either their own soldiers or British troops.[18]

Furious that Pershing would provide no support for the British offensive, Haig rebuffed his requests for armor to support the American attack on the St. Mihiel salient. Moreover, Haig, behind Pershing's back, coaxed Foch in the interests of Allied harmony to order Pershing to keep the U.S. Twenty-seventh and Thirtieth Divisions with the British army. He also met privately with Foch to discuss Pershing's proposed offensive and pointed out the numerous flaws he saw with the plan, the most apparent being that it offered no support to the British offensive in Flanders. The British commander pointed out how well his offensive and those of the French, which had begun on 8 August, were going but that the proposed American drive would not lend any support to these attacks because it would be launched too far away from the main battle zone in the north. Haig argued that the American attack should be directed northward astride the Meuse River and through the dense Argonne Forest, where it would lend greater support to the overall Allied offensive and threaten the left flank of the German armies.[19]

Foch was eager to exploit the French and British successes in the north and thus agreed to Haig's suggestions, even though this meant that months of planning by the Americans would be ruined and, under Foch's revised plan, that American divisions and corps would have to be placed under French army command again in order to exploit the deteriorating German defenses quickly. Foch believed that the St. Mihiel offensive should be vastly scaled back or perhaps even canceled altogether and that American divisions should be immediately shifted northwest to be assigned to the French Fourth and Second Armies for the new attack astride the Meuse.

Aside from these tactical and political considerations, Foch had become increasingly annoyed by Pershing's grocery lists requesting support troops, artillery, tanks, aircraft, and other items necessary for the formation of the U.S. First Army. These had to come from the already depleted and overstretched ranks of the French army. Moreover, Pershing's preparations seemed to be taking an inordinate amount of time, and increasingly, Foch believed that a great opportunity to defeat the Germans might be missed. He reasoned that if the Americans did not have the necessary support troops to form their own army immediately, then why waste precious time?

According to Foch's revised plan of attack, American divisions could enter the battle right away, modeling their service on their brilliant performance in the Second Battle of the Marne. Their new avenue of attack would be much closer to the battles being waged by the British and French and thereby provide far greater support to these offensives. Foch's cry since July had been *"Tout le Monde à la Bataille!"* (everyone into the battle!); and with the arrival of the Americans, he believed that the German front might crack, depending of course on their offensive being launched immediately and in the proper location. To Foch, such an opportunity was too good to pass up for an idea as ephemeral, to him anyway, as American military autonomy.

Pershing was stunned when on 30 August Foch announced his intention to scale down the St. Mihiel attack drastically in order immediately to launch an attack west of the Meuse that would provide direct support to the ongoing French and British offensives. Pershing protested that his army was not capable of launching both the St. Mihiel offensive and the new attack. Foch retorted that if that were the case, then the St. Mihiel operation should be abandoned. He further stated that in order to facilitate the immediate opening of the new attack, American divisions would be placed under French corps and army command, at least for the duration of the offensive.

When Pershing realized that Foch's new plan meant not only a cancellation of the St. Mihiel attack but also an indefinite delay in the formation of the U.S. First Army, his shock gave way to anger, and he categorically refused to go along with the scheme. Foch, growing weary of Pershing's intransigence, queried, "Do you wish to give battle?" Pershing replied, "Yes, but as an American army." A heated exchange ensued between the two commanders, at the end of which Foch left, both men visibly angry and neither conceding the other's point of view.[20]

Many writers have used this incident and the strained relationship that existed between Foch and Pershing throughout the autumn campaign as evidence of acrimony between the two armies during the war. They have asserted that there were dark political motivations behind Foch's decision to shift the focus of the American offensive, arguing that Clemenceau, Foch, Lloyd George, and Haig acted in conjunction to reach the common goal of reducing the role of the American forces in the final campaign of 1918 in the hopes of also reducing President Wilson's influence at the peace table.[21]

On closer examination, however, this conspiratorial argument lacks merit. The motivations behind Foch's change of plan have been misconstrued by individuals who have too quickly seized upon the most negative and sinister interpretations possible for the proposed alterations in the American offensive. Foch has often been portrayed as being far more complex than he actually was; in reality, what you saw was what you got. Indeed, there was little about Foch that was subtle, much less devious, in terms of his personality or his leadership style. To ascribe a nefarious political objective to his decision to alter a military operation is an error; it would have been completely out of character for him. Such a motive also suggests a level of cooperation between Foch and Clemenceau on military policy and postwar political policy that simply did not exist. Although each man had a certain degree of respect for the other, there was no cordiality between them; they repeatedly clashed in 1918 and immediately after the war over many different issues, including, significantly, Foch's defense of Pershing and the American army.

In regard to the dispute between Foch and Pershing, the former had an extremely volatile personality and clashed repeatedly with Joffre, Clemenceau, Pétain, and Haig (to name but a few) during the course of the war. It is no surprise that he would clash with Pershing as well. Pershing himself was stern, bristled at criticism, and was quick to anger over any proposal he believed infringed on his vision of military autonomy. Two such strong-willed individuals, placed in a stressful environment with each holding a different vision of the best method to obtain the common goal, would seem predestined to clash, as indeed they did.

Further, historians who have sought to use this dispute, and future ones, between Foch and Pershing as evidence of discord between the French and American armies neglect the fact that Pétain, not Foch, commanded the French army. Holding the position of commanding general of the Armies of the North and Northeast, Pétain exercised direct authority over all French forces on the western front. He was under Foch's overall command, to be sure, but in the same fashion that British Field Marshal Haig and General Pershing were under Foch's orders. Like his British and American counterparts, Pétain had to yield to Foch occasionally on certain matters, such as the timing for the counteroffensive along the Marne in July 1918, but he retained considerable autonomy in his conduct of military operations.

Pétain knew that the formation of an autonomous American army with its own sector of the front was good not only for the United States but also for France as well. He had worked miracles with the French army during 1917 and 1918, but he recognized that it was fragile and desperately needed American support and cooperation in the form of large numbers of combat divisions to assume responsibility for their own sector. Since the American army would enter the French sector, its arrival would bring troops for the relief of numerous French divisions for service elsewhere or enough manpower to bring existing divisions up to full strength.

Although the French needed the Americans, Pétain also realized that the Americans needed French artillery, tanks, aviation, and supplies. The answer, therefore, was mutual support rather than complete autonomy for either party. He immediately set to work to help both Pershing and Foch realize the mutual benefits that would be derived from the continuation of the close association between the two armies.

Pétain agreed with Pershing that canceling the attack on the St. Mihiel salient would be a mistake and that splitting up the American army just as it was forming was foolish. He told Pershing that in his view, Foch had overstepped his authority by interfering with the American plan of operations. Nevertheless, Pétain agreed with Foch and Haig's view that given the new tactical situation on the western front, the St. Mihiel attack should be limited to reducing the salient itself. The main U.S. attack, Pétain argued, should be delivered through the Argonne but made as an autonomous army, with French support of course.

Foch arranged a conference for 2 September so that he, Pershing, and Pétain could resolve the impasse. Pershing argued that with the St. Mihiel operation scheduled to begin within two weeks, it was imperative for the prestige of the new American army that it be launched, pointing out that successfully clearing the salient would greatly ease German pressure near Verdun. At the very least, the operation would then enable this region to be used as a base for Foch's proposed offensive west of the Meuse. Pétain wholeheartedly supported Pershing's position and pointed out to Foch that the American attack at St. Mihiel would not, and should not, preclude a large-scale operation in the Meuse-Argonne region, provided that the French lent support to both operations.[22]

Foch insisted that the attack at St. Mihiel would still need to be scaled down, and both Pershing and Pétain agreed that the assault would seek only the limited objective of the elimination of the salient rather than the originally envisioned breakthrough toward Metz. Foch asserted that Pershing must also agree to launch the proposed offensive through the Argonne before the month was out. Pershing said that after the elimination of the salient, he could then pivot his forces and launch the main offensive when and where Foch wanted, but as an American army.[23]

Pétain announced that he would turn over a greater area of the French sector of the western front to the Americans while also providing the necessary support troops and even augmenting Pershing's forces with French infantry divisions for both the St. Mihiel operation and the Argonne attack. Pershing's forces would work in close cooperation with the French Fourth and Second Armies throughout the course of each operation, and Pétain would serve as army group commander for both offensives. This satisfied Foch, as it allowed a greater degree of French input on the conduct of the campaigns; he formally approved both offensives. Although lauded by many American officers and historians as a triumph for American autonomy, the 2 September conference established the U.S. First Army as a Franco-American force. The agreement ensured overall French direction and direct support to the AEF during the largest American campaigns of the war.[24]

On 12 September, the U.S. First Army launched its attack against the St. Mihiel salient. Donald Smythe has referred to the operation as "the birth of an American army."[25] In reality, St. Mihiel marked the birth of a Franco-American army (see Table 2).[26]

The U.S. First Army at St. Mihiel was composed of a total of 550,000 American and 110,000 French soldiers. It possessed 3,010 French artillery pieces, approximately one-third of which were manned by French gun crews, and all the shells fired in support of the operation were of French manufacture. In addition, 267 tanks, all of French manufacture and 113 of them manned by French crews, supported the assault, and over 1,400 aircraft supported the ground attack, with 600 of these flown by French pilots.[27]

Table 2. Order of Battle, U.S. First Army, 12 September 1918

U.S. V Corps	French II Colonial Corps	U.S. IV Corps	U.S. I Corps
French 15th Colonial Division	French 2d Cavalry Division (dismounted)	U.S. 1st Division	U.S. 2d Division
U.S. 4th Division	French 26th Division	U.S. 42d Division	U.S. 5th Division
U.S. 26th Division	· French 29th Colonial Division	U.S. 89th Division	U.S. 90th Division
			U.S. 82d Division

As the force readied itself for battle, French soldiers throughout the sector expressed confidence in their American allies. In their letters home, the French praised American professionalism, organizational skill, and "warrior spirit." The massive numbers of U.S. infantry and artillery swarming into eastern France also greatly impressed the French, and rumors swept the ranks of the French army that St. Mihiel was just the first phase of a massive American offensive that would rip open the western front. Soldiers from the French divisions slated to be attacking with the Americans proclaimed "great confidence" in the forthcoming operation. The French high command noted that any expression of skepticism over the outcome of the operation was virtually nonexistent and that because of the Americans, "optimism is the order of the day." The French army had come a long way from the mutinies of 1917, and the impact on morale of having the Americans fighting with them was a major reason for their renewed spirit and confidence.[28]

The St. Mihiel offensive was indeed a smashing success, as concentric attacks by the U.S. I Corps and U.S. IV Corps from the south, the U.S. V Corps from the north, and the French II Colonial Corps from the west rolled over the surprised German defenders. Indeed, after all the buildup, the event itself was anticlimactic, as German forces had just begun evacuating their exposed positions in the salient when the French and Americans struck. By the morning of 13 September, the northern and southern pincers of the Franco-American forces had met and completely cut off the entire salient, which they then methodically mopped up. The forces advanced to the German's Michel I line, constructed across the base of the salient as a final defensive position, and launched a couple of desultory probes but, pursuant to orders, made no serious attempt to breach the line.[29]

The fortress of Metz, a vital rail and communication center that had been in German hands since the Franco-Prussian War of 1870–1871, loomed nearby, and many American officers, including Douglas MacArthur, later expressed regret at not being able to exploit their attack as originally planned. This opinion was far from unanimous, however. Major General Hunter Liggett, commander of the U.S. I Corps during the St. Mihiel operation and the future commander of the U.S. First Army, claimed that such an offensive inevitably would have bogged down in the mud of the Woëvre plain and that the Americans would have spent months in vain assaults against the fortress complex. The new attack plan of 2 September rendered the issue moot, but Liggett's opinion is significant in considering the wisdom of Foch's decision to make the St. Mihiel attack a limited offensive.[30]

A jubilant Pétain drove to Pershing's headquarters to congratulate him, and together the two men headed off to inspect the liberated salient. They were met by crowds of French civilians, waving French flags and jubilant over their liberation after four years of German occupation. A great throng of people gathered at the Hôtel de Ville in the center of the city, and Pétain addressed the crowd. He explained to the civilians that although French troops had captured St. Mihiel, they were "part of the American Army and were able to reoccupy the town because the American attacks had crushed in the salient."[31]

On 13 September Foch rather magnanimously wired his congratulations to Pershing for the success of the attack: "The First American Army, under your command, on this first day has won a magnificent victory by a maneuver as skillfully and expertly prepared as it was valorously executed. I extend to you as well as to the officers and to the troops under your command my warmest compliments."[32]

Pershing sent a courteous reply to Foch but reserved his warmest message for Pétain: "May I express my heartfelt thanks to you and to the armies under your command for the cordial cooperation and support which has been universal throughout the recent operations of the First American Army. Every request has met a quick and helpful response. Your continued interest and valuable advice, and the cordial assistance of all officers under your command are deeply appreciated."[33]

The average French soldier was electrified by the news of the Franco-American victory at St. Mihiel, and they spoke of it constantly in their letters home. Everywhere, and especially in the French Second Army (the one most directly associated with the AEF at this time), the Americans were referred to in glowing terms. The French high command noted that "our men speak of the Americans with great admiration and friendship," and they expressed pride in the American victory at St. Mihiel. They were especially impressed with the ease with which the Americans had burst through the German lines and with the large number of prisoners taken. Although the French soldier still had a strong desire for peace, he now had a desire for a victorious peace, which was ascribed to his faith in the growing power and stellar accomplishments of the U.S. Army.[34]

With each successive military operation in 1918, the Americans had earned more accolades from the French, along with increasing responsibility. After St. Mihiel, the First Army began to redeploy rapidly to the northwest in preparation for its projected offensive north along the Meuse River Valley and through the Argonne forest. This new area, assigned to them at Pétain's suggestion, reflected the French commander in chief's increasing faith in their capabilities, for as the army shifted northwest, it was in charge of the defense of the Verdun sector.

Verdun symbolized the defiance, determination, and sacrifice of France in the Great War, "the glory and the misery of Verdun," as soldier deputy André Maginot described the ten-month long ordeal. This was the longest and bloodiest battle in French history. During the war, Americans noted that when they asked a French soldier how long he had been in the army, he would respond with the number of years of service but then conclude by specifically stating the number of months he had fought at Verdun. The French considered service at Verdun a mark of great martial achievement; they took took great pride in the victory they had won there.[35]

The approximately 400,000 French casualties at Verdun had made the ground sacred to France and to its army, yet the French were willing to allow the newly formed U.S. First Army to assume the responsibility for its defense. Pétain, forever immortalized as the victor of Verdun, was most certainly aware of the significance of the sector he was handing over to the Americans. Indeed, Pershing's new headquarters was set up in the same building in the village of Souilly where Pétain had had his headquarters when he commanded the French Second Army during the battle two years earlier. The monumental significance of the assignment of such precious French soil to American care was not lost on Pershing or his officers. As Pershing later recalled:

As Verdun was soon to become a part of my command, I went on [September] 21st to see the town and make a casual inspection of the citadel. The commanding officer showed me the various chambers, including those occupied by the local civil authorities during the period of the German drive to wrest the stronghold from the French, and finally we reached the Officers' Club. As we entered, my eye fell upon Pétain's famous declaration, "*On ne passe pas,*" in bold letters on the wall opposite me. It would be difficult to describe my feelings, and as I stopped in my tracks the party, realizing the reason, with one accord remained silent for some minutes.[36]

Pershing was also well aware of the traumatic effect the battle had had on his close friend, and during a speech he delivered after the war at the dedication of the famous Ossuaire at Douaumont, he reflected on this:

I have often felt, when you and I were together, that I could read your thoughts and follow your mind as it reviewed the days and weeks of your struggles on this soil, when your country's fate hung in the balance. Only those who know the kindness of your heart can appreciate the weight of sorrow which it carried. The fall of each one of your soldiers was a stab in the heart of his general, and the impassive expression under which you hide your feelings masked constant and unremitting grief.[37]

The French decision to assign the AEF to the Verdun sector was perhaps the finest and highest compliment they could pay to the military capabilities of the Americans and their commander General John J. Pershing. Moreover, the close friendship between the commanders of the two armies, and indeed the men of the two armies as well, meant that the French were entrusting this sacred place to people who were more than just Allies but were indeed brothers in arms.

On 26 September the AEF began their largest operation of the Great War, and the largest battle in American history, the Meuse-Argonne offensive (see Table 3).[38] As at St. Mihiel, this offensive was to be a Franco-American battle from first to last as Pershing's First Army once more had a powerful force of French artillery, tanks, and aviation units assigned to provide direct support. French infantry divisions and two French army corps were also assigned to the U.S. First and served directly under American command. Meanwhile, in a further integration of the two armies, U.S. divisions were assigned to French corps commanders.

The American First Army served as part of a French Army Group from 26 September to 12 October, under the overall command of General Pétain, who was Pershing's superior officer in this arrangement. Although the main attack west of the Meuse was to be delivered by the U.S. I, V,

Table 3. Order of Battle (West to East), U.S. First Army, 26 September 1918

U.S. I Corps	U.S. V Corps	U.S. III Corps	French XVII Corps	French II Colonial Corps	U.S. IV Corps
U.S. 77th Division	U.S. 91st Division	U.S. 4th Division	French 18th Division	U.S. 79th Division	U.S. 89th Division
U.S. 28th Division	U.S. 37th Division	U.S. 80th Division	French 10th Colonial Division	French 2d Cavalry Division (dismounted)	U.S. 78th Division
U.S. 35th Division	U.S. 79th Division	U.S. 33d Division	French 15th Colonial Division	French 39th Division	U.S. 90th Division
					French 69th Division

and III Corps, which contained no French divisions, these corps were supported by over 100 French tanks and more than 1,000 French guns. The French XVII Corps, operating east of the Meuse, was assigned to feint an attack against the German positions on its front and to maintain a lively fire with its artillery.

The U.S. First Army was part of an army group that included the French Fourth Army on its left flank, which would attack simultaneously with and in support of the American offensive. Pétain handled the assignment of heavy artillery and reserves as well as coordinating the attack. Thus, the U.S. First Army was indeed an autonomous military force responsible for its own sector, but it contained over 100,000 French soldiers under its command and was under the strategic direction of the French. Nevertheless, the French high command gave Pershing a great deal of freedom in terms of arranging the tactical disposition of his forces, timing the attack, arranging the preparatory artillery barrage, and supervising the logistical aspects.[39]

On 26 September a massive barrage by 2,700 guns and howitzers, almost all of French manufacture and half of which were manned by French gun crews firing ammunition almost exclusively of French manufacture, thundered just north of Verdun, along the west bank of the Meuse. The American journalist Frederick Palmer toured the rear area of the First Army and noted the large number of French gunners lounging casually, defiantly even, "as if French democracy were flouting Prussian militarism." With the order to ready their guns for action, the French artillerymen sprang into action with an alertness that Palmer compared to a "batter stepping up to the plate." He noted the ease and casual professionalism that the French soldiers displayed, working their guns with the skill of veteran soldiers at home on the battlefield. Of the presence of the French in the First Army, Palmer wrote: "Never were guests more welcome than they to our army. We could not have too many French guns."[40]

After a fierce three-hour bombardment, the First Army went over the top and into the teeth of one of the most heavily fortified positions on the entire western front. The region was later described by Pershing and U.S. Army historians as "ideal for defensive fighting," with numerous ridges and wooded hills that had been linked into the German trench system and that provided natural strongpoints and superb observation posts for directing artillery fire. The gloaming depths of the Argonne Forest were assigned as an objective to the U.S. I Corps, where liaison was supposed to be maintained with General Gouraud's Fourth Army. As part of Pétain's ad hoc army group, it was launching a simultaneous offensive to the west of the U.S. First Army.[41]

While the Fourth Army's artillery hammered away for twelve hours against the German positions to their front, Pershing kept the First Army's bombardment brief in order to secure the element of surprise. He hoped that with surprise and speed his infantry could rapidly overrun the initial line of German defenses and press on to the main defense line, some ten miles distant, before the Germans had time to react. Unfortunately for the Americans, however, the Germans had learned of the planned assault through the Argonne. Thus, there was no element of surprise, and due to the brevity of the barrage, many powerful German defensive positions remained untouched by the artillery fire. Nevertheless, the American assault divisions, supported by 189 French Renault tanks, 47 manned by French crews, pushed forward and overran the thinly held German front line. Much like the German barrage at Reims three months earlier, the Franco-American artillery had blasted to pieces only a thinly held front line, leaving the main German defensive positions farther back, relatively unscathed. The twisted, broken terrain of the region, torn up even more by the bombardment, proved to be a great hindrance to movement, but the big American divisions still shouldered their way forward against determined German resistance.[42]

The German bastion of Montfaucon stood prominently astride the center of the First Army's advance and provided the only serious check to the Americans on the first day of the offensive. It was the highest point on the battlefield and was also perhaps the most heavily fortified German position in the sector. The headquarters of the German Crown Prince had been located there during the Battle of Verdun, and with good reason, for the position provided a commanding view of the surrounding country-side and was invaluable for directing artillery fire on any assailants attempting to move toward or past it. Pershing had made Montfaucon a primary objective for the first day of the offensive, but the attack of the U.S. V Corps, assigned to take the position, was bloodily repulsed. Although the V Corps did not manage to take it on the first day, the advance of other American forces on either flank of the German bastion compromised it to the point that it finally fell on the afternoon of the second day of the battle, but not before seriously altering Pershing's strict schedule for the advance.[43]

On 27 September the offensive noticeably slowed, as Pershing was forced to displace his artillery forward over the broken ground to maintain support fires for his advancing troops. Meanwhile, the German artillery, much of it located on the heights east of the Meuse, was becoming increasingly active and deadly, directed by observers occupying the high ground in the sector. The American infantry staggered under the combination of high explosive shell and poison gas raining down. Pershing's oversized divisions (twice as large as German, French, or British) proved unwieldy, as Joffre had cautioned as far back as April 1917, and the dense formations suffered heavily from the German fire as they clumsily pressed their way forward in the face of increasingly determined resistance. German divisions were being rushed into the sector at a far greater rate than Pershing or his staff had predicted, and by the end of the second day it was apparent that the Americans were engaged in their hardest fight of the war.

More armor, French and American, was brought up, and with renewed artillery support the attack began again in earnest on 28 September, as the First Army overran the secondary defensive position and at last penetrated to the third, and strongest, defensive line, the *Kriemhilde Stellung*, part of the infamous Hindenburg Line. On 29 September American probes of this formidable position were met with vicious German counterattacks, launched by fresh divisions that Ludendorff had rushed to the threatened sector to halt the American assault. The German high command also moved more guns into the sector, and the Americans noted a sharp increase in the intensity of the artillery fire on their forces. Renewed American assaults on 30 September were also bloodily repulsed, and the offensive faltered. Pershing and his staff had overoptimistically planned to breach the *Kriemhilde Stellung* within twenty-four hours of the start of the offensive, but it was painfully obvious that extensive preparations had to be made before this formidable obstacle could be attacked in a set-piece assault.[44]

The battle at St. Mihiel had provided a dangerous reinforcement to Pershing's illusion that American ardor and bayonets could swiftly and easily overcome an entrenched opponent. As casualties continued to mount, it became increasingly clear that the fighting in the Meuse-Argonne was going to be completely different from what Pershing or his staff had envisioned. Yet despite their casualties, the Americans continued to bash their way forward. There was no subtlety to their attacks as there were no flanks to turn. Rather, the offensive became a brutal frontal assault that repeatedly slammed into the German defenders.

Pershing, somewhat discouraged, began the difficult process of rotating fresh divisions into the line and pulling back his more depleted divisions for rest and refitting. The poor road network that ran along the west bank of the Meuse, the broken nature of the terrain, the maze of German entrenchments, and the cratered landscape caused by the heavy fighting of the past several days combined to make even the simplest of movements difficult. To compound these problems, the weather turned bad. Heavy rains began to fall on the first day of the battle and swiftly turned the three narrow roads, the only routes of communication into this sector, into quagmires. Logistical problems were overwhelming for Pershing's staff, and during attempts to relieve worn-out divisions by pressing fresh troops forward over these same clogged arteries, gridlock set in with traffic jams that backed up men, guns, vehicles, and animals for miles. The First Army had pushed forward approximately eight miles in four days, but the attack had clearly run out of steam still short of the first day's objectives.[45]

Foch had mixed emotions regarding the Americans' performance. It was evident from reports and the high casualties that the American infantry was once more fighting bravely, if not particularly skillfully, yet the attack's progress had clearly come to a halt. Foch and his staff believed that the lull in operations was not caused by any lack of ardor but because Pershing and his staff officers simply lacked experience in conducting major operations. He believed that the logistical difficulties and traffic jams, caused by poor staff work, were the real culprits in the Americans' failure to complete their ten-mile dash to the *Kriemhilde Stellung*.[46]

The logistical situation of the First Army had become absolutely nightmarish by 1 October, and the advance had indeed stalled. Yet in assessing this initial stage of the Meuse-Argonne operation, the offensive must be placed in context. Whatever its shortcomings, the attack had pushed forward eight miles before faltering. Though short of expectations, it was a far larger gain than any French or British offensive ever made on the western front from 1915 to 1917. American casualties were high, but nowhere did they approach the British death toll at the Somme or Passchendaele or the French losses in the Nivelle offensive or in Champagne or Artois, for that matter.

One could argue that the western front of 1918 was far more fluid than it was from 1915 to 1917, but this was not the case in the Meuse-Argonne sector. Here, the Germans had not moved, or been moved by French attacks, since they arrived in 1914, and they were heavily entrenched in excellent defensive terrain. One might compare the attack by Mangin's Tenth Army on 18 July 1918 with the U.S. First Army's offensive of 26 September. Mangin's forces struck an overextended German army occupying poorly constructed defenses in otherwise open terrain, took them completely by surprise, and rolled forward approximately the same distance in four days of fighting that Pershing's First Army did in the Meuse-Argonne. And Mangin's offensive lost its momentum at almost the same time (after four days) that Pershing's did. Yet Mangin's attack is considered to be a great victory, and rightly so, but the attack by the U.S. First Army has been roundly criticized.

Without question, the initial phase of the Meuse-Argonne offensive (26 September–1 October) did not achieve the expected results and this failure to meet the high expectations was, and remains, the basis for criticisms. Yet the lofty goals that Foch, Pétain, Haig, and Pershing envisioned for this operation were completely unrealistic. Estimates of how far the advance could be pressed, and how quickly, were based on the recent Franco-American success at St. Mihiel and on the formidable reputation that the American soldiers had forged for themselves during the battles of spring and summer. Thus, the superlative performance of American units in these early battles had caused the Allies, and the Americans themselves, to see their big divisions as their own Stürmtruppen, which could replicate the spectacular advances of the Germans during their 1918 offensives. These estimates ignored the critical facts that the situation confronting the AEF in the Meuse-Argonne was more complex than anything the inexperienced Americans had encountered before. It also ignored the fact that U.S. divisions were not created equal. The best AEF divisions (the First, Second, Third, and Forty-second) did not participate in the initial assault; instead, inexperienced divisions, many of which were seeing their first action of the war, carried it out.

Another major factor contributing to the failure was that the First Army had to be disengaged from St. Mihiel and then shifted approximately sixty miles to the northwest over a poor road and rail network by inexperienced staff members who had little time to prepare the operation. St. Mihiel had proven that the Americans could conduct a major operation, with French assistance, but they had planned that attack for many months in advance. The first news anyone had of an attack through the Argonne came on 30 August and was not official until 2 September. The shifting into place of over 600,000 men in such a short period of time while simultaneously conducting a major battle was a feat of staff work and logistical skill that would have sorely tried the most battle-hardened and experienced staff of any army. A tremendous amount of credit is given to the U.S. First Army chief of staff, Colonel George C. Marshall, for this achievement. However, it was the French Service Automobile that actually transported the overwhelming majority of American troops, ammunition, and guns, as well as their own forces, into and out of the designated sector. Indeed, it was miraculous that the Franco-American forces designated for the Meuse-Argonne offensive were able to mass at the jump-off point by 26 September.[47]

Even though the troops, artillery, and supplies arrived in time, the planning for the operation was less than perfect, due to the short time frame in which it was organized. The plan of attack, including future tactical movements and supply of the forces engaged that should have been carefully prepared over a period of months, was instead improvised over a period of a few weeks. It is a tragic irony that the bulk of American planning and preparation was directed at the St. Mihiel operation, which because of Foch's change of plan, at Haig's instigation, became a minor affair. Meanwhile, the greatest offensive of the AEF, the largest and bloodiest battle the U.S. Army had waged, was prepared when its staff's attention and time were divided and unfocused. It is indeed a testament to the skill of Pershing and his staff that the offensive went forward on schedule and that the First Army was not disastrously defeated at the very outset of the attack.

Criticism of the offensive, fair or not, reached such proportions that Foch called a meeting with Pétain and Pershing to discuss the stalled advance. The French leaders arrived equipped with a solution. Since the left flank of the American advance, which had to slug through the Argonne Forest, was encountering some of the stiffest resistance, Pétain proposed to insert the French Second Army into the front at this point. It would be assigned to clear the remainder of the wood and to straighten out the salient that had developed between the First Army on the east and Gouraud's Fourth Army in the west.[48]

Since several American divisions were already heavily engaged in the

Argonne Forest, Foch proposed to incorporate these units temporarily into the French Second Army for the duration of the operation. He reasoned, quite correctly, that any attempt to relieve these divisions would only add to the already formidable congestion on the inadequate transportation network. Pershing would be provided with extra French divisions to reinforce his troops on the east bank of the Meuse and could then use them to broaden the front of his attack to include a thrust up the east bank of the river. Foch concurred in principal with Pétain's proposal but was anxious to have Pershing's approval before giving his final authorization to the plan.[49]

This meeting is often held up as evidence of a Franco-American dispute. Proponents of this argument allege that dark political motivations fueled the French proposal, which, much like Foch's earlier plans for the offensive itself, was designed to minimize America's military effort as the end of the war drew near in order to destroy President Wilson's leverage at the future peace conference. Yet such allegations, aside from assuming the worst possible motivations for Foch's actions, ignore certain realities.

First, from a purely military point of view, the Foch-Pétain plan had much to offer. An attack on the east bank of the Meuse was a superlative suggestion. Most of the German artillery, which had been so lethal in opposing the Franco-American advance, was located here. Aside from occasional counterbattery fire, these guns had been relatively untouched; operating in complete safety on commanding ground, they had sent plunging fire into the flank of the U.S. First Army's advance from the opening of the assault. The Germans themselves were somewhat surprised that no attack had yet been made on the east bank. General Von Gallwitz, commanding the German Army Group holding this sector, was convinced that the Franco-American attack west of the Meuse would be unable to advance until they captured the heights east of the river and knocked out or displaced the German artillery there. Indeed, one of the great criticisms of the German offensive in this region in 1916 was their failure to simultaneously attack down both sides of the Meuse. Consequently, like Pershing's forces, they had been severely punished by artillery operating unmolested on the far bank.[50]

Further, the big American divisions were horribly jammed on the narrow attack frontage Pershing had assigned to them. Foch argued that by widening the focus of the attack, there would be considerably more room for maneuver and an easing of the strain on the overburdened roads on the west bank. Pétain agreed and believed that by augmenting the French XVII Corps, on the east bank and already assigned to the First Army, with additional French and American divisions, it could not only seize the heights but also threaten to cut off German forces on the west bank, thus precipitating a general German withdrawal from the Argonne.

Yet Pershing rejected this plan, ostensibly because he believed it impinged on the autonomy of the First Army by removing American divisions from his command. His objections probably were also based on the new plan's implication that he was unable to accomplish what he had set out to do on 26 September. Pershing argued that the French suggestions were unnecessary and that he would straighten out his logistical problems shortly and resume the offensive soon. If Foch wanted the attack broadened to include the east bank of the Meuse, then he would consider that, but not as part of a deal that he believed compromised American military autonomy. Pershing was determined to clear out the Argonne, regardless of how long it took or how many casualties it cost, because it was an American objective. He believed that the honor of his army, and indeed the honor of the United States, was at stake. In actuality, it was Pershing's honor that was at stake, and this was perhaps the deciding factor. He would not admit that he could not accomplish a task assigned to his army, and he was determined to press on, regardless of the consequences.

Critics of the Franco-American military relationship point to this conference as evidence that the French high command lacked faith in the leadership capabilities of Pershing and his higher ranking officers. Yet if this had been the case, then why did Foch and Pétain not only allow Pershing to retain control of French divisions and corps but also suggest that more French units be placed under his command? Would Foch or Pétain have really placed more of their own rapidly dwindling infantry force in the hands of a man they deemed to be incompetent? One must consider the French criticisms for what they were. The U.S. First Army's attack was not progressing at the pace Foch and Pétain had hoped for, and as Pershing's superior officers, they criticized his performance while also offering a possible solution to the problem. Foch and Pétain also admonished General Gouraud, whose Fourth Army had also failed to live up to expectations. National rivalries or leverage at the peace conference certainly had nothing to do with the criticism of Gouraud, and such considerations had nothing whatsoever to do with Foch and Pétain's criticisms of Pershing, which were entirely of a military nature.

The French leaders were criticizing professional performance, not the United States. Nor did their criticism indicate a lack of belief in Pershing's competency. Indeed, if Foch and Pétain had not held a high opinion of Pershing and the U.S. Army, there would have been no reason to be dissatisfied. The Americans had made a solid, if not spectacular, advance; their casualties were high but not catastrophic. If Foch and Pétain had truly possessed a low opinion of Pershing's capabilities, then they would have been pleased with even modest gains from an incompetent commander. Instead, because they held Pershing and the Americans in such esteem, their criticism was harsh, for their expectations were high for this powerful military force that had been assembled, at no small effort by the French, for this offensive.

Although Pershing was displeased, he accepted the criticism of his French superiors because the offensive had thus far not lived up to his own optimistic forecasts. Shortly after his conference with Foch and Pétain, he began a major overhaul of the First Army. He almost completely replaced the initial assault force with fresh veteran divisions and ordered an early resumption of the offensive. He was determined to break through the main German defense lines, no matter what the cost.

The German high command, reacting to the crisis posed by the Franco-American advance, began to send large numbers of reinforcements into the *Kriemhilde Stellung* to hold this critical sector. When the First Army attacked on 26 September, only five German divisions were arrayed against them. Yet by 1 October U.S. Army intelligence had identified twenty-seven separate German divisions in the main defense system, with an estimated thirteen more German and Austrian divisions in reserve. Granted, many of the German divisions were actually only elements of these units. Nevertheless, the Franco-American offensive west of the Meuse had provoked the Germans to commit a large number of their rapidly dwindling reserves to the sector.[51]

By 1 October the Germans had definitely recognized the advance of the First Army between the Meuse and the Argonne as a serious threat. Unlike in Flanders, where the German army had traded space for time by executing a series of fighting withdrawals in the face of Haig's advancing British forces, the German forces in the Meuse-Argonne had no room for maneuver. A retreat on the scale of the one executed in the north would have allowed the French and Americans to cut the main railway supplying all the German forces in Belgium, completely isolating them there. The Germans instead reinforced the *Kriemhilde Stellung*, determined to make a stand and to hold this position at all costs. There was no way around this formidable obstacle; only a brutal frontal assault as part of a vicious contest of attrition could break through the German line. Pershing began to ready his army for this daunting task.

Pétain knew that Pershing's work would be easier if Gouraud's Fourth Army could push forward to provide support to the First Army's new attack, and he gave orders for Gouraud immediately to resume his offensive. The Fourth Army's advance had halted in front of a dominating ridgeline, Le Massif de Blanc Mont, a seemingly impregnable position that stood athwart the main axis of Gouraud's advance. The French had lost tens of thousands of men unsuccessfully assaulting this ridge in 1915, and the Germans had spent the ensuing three years fortifying the position even further. Any renewed advance by Gouraud would have to begin by seizing Blanc Mont, and he did not believe his troops could do so. Pétain recognized this, and with Pershing's grudging assent, released the U.S. Second and Thirty-sixth Divisions from the army group reserve and ordered them to move to Gouraud's sector to assist in jump-starting the stalled French offensive.[52]

Although the relationship between Foch and Pershing was at times strained over the course of the autumn campaign, the relationship between French and American officers and among the common soldiers themselves remained strong. Nowhere was it stronger than with the American divisions that remained under French command. The service of the U.S. Second Division with the Fourth Army in October provides an excellent example of the camaraderie that existed between the armies, even when their high commands bickered.

The officers and men of the Second Division were no strangers to the French by autumn. The French had trained this division and had gone into battle with it at Belleau Wood and the Second Battle of the Marne. Gouraud was extremely pleased to have American soldiers once more under his command and was particularly gratified to have the Second Division, whose reputation preceded it. The division had a new commander in September 1918, Major General John A. Lejeune, a graduate of the U.S. Naval Academy and a tough, veteran marine who had served in a variety of positions during the war before being named to command the Second.[53]

Lejeune and Gouraud met for the first time on the eve of the great offensive and, like virtually every American commander before him, Lejeune was immediately impressed by the colorful and brilliant French general. Lejeune recalled that at his first meeting with Gouraud, "I sensed that he was a man of power with a will of iron, but kindly withal. I acquired confidence in his judgment and in his justness. I believed him to be a General whom it would be a delight to follow."[54]

During the course of their meeting, Lejeune was shown the situation map detailing the attacks by the Fourth Army since 26 September. Gouraud gave the briefing in French, but Lejeune had picked up enough of the language to be able to follow him. Gouraud spoke slowly and clearly, which Lejeune thought quite courteous, as it immensely aided his understanding. Gouraud pointed out the dominating heights of Blanc Mont and informed the American that the position was heavily fortified and held in strength. He stated that his men regarded the position as nearly impregnable, and he was attempting a complicated maneuver with the French Fifth Army to his west in order to try to flank the position. He was not sure the plan would work, but after three days of fighting his forward units were badly in need of rest and replacements and were thus in no position to attack the commanding heights head-on.

Lejeune saw that the Second Division could play a vital role in the coming battle, but he informed Gouraud there were rumors that the French intended to split up his big division in order to reinforce the depleted French divisions in the Fourth Army's front line. Gouraud denied this, informing Lejeune that he had no intention of breaking up such a fine assault division. Lejeune told Gouraud that if the French would keep his division together, then he promised that his men would take Blanc Mont in a single attack and hold it.[55]

Gouraud was immensely pleased but quickly stated that he would need Pétain's permission to use the Second Division. Lejeune agreed and began immediate preparations for the operation. The following day, he arrived at Fourth Army headquarters to find Gouraud jubilant. Pétain had arrived earlier that morning and after inspecting the plan had approved the use of the Second Division to spearhead a new thrust by the Fourth Army. The American division was assigned to the French XXI Corps and given the daunting task of taking Blanc Mont, with French divisions attacking on either flank in support.[56]

On 3 October the U.S. Second Division began its assault on Blanc Mont. The fight proved to be the bloodiest engagement of the war for the veteran division. The attack was well coordinated, but the troops had to overcome fierce resistance from German forces heavily entrenched in a small wood and a fortified village at the base of Blanc Mont before they could begin their attack against the ridge itself. Some American writers have criticized the French for not being aggressive enough in supporting the American attack, but Lejeune was most emphatic in later praising the French infantry on both his flanks for attacking with great élan and pressing their assaults, despite heavy casualties. He later wrote:

In spite of four years warfare and in spite of their depleted ranks, the French divisions were full of the fighting spirit. I personally examined [the battlefield] and counted over one hundred dead Frenchmen in a two-acre lot, not to mention many more locked in the embrace of death with German soldiers in Essen Trench. The place was a shambles and the number of French dead spoke far more eloquently than words of the desperate attacks by the French troops.[57]

With the assistance of the French divisions on their flanks and with French artillery and armor in support, the soldiers and marines of the Second Division made their general's word good by storming the imposing heights of Blanc Mont at bayonet point. Not content with this success, the division continued to press forward in relentless attacks for almost a week until the U.S. Thirty-sixth Division finally relieved them and continued to exploit the initial success. This victory tore open the German defenses and enabled the Fourth Army to advance approximately fifteen miles to the Aisne River by 12 October.[58]

The French were overjoyed by the Americans' performance at Blanc Mont. Pétain called the attack one of the greatest feats of arms in the history of the war, and he cited every battalion, every regiment, both brigades, and the division itself in the French Army's Order of the Day. In addition to the unit citations, approximately 2,000 individual Croix de Guerre were awarded to American soldiers who took part in the battle, and Lejeune himself was made a commander of the Legion of Honor.[59]

The U.S. First Army, reorganized and readied for a grueling slugfest, lunged forward on 4 October in the first of a series of attacks that continued until mid-October against the *Kriemhilde Stellung* to the north, the Argonne Forest to the west, and the heights of the Meuse to the east (see Table 4).[60] Once more, French units played a vital role in these operations, their corps and divisions participating in the fighting and their artillery, air, and armor supporting the offensives. The Meuse-Argonne offensive was indeed a Franco-American offensive from first to last.

The Germans repulsed most of the First Army's attacks of 4–5 October, but only after heavy fighting and heavy loss by both sides. Yet with a determination and courage bordering on fanaticism, the U.S. First Division devastated its opposition and wrested a solid foothold in the *Kriemhilde Stellung*. This tactical success enabled the rest of Major General Hunter Liggett's U.S. I Corps gradually to outflank the German positions in the Argonne Forest. On 10 October, the Argonne at last fell to Liggett's men, but the German defenders managed deftly to extricate themselves and fall back to an even more formidable defensive line along commanding high ground to the northeast of the smoldering wood. Undaunted, the First Army continued to hammer its way forward against fierce resistance. The fighting was by far the fiercest and most desperate combat the Americans had yet seen, as the Germans, with no room for withdrawal, bitterly contested every yard of the advance.[61]

On 8 October Pershing at last launched an attack east of the Meuse River with the French XVII Corps, which he reinforced with the U.S. Thirty-third Division and elements of the U.S. Twenty-ninth Division for

Table 4. Order of Battle (West to East), U.S. First Army, 4 October 1918

	U.S. I Corps	U.S. V Corps	U.S. III Corps	French XVII Corps	French II Colonial Corps	U.S. IV Corps
In front line	U.S. 77th U.S. 28th U.S. 1st	U.S. 32d U.S. 3d	U.S. 80th U.S. 4th U.S. 33d	French 18th French 10th French 5th	U.S. 26th French 2d French 39th	U.S. 89th U.S. 78th U.S. 90th French 69th
Corps Reserve	U.S. 82d French 5th Cavalry	U.S. 42d U.S. 91st		French 26th	U.S. 79th	U.S. 5th U.S. 7th U.S. 37th
Army Reserve	U.S. 92d U.S. 35th	U.S. 29th				

this operation. After a series of early successes, this attack ground to a halt in the face of heavy German resistance, backed by massive artillery barrages in which poison gas was liberally used against the inexperienced American divisions. Pershing viewed this assault only as a subsidiary operation to his main drive west of the Meuse and thus did not fully support the attack, as he should have. Nevertheless, although the French XVII Corps's offensive failed to clear the heights east of the Meuse completely, it did divert the attention, and the fire, of the German guns, forced some of their artillery to displace to the rear, and helped to relieve pressure on the rest of the U.S. First Army. This support proved invaluable in the vicious struggle raging to the west, between the Meuse and the Argonne.[62]

On 11 October the First Army finally penetrated the *Kriemhilde Stellung* in force, and by 16 October attacks by the U.S. Forty-second and Thirty-second Divisions cracked open the infamous German defense system. After weeks of vicious battle, Pershing called a halt in order to regroup and reorganize the First Army for a fresh offensive. He later recalled that early October 1918 was a time that "involved the heaviest strain on the army and on me," and Donald Smythe has noted that on several occasions during this period the stress of the battle brought Pershing to the breaking point.[63]

Meanwhile, Clemenceau, upset at what he deemed to be Pershing's inept performance and by his intransigence on sharing American divisions with the French or British armies, began a series of ever more strident requests for Marshal Foch to relieve him from command. Pershing later stated that Clemenceau's actions were designed to discredit the American contribution, with victory increasingly imminent, and hence to undermine Wilson's influence at the postwar peace conference, and some historians have agreed with him. This accusation assumes that the French premier had the luxury of watching an inevitable victory unfold and already had one eye on the peace conference; this simply was not the case. France had already suffered a frightful death toll in this conflict, and each day more men died. Victory was close, but it was by no means certain that France would survive to see it. Clemenceau's primary motivation during autumn 1918 was to achieve a quick and decisive victory with the least possible loss of French lives. Although he wanted Pershing relieved from command, he genuinely believed that the general was mishandling the campaign, and he did not act from a devious desire to manipulate the postwar world. There were political considerations in all of Clemenceau's actions, but in this case they were secondary to his desire for a better commander to handle the American forces. At any rate, Marshal Foch, no great friend of Pershing, refused Clemenceau's demands and insisted on maintaining the general as head of the AEF.

Pershing's biographer Frank Vandiver has asserted that Foch wanted to relieve him from command and even issued the orders to remove him, but Pershing refused to accept his relief, at which point the matter was dropped. I could find no evidence in the French army archives that Foch ever ordered Pershing to be relieved from command. To the contrary, there is considerable evidence that Foch instead defended Pershing from Clemenceau's designs, and thus I believe his alleged relief never occurred.[64]

Foch's defense of Pershing created a great deal of enmity between him and Clemenceau, the most powerful political figure in the history of the Third Republic. It is significant that a French marshal would put his own career and position at risk by defending an American general, to whom he was not particularly close, and thus antagonize the French premier and minister of war. Foch's own criticisms of Pershing's performance had been designed to spur him along, not to destroy the U.S. First Army, its commander, or the position of the United States in the postwar world. Thus the close relationship between the French and American armies, whose operations remained intricately entwined throughout the course of the war, stayed strong, even when the machinations of the French political leadership threatened to disrupt it.

Foch's decision to stand beside Pershing reveals that the supreme Allied commander appreciated and sympathized with the difficult position

Pershing's forces were in. Foch later acknowledged that the First Army had faced extremely stiff resistance from the Germans during the battle, noting that the sector it was attacking was composed of challenging terrain: a rugged landscape combined with a poor road network, making "the effective handling of large forces particularly difficult."[65]

Foch informed Clemenceau that the only thing wrong with the U.S. First Army was its lack of experience, which was beyond the power of any one individual to control and could be obtained only by allowing the Americans to plow through their difficulties and overcome them. As Foch reasoned, "In these circumstances, then, was it to our interests to precipitate a crisis in the American High Command, to raise an outcry, to bring Wilson himself into the matter?" Foch thought not, and despite Clemenceau's repeated objections, he refused to bow to the French premier's wishes on this issue and would not consider the matter again.[66]

With the front of his attack broadening and the battle entering a new phase, Pershing decided to relinquish command of the First Army and appointed Lieutenant General Hunter Liggett in his place. At the same time, Pershing formed the U.S. Second Army, which, like the First, also contained a strong contingent of French forces, and placed Lieutenant General Robert L. Bullard in command. The new command arrangement made Pershing an army group commander and thus removed Pétain from this role in relation to the AEF. Nevertheless, Pétain still retained a great degree of input on the conduct of these operations because of the large numbers of French troops serving with both American armies and because these armies were to coordinate their attacks with French armies on their flanks.[67]

Liggett took approximately two weeks to sort out the First Army's logistical problems and to allow his tired and depleted divisions time to recover from the brutal battle they had just waged. As the French and Americans regrouped along the Meuse, Germany began to slide rapidly toward the brink of collapse. The battles of October had shattered the best divisions of the Imperial German Army, and there were no more replacements for their devastated ranks. The bitter fighting along the *Kriemhilde Stellung*, in particular, had bled their forces grievously in their desperate and ultimately futile defensive stand against the First Army. Ludendorff later wrote, "In the October battles for the possession of the Meuse line, which we had held for four years and heavily fortified, the Americans must be credited with [a] decisive victory. By frontal pressure against the troops opposing them, they forced us to abandon the Aisne position and retreat behind the Meuse."[68]

On 25 October Liggett visited General Gouraud's headquarters and arranged for a renewal of the offensive at an early date. By this time over

2 million American soldiers were in France, with more arriving every week, and the U.S. Second Army would soon be conducting its own operations east of the Meuse. Yet even at this late date, French divisions and corps remained assigned to the First Army, and its tactical movements were still coordinated with the French Fourth Army. Indeed, despite the rest, refitting, and heavy reinforcement of the First Army that Liggett had supervised for approximately two weeks, he still believed that it was absolutely vital for the Fourth Army to attack in conjunction with his army. Gouraud agreed on a joint attack, and Pershing and Foch both quickly approved the operation, which was scheduled to begin on 1 November.[69]

As the Franco-American armies prepared to launch their next drive, Imperial Germany began to fall apart. Under increasing pressure from both the Left and the Right in the civilian government, and having lost the confidence of the kaiser and many of his own officers, a bitter Ludendorff was forced to resign his position as first quartermaster general of the German army on 26 October, leaving his superior, Field Marshal Paul von Hindenburg, without his chief counsel and adviser for the first time in the war. With revolution in the air in the streets of Berlin, and the soldiers on the western front exhausted and on the verge of collapse, the German government began seriously to consider the possibility of surrender. By late October Germany's last ally, Austria-Hungary, had collapsed, as the ancient Hapsburg monarchy and its multiethnic empire erupted into revolution. Clearly, the end was near, and one more push could send the German Empire over the brink and into the abyss.[70]

On 1 November the reorganized and rested First Army surged forward and shattered the German line opposite its positions, pushing forward and exploiting the rapidly deteriorating morale and physical strength of the Imperial German Army. Gouraud's Fourth Army simultaneously burst through the German lines, and the two Franco-American armies raced for the prize of Sedan that, if taken, would effectively isolate the remaining German armies in Belgium. The U.S. Second Army also began an offensive, pushing forward against surprisingly stiff German resistance. Whatever the criticisms of the AEF's performance in the early stages of the Meuse-Argonne offensive, no one can contest that the attacks from 1 November to 11 November were carried out with daring and tremendous professional skill.

As the Allied offensives continued their steady pressure, Germany began to unravel. Hindenburg later recalled that given the incessant pounding of the American, French, and British armies against the tattered remnants of the Imperial German Army on the western front, "It was plain that this situation could not last. Our armies were too weak and too tired. Moreover the pressure which the fresh American masses were putting upon our most sensitive point in the region of the Meuse was too strong. . . . The strain had become almost intolerable. Convulsions anywhere, whether at home or in the Army, would make collapse inevitable."[71]

On 5 November the new commander of the Imperial German Army, General Wilhelm Groener, assured the war council in Berlin that the western front would hold until a reasonable peace could be negotiated with the Allies. The following day, however, Groener visited Sedan and was dismayed to learn of the rapid advance of the Franco-American armies on this critical objective. The crown prince informed Groener that his men would be unable to hold the city long in the face of the furious Franco-American attacks breaking across his front. Given this new development, Groener immediately changed his estimate on the stability of the western front and urged his government to make peace immediately, before it was too late.[72]

Events overtook them as a revolution broke out in Germany on 8 November, and the government and army rapidly collapsed. On 11 November 1918, representatives of the new German government signed the armistice that ended the Great War, and peace settled over Europe for the first time in four years. That same day, a jubilant Pershing telegraphed his friend Pétain: "My dear General: On the occasion of the signing of the terms of the armistice and the cessation of hostilities on the Western front, I send to you and your gallant Armies the most cordial greetings and hearty congratulations of myself and the officers and men of the American Expeditionary Forces. It has indeed been a proud privilege and pleasure to participate in this great war and battle by the side of the veteran French Armies and to march with them to victory."[73]

The significance of America's military contribution to the final Allied victory in November has been questioned and even denigrated by some historians, but the Meuse-Argonne offensive inflicted grievous damage to the German army, and its importance cannot be overstated. The Germans considered the American effort as a vital, indeed essential, component of the final Allied triumph. Ludendorff recalled, "It was most assuredly the Americans who bore the heaviest brunt of the fighting on the whole battle front during the last few months of the war." He also stated that during the final Allied offensives of 1918, American soldiers were "much more aggressive in attack than either the English or the French" and that the Germans had been unable to "withstand the incessant force of intrepidity of the American attack."[74]

General Max von Gallwitz, who served both as an army group commander and an army commander against the Franco-American forces in the Meuse-Argonne campaign, later recalled, "We were surprised by the vastness and vigor of America's military expansion. We admired the intensity with which a big army had been created, with marvelous all-around equipment. The American army had numerically strong, well-set-up, substantial, human material, endowed with great energy. . . . After all, it was the astonishing display of American strength which definitely decided the war against us."[75]

Yet in the final analysis, the Allied victory in 1918 was just that, an Allied triumph brought about by the concerted military efforts of the great armies of the west against the forces of Imperial Germany. British historians, in particular, have often claimed the lion's share of credit for winning the war during this final campaign. Without question, the British and Commonwealth forces fought with tremendous skill during the autumn campaign and displayed an amazing tenacity and determination, given the horrific losses they had suffered over the course of four years of the bloodiest war in human history. Yet French and Belgian armies, which had three American divisions assigned to them, participated in the British drive in Flanders, as did two American divisions assigned to the British. Thus the British campaign was actually an Allied campaign, and their successes, if not dependent upon, certainly were assisted by these Allied forces.

Although token U.S. forces took part in other sectors, America's main military effort in that autumn was in the Meuse-Argonne sector and was inextricably linked with the French army. The offensives at St. Mihiel and the Meuse-Argonne remain the most significant American contributions to the campaign, indeed to the entire Allied war effort, and in every phase of these two offensives, the French and Americans fought as a combined force.

Far too often historians have attempted to cite the various Allied military contributions in terms of prisoners taken or miles advanced as indicative of a particular nation's contributions to the final victory. Yet one can never begin to unravel national totals of such statistics from a French army group with U.S. divisions assigned to it or from an American army containing French corps and divisions. Moreover, the French corps assigned to the U.S. First Army contained U.S. Army divisions, and the American corps of the U.S. First Army contained French divisions, artillery batteries, armor companies, and aviation units. The great story of America's military contribution to the Allied victory was not an autonomous American effort, for such a concept was always illusory, but rather the establishment of a Franco-American force that was instrumental in the final defeat of Germany.

Pershing did not forget the Frenchmen who had helped make the victory possible, and on 13 November 1918 he drove to Paris for a final meeting with Marshal Joffre to award him the Distinguished Service Medal. Pershing recalled, "This grand old French Commander-in-Chief was very proud of this recognition by our Government." Later that same day he visited General Pétain to confer upon him the same decoration. Pershing later wrote of the ceremony, "Facing General Pétain . . . I spoke a few words regarding his exceptional service to his country and thanked him for his uniform consideration and great assistance to our armies, and pinned on the medal. It was especially gratifying to me to decorate Pétain, as my relations with him were always closer than with any of the other Allied officers and we had become fast friends."[76]

After a perfunctory appearance at Field Marshal Haig's headquarters, Pershing journeyed to Paris to see Clemenceau for the first time since the war had ended. He recalled "When we met he was much affected, and indeed demonstrative. We fell into each other's arms, choked up and had to wipe our eyes. We had no differences to discuss that day."[77]

Thus the fraternity of arms that existed between the U.S. Army and the French army, whose foundation had been laid by Joffre and had been nurtured and developed by Pershing, Pétain, and Foch, proved to be absolutely essential to the military efforts of both nations in the war's final year. Together they achieved the goal that could not have been reached without the cooperation, sacrifices, and determined desire to triumph that the armies of the two republics shared in their final drive for victory in autumn 1918.

CHAPTER 9

• • • • • • • • • • • • • •

Conclusion

The AEF and the French army enjoyed a close relationship throughout America's involvement in the Great War. American and French soldiers cooperated magnificently on the battlefield, winning brilliant victories and together providing a significant military contribution to the final Allied victory that neither could have achieved alone. After the guns fell silent, however, differences arose between the United States and France that resulted in a distortion of the historical view of Franco-American military relations during the war. A common struggle against a common foe on the battlefield gave way to differences over the treatment of the defeated Germans, the reparations and territory that France was entitled to, and the methods for safeguarding the peace of postwar Europe.

On 17 November 1918, six days after the signing of the Armistice, the newly created U.S. Third Army moved across the Armistice line and entered the area of western Germany known as the Rhineland. The French Tenth Army advanced on its right and the French Fifth Army on its left; British and Belgian forces moved into the Rhineland farther north. In addition to the zones of occupation, Allied forces occupied bridgeheads on the east bank of the Rhine, with the British at Cologne, the Americans at Coblenz, and the French at Mainz. Supreme Allied commander Marshal

Foch dictated that although the Allied armies would have their own zones in the Rhineland, the bridgeheads would be occupied by interallied forces with sizable contingents of French troops stationed in the American and British bridgeheads.[1]

Many French military and political leaders were concerned that Germany might renew hostilities at any moment, even though it was in tatters and rocked by revolution in the wake of the collapse of the Hohenzollern monarchy and the German Empire. This internal turmoil and the utter collapse of its armed forces had neutralized it as a military threat, but it was much easier for Americans to accept this than the French, given the historical experience of the two nations in regard to Germany.

The United States had never been defeated by Germany, foreign invaders had not landed on its soil since the British were driven from New Orleans in 1815, and it had never lost any of its national territory in war. President Wilson publicly stated in 1918 that although America insisted that Germany's "military masters" had to be removed from power and a democracy established, the United States did not seek war reparations and was opposed to a "conqueror's peace." Because the Germans had formed a republic, albeit a shaky one, the United States was willing to accept it as a fellow democratic nation; it was no longer the autocracy against whom the war had been fought. American soldiers were received kindly by the Germans, and they quickly warmed to the population. Many Germans hoped that the United States would be a moderating influence at the Paris peace conference, where the victorious Allies would decide what to do with their country, and they were much friendlier to American soldiers than to the French or British. A later U.S. Army study concluded that American soldiers rarely took into account "the fact that it was good policy for the German people to make the best possible impression on their American visitors." Still, American soldiers quickly made friends with the Germans, much to the consternation and fear of the French.[2]

Indeed, fear was a prime motivating factor in French attitudes toward Germany, even though this seemed irrational to many Americans. Prussian/German armies had invaded and occupied France in 1814, 1815, 1870, and 1914.[3] Though the French emerged victorious in the Great War, the victory had been close and dearly bought. A broad swathe of northeastern France had been devastated by the fighting and by wanton acts of destruction committed by German soldiers. Millions of French people had lived under the iron hand of German military occupation, including those of Alsace and Lorraine, which had been held by the Germans since 1870 and for whose liberation France had sacrificed a generation of her youth.

The terrible casualties France suffered in the war heavily influenced their postwar attitude. "Approximately 1,375,800 Frenchmen had died and another 4,266,000 had been wounded, including over 800,000 who were classified as permanently disabled by their wounds. The overwhelming majority of these casualties had occurred on the western front as the French defended their homeland. In contrast, the United States lost approximately 126,000 killed and 234,300 wounded, which, though heavy by modern standards, was modest compared to the horrific casualties suffered by France and the other European great powers. France, with a population roughly one-third that of the United States in 1914, suffered more casualties in the war than the United States has suffered in all its wars, from the American Revolution to the present time, combined. Americans were able to put aside their fear and hatred of the Germans when the war was over, but for the French there were issues that needed to be settled with their ancient enemy.

The French were eager to repay the Germans in kind for the numerous occupations they had endured. They also wanted to impress upon the Germans that France was strong and would never be vulnerable to German invasion again. Therefore, the French army pursued a heavy-handed occupation policy in their zone of the Rhineland and encouraged the Americans to follow suit. Americans were angered by what they saw as French bullying of a defeated people, the equivalent of kicking a man while he's down. Consequently, in general, American opinion of the French dropped significantly because they viewed the occupation policies of the French army as unnecessarily harsh.[4]

Americans also were concerned about the political machinations of leading figures in the French army high command who desired to annex the Rhineland, which they believed was part of their rightful share in the spoils of victory. The senior leadership of the French army, along with certain segments of the French Right, hoped that this significant territorial acquisition would permanently cripple Germany while reestablishing the power of France. They also believed that the Rhine would provide a defensible frontier for the postwar era.

Early in the war Premier Clemenceau had won British, and later, American support for French demands that Alsace and Lorraine be returned to France. These territories had been reclaimed and occupied by French forces within days of the Armistice. Clemenceau entertained hopes of annexing the Rhineland as well, but he received absolutely no support for this plan from President Wilson or Prime Minister Lloyd George, who did not want a new form of the old Alsace-Lorraine dispute sowing the seeds for a future Franco-German war. In his heart Clemenceau believed annexation was in the best interest of France, but he was enough of a pragmatist to realize that neither the Americans nor the British would ever accept it, and he subsequently dropped this issue at the peace conference. This decision quickly provoked a general outcry from the senior leadership of the French army, including Marshal Foch.[5]

Foch believed that annexation of the Rhineland was essential to the future security of France, and he angrily disputed Clemenceau's decision to drop the matter. Foch had some political support from the French Right on this issue, and a considerable amount of sympathy from the French officer corps, including General Mangin, who commanded the Tenth Army in the Rhineland. Following Clemenceau's decision, Foch and Mangin endeavored to use the French occupation forces to make a statement to their government, to the Germans, and in some ways, to the Americans and British, that France claimed the region. Foch conducted numerous displays of military strength, during which French troops sometimes crossed into American or British zones of occupation, or both, in an effort to assert French hegemony in the region. When Clemenceau made it clear that annexation would never happen, Foch and Mangin became involved with various Rhenish separatist groups in the hopes of setting up a French puppet state in the Rhineland.[6]

These political machinations had a negative impact on the general view that Americans had of their French comrades and disillusioned a naive nation that had truly hoped if not actually believed that the "War to End All Wars" had been fought and won. Americans did not want to hear about the need to prepare for a future war with Germany. They believed that victory in the Great War and the conversion of Germany to a democracy was enough to end the menace; Americans were unwilling to do more. The U.S. Senate's rejection of the Treaty of Versailles and refusal to join the League of Nations signaled an American withdrawal from the affairs of Europe, a retreat from greatness that was soon matched by the early withdrawal of American occupation forces from the Rhineland, which surprised and hurt the French. As the Americans sailed away, French leaders were convinced that the Germans would come again and that France would have to face them alone.

These postwar political disputes created a degree of bitterness between France and the United States, an acrimony that in the 1920s served to distort the historical reality of the cooperation that had flourished between the armed forces of the two republics on the battlefield. As a U.S.

Army study concluded, these postwar developments bore no resemblance to Franco-American military relations during the war.[7]

Despite these political differences, there remained a powerful bond between the two countries that had been forged on the battlefields. Perhaps this was best exemplified by an experience Pershing had in 1919. Shortly after yet another confrontation with Foch over occupation policy in the Rhineland, Pershing decided to tour one of the Meuse-Argonne battlefields. Fuming from his latest argument, he distracted himself from it by walking the wooded hills where the scars of battle were still fresh and the ferocity of the fighting was evidenced by the numerous American soldiers buried there. As he stood near a local cemetery noting the large number of American graves, he was surprised to see a sizable group of French civilians from the local village walking up the hill toward the graveyard carrying flowers. As the people arrived at the top of the hill, Pershing spoke to an elderly gentleman in the group and asked what they were doing.

In broken English, the old gentleman explained that they were taking the flowers to decorate the graves of the American soldiers. He told Pershing that the people of his village would never forget the Americans who liberated them from the Germans and would always care for the burial places of these fallen heroes from across the sea. The normally stoical Pershing had to choke back tears as he told the man, "It is very hard for us to say 'Good-bye' for the last time to our dear comrades. . . . But since they cannot go home with us, there is no land save their own in which we would rather have them rest—no people with whom we can more surely leave their ashes to tender care and lasting memory than the dear people of France. I thank you in the name of their bereaved and in the name of our whole people who are mourning them today and whose hearts are here."[8]

The soldiers of America and France had trained, fought, bled, and died, side by side on the battlefields of the Great War, and it was this shared sacrifice in a common cause that forged an unbreakable bond of fraternity between the two republics. Almost three years after the end of the war, the final act was performed that affirmed the solemn union.

On 22 October 1921, the U.S. Army conducted a somber martial ceremony at the four major American military cemeteries in France, as the body of one unknown American soldier was exhumed from each. A U.S. Army truck brought the four bodies to the town square of the French city of Châlons-sur-Marne, where a French honor guard composed exclusively of decorated veterans of the Great War received the bodies with full military honors. The people of the town packed the square and watched silently, heads uncovered, as the French soldiers carried the four plain wooden coffins, each draped with an American flag, into a dimly lit antechamber of the city hall.[9]

An American honor guard was stationed inside the room to stand vigil over the coffins, and the French army posted another honor guard in the adjoining rooms and outside the building. Throughout the night, the villagers of Châlons-sur-Marne and nearby towns filed past the caskets of the unknown American dead and laid mounds of flowers at the foot of each one. An American eyewitness to these events, Captain A. E. Dewey, later recalled, "Each person in that long, steady line . . . bowed [his] head, offering a silent prayer, a prayer of sorrow and of thanksgiving, for the eternal rest of the souls of those Unknowns, far from home, who had given their lives in assisting France."[10]

There were large numbers of French war widows in the procession, recognizable because they had once more put on their black armband of mourning, a common fashion during the war but one rarely seen since the Armistice. American observers remarked on how young the widows were; almost all of them were in their twenties. Many of them became increasingly emotional as they drew nearer to the flag-draped coffins, and as they laid their flowers on the caskets some of them completely broke down into uncontrollable fits of weeping.[11]

Perhaps the fallen Americans were too strong a reminder of the widows' own husbands who had died in the same war, perhaps even in the same battle. The thought that somewhere on the other side of the Atlantic there were other young women who grieved as they did brought no solace, only a greater sorrow. Their surviving family members rushed to support these young women, whose sacrifice to France had been so great and was almost too terrible to bear. The absence of young men in these families was painful to see, for not just husbands but fathers, lovers, sons, and brothers had fallen in defense of the Republic, and hardly a family in France had not been touched by the war. These shattered families gathered around the young widows and led them away from this place of dark remembrance.[12]

The following morning, U.S. Major General Henry T. Allen, commander of the American forces on the Rhine, along with his staff, escorted Sergeant Edward F. Younger into the antechamber where the unknowns lay in state, while outside in the courtyard a French military band played Chopin's funeral march. Younger was a decorated veteran of the AEF who had been wounded in combat and had been selected "to choose from among the four Americans the one who will forever symbolize the sacrifice of American sons in the war."[13] Younger was given a single white rose to mark the casket he had chosen, and then he was left alone in the room. As he later recalled, "I went into the room and walked past the caskets. I walked around them three times. Suddenly I stopped. It was as though something had pulled me. A voice seemed to say: 'This is a pal of yours.' I put the rose on the coffin in front of me and went back into the sunlight. I still remember the awed feeling I had, standing there alone."[14]

The three soldiers not chosen were removed and buried with full honors in a joint Franco-American ceremony at the new American military cemetery at Romagne-sous-Montfaucon, a scene of fierce fighting during the Meuse-Argonne offensive. The casket of the chosen Unknown Soldier remained lying in state until that evening, as many more French villagers filed past to pay their respects. Then America's Unknown Soldier began his long journey home.

The Unknown Soldier was carried from the town hall by a group of six noncommissioned officers of the U.S. Army, who served as pallbearers. A French honor guard escorted them into the town square of Châlons-sur-Marne, which was packed with French soldiers and civilians, and the casket was placed on a flag-draped and flower-bedecked caisson for transport to the train station. Slowly and solemnly, with arms sloped, French soldiers marched in column on both sides of the road along the length of the parade route to the station. The body was then transferred into a special black casket bearing the inscription, "An unknown soldier who gave his life in the Great War," and then the entire French Sixth Infantry Division marched past, by companies. Captain Dewey recalled, "Each company as it passed dipped its torn and bloody battle standards, the officers presented sabers, the men executed 'eyes right' and presented arms." The casket was then placed aboard a special train provided by the French army to transport the Unknown Soldier to the port of Le Havre.[15]

When the train arrived in Le Havre, the casket was transferred to a caisson for a solemn procession through town to the docks. The French 129th Infantry Regiment was formed into two ranks along both sides of the road. The French soldiers marched with sloped arms, escorting the caisson, which was driven by a French soldier. Along with General Allen and the American honor guard, French children carrying flowers walked in the procession, as did one hundred former *poilus,* each bearing a wreath representing a different French veteran's organization. As the parade moved slowly through town, the bells of all the churches in Le Havre began to toll and continued to chime mournfully throughout the procession and ceremony that followed.

An enormous crowd lined the parade route, quiet, solemn, and dignified; not a single policeman was used to maintain control. At the dock a detachment of U.S. Marines stood at attention ready to receive the Unknown Soldier, whose flag-draped casket still bore the single white rose that Sergeant Younger had placed upon it. The ceremonies began with the awarding of the Légion d'honneur, France's highest award for bravery, to America's Unknown Soldier.[16] André Maginot, France's soldier deputy, a hero who had lost a leg during the war and was a powerful force in the Chamber of Deputies, spoke to the gathered crowd and told them that France would never forget what the American soldiers had done for her. Maginot then faced the casket and said, "You came over here for no material or selfish purpose, but in exhibition of a noble spirit. American brother, they now take you back to the great country whence you came, but France will conserve you forever in pious memory, and her soil will never forget that to it you confided your last dream."[17]

The coffin was then carried by American soldiers to the gangways leading up to the USS *Olympia*, whose decks were covered with French and American flags, and transferred to a detachment of U.S. Marines.[18] As the ship's band played "La Marseillaise," the marines carried the casket aboard and placed it on the aft deck of the ship. The band then played the "Star Spangled Banner" and finally "Taps." As the last mournful tones were played, the children of Le Havre, led by village priests and nuns, came aboard and placed flowers on the coffin until it virtually disappeared from sight. They then silently filed off the ship, and the *Olympia* slipped away from the docks. Two French war vessels took their places alongside the American cruiser to escort it out of the harbor while a nearby French battleship began to fire a thunderous salute as France bid farewell to a fallen brother in arms.

The casket bearing the remains of the Unknown Soldier lay in state in the rotunda of the U.S. Capitol on 10 November 1921 as masses of people came to pay their respects. The *New York Times* reported, "While this American warrior lay in his simple black coffin, a steady throng filed past, all through the day and nearly to midnight. Old and young, black and white, crippled and stalwart, soldier and sailor and civilian, they moved steadily on, each craving the privilege of tendering to this symbolic man reverence and honor."[19]

The following day marked the third anniversary of the end of the war. A solemn procession, which included Medal of Honor winners from the American Civil War and Gold Star mothers who had lost a son in the Great War, escorted the Unknown Soldier from the Capitol, across the Potomac River, and into Arlington, where an international delegation and an enormous crowd awaited. President Harding addressed the throng:

Burial here is rather more than a sign of the Government's favor, it is a suggestion of a tomb in the heart of the nation, sorrowing for its noble dead. Today's ceremonies proclaim that the hero unknown is not unhonored. Here the inspirations of yesterday and the conscience of today forever unite to make the Republic worthy of his death for flag and country. . . . Conscious that all America has halted to share in the tribute of heart and mind and soul to this fellow American and knowing that the world is noting this expression of the Republic's mindfulness, it is fitting to say that his sacrifice, and that of the millions dead, shall not be in vain.[20]

Harding then pinned the Medal of Honor and the Distinguished Service Cross to the American flag that covered the casket and stepped back as a long procession of distinguished foreign soldiers representing all the Allied nations came forward to present their country's highest military awards. The entire ceremony was conducted with much solemnity and martial dignity, as the various military officers each gave his own tribute. The French representative was Marshal Foch. With tears brimming in his eyes, Foch, whose only son had been killed in the war, stepped up to the side of the flag-draped casket to present the Croix de Guerre (avec palme) and the Medaille Militaire to the fallen American soldier. Addressing the casket, he said, "Unknown Soldier of the American Army, noble son of the great Republic of the United States which you so well personify! For your disinterestedness, your valor, your devotion as far as the supreme sacrifice to the cause of liberty, you are forever inscribed on the rolls of honor of the French Armies. In testimony whereof I place these decorations which France bestows upon your immortal memory."[21]

At the conclusion of the ceremonies, Chief Plenty Coups of the Crow Nation recited an ancient warrior prayer and then placed his ancestral warbonnet and coup stick on the coffin as it was slowly lowered into the tomb. At the bottom of the crypt, on the hallowed ground of America's Valhalla, a two-inch deep layer of French soil, gathered from the battlefields of the western front where the French army and American army had fought side by side, had been spread. Here the Unknown American Soldier of the Great War rests for all eternity.[22]

Prior to 1917, the United States had waged its wars unilaterally, with the exception of the American Revolution, when it formed the first military alliance in its history with France. Though not a formal military alliance, the association between the AEF and the French army played a vital role in the maturation of the United States as a world military power. In addition to the vital role that Franco-American forces had played in the 1918 campaign, America's special relationship with France provided the officers of the U.S. Army, including MacArthur, Marshall, and Patton, their first experience in modern warfare and the opportunity to command multinational forces as part of an international military coalition. When one considers that in every major conflict since World War I the United States has waged war as the leader of a multinational coalition, the significance of this Franco-American military relationship becomes truly evident. But it was more than just a marriage of convenience, for a true bond of friendship existed between the soldiers of the two republics.

Nevertheless there have been those on both sides of the Atlantic, even as early as the 1920s, who have sought for their own purposes to discredit the value, importance, and uniqueness of the Franco-American military relationship in the Great War. In the final days before his death, Marshal Joffre, the man who had done more than any other to forge the modern military bond between France and America, wrote:

Politics, influenced as they so often are by despicable motives, have since found means, from time to time, to embitter feelings between Americans and ourselves; but when I look back upon those few brief weeks in the spring of 1917 and live through them again in writing these lines, when I remember those eager faces, those hands stretched out to clasp our own, when I hear again the shouts of joy which greeted our passage, I cannot believe that these misunderstandings can ever persist. And I wish to die sustained by the hope that France and the United States will never forget that at two tragic moments in their history they drew their swords to fight side by side for right and liberty, and did not sheathe them again until, by a victory won together, they had saved the most sacred of all causes.[23]

France and America have often had different views on various political subjects, sometimes quite different indeed. But beneath these differences remains a fraternity of arms among the soldiers of the great republics that forms the bedrock of Franco-American relations.

APPENDIX: MAPS

● ● ● ● ● ● ● ● ● ● ● ● ●

Maps courtesy of American Battle Monuments Commission from *American Armies and Battlefields in Europe* (Washington, DC: GPO, 1938).

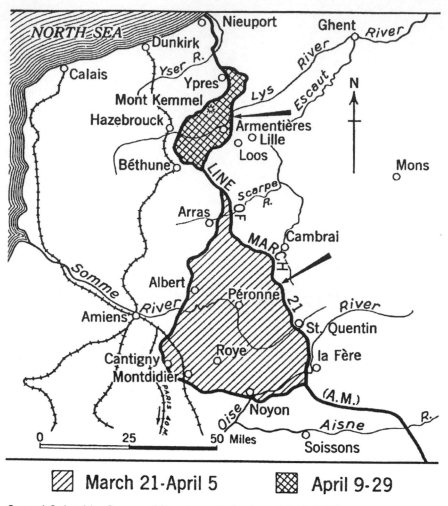

North Sea

Nieuport

Ghent

River

Dunkirk

Calais

Yser R.

Lys River

Escaut

N

Ypres

Mont Kemmel

Hazebrouck

Armentières

Lille

Loos

Mons

Béthune

LINE OF MARCH 21

Scarpe R.

Arras

Cambrai

Albert

Péronne

St. Quentin

River

Amiens

Somme River

Cantigny

Montdidier

Roye

la Fère

PARIS 40 M.

Oise

Noyon

(A.M.)

Aisne

R.

Soissons

0	25	50 Miles

March 21-April 5   April 9-29

Ground Gained by German Offensives of March and April 1918.

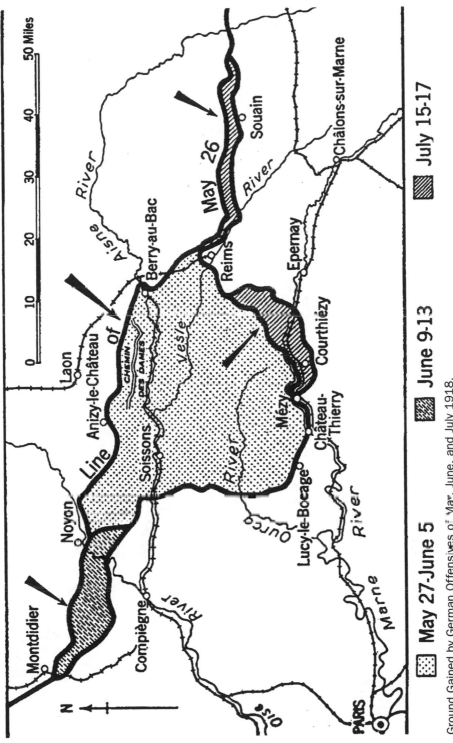

50 Miles

Aisne River

Laon

Anizy-le-Château

Noyan

Line

of

Montdidier

Compiègne

Oise River

CHEMIN DES DAMES

Soissons

Berry-au-Bac

Reims

Vesle River

Mézy

Château-Thierry

Lucy-le-Bocage

Ourcq

River

Marne River

May 26

Souain

River

Epernay

Courthiézy

Châlons-sur-Marne

PARIS

Oise

N

☐ May 27–June 5   ☐ June 9–13

☐ July 15–17

Ground Gained by German Offensives of May, June, and July 1918.

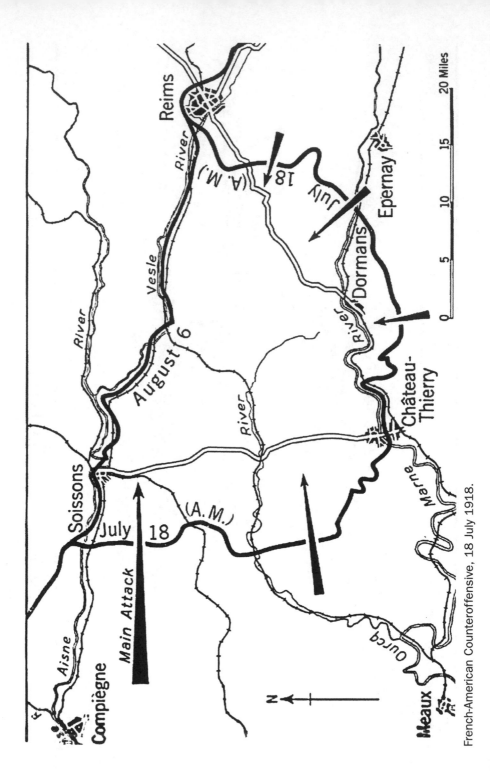

Reims

Epernay

Dormans

Château-Thierry

Vesle River

River

Aisne River

Soissons

Compiègne

July 18

Main Attack

(A. M.)

August 6

July 18 (A.M.)

Marne

Ourcq

Meaux

N

0 5 10 15 20 Miles

French-American Counteroffensive, 18 July 1918.

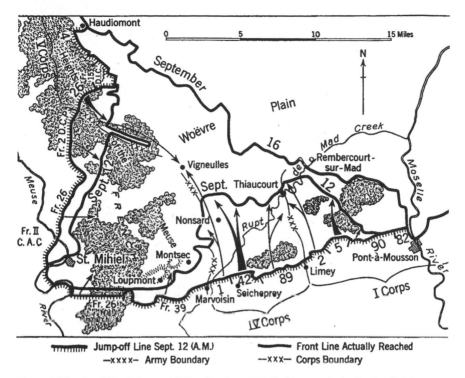

Plan of Attack of First Army, 12 September 1918. (Numerals indicate divisions; arrows indicate direction and weight of attacks.)

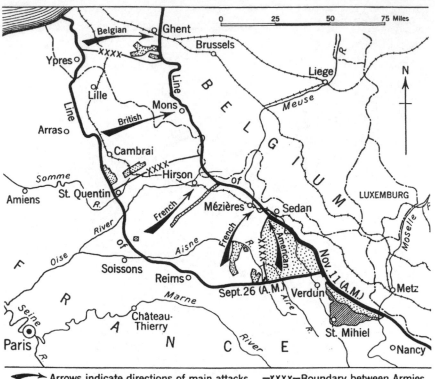

Arrows indicate directions of main attacks   —xxxx—Boundary between Armies
Ground gained by American units Sept. 12-16, 1918
Ground gained by American units Sept. 26-Nov. 11, 1918

American and Allied Attacks on the Western Front, 26 September–11 November 1918.

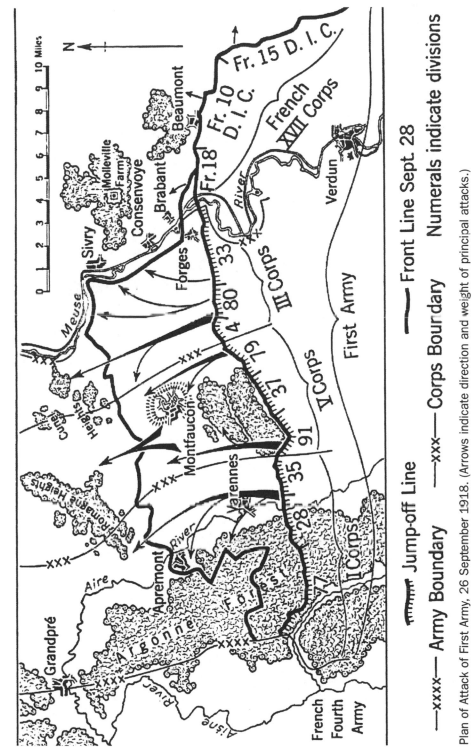

Plan of Attack of First Army, 26 September 1918. (Arrows indicate direction and weight of principal attacks.)

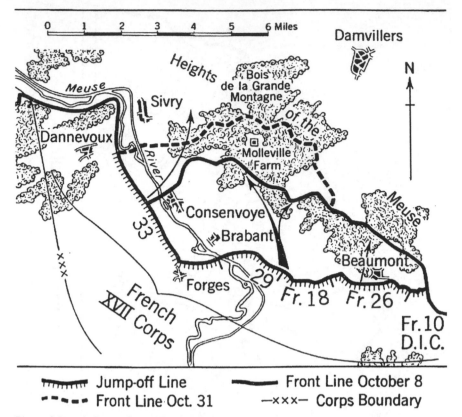

Jump-off Line — **Front Line October 8**
Front Line Oct. 31 —×××— **Corps Boundary**

Plan of Attack East of the Meuse, 8 October 1918. (Numerals indicate divisions; arrows indicate direction and weight of attacks; American 29th Division attached to French 18th Division for this attack.)

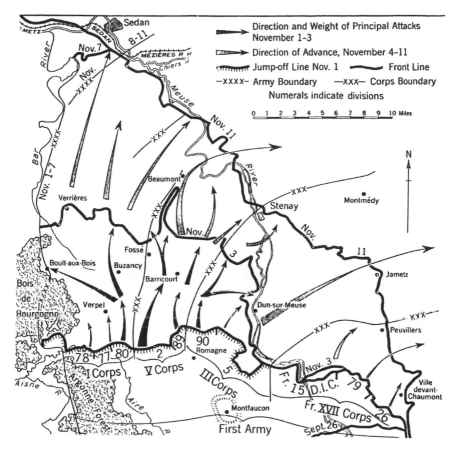

Operations of First Army, 1–11 November 1918.

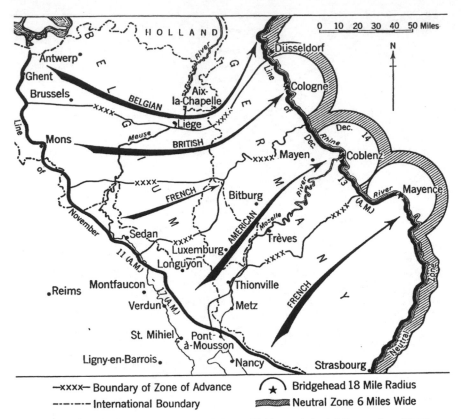

American and Allied Advance to the Rhine, 17 November–14 December 1918.

—xxxx— Boundary of Zone of Advance

- - - - - - International Boundary

Bridgehead 18 Mile Radius

Neutral Zone 6 Miles Wide

NOTES

• • • • • • • • • • • • • • •

Chapter 1. American Volunteers in France

1. Address by President Woodrow Wilson, 18 August 1914, in *The Papers of Woodrow Wilson*, ed. Arthur S. Link et al., 69 vols. (Princeton: Princeton University Press, 1966–1994), 30: 393–94 (hereafter *PWW*).

2. The Rockwell brothers were independently wealthy and therefore did not rely on income from their writing to support themselves.

3. Kiffin Rockwell, *War Letters of Kiffin Yates Rockwell, Foreign Legionnaire and Aviator: France 1914–1916*, with memoir and notes by Paul Ayres Rockwell (1917; reprint, Garden City, N.Y.: Country Life Press, 1925), xvii. Without question, the tales that their grandfathers told them about the American Civil War also fueled their romantic notions of warfare.

4. Ibid., xvii.

5. Ibid., xviii–xix.

6. T. Bentley Mott, *Myron T. Herrick, Friend of France: An Autobiographical Biography* (Garden City, N.Y.: Doubleday, Doran, 1929), 115–17 and 393–98. Herrick, a staunch Republican, had tendered his resignation shortly after Woodrow Wilson's election in November 1912. But Wilson failed to act upon the letter because his original nominee, William F. McCombs, spent months mulling over whether to accept the post before finally declining it. The new appointee, William G. Sharp, did not arrive in France until July 1914. Herrick was scheduled to hand over his post officially on 8 August 1914, but with the outbreak of hostilities, he was asked to stay to aid Sharp until his successor could become acclimated to his

new position. Thus America had both an ambassador and an ambassador-designate in France until late September 1914. Herrick became ambassador to France again in 1921 when the Harding administration took office.

7. Ibid., 143–44.

8. This flag remained with the American volunteers until 1915 when, after seeing heavy fighting in Champagne, they sent it back to Paris for safekeeping. In 1917 it was formally presented to the Musée de l'Armée at the Hôtel des Invalides in Paris, where it remains to this day.

9. Paul Ayres Rockwell, *American Fighters in the Foreign Legion, 1914–1918* (Boston: Houghton Mifflin, 1930), 4–7.

10. Ibid., 11.

11. Letter from Kiffin Rockwell to his mother, 31 August 1914, Rockwell, *War Letters*, 5.

12. Irving J. Newman, "A Biography of Colonel Thaw II," *Popular Aviation*, 19 November 1934, 281–83.

13. Victor Chapman, *Victor Chapman's Letters from France*, edited and with memoir by John J. Chapman (New York: Macmillan, 1917), 22. John J. Chapman's memoir of his late son is an amazingly candid portrayal of Victor and of the Chapman family; this candor extended to his editing of Victor's letters.

14. Edwin C. Parsons, *I Flew with the Lafayette Escadrille* (Indianapolis: E. C. Seale, 1963), 11.

15. James Norman Hall and Charles Bernard Nordhoff, eds., *The Lafayette Flying Corps*, 2 vols. (Boston: Houghton Mifflin, 1920), 1: 330–31.

16. *New York Herald Tribune*, 13 March 1948.

17. Parsons, *I Flew with the Lafayette Escadrille*, 8–10. Parsons was one of the most colorful members of the Escadrille Lafayette, and although he firmly believed in the justness of the cause he was fighting for, he definitely fit into the category of adventurer. After his service in the war, he worked in Hollywood as a technical adviser and screenwriter before quitting that job to become an FBI agent. During World War II he joined the U.S. Navy and rose to the rank of rear admiral.

18. Edward Morlae, *A Soldier of the Legion* (Boston: Houghton Mifflin, 1916), 8.

19. Rockwell, *American Fighters*, 137–38 and letter from Alan Seeger to his *marraine*, 1 June 1916, in Alan Seeger, *Letters and Diary of Alan Seeger* (New York: Charles Scribner's Sons, 1917), 202. A *marraine* (godmother) or, more properly in this context, *marraine de guerre* (war godmother), was a French woman who volunteered to adopt a French soldier at the front to correspond with, send packages to, and so on. The program was an important part of French efforts to sustain soldiers' morale by maintaining a positive contact between them and women on the home front. See Margaret H. Darrow, *French Women and the First World War: War Stories of the Home Front* (New York: Berg, 2000), 79–86.

20. The French soldier in World War I wore a *horizon bleu* uniform from 1915 to the end of the war. Alan Seeger, *Poems* (New York: Charles Scribner's Sons, 1917), 171. A portion of this stanza is inscribed on the memorial in Paris to the American volunteers who died in the Great War.

21. Ibid., 165–66.

22. Douglas Porch, *The French Foreign Legion: A Complete History of the Legendary Fighting Force* (New York: HarperCollins, 1991), 335–40.

23. Ibid.

24. Paul Rockwell never fully recovered and was discharged from the Foreign Legion in 1915. Nevertheless, he remained in France and served for the rest of the war as an ambulance driver. He was an ardent supporter and a great friend to the other American volunteers in France, whom he assisted with his fortune and connections whenever he could.

25. Letter from Kiffin Rockwell to Paul Rockwell, 26 December 1914, Rockwell, *War Letters,* 12.

26. Ibid., 21 January 1915, 22.

27. Ibid., 1 February 1915.

28. Rockwell, *American Fighters,* 72.

29. Letter from Kiffin Rockwell to Paul Rockwell, 13 May 1915, in Rockwell, *War Letters,* 46–47.

30. Letter from Paul Pavelka to Alice Weeks, 3 October 1915, in Alice S. Weeks, ed., *Greater Love Hath No Man* (Boston: Bruce Humphries, 1939), 139–40. Musgrave was also an American volunteer.

31. Philip M. Flammer, *The Vivid Air: The Lafayette Escadrille* (Athens: University of Georgia Press, 1981), 6–7. Kenneth Weeks was never found, and after the war, when he failed to return after the prisoner exchanges, his status was changed to killed in action.

32. *La gamelle* (the mess tin) was a common insult hurled by the veterans at the volunteers who joined the Foreign Legion in 1914. It implies that the new men joined not out of patriotism or high ideals but only because they could not find work and needed food and money. Letter from Kiffin Rockwell to Paul Rockwell, 26 August 1915, in Rockwell, *War Letters,* 74.

33. Rockwell, *American Fighters,* 159–70.

34. Porch, *French Foreign Legion,* 364–65.

35. Diary entry, 1 September 1915, in Seeger, *Letters and Diary,* 154.

36. Ibid.

37. Porch, *French Foreign Legion,* 363. Part of the Legion was at Salonika, Greece, and the rest was in French North Africa helping to maintain order among the volatile Arab population.

38. Letter from Alan Seeger to his *marraine,* 4 June 1916, in Seeger, *Letters and Diary,* 206–7.

39. Ibid., letter from Alan Seeger to "A Friend," 28 June 1916, 211.

40 . Ibid., written statement of Legionnaire Rif Baer, 214.

41. Rockwell, *American Fighters,* 180, and Seeger, *Poems,* 144.

42. Reprinted in Paul Rockwell, *American Fighters,* 185.

43. Porch, *French Foreign Legion,* 368.

44. Citation à l'ordre du jour de la Division du Maroc, 25 décembre 1916, reprinted in Seeger, *Letters and Diary,* iii.

45. Rockwell, *American Fighters,* xiv.

46. By a strange coincidence, Pau was one of the major training facilities for

French pilots during the Great War, and Prince himself had his military flight training there.

47. The Service Aéronautique, like most aviation forces in World War I, was not an independent branch but a part of the French army.

48. Hall and Nordhoff, eds., *Lafayette Flying Corps*, 1: 243 and 392. Prince sailed for France on 20 January 1915 aboard the aptly named SS *Rochambeau*. By an odd coincidence, Edmond Genet, who had deserted from the U.S. Navy in order to go to France to join the Foreign Legion, was on board the same ship. After fifteen months of service in the trenches with the Legion, Genet transferred to the Escadrille Lafayette, where he became one of its most beloved pilots. A direct descendant of Citizen Genet, he was killed in action flying for France in April 1917.

49. See Harry Ammon, *The Genet Mission* (New York: Norton, 1973), and John C. Miller, *The Federalist Era, 1789–1801* (New York: Harper and Row, 1960), 126–39.

50. Hall and Nordhoff, ed., *Lafayette Flying Corps*, 1: 67–68.

51. Ibid. It is an interesting coincidence that the Vanderbilt family estate was in Asheville, North Carolina, the hometown of Paul and Kiffin Rockwell.

52. Because the Rockwell family was quite wealthy and socially well connected, Georges Leygues eagerly approved of the match. After the war, he became premier of France.

53. Flammer, *Vivid Air*, 18–19.

54. Hall and Nordhoff, eds., *Lafayette Flying Corps*, 10–11. The original Franco-American Committee was composed of Robert Bacon, Dr. Edmond Gros, Dr. William White, Senator Menier, Jarousse de Sillac, and Léon Bourgeois.

55. Parsons, *I Flew with the Lafayette Escadrille*, 43–45.

56. Letter from Kiffin Rockwell to Paul Rockwell, 27 September 1915, in Rockwell, *War Letters*, 87–88.

57. Parsons, *I Flew with the Lafayette Escadrille*, 15.

58. Flammer, *Vivid Air*, 25.

59. Ibid.

60. Jules Witcover, *Sabotage at Black Tom: Imperial Germany's Secret War in America, 1914–1917* (Chapel Hill, N.C.: Algonquin Books, 1989), 120–29.

61. Flammer, *Vivid Air*, 25–26.

62. Ibid., 26. Further German diplomatic protests did prompt a change in the name of the squadron from Escadrille Américaine to its more famous moniker, Escadrille Lafayette, in December 1916.

63. Letter from Kiffin Rockwell to his mother, 18 October 1915, in Rockwell, *War Letters*, 98–100: "Long live the American Aviator [who] Volunteered for France," and "I love the Aviator."

64. Parsons, *I Flew with the Lafayette Escadrille*, 61.

65. The French assigned squadron numbers based on a letter prefix designating the type of aircraft flown by the squadron and followed by a number. In the case of the Escadrille Américaine, the *N* stood for Nieuport, which referred to the Nieuport-11, and later for the Nieuport-17. When the squadron was later upgraded with the new SPAD-VII fighter, the designation was changed to SPA-124.

66. Georges Thénault, *The Story of the Lafayette Escadrille* (Nashville: Battery Press, 1990), 14–17.

67. Parsons, *I Flew with the Lafayette Escadrille,* 4–6.

68. When Thaw died in the United States, shortly after the war, his family found the empty bottle among his small collection of personal effects. It was sent to France and is now in the National Museum of Franco-American Cooperation in Blérancourt.

69. Erich von Falkenhayn, *General Headquarters and Its Critical Decisions, 1914–1916,* (London: Hutchinson, 1919), 210–11.

70. Ministère de la Guerre, *Les armées françaises dans la grande guerre,* vol. 4; *Verdun et la Somme;* vol. 3, *Bataille de la Somme (fin), offensives françaises à Verdun (3 septembre–fin décembre 1916)* (Paris: Imprimerie Nationale, 1936), 509.

71. Service Historique de l'Armée de Terre, *1916: Année de Verdun* (Paris: Charles Lavauzelle, 1996), 168–70. For details of the aerial battle in the skies over Verdun, see François Pernot, "Verdun 1916: Naissance de la chasse française," *Revue historique des armées* 2 (1996): 39 50, and Général Voisin, *La doctrine de l'aviation française de combat: Au cours de la guerre, 1915–1918* (Paris: Editions Berger-Levrault, 1932).

72. James R. McConnell to Marcelle Guerin, letter, 18 July 1915, James Rogers McConnell Memorial Collection, University of Virginia, Charlottesville (hereafter McConnell Collection).

73. James R. McConnell, *Flying for France: With the American Escadrille at Verdun* (Garden City, N.Y.: Doubleday, Page, 1917), 53–55.

74. *Outlook,* 15 September 1915, and Hall and Nordhoff, eds., *Lafayette Flying Corps,* 342–43.

75. James R. McConnell to Marcelle Guerin, letter, 13 June 1916, McConnell Collection.

76. Ibid. The Fokker E-III was a fast and agile monoplane armed with a synchronized machine gun. These were the premier German fighters in early 1916 and dominated the skies over Verdun until the introduction of the French Nieuport-17, during summer, tipped the scales back in favor of the French.

77. Edwin C. Parsons, *I Flew with the Lafayette Escadrille,* 150 51.

78. Thénault, *Lafayette Escadrille,* 60–61.

79. Letter from Kiffin Rockwell to Paul Rockwell, 23 June 1916, in Rockwell, *War Letters,* 136–38.

80. Ibid., letter from Kiffin Rockwell to Mrs. John J. Chapman, 30 June 1916, 139–43.

81. Theodore Roosevelt, "Lafayettes of the Air: Young Americans Who Are Flying for France," *Colliers,* 29 July 1916. For added emphasis Roosevelt dated his article "July 4th."

82. Thénault, *Lafayette Escadrille,* 61. One year later, on 4 July 1917, General John J. Pershing, the newly designated commander of the American Expeditionary Forces, took part in similar ceremonies at Picpus Cemetery, where his aide uttered the famous cry, "Lafayette, we are here!"

83. Flammer, *Vivid Air,* 74.

84. Thénault, *Lafayette Escadrille*, 104–5.

85. Letter from Kiffin Rockwell to Paul Rockwell, 27 July 1916, in Rockwell, *War Letters*, 146.

86. Thénault, *Lafayette Escadrille*, 157.

87. Parsons, *I Flew with the Lafayette Escadrille*, 253.

88. For photographs and descriptions of these memorials, see Paul Rockwell, *American Fighters*, 354–55.

89. Ibid., 356.

90. Flammer, *Vivid Air*, 202–3.

Chapter 2. America Embraces France

1. William Graves Sharp, *The War Memoirs of William Graves Sharp, American Ambassador to France, 1914–1919* (London: Constable, 1931), 182.

2. Alexandre Ribot, *Journal d'Alexandre Ribot et correspondances inédits, 1914–1922* (Paris: Plon, 1936), 52.

3. Sharp, *War Memoirs*, 182–83.

4. Ambassador William Graves Sharp to the U.S. State Department, telegram, 23 April 1917, reprinted in ibid., 183–84. See also Beckles Willson, *America's Ambassadors to France, 1777–1927* (New York: Frederick A. Stokes, 1928), 409. There was tremendous symbolism attached to this event. The statue of Washington evoked the memory of the Franco-American alliance in the American Revolution, and it was located at the Place d'Iéna, named for Napoleon's great victory over the Prussians in 1806, a happy coincidence that was not lost on the crowd in attendance.

5. General Robert Nivelle to General Hugh Scott, letter, 8 April 1917, Box 28, Papers of Hugh L. Scott, Library of Congress, Washington, D.C. (hereafter Scott Papers). Significantly, no similar message was ever sent to Scott by the British high command.

6. Ibid., General Hugh Scott to General Robert Nivelle, letter, 12 April 1917.

7. Sharp, *War Memoirs*, 189.

8. Joffre's critics have asserted that his poor class standing made him choose a military career instead of a more lucrative one as a civilian engineer with the French government. Yet he graduated in the middle of his class and could have gone either way in his career choice, so money was far from a motivating factor in this decision making process. Strong evidence shows that even before the war, Joffre was considering a military career, and his participation in the defense of Paris fueled his desire to devote his life to service in the French army.

9. In 1894 Captain Alfred Dreyfus was falsely accused of selling military secrets to Germany; the following year he was found guilty and sentenced to life imprisonment. The French Left was convinced that Dreyfus was innocent and believed his prosecution to be evidence of corruption within the French army's officer corps. After a bitter political battle that lasted years, the Left succeeded in using the affair to catapult themselves into control of the government. The *affaire*

des fiches erupted in 1904 when it was revealed that the French minister of war maintained files on every officer's political and religious beliefs, with information provided by the Freemasons, in order to block promotion of officers whose views did not coincide with those of the French Left. For a good, concise account of these scandals and their impact on the French army, see Douglas Porch, *The March to the Marne: The French Army, 1871–1914* (London: Cambridge University Press, 1981), 54–104.

10. In spite of the critically important role he played in the Great War, Joffre is an understudied French figure of that conflict, lost in the shadow of Marshal Ferdinand Foch and Marshal Philippe Pétain and virtually ignored by the Anglophonic historical community. The standard biographical works on Joffre are Arthur Conte, *Joffre* (Paris: Perrin, 1998); Pierre Varillon, *Joffre* (Paris: Libraire Artheme Fayard, 1956); Raymond Recouly, *Joffre* (Paris: Éditions des portiques, 1931); and Jean Fabry, *Joffre et son destin* (Paris: Charles Lavauzelle, 1931). See also Jean Blondel, "Joffre raconté par lui-même," *Revue historique des armées*, 11, 1 (1984): 30–41.

11. Jean de Pierrefeu, *French Headquarters, 1915–1918,* trans. C. J. C. Street (London: Geoffrey Bles, 1924), 29–30. On the First Battle of the Marne and Joffre's role in it, see also Commandant Muller, *Joffre et la Marne* (Paris: G. Grès, 1931); Henri Isselin, *La bataille de la Marne* (Grenoble: Arthaud, 1964); Georges Blond, *La Marne* (Paris: Les Presses de la Cité, 1962); and B. H. Liddell-Hart, *Reputations: Ten Years After* (Boston: Little, Brown, 1928). Joffre's exact role in the First Battle of the Marne is a matter of some debate. Initially, the French press (and the Allied and neutral nations' press corps as well) acclaimed Joffre as the "victor of the Marne" and heaped accolades upon him. During the interwar period, his command at the Marne was called into question by historians such as B. H. Liddell-Hart, who severely criticized his abilities as a commander and gave credit for the victory to the French military governor of Paris, General Joseph Simon Gallieni. Later historians such as Henri Isselin and Georges Blond have challenged Liddell-Hart's scathing criticisms and, though acknowledging Gallieni's importance in the battle, argue that Joffre still played the pivotal role in the French decision to make a stand before Paris and to launch the successful counteroffensive.

12. Jere Clemens King, *Generals and Politicians: Conflict Between France's High Command, Parliament and Government, 1914–1918* (Berkeley: University of California Press, 1951), 11–66.

13. Le Général Commandement en Chef les Armées Françaises à Monsieur le Ministre de la Guerre, 14 décembre 1916, 1 K 268, Service Historique de l'Armée de Terre, Archives de la Guerre, Château de Vincennes, Vincennes, France (hereafter SHAT).

14. Joseph Jacques Césaire Joffre, *Journal de marche de Joffre (1916–1919),* ed. Guy Pedroncini (Vincennes: Service Historique de l'Armée de Terre/Fondation pour les études de Défense nationale, 1990) (hereafter *Journal de marche*), entrevue du général en chef et de M. Briand, le 3 décembre 1916, 174–76; conversation du général en chef avec M. Briand, le 12 décembre, 180–81; and entries for 27 December 1916, 194–96. See also King, *Generals and Politicians,* 89–114, 135–39, and Joseph

Joffre, *The Personal Memoirs of Joffre, Field Marshal of the French Army*, trans. T. Bentley Mott, 2 vols. (New York: Harper and Brothers, 1932), 2: 541–43. General Robert Nivelle succeeded Joffre as commanding general of the French army with the new title of commander in chief of the French Armies of the North and Northeast.

15. Deuxieme Bureau, État-Major de l'Armée au Ministère de la Guerre, 1 avril 1917, 7 N 1720, SHAT, and Joffre, *Journal de marche*,1 avril 1917, 207.

16. Joffre, *Memoirs*, 2: 566–67.

17. Letter from Robert Lansing to Woodrow Wilson, 6 April 1917, 41: 553–54, and letter from Woodrow Wilson to Robert Lansing, 8 April 1917, 42: 14, both in *PWW*.

18. Jean Jules Jusserand au Ministère des Affaires Étrangères, télégramme, 10 avril 1917, 14 N 26, SHAT, and Sharp, *War Memoirs*, 190.

19. Jean Jules Jusserand to Major General Hugh L. Scott, letter, 13 April 1917, Box 28, Scott Papers. Accounts that have asserted or implied that the British and French missions were allied are numerous and include (but are not limited to) Robert H. Ferrell, *Woodrow Wilson and World War I, 1917–1921* (New York: Harper and Row, 1985); Daniel R. Beaver, *Newton D. Baker and the American War Effort, 1917–1919* (Lincoln: University of Nebraska Press, 1966); and Edward M. Coffman, *The War to End All Wars: The American Military Experience in World War I* (New York: Oxford University Press, 1968).

20. Paul Painlevé au Attaché Militaire [Colonel P. Vignal] à Washington, D.C., 24 mars 1917, 14 N 27, SHAT.

21. Ibid., Général Robert Nivelle à Monsieur le Ministère de la Guerre [Paul Painlevé] 11 Mai 1917, 14 N 27.

22. Chief of the Military Mission, Paris [Colonel James A. Logan] to chief of the Army War College, War College Division, G. S. [Brigadier General Joseph E. Kuhn], letter, 13 April 1917, 10050-2, RG 165, National Archives and Records Administration (NARA).

23. Paul Painlevé to Attaché Militaire [Col. P. Vignal] at Washington, letter, 14 April 1917, 10050-7, RG 165, NARA.

24. Joffre, *Memoirs*, 2: 568.

25. Joseph Joffre to Paul Painlevé, letter, 20 May 1917, in U.S. Army Dept., *The United States Army in the World War, 1917–1919*, 17 vols. (Washington, D.C.: GPO, 1948), 2: 4 (hereafter *USAWW*), and Joffre, *Memoirs*, 2: 568.

26. Joffre, *Memoirs*, 2: 569; Recouly, *Joffre*, 344; and Pierre Lesouef, "La mission du maréchal Joffre aux États-Unis au moment de leur entrée en guerre," *Revue historique des armées* 11 (March 1984): 23. For details of the Nivelle offensive and its disastrous consequences, see Général Charles Mangin, *Comment finit la guerre* (Paris: Plon, 1920), 128–53, and Jean de Pierrefeu, *French Headquarters: 1915–1918* (London: Geoffrey Bles, 1924), 144–83. For details on the French army mutinies, see Guy Pedroncini, *Les mutineries de 1917* (Paris: Presses Universitaires de France, 1967); Richard M. Watt, *Dare Call It Treason* (New York: Simon and Schuster, 1963); and Leonard V. Smith, *Between Mutiny and Obedience: The Case of the French Fifth Infantry Division During World War I* (Princeton: Princeton University Press, 1994).

27. Joffre, *Memoirs*, 2: 570.

28. Fabry, *Joffre et son destin*, 246.

29. *New York Times*, 25 April 1917, and *New York Evening Post*, 25 April 1917.

30. Thomas W. Brahany, Diary, 25 April 1917, *PWW*, 42:132–33.

31. Francis W. Halsey, ed., *Balfour, Viviani and Joffre: Their Speeches and Other Public Utterances in America* (New York: Funk and Wagnall's, 1917), 9.

32. Palmer C. Ricketts to General Hugh L. Scott, letter, 30 April 1917, Scott Papers.

33. Edward M. House, Diary, 30 April 1917, *PWW*, 42: 169–70, and Recouly, *Joffre*, 346.

34. Address of Marshal Joseph Joffre to the U.S. Army War College, 27 April 1917, 9971-C-4, RG 165, NARA.

35. Major General Harrison Otis to Major General Hugh Scott, telegram, 2 April 1917, and Major General Hugh Scott to Major General Harrison Otis, letter, 3 April 1917, Box 28, Scott Papers.

36. Ibid., Major General Hugh Scott to Brigadier General James A. Buchanan, letter, 25 April 1917.

37. Paraphrase of confidential conference between Marshal Joffre and the chief of staff [Major General Hugh Scott] at the Army War College on 27 April 1917, 9971-C-4, RG 165, NARA.

38. Ibid.

39. Ibid.

40. Frederick Palmer, *Newton D. Baker: America at War*, 2 vols. (New York: Dodd, Mead, 1931), 1: 184, 193; Beaver, *Newton D. Baker and the American War Effort*, 30–35; and John W. Chambers II, *To Raise an Army: The Draft Comes to Modern America* (New York: Free Press, 1987), 125–77.

41. Sharp, *War Memoirs*, 191; Fabry, *Joffre et son destin*, 250–51; and Colonel de Chambrun and Captain Marenches, *The American Army in the European Conflict* (New York: Macmillan, 1919), 12–13.

42. Joffre, *Memoirs*, 2: 572.

43. Edward M. House, Diary, 30 April 1917, *PWW*, 42: 169–70.

44. Ibid., from "Narrative by an Unknown Person," 30 April 1917, 42: 173–74. The unknown person was an unidentified member of Jusserand's staff.

45. Ibid., Jean Jules Jusserand to the [French] Foreign Ministry, telegram, 1 May 1917, 42: 183–84, and *New York Times*, 1 May 1917.

46. *Washington Post*, 2 May 1917; *New York Times*, 2 May 1917; *New York World*, 2 May 1917; Halsey, ed., *Balfour, Viviani and Joffre*, 50; and Conte, *Joffre*, 403.

47. Minutes of Woodrow Wilson's conversation with Joseph-Jacques-Césaire Joffre, 2 May 1917, *PWW*, 42: 186–91, and Fabry, *Joffre et son destin*, 253–60.

48. *PWW*, 42: 186–91.

49. Joffre, *Memoirs*, 2: 575.

50. *Washington Post*, 4 May 1917, and ibid.

51. Arthur S. Link, *Woodrow Wilson and the Progressive Era, 1910–1917* (New York: Harper and Row, 1954), 218–22.

52. John Patrick Finnegan, *Against the Specter of a Dragon: The Campaign for*

American Military Preparedness, 1914–1917 (Westport, Conn.: Greenwood Press, 1974), 175–76.

53. Kenneth J. Hagan, *This People's Navy: The Making of American Sea Power* (New York: Free Press, 1991), 255.

54. Ibid., 257–80; David M. Kennedy, *Over Here: The First World War and American Society* (New York: Oxford University Press, 1980), 324–26, and Thomas Wildenberg, "In Support of the Battle Line: Gunnery's Influence on the Development of Carrier Aviation in the U.S. Navy," *Journal of Military History* 65 (July 2001): 697–711.

55. Joseph Edward Cuddy, *Irish-America and National Isolationism, 1914–1920* (New York: Arno Press, 1976), 107–16. On the role of the United States in the Irish nationalist movement, see Charles C. Tansil, *America and the Fight for Irish Freedom: 1866–1922* (New York: Devin-Adair, 1957). There are numerous works on the Irish Easter Rising and the Irish independence movement during World War I. Among the best are Peter de Rosa, *Rebels: The Irish Easter Rising of 1916* (New York: Fawcett Columbine 1990), and Ulick O'Connor, *Michael Collins and the Troubles: The Struggle for Irish Freedom, 1912–1922* (New York: Norton, 1996).

56. *Chicago Daily Tribune,* 1 May 1917.

57. *New York World,* 30 April 1917.

58. Ibid.

59. Robert Lansing, *War Memoirs of Robert Lansing* (Indianapolis: Bobbs-Merrill, 1935), 277.

60. *New York World,* 25 April 1917.

61. John J. Pershing, *My Experiences in the First World War,* 2 vols. (New York: Da Capo, 1995), 1: 32, and Coffman, *The War to End All Wars,* 9–10.

62. Major General Hugh L. Scott to Captain Frank R. McCoy, letter, 30 April 1917, Box 28, Scott Papers.

63. General G. T. M. Bridges to Major General Hugh Scott, letter reprinted in Pershing, *My Experiences,* 1: 32–33.

64. Newton D. Baker to Woodrow Wilson, letter, 2 May 1917, 42: 192, and Woodrow Wilson to Newton D. Baker, letter, 3 May 1917, 42: 202, both in *PWW.*

65. Joffre, *Memoirs,* 2: 575.

66. *Chicago Herald,* 28 April 1917, and *Chicago Daily Tribune,* 28 April 1917.

67. *Chicago Daily News,* 3 May 1917.

68. *Chicago Herald,* 4 May 1917, and *Chicago Daily Tribune,* 4 May 1917.

69. *Chicago Herald,* 4 May 1917, and *Chicago Daily Tribune,* 4 May 1917.

70. *Chicago Herald, Chicago Daily Tribune,* and *Chicago Daily News,* 4 May 1917, and Halsey, ed., *Balfour, Viviani and Joffre,* 114.

71. *Chicago Daily Tribune,* 2 May 1917.

72. Ibid., 5 May 1917, and *Chicago Daily News,* 4 May 1917.

73. *Chicago Daily Tribune,* 8 May 1917. Thompson had a difficult time recovering from his error in opposing the visit of the French mission; he left the city while it was still there and went on a retreat. When he returned, he refused to give interviews to the press or to hold press conferences for some time, claiming that the Chicago press had distorted his remarks.

74. *Chicago Herald,* 5 May 1917.

75. Ibid. A song sheet that included the words to the "Marseillaise" had been distributed to the crowd.

76. *Chicago Daily Tribune,* 5 May 1917, and *Chicago Herald,* 5 May 1917.

77. *Chicago Daily News,* 7 May 1917, and Associated Press reports for 7 May 1917 appearing in numerous papers.

78. *Current History* 6, 3 (June 1917): 397.

79. *Chicago Daily Tribune,* 5 May 1917.

80. *Boston Herald,* 13 May 1917.

81. Ibid., 3 May 1917.

82. Ibid., 13 May 1917.

83. René Viviani and Joseph Joffre, *Addresses in the United States by M. René Viviani and Marshal Joffre, French Mission to the United States, April–May 1917* (Garden City, N.Y.: Doubleday, Page, 1917), 149. Doubleday, Page donated all proceeds from the sale of this book to "the orphan children of France."

84. Le Maréchal Joffre à Monsieur le Ministère de la Guerre [Paul Painlevé], 20 mai 1917, 7 N 1720, SHAT.

85. This became a prerogative that Pershing exercised during America's involvement in World War I, much to the exasperation of the French.

86. The U.S. Army's only experience with such large formations had been in the American Civil War. From 1865 to 1917, the largest independent formations deployed in battle were brigades consisting of two regiments each. Indeed, the entire U.S. expeditionary force sent to Cuba during the Spanish-American War was designated the U.S. V Corps; and at a strength of approximately 17,000 men, it was smaller than a single division in the U.S. Army during the Great War.

87. Le Maréchal Joffre à Monsieur le Ministère de la Guerre [Painlevé], 20 mai 1917, 7 N 1720, SHAT.

88. Ibid.

89. Ibid.

90. Ibid.

91. Sharp, *War Memoirs,* 181.

92. Joffre, *Journal de marche,* lettre reçue par le maréchal chez lui, le dimanche 3 juin.

93. Ibid., 11 juin 1917, note, à joindre au procès-verbal de la conference du 11 juin relative à la cooperation américaine.

Chapter 3. The Arrival of the American Expeditionary Force in France

1. Donald Smythe, *Pershing: General of the Armies* (Bloomington: Indiana University Press, 1986), 5, and Frederick Palmer, *Newton D. Baker: America at War,* 2 vols. (New York: Dodd, Mead, 1931), 1: 7–10.

2. The other two serious candidates for the position were Major General Thomas H. Barry and Major General J. Franklin Bell, both of whom were quickly ruled out by Secretary of War Baker and U.S. Army Chief of Staff General Hugh

Scott, due to their age and ill health. Scott was only a few months short of retirement, and thus he was not a contender for the position, either. See Palmer, *Baker*, 1:161–62.

3. Wood was promoted to the rank of major general in 1903; Pershing was promoted to major general in 1906.

4. The best biography of Wood is Jack C. Lane, *Armed Progressive: General Leonard Wood* (San Rafael, Calif.: Presidio Press, 1978).

5. Lane, *Armed Progressive*, 145–47; Smythe, *Pershing*, 3; Palmer, *Baker*, 1: 165; and Peyton C. March, *The Nation at War* (Garden City, N.Y.: Doubleday, Doran, 1932), 59. Wood's desk had been temporarily moved to a new location by an orderly who was cleaning the general's office. Wood was seated at the relocated desk when he was called to another room. Rising quickly from his chair, he severely banged his head against a low-hanging chandelier that he had forgotten was hanging over his desk in its new location and was knocked senseless. He seemed to recover quickly but soon developed severe headaches and even had seizures. After several surgeries, his health improved only slightly, and he had to wear a steel plate in his head. Moreover, the nerve damage he had suffered as a result of the accident and subsequent surgeries caused him to develop a serious limp. By 1917 his left leg was essentially useless, and he dragged it when he walked.

6. March, *Nation at War*, 60.

7. Joseph L. Gardner, *Departing Glory: Theodore Roosevelt as ex-President* (New York: Charles Scribner's Sons, 1973), 337–39. On the rivalry between Roosevelt and Wilson, see John Milton Cooper Jr., *The Warrior and the Priest: Woodrow Wilson and Theodore Roosevelt* (Cambridge: Harvard University Press, 1983). In 1916 Wood further alienated himself from Wilson when he ran as a candidate in the Republican presidential primary election.

8. John J. Pershing, *My Experiences in the First World War*, 2 vols. (1935; reprint New York: Da Capo, 1995), 1: 1.

9. Ibid. Pershing later freely admitted that he had exaggerated his abilities in French because he suspected that a large, important assignment was at stake.

10. Avery D. Andrews, *My Friend and Classmate John J. Pershing* (Harrisburg, Pa.: Stackpole Books, 1939), 75.

11. Frank E. Vandiver, *Black Jack*, 2 vols. (College Station: Texas A&M University Press, 1977), 32.

12. For Pershing's service in the Spanish-American War, see his essay in Herschel V. Cashin et al., *Under Fire with the Tenth U.S. Cavalry* (London: Tennyson, 1899), and Donald Smythe, "John J. Pershing in the Spanish-American War," *Military Affairs* 30 (spring 1966): 25–33. For details of Pershing's service in the Philippines, see Donald Smythe, *Guerrilla Warrior: The Early Life of John J. Pershing* (New York: Scribner's, 1973).

13. See John S. D. Eisenhower, *Intervention! The United States Involvement in the Mexican Revolution, 1913–1917* (New York: Norton, 1993), and Herbert Molloy Mason, *The Great Pursuit: Pershing's Expedition to Destroy Pancho Villa* (New York: Random House, 1970).

14. [Jean Jules] Jusserand au Ministère d'Affaires Étrangères, telegramme, 20 mai 1917, 14 N 26, SHAT.

15. Ironically, the *Baltic* was a British liner. During the course of the Great War, British vessels transported approximately 50 percent of the U.S. soldiers sent to Europe, yet upon arrival the vast majority were immediately assigned to the French army zone for training and eventual combat duty, a fact that bothered the British no end.

16. Pershing, *My Experiences,* 1: 78.

17. James G. Harbord, *The American Expeditionary Forces: Its Organization and Accomplishments* (Evanston, Ill.: Evanston Publishing, 1929), 5–7, and Pershing, *My Experiences,* 1: 19. Theodore Roosevelt had offered Harbord command of a brigade in the Volunteer Division that Roosevelt was attempting to organize, but Harbord turned it down.

18. James G. Harbord, *Leaves from a War Diary* (New York: Dodd, Mead, 1925), 6–7.

19. Pershing, *My Experiences,* 1: 43.

20. James G. Harbord, *The American Army in France, 1917–1919* (Boston: Little, Brown, 1936), 73.

21. Letter from George S. Patton Jr. to Beatrice Patton, 1 June 1917, in Martin Blumenson, ed., *The Patton Papers, 1885–1940,* 2 vols. (Boston: Houghton-Mifflin, 1972), 1: 424.

22. Harbord, *War Diary,* 17–18.

23. Pershing, *My Experiences,* 1: 46.

24. Ibid, 1: 48.

25. Ibid., 1: 52, and Vandiver, *Black Jack,* 1: 3.

26. Vandiver, *Black Jack,* 2: 711.

27. James S. Olson, *The Ethnic Dimension in American History* (New York: St. Martin's Press, 1979), 208. See also Alan M. Kraut, *The Huddled Masses: The Immigrant in American Society, 1880–1921* (Arlington Heights, Ill.: Harlan Davidson, 1982).

28. Kendrick A. Clements, *The Presidency of Woodrow Wilson* (Lawrence: University Press of Kansas, 1992), 19–20; Arthur S. Link, *Woodrow Wilson and the Progressive Era, 1910–1917* (New York: Harper and Row, 1954), 245–46; and Cooper, *Warrior and the Priest,* 308.

29. Harbord, *War Diary,* 41.

30. Ibid.

31. See the photograph of James G. Harbord interrogating a German prisoner during the Battle of Belleau Wood in photo section. See also the frontispiece to Harbord, *American Expeditionary Forces.*

32. Pershing, *My Experiences,* 1: 57.

33. General John J. Pershing to adjutant general in Washington, D.C., cable, 13 June 1917, *USAWW,* 2: 13.

34. Ibid.; Pershing, *My Experiences,* 1: 58–59; Patton, *Patton Papers,* 1: 429.

35. Harbord, *War Diary,* 43, and Pershing, *My Experiences,* 1: 59.

36. The Hôtel des Invalides remains to this day a supreme monument to the glorious history of the French army. It is also a veterans' home.

37. William Mitchell, *Memoirs of World War I: From Start to Finish of Our Greatest War* (New York: Random House, 1960), 140–41; Harbord, *War Diary*, 86; Patton, *Patton Papers*, 1: 429.

38. Pershing, *My Experiences*, 1: 60–61.

39. He had replaced Joffre in December 1916.

40. Guy Pedroncini, *Pétain: Le soldat et la gloire, 1856–1918* (Paris: Perrin, 1989), 156–59.

41. See chapter 2 for details on Joffre's relief.

42. Gabriel Terrail, *Nivelle et Painlevé: La deuxieme crise du commandement* (Paris: P. Ollendorf, 1919), 13–14. For details on the relationship between the French government and the French army during World War I, see Jere Clemens King, *Generals and Politicians: Conflict Between France's High Command, Parliament and Government, 1914–1918* (Berkeley: University of California Press, 1951).

43. Général B. Palat, *La Grande Guerre sur le front occidental*, vol. 12, *L'Annee d'angoisse, 1917* (Paris: Berger-Levrault, 1927), 15–45; Général Charles Mangin, *Comment finit la guerre* (Paris: Librairie Plon, 1920), 112–15; Pedroncini, *Pétain: Le soldat et la gloire*, 159–60.

44. Jean de Pierrefeu, *French Headquarters, 1915–1918,* trans. C. J. C. Street (London: Geoffrey Bles, 1924), 119.

45. Rapport sur la correspondance des troupes du 10 au 25 fevrier 1917, GQG Controle Postal, 16 N 1485, SHAT.

46. Mangin, *Comment finit la guerre*, 117–18, and Rod Paschall, *The Defeat of Imperial Germany, 1917–1918* (1989; reprint, New York: Da Capo, 1994), 36.

47. Erich Ludendorff, *Ludendorff's Own Story*, 2 vols. (New York: Harper and Brothers, 1920), 2: 4–9.

48. Ibid., 2: 4, 8–9. Given the code name Operation Alberich, after the destructive dwarf in the *Nibelungen* saga, Ludendorff's order to destroy this region of France was widely condemned both during and after the war and was described by S. L. A. Marshall as "one of the most fiendish affairs in modern history" (S. L. A. Marshall, *World War I* [New York: American Heritage, 1985], 289). Ludendorff defended his actions by claiming they were militarily necessary and were "in accordance with the laws of warfare and had not even gone so far as the belligerents in the American Civil War."

49. In fact, the new Kerensky government made herculean efforts to keep Russia in the war and even launched a brief offensive in July 1917. The attack quickly broke down, however, and with it the last will to fight of the Russian army, as Russia collapsed into anarchy and civil war. See Norman Stone, *The Eastern Front, 1914–1917* (London: Penguin, 1998), 282–301.

50. Paul Painlevé, *Comment j'ai nommé Foch et Pétain* (Paris: Librairie Féix Alcan, 1923), 30–31.

51. Ibid.

52. Ibid., 41–43, and Edward L. Spears, *Prelude to Victory* (London: Cape, 1930), 338.

53. Palat, *L'Année d'angoisse*, 163–67.

54. Ibid., 168.

55. King, *Generals and Politicians*, 156–58.

56. Mangin, *Comment finit la guerre*, 124, and Richard M. Watt, *Dare Call It Treason* (New York: Simon and Schuster, 1963), 169.

57. Painlevé, *Comment j'ai nommé Foch et Pétain*, 52–54; Stephen Ryan, *Pétain the Soldier* (New York: Barnes, 1969), 112; King, *Generals and Politicians*, 158.

58. Alexandre Ribot, *Lettres à un ami* (Paris: Bossard, 1924), 190; Watt, *Dare Call It Treason*, 169–70; King, *Generals and Politicians*, 158–59; and Painlevé, *Comment j'ai nommé Foch et Pétain*, 52–54.

59. Rapport sur la correspondance des troupes du 10 au 25 avril 1917, 16 N 1486, SHAT.

60. Palat, *L'Année d'angoisse*, 237–70. For more information on the Nivelle offensive, see also R. G. Nobecourt, *Les fantassins du Chemin des Dames* (Paris: Robert Laffont, 1965), and Général Hellot et al., *Histoire de la guerre mondiale: Collection de memoires, études et documents pour servir à l'histoire de la guerre mondiale*, 4 vols. (Paris: Payot, 1936–1937), vol. 3, *Le commandement des généraux Nivelle et Pétain, 1917.*

61. Palat, *L'Anné d'angoisse*, 237–70.

62. Ibid.; John H. Morrow Jr., *The Great War in the Air* (Washington, D.C.: Smithsonian Institution Press, 1993), 198–99; John H. Morrow Jr., *German Air Power in World War I* (Lincoln: University of Nebraska Press, 1982), 91; and Norman Franks et al., *Under the Guns of the Red Baron* (New York: Barnes and Noble, 1998), 89–136.

63. Palat, *L'Année d'angoisse*, 269–70; Mangin, *Comment finit la guerre*, 132–35; Pedroncini, *Pétain: Le soldat et la gloire*, 161–62.

64. France, Armée, État-major, Service Historique, *Les armées françaises dans la Grande Guerre*, 11 tomes, 132 vols. (Paris: Imprimerie Nationale, 1922–1939), tome 5, vol. 1, 689–712 (hereafter AFGG).

65. Ryan, *Pétain the Soldier*, 115–16.

66. Rapport sur la correspondance des troupes du 10 au 25 avril 1917, 16 N 1486, SHAT.

67. Ibid., rapport sur la correspondance des troupes du 25 avril au 10 mai 1917, 16 N 1486, and État-Major de l'Armée, Deuxieme Bureau, L'État de l'Opinion en France, 15 avril–15 mai 1917 et 15 mai–15 juin 1917, 7 N 867.

68. Pedroncini, *Les mutineries*, 181–278; Jean-Baptiste Duroselle, *La Grande Guerre des français, 1914–1918* (1994; reprint, Paris: Perrin, 1998), 203; and Watt, *Dare Call It Treason*, 177–78.

69. Jean-Jacques Becker, *The Great War and the French People*, trans. Arnold Pomerans (1985; reprint, Providence, R.I.: Berg, 1993), 205–16; Margaret H. Darrow, *French Women and the First World War* (New York: Berg, 2000), 194–97; and Patrick Fridenson, ed., *The French Home Front, 1914–1918* (New York: Berg, 1992), 203–7. There has been some speculation that the female factory workers went on strike in support of their men on strike at the front, but there is little evidence that the French people knew much about the mutinies at the time, other than rumors.

70. Rapport sur les letters subversives parvenus au GQG, 6 juin 1917, 16 N 1486, SHAT.

71. Ryan, *Pétain the Soldier,* 117.

72. Charles de Gaulle, *France and Her Army,* trans. F. L. Dash (London: Hutchinson, 1945), 103.

73. Guy Pedroncini is the leading authority on Pétain. His large body of work on this controversial French marshal has accomplished much toward a defense of Pétain's reputation by highlighting his accomplishments and service to France during the Great War.

74. Philippe Pétain, "A Crisis of Morale in the French Nation at War," trans. Rivers Scott, in Edward Spears, *Two Men Who Saved France: Pétain and de Gaulle* (New York: Stein and Day, 1966), 99–104.

75. See, for example, Leon Wolff, *In Flanders Fields: The 1917 Campaign* (New York: Viking, 1958).

76. Guy Pedroncini, *Les mutineries,* 183–231, and Marc Ferro, *The Great War* (London: Routledge and Kegan Paul, 1977), 184.

77. Pétain, "Crisis of Morale," 112.

78. Ibid., 112–13.

79. Ibid., 112.

80. Ibid., 115.

81. Ibid., 110–11, 123–24, and Guy Pedroncini, *Pétain, général en chef, 1917–1918,* 2d ed. (Paris: Presses Universitaires de France, 1997), 63–91.

82. Pierrefeu, *French Headquarters,* 180.

83. Pétain, "Crisis of Morale," 106.

84. Général Laure, *Le commandement en chef des armées françaises: du 15 mai 1917 à l'armistice* (Paris: Éditions Berger-Levrault, 1937), 8; Pedroncini, *Pétain: Le soldat,* 170–81; and Pierre Miquel, *La Grande Guerre* (Paris: Fayard, 1983), 407.

85. Spears, *Two Men Who Saved France.*

86. The major work that espouses this view is Leonard V. Smith, *Between Mutiny and Obedience: The Case of the French Fifth Infantry Division* (Princeton: Princeton University Press, 1994).

87. Jay Luvaas, ed., *Napoleon on the Art of War* (New York: Free Press, 1999), 61.

88. Specifically, his views clashed with those of supreme Allied commander Marshal Ferdinand Foch and French Premier Georges Clemenceau.

89. General Philippe Pétain, "Note on the Utilization of the Resources of the United States," April 26, 1917, 10050-18, RG 165, NARA.

90. Colonel James A. Logan Jr., chief of the military mission [to France] to chief of the War College Division [Brigadier General Joseph Kuhn], General Staff, Washington, D.C., letter, 10 May 1917, 6718-91, RG 165, NARA.

91. Maréchal Joffre au Général Pétain 9 juin 1917, 14 N 26, SHAT.

92. Joffre, *Journal de marche,* 11 juin 1917, note, à joindre au procès-verbal de la conference du 11 juin relative à la cooperation américaine; see also chapter 2.

93. Maréchal Joffre au Ministre de la Guerre [Painlevé] 10 juin 1917, 14 N 26, SHAT.

94. Ibid., entrevue du Maréchal Joffre et du Général Pershing 16 juin 1917, 14 N 26, SHAT.

95. Marshal Joffre to General Pershing, letter, 16 June 1917, 2: 13, and final report of General John J. Pershing, 1 September 1919, 12: 75, both in *USAWW*.

96. Robert A. Doughty, "More Than Numbers: Americans and the Revival of French Morale in the Great War," *Army History* 52 (spring 2001): 1–10.

97. Pershing, *My Experiences,* 1: 63.

98. Harbord, *War Diary,* 52.

99. Ibid.

100. Ibid., 48, and Charles Rearick, *The French in Love and War: Popular Culture in the Era of the World Wars* (New Haven: Yale University Press, 1997), 28.

101. Harbord, *War Diary,* 48.

102. Marianne has been used as a symbol for the Republic since the early nineteenth century and was first depicted in Eugene Delacroix's famous painting *Liberté Guidant la Peuple,* which showed a young bare-breasted woman with tricolor in hand leading the citizens of Paris in the 1830 revolution.

103. George C. Marshall, *Memoirs of My Service in the World War, 1917–1918* (Boston: Houghton Mifflin, 1976), 12. Marshall had meant to say, "Il fait très beau aujourd'hui" (The weather is very beautiful today), but instead had said, "Je suis très beau aujourd'hui" (I am very handsome today).

104. General Order no. 91 from *Grand Quartier Général des Armées du Nord et Nord Est,* 3 July 1917. See papers of John J. Pershing, Box 160, Library of Congress, Washington, D.C. (hereafter Pershing Papers).

105. Pershing, *My Experiences,* 1: 92.

106. Harbord, *War Diary,* 86–87.

107. Ferdinand Foch, "The American Soldier in the World War as Seen by a Friend," in *As They Saw Us: Foch, Ludendorff and Other Leaders Write Our War History,* ed. George S. Viereck (Garden City, N.Y.: Doubleday, Doran, 1929), 8–9.

108. Pershing, *My Experiences,* 1: 92; Patton, diary entry, 4 July 1917, *Patton Papers,* 1: 437; Harbord, *War Diary,* 87–88; and Smythe, *Pershing,* 33.

109. André Kaspi, *Le temps des Américains, 1917–1918* (Paris: Publications de la Sorbonne, 1976), 129.

110. Pershing, *My Experiences,* 1: 92.

111. "Lafayette, we are here!" Pershing, *My Experiences,* 1: 93; and Smythe, *Pershing,* 33.

112. Letter from Quentin Roosevelt to his family, 18 August 1917, in Quentin Roosevelt, *Quentin Roosevelt: A Sketch with Letters,* ed. Kermit Roosevelt (New York: Charles Scribner's Sons, 1921), 42–43.

113. General John J. Pershing to Secretary of War Newton D. Baker, cable, 6 July 1917, *USAWW,* 2: 17.

114. Ibid.; the AEF eventually numbered close to 2 million men by the time the war ended.

Chapter 4. The Role of France in Arming and Training
the American Expeditionary Forces

1. From 1898 to 1917 the U.S. Army had participated in two major wars, the Spanish-American War of 1898 and the Philippine Insurrection of 1899–1902. American soldiers and marines also had taken part in suppressing the Boxer Rebellion in 1900 and in the Moro campaigns in the Philippines from 1902 to 1905. In addition, the United States sent armed forces into Cuba in 1906 and into Honduras and Nicaragua in 1912; occupied Veracruz, Mexico, in 1914; intervened in Haiti in 1915; and launched the Punitive Expedition into Mexico in 1916. For specific details of these campaigns and a general overview of the army during this period, see David Trask, *The War with Spain in 1898* (New York: Macmillan, 1981); Brian Linn, *The Philippine War, 1899–1902* (Lawrence: University Press of Kansas, 2000); John S. D. Eisenhower, *Intervention! The United States and the Mexican Revolution, 1913–1917* (New York: Norton, 1995); Max Boot, *The Savage Wars of Peace: Small Wars and the Rise of American Power* (New York: Basic Books, 2002); and Timothy K. Nenninger, *The Leavenworth Schools and the Old Army: Education, Professionalism, and the Officer Corps of the United States Army, 1881–1918* (Westport, Conn.: Greenwood Press, 1978).

2. Leonard P. Ayres, *The War with Germany: A Statistical Summary* (Washington, D.C.: GPO, 1919), 11, 16, 21.

3. Men such as John C. Frémont, Franz Sigel, and Benjamin Butler (to name a few) had attained their commissions as generals because of their political connections and retained their high rank because of them, even after proving themselves to be utterly inept on the battlefield. For an excellent discussion of these political generals and the problems they caused, see T. Harry Williams, *Lincoln and His Generals* (New York: Knopf, 1952).

4. For details on the debate in the United States over whether to raise a volunteer or a conscript army during World War I, see John W. Chambers II, *To Raise an Army: The Draft Comes to Modern America* (New York: Free Press, 1987).

5. Ayres, *The War with Germany*, 16, and James W. Rainey, "The Questionable Training of the AEF in World War I," *Parameters* 22, 4 (winter 1992–1993): 89–103.

6. The modern parallel to this system of training would be the basic training given to all army recruits, which is then followed by advanced individual training, where the recruits are sent to advanced schools to learn their specific specialty.

7. Ayers, *War with Germany*, 31. The British sent over 261 training officers as well.

8. Rainey, "Questionable Training," 92–99.

9. Final report of General John J. Pershing, 1 September 1919, *USAWW*, 12: 76.

10. John J. Pershing, *My Experiences in the First World War*, 2 vols. (1935; reprint, New York: Da Capo, 1995), 1: 107.

11. Boyd L. Dastrup, *King of Battle: A Branch History of the U.S. Army's Field Artillery* (Washington, D.C.: U.S. Army Center of Military History, 1993), 164–65. Ironically, the original M1902 3-inch gun, although scarce, was at least available

and suffered from none of the problems that the improved M1916 3-inch gun did. In fact, in tests conducted after the war, the M1902 3-inch gun performed almost as well, and some said better, than the famed French M1897 75mm gun that the U.S. Army used during the war.

12. William J. Snow, *Signposts of Experience: World War Memoirs* (Washington, D.C.: U.S. Field Artillery Association, 1941), 242.

13. Report by French GQG G-4, 25 October 1917, 403-40.9, RG 165, NARA.

14. Harvey A. De Weerd, "The American Adoption of French Artillery, 1917–1918," *Journal of American Military Institute* 3 (summer 1939): 104–16; final report of General John J. Pershing, 1 September 1919, *USAWW*, 12: 76.

15. De Weerd, "American Adoption of French Artillery, 1917–1918," 104–16.

16. James A. Huston, *The Sinews of War: Army Logistics, 1775–1953* (Washington, D.C:. U.S. Army Center of Military History, n.d.), 322, and Edward M. Coffman, *The War to End All Wars: The American Military Experience in World War I* (New York: Oxford University Press, 1986), 39.

17. Because the Colt-Marlin was the most abundant machine-gun model available and was already in production, American ordnance officers searched for some way to employ the outdated weapons. In the process they developed a modified version of the Colt-Marlin that was used successfully as a machine gun on aircraft of the U.S. Air Service during the war (see Huston, *Sinews of War,* 322).

18. Ibid., 298. See also David A. Armstrong, *Bullets and Bureaucrats: The Machine Gun and the United States Army, 1861–1916* (Westport, Conn.: Greenwood Press, 1982).

19. Pershing, *My Experiences,* 1: 132.

20. Letter from the assistant French minister of war to General John J. Pershing, "Problem of Equipping American Divisions with Machine Guns and Rifles," 5 July 1917, 400-40-1, RG 165, NARA.

21. Marcel Vigneras, *Rearming the French: U.S. Army in World War II Special Studies* (Washington, D.C.: CMH, 1957), 3; Huston, *Sinews of War,* 324–27; and James J. Hudson, *Hostile Skies: A Combat History of the American Air Service in World War I* (Syracuse, N.Y.: Syracuse University Press, 1968), 2–3.

22. Vigneras, *Rearming the French,* 4, and Huston, *Sinews of War,* 334–35.

23. Preliminary report of the commander in chief, AEF, 19 November 1918, *USAWW*, 12: 5–6.

24. Jack C. Lane, *Armed Progressive* (San Rafael, Calif.: Presidio Press, 1978), 220–21; and Donald Smythe, *Pershing* (Bloomington: University of Indiana Press, 1986), 86; see chapter 5 for details of this event.

25. Henri Truchy, *Les finances de la guerre de la France* (Paris: Les Presses Universitaires de France, 1926), 285–86, and André Kaspi, *Le temps des Américains à la France en 1917–1918* (Paris: Publications de la Sorbonne, 1976), 47–69.

26. Truchy, *Les finances,* 315–16.

27. Jean-Baptiste Duroselle, *La Grande Guerre des français, 1914–1918* (Paris: Perrin, 1994), 171.

28. Ibid., 173.

29. Huston, *Sinews of War,* 333.

30. Ayres, *The War with Germany*, 78.

31. Letter from Colonel Frank Parker, chief of Liaison Group, GQG French Armies in France, to chief of American military mission, Paris, France, 28 May 1917, *USAWW*, 3: 238–40.

32. Ibid.

33. Pershing, *My Experiences*, 1: 80.

34. Ibid., 1: 80–84, and Smythe, *Pershing*, 27.

35. Général Eugène Debeney à Général Ferdinand Foch, letter, 22 May 1917, 403-30.1, RG 165, NARA.

36. Entrevue du Maréchal Joffre et du Général Pershing, 15 juin 1917, 14 N 26, SHAT.

37. George C. Marshall, *Memoirs of My Services in the World War, 1917–1918* (Boston: Houghton Mifflin, 1976), 18.

38. Ibid.

39. Ibid., 17.

40. Ibid., 26.

41. Ibid.

42. Joseph T. Dickman, *The Great Crusade* (New York: Appleton, 1927), 42–43.

43. Letters from Private Lloyd G. Short, Sixth USMC Regiment, U.S. Second Division, to his parents, 13 June 1918 and 11 July 1918, AEF Questionnaire File, U.S. Army Military History Institute, Carlisle Barracks, Carlisle, Pennsylvania (hereafter AEF USAMHI).

44. Ibid., letter from Sergeant Lloyd Norris, Twenty-third Infantry Regiment, U.S. Second Division, to his parents, 5 August 1918, and letter from Mme. F. Abray to Mrs. Norris, 19 August 1918.

45. Robert Lee Bullard, *Personalities and Reminiscences of the War* (Garden City, N.Y.: Doubleday, Page, 1925), 53–54.

46. Ibid., 54.

47. Editorial in *L'Echo de tranchées-villes*, 18 November 1915, quoted in Stéphane Audoin-Rouzeau, *Men at War, 1914–1918: National Sentiment and Trench Journalism in France During the First World War* (Oxford: Berg, 1995), 116.

48. Bullard, *Personalities and Reminiscences*, 53–58.

49. AEF General Order no. 7, 3 August 1917, *USAWW*, 16: 12.

50. Sergeant Major Vernon C. Mossman, Eighteenth Infantry Regiment, U.S. First Division, AEF USAMHI.

51. Bullard, *Personalities and Reminiscences*, 56–57.

52. Marshall, *Memoirs*, 18.

53. Stephen Ambrose, *Duty, Honor, Country: A History of West Point* (Baltimore: Johns Hopkins Press, 1966), 63.

54. Ibid., 64–67.

55. Ibid., 138–39; George S. Pappas, *The Point: The United States Military Academy, 1802–1902* (Westport, Conn.: Praeger, 1993), 263–64; and Stephen W. Sears, *George B. McClellan: The Young Napoleon* (New York: Ticknor and Fields, 1988), 31.

56. Timothy D. Johnson, *Winfield Scott: The Quest for Military Glory* (Lawrence: University Press of Kansas, 1998), 4, 67–68, and John D. Morris, *Sword of the Bor-*

der: *Major General Jacob Jennings Brown, 1775–1828* (Kent, Ohio: Kent State University Press, 2000), 156.

57. The American designed 10-pound Parrott, a rifled gun, was the other main field-artillery piece used. Most gunners preferred the Napoleon because of its capacity to fire massive loads of canister when infantry closed within short range and because its bronze barrel was less prone to bursting than the iron-barreled Parrott.

58. The bullet was invented and developed by Captain Claude Minié of the French army.

59. James I. Robertson Jr., *Stonewall Jackson: The Man, the Soldier, the Legend* (New York: Macmillan, 1997), 42–43, 84, 517; Sears, *McClellan*, 11–12, 31, and 282–83. See also Edward Hagerman, *The American Civil War and the Origins of Modern Warfare* (Bloomington: Indiana University Press, 1988), and William B. Skelton, *An American Profession of Arms: The Officer Corps, 1784–1861* (Lawrence: University Press of Kansas, 1992).

60. Bullard, *Personalities and Reminiscences*, 59; and Douglas V. Johnson and Rolfe L. Hillman, *Soissons 1918* (College Station: Texas A&M University Press, 1999), 22.

61. "A Study of Anglo-American and Franco-American Relations During World War I, Part II, Franco-American Relations," 7200 E, RG 165, NARA.

62. Confidential instructions from General Pétain, commander in chief of the Armies of the North and Northeast, to the liaison officers and officers acting as instructors with the American Expeditionary Forces, 8 May 1918, 3: 296–97, and AEF General Orders no. 41, 24 September 1817, 16: 84, both in *USAWW*.

63. Rapport de Mission au Division Américaine, 18 juillet 1917, 14 N 27 SHAT.

64. Ibid., Général d'Armand de Poudrygain à Général en Chef [Pétain] and Général Commandant le G.A.E. [Général Nöel de Castelnau] 31 juillet 1917.

65. Ibid.

66. Sergeant Major Vernon C. Mossman, Eighteenth Infantry Regiment, U.S. First Division, and Corporal Frederick Shaw, Eighteenth Infantry Regiment, U.S. First Division, both in AEF USAMHI.

67. Oral history interview with Lieutenant General Edward M. Almond, US-AMHI Oral History Project.

68. Memorandum for [AEF] chief of staff from Colonel Harold B. Fiske, 4 July 1918, *USAWW*, 3: 330–31. Although written in 1918, this message neatly sums up the general concerns that Pershing and the AEF high command had concerning French and British tactical doctrine.

69. Telegram from General John J. Pershing to U.S. Army adjutant general, War Department, 19 October 1917, *USAWW*, 14: 316.

70. Pershing, *My Experiences*, 1: 153.

71. See Louis Loyzeaux de Grandmaison, *Dressage de l'infanterie en vue du combat offensif* (Paris: Berger-Levrault, 1906); Ferdinand Foch, *De la conduite de la guerre* (Paris: Economica, 2000); Charles Ardant du Picq, *Battle Studies: Ancient and Modern*, in *Roots of Strategy*, Book 2 (Harrisburg, Pa.: Stackpole Books, 1987); Douglas Porch, *The March to the Marne* (London: Cambridge University Press, 1981),

213–31; and Joseph C. Arnold, "French Tactical Doctrine: 1870–1914," *Military Affairs* 42 (1976): 60–67.

72. Pershing, *My Experiences,* 1: 152.

73. Peyton C. March, *The Nation at War* (Garden City, N.Y.: Doubleday, Doran, 1932), 269–70.

74. B. H. Liddell-Hart, *Reputations: Ten Years After* (Boston: Little, Brown, 1928), 308–9.

75. Rainey, "The Questionable Training of the AEF," 91–92.

76. Allan R. Millett, *The General: Robert L. Bullard and Officership in the United States Army, 1881–1925* (Westport, Conn.: Greenwood Press, 1975), 315.

77. There have been several superlative studies of how the battlefield tactics of the major belligerents on the western front evolved over the course of the war. See Hubert C. Johnson, *Breakthrough! Tactics, Technology and the Search for Victory on the Western Front in World War I* (Novato, Calif.: Presidio Press, 1994); Timothy Travers, *The Killing Ground: The British Army, the Western Front, and the Emergence of Modern Warfare, 1900–1918* (London: Allen and Unwin, 1997); Bruce Gudmundsson, *Stormtroop Tactics: Innovation in the German Army, 1914–1918* (New York: Praeger, 1989); David T. Zabecki, *Steel Wind: Colonel Georg Bruchmüller and the Birth of Modern Artillery* (Westport, Conn.: Praeger, 1994); and Timothy T. Lupfer, *The Dynamics of Doctrine: The Changes in German Tactical Doctrine During the First World War* (Leavenworth, Kans.: Combat Studies Institute, 1981).

78. Marshall, *Memoirs,* 21–22.

79. The French Army Group boundaries were redrawn by Pétain in summer 1917, and thus Gondrecourt, formerly in the GAC sector, was in the GAE sector in July 1917.

80. Marshall, *Memoirs,* 39.

81. Ibid.

82. General Pétain au Ministre de la Guerre [Painlevé], letter, 14 juin 1917, 14 N 27, SHAT.

83. Barthélemy E. Palat, *La Grande Guerre sur la front occidental,* 14 tomes (Paris: Berger-Levrault, 1917–1929), 12, *L'Année d'angoisse, 1917* (Paris: Berger-Levrault, 1927), 560–71. The final front line established by this offensive would be the jumping-off point for the Meuse-Argonne offensive in September 1918.

84. Ibid., 581–90.

85. Stephen Ryan, *Pétain the Soldier* (New York: Barnes, 1969), 156–57.

86. Mark E. Grotelueschen, *Doctrine Under Trial: American Artillery Employment in World War I* (Westport, Conn.: Greenwood Press, 2001), 5.

87. March, *Nation at War,* 31.

88. Ibid., 33.

89. Ibid., and Grotelueschen, *Doctrine Under Trial,* 21.

90. Letter from Captain George S. Patton Jr. to General John J. Pershing, 3 October 1917, reprinted in *The Patton Papers, 1885–1940,* ed. Martin Blumenson, 2 vols. (Boston: Houghton-Mifflin, 1972), 1:462.

91. Ibid., letter from George S. Patton Jr. to Beatrice Patton, 29 May 1918, 1: 581–82.

92. Baron Anthoine Jomini was actually Swiss, but Switzerland was annexed by France in 1799 and remained so until the collapse of the French Empire in 1814. Jomini served as a staff officer in Napoleon's Grande Armée until 1813 and wrote his works on military theory and philosophy in French.

93. Carlo D'Este, *Patton: A Genius for War* (New York: Harper Perennial, 1996), 320–29; and Martin Blumenson, *Patton: The Man Behind the Legend, 1885–1945* (New York: Berkley Books, 1985), 29.

94. Patton, *Patton Papers*, 1: 480.

95. Ibid.

96. There are a host of fine biographies of Georges Clemenceau. The best of these, in no particular order, are Jean-Baptiste Duroselle, *Clemenceau* (Paris: Fayard, 1989); Gaston Monnerville, *Clemenceau* (Paris: Fayard, 1969); David S. Newhall, *Clemenceau: A Life at War* (Lewiston, N.Y.: Edwin Mellen Press, 1991); David Robbins Watson, *Georges Clemenceau: A Political Biography* (New York: McKay, 1974); and Edgar Holt, *The Tiger: The Life of Georges Clemenceau, 1841–1929* (London: Hamish Hamilton, 1976).

97. Watson, *Georges Clemenceau*, 36–55.

98. Newhall, *Clemenceau*, 303. Clemenceau had been premier of France from 1906 to 1909, and during his tenure his stance on various labor disputes, as well as on other issues, had alienated him from the French Left, to which he had once firmly belonged.

99. Ibid., 309–37.

100. Jere Clemens King, *Generals and Politicians* (Berkeley: University of California Press, 1951), 192. Clemenceau's official title was Monsieur le Président du Conseil, Ministre de la Guerre. In order to distinguish him more readily from Président de la Republique Raymond Poincaré, the title Président du Conseil is usually translated as either prime minister or premier. I have used the latter throughout this book but at all times have retained the title used in direct quotations from documents of the time.

101. Richard M. Watt, *Dare Call It Treason* (New York: Simon and Schuster, 1963), 287. *Cochon* means pig and *salaud* is a vulgar insult usually translated as meaning a dirty person or slut.

102. The larger than life bronze statue of Clemenceau at the Place de Clemenceau in Paris depicts the French premier dressed in this attire, heading out to tour the front.

103. March, *Nation at War*, 31–32.

104. Ibid., 32.

105. Bullard, *Personalities*, 155.

106. Ibid.

107. Marshall, *Memoirs*, 42.

108. Laurence Stallings, *The Doughboys: The Story of the AEF, 1917–1918* (New York: Harper and Row, 1963), 36.

109. Ibid., 37.

110. General Eugène Savatier, "The American Doughboy Goes into Action" in *As They Saw Us*, ed. George S. Viereck (Garden City, N.Y.: Doubleday, Doran,

1929), 69–70. The American unit assigned to Savatier was the Twenty-third Regiment of the U.S. Second Division.

111. Stallings, *Doughboys*, 38.

112. Ibid., 39.

113. Marshall, *Memoirs*, 46–47.

114. Ibid., 49–50. The monument referred to by General Bordeaux was indeed built, with money donated by the local citizens, next to the graves of the three American soldiers who were killed in action. It is a large Lorraine cross upon which is inscribed, "Here rest the first soldiers of the United States to fall on the soil of France in the cause of Justice and Liberty." See Colonel de Chambrun and Captain de Marenches, *The American Army in the European Conflict* (New York: Macmillan, 1919), 120.

Chapter 5. The Amalgamation Controversy

1. For details on Passchendaele and Cambrai, see Robin Prior and Trevor Wilson, *Passchendaele: The Untold Story* (New Haven: Yale University Press, 1998); Philip Warner, *Passchendaele: The Tragic Victory of 1917* (New York: Atheneum, 1988); and Bryan Cooper, *Ironclads of Cambrai* (London: Cassell, 2002). For the situation on the Italian front in 1917, see J. Wilks, *Caporetto and the Italian Campaign, 1915–1918* (London: Leo Cooper, 1997).

2. The armistice was signed on 15 December 1917, but the final Treaty of Brest-Litovsk, was not formally signed until 3 March 1918.

3. Holger Herwig, *The First World War: Germany and Austria-Hungary, 1914–1918* (New York: St. Martin's Press, 1997), 381–94, and Max Hoffman, *The War of Lost Opportunities* (Nashville: Battery Press, 1999), 195–243. Because of the fear of Russian forces (Red or White) taking advantage of the German commitment on the western front to undo the Treaty of Brest-Litovsk, there were still forty German infantry divisions and three cavalry divisions on the eastern front when the great German offensives began in the West on 21 March 1918.

4. Hubert Essame, *The Battle for Europe: 1918* (New York: Charles Scribner's Sons, 1972), 32; Stephen Ryan, *Pétain the Soldier* (New York: Barnes, 1969),156–57; B. H. Liddell-Hart, *The Real War, 1914–1918* (Boston: Little, Brown, 1930), 366; and Herwig, *The First World War*, 351–54. The Central Powers were also facing critical manpower shortages, and the Germans were able to grow stronger on the western front only because of the collapse of Russia and the subsequent redeployment of the divisions serving there to the western front.

5. Général Laure, *Le commandment en chef des armées françaises: du 15 mai 1917 à l'armistice* (Paris: Berger-Levrault, 1937), 38–40; Jean-Baptiste Duroselle, *La Grande Guerre des français, 1914–1918* (Paris: Perrin, 1994), 347–48, and Ryan, *Pétain*, 156–57.

6. Woodrow Wilson to Edward M. House, letter, 21 July 1917, *PWW*, 43: 238.

7. Edward M. Coffman, *The Hilt of the Sword: The Career of Peyton C. March* (Madison: University of Wisconsin Press, 1966), 50–51.

8. Ibid., 52–94, and Peyton C. March, *The Nation at War* (Garden City, N.Y.: Doubleday, Doran, 1932), 69–103.

9. See chapter 2.

10. Le Maréchal Joffre à Monsieur le Ministère de la Guerre [Painlevé], 20 mai 1917, 7 N 1720, SHAT. Joffre was right, of course, but as events turned out, the Americans were able to participate only in the middle and end portions of the great campaign of 1918. The French and British still had to stand essentially on their own when the German offensive struck on 21 March.

11. Guy Pedroncini, *Pétain: Le soldat et la gloire, 1856–1918* (Paris: Perrin, 1989), 239–43, and Guy Pedroncini, *Pétain: Général en chef, 1917–1918*, 2d ed. (Paris: Presses Universitaires de France, 1997), 174–77.

12. John J. Pershing, *My Experiences in the First World War*, 2 vols. (1935; reprint, New York: Da Capo, 1995), 1: 272–73, and Pedroncini, *Pétain: Général en chef*, 181.

13. Pershing, *My Experiences*, 1: 272–73.

14. "A Study of Anglo-American and Franco-American Relations During World War I, Part II, Franco-American Relations," 7200 E, RG 165, NARA.

15. Georges Clemenceau, *The Grandeur and Misery of Victory*, trans. F. M. Atkinson (New York: Harcourt Brace, 1930), 63–65.

16. Sir Cecil Arthur Spring Rice to Edward Mandell House, letter, 17 December 1917, *PWW*, 45: 316–17.

17. Enclosure with ibid.

18. Ibid., Newton D. Baker to John J. Pershing, cable, 18 December 1917, 45: 328.

19. Ibid., Raymond Poincaré to Woodrow Wilson, letter, 28 December 1917, 45: 372.

20. Ibid., Newton D. Baker to Woodrow Wilson, letter, 3 January 1918, 45: 438.

21. James G. Harbord, *Leaves from a War Diary* (New York: Dodd, Mead, 1925), 215.

22. General John J. Pershing to Georges Clemenceau, letter, 5 January 1918, Box 47, Pershing Papers.

23. Ibid., Georges Clemenceau to John J. Pershing, letter, 6 January 1918.

24. Newton D. Baker to Woodrow Wilson, letter, 3 January 1918, *PWW*, 45: 438.

25. Ibid., John J. Pershing to Newton D. Baker, cable, 2 January 1918, 45: 439–40.

26. Ibid.

27. Ibid.

28. Jack C. Lane, *Armed Progressive* (San Rafael, Calif.: Presidio Press, 1978), 214–15.

29. Ibid., 215–17.

30. Ibid., 218–19.

31. Ibid., 219.

32. March, *The Nation at War*, 61–62.

33. Donald Smythe, *Pershing* (Bloomington: University of Indiana Press, 1986), 85.

34. The story of Clemenceau's alleged request to the Wilson administration on the subject of replacing Pershing with Wood can be found in Lane, *Armed Progressive*, 220. Lane presents this story as fact, but there is no reference to it in the Woodrow Wilson Papers, Newton D. Baker papers, or the remnants of Clemenceau's papers, most of which he destroyed before he died. For his evidence Lane cites an entry in the diary of Henry L. Stimson, former secretary of war under William Howard Taft and a close confidant and friend of Leonard Wood. Since the diary entry was made in 1923, five years after the event in question, and since Stimson had little if any access to the internal operation of the Wilson administration during the war, the story can hardly be treated as anything more than rumor.

35. Lane, *Armed Progressive*, 220–21, and Smythe, *Pershing*, 86.

36. March, *Nation at War*, 61–63.

37. Smythe, *Pershing*, 85, and March, *Nation at War*, 61–63.

38. Smythe, *Pershing*, 75.

39. Ibid.

40. John J. Pershing to Newton D. Baker, 17 January 1918, letter reprinted in Pershing, *My Experiences*, 1: 293–97.

41. Ibid., 1: 291.

42. On the friendship between Pershing and Pétain, see Smythe, *Pershing*, 22–23.

43. In other words, the four regiments had no division- or brigade-level headquarters, supply, communications, transport, or other support troops necessary for the formation of an actual division. These four were the 369th, 370th, 371st, and 372nd Infantry Regiments, and they were the only American infantry regiments that were amalgamated directly into the French army during World War I. The 369th Infantry Regiment, the Harlem Hellfighters, particularly established itself as a superior unit while serving with the French army and was one of the most heavily decorated American regiments of the war. The 370th Regiment had a more spotty record and was criticized by the French divisional commanders it fought under. Pershing, *My Experiences*, 1: 291.

44. John J. Pershing to Georges Clemenceau, 16 January 1918, telegram, Box 47, Pershing Papers.

45. John J. Pershing to Newton D. Baker, 17 January 1918, letter reprinted in Pershing, *My Experiences*, 1: 294–95.

46. Smythe, *Pershing*, 72. For charges of Pershing's alleged racism, as well as that of other senior AEF commanders, see Arthur E. Barbeau and Florette Henri, *The Unknown Soldiers: African-American Troops in World War I*, 2d ed. (New York: Da Capo, 1996).

47. See chapter 2.

48. Pershing, *My Experiences*, 1: 315–16.

49. Le Ministre de la Guerre [Painlevé] à Monsieur le Maréchal [Joffre], 3 juin 1917, 7 N 1720, SHAT, and Joffre, *Journal de marche*, 218.

50. Conversation avec le général Pershing (54, rue Michel-Ange) 26 janvier 1918, Joffre, *Journal de marche*, 257–59, and Pershing, *My Experiences*, 1: 305–6.

51. Joffre, *Journal de marche*, 257–59, and Pershing, *My Experiences*, 1: 305–6.

52. Joffre, *Journal de marche*, 257–59, and Pershing, *My Experiences*, 1: 305–6.

53. Joffre, *Journal de marche*, 257–59, and Pershing, *My Experiences*, 1: 305–6.

54. Joffre, *Journal de marche*, 257–59, and Pershing, *My Experiences*, 1: 305–6.

55. Smythe, *Pershing*, 78–79.

56. John J. Pershing to Henry Pinckney McCain, cable, 31 January 1918, *PWW*, 46: 196–98. It is unclear why Pershing sent this message to McCain rather than to Baker. Perhaps it was because Pershing was withdrawing his earlier support for the amalgamation scheme and was insinuating that there had been some mistake made at the War Department regarding his views on the subject instead of admitting that he had changed his mind. Such a message would have far less political and personal fallout if directed to McCain rather than to Baker.

57. Woodrow Wilson to Newton Diehl Baker, letter, 4 February 1918, *PWW*, 46: 236–37.

58. "Relations Between AEF and BEF, 1917–1920" 7200 E, RG 165, NARA. Small elements of two other American divisions also saw limited duty with the British, but the divisions themselves were transferred to French, and later to American, command in spring 1918.

59. Ibid.

60. Ibid., "A Study of Anglo-American and Franco-American Relations During World War I. Part II: Franco-American Relations."

61. Ibid., "Relations Between AEF and BEF, 1917–1920."

62. Joseph T. Dickman, *The Great Crusade* (New York: Appleton, 1927), 32–33.

63. Edward M. Coffman, *The War to End All Wars: The American Military Experience in World War I* (New York: Oxford, 1968), 285.

64. Erich Ludendorff, "The American Soldier in the World War as Seen by a Foe," in *As They Saw Us: Foch, Ludendorff and Other Leaders Write Our War History*, ed. George S. Viereck (Garden City N.Y.: Doubleday, Doran, 1929), 49–50.

65. Minutes of Supreme War Council Meeting, 1 February 1918, Box 252, Tasker H. Bliss Papers, Library of Congress, Washington, D.C.

66. Ibid. (emphasis in original).

Chapter 6. Springtime of War

1. The first offensive was named for the Archangel Michael, the patron saint of Imperial Germany; ironically, he is also a patron saint of France.

2. For details on the preparations, planning, and execution of Operation Michael and the overall German plan for victory in 1918, see Erich Ludendorff, *Ludendorff's Own Story*, 2 vols. (New York: Harper and Brothers, 1920) 2: 158–325; Holger Herwig, *The First World War* (New York: St. Martin's Press, 1997), 392–432; and Robert Asprey, *The German High Command at War: Hindenburg and Ludendorff Conduct World War I* (New York: William Morrow, 1991), 381–418. The two essential works on the development and implementation of the infantry and artillery components of German stormtroop tactics are Bruce I. Gudmundsson, *Stormtroop*

Tactics: Innovation in the German Army, 1914–1918 (1989; reprint, Westport, Conn.: Praeger, 1995) and David T. Zabecki, *Steel Wind: Colonel Georg Bruchmüller and the Birth of Modern Artillery* (Westport, Conn.: Praeger, 1994).

3. Admiral Georg Alexander von Müller, diary entries for 23 March 1918 and 26 March 1918, in Admiral Georg Alexander von Müller, *The Kaiser and His Court: The Diaries, Note Books and Letters of Admiral Georg Alexander von Müller, Chief of the Naval Cabinet, 1914–1918,* ed. Walter Görlitz. (1959; reprint, New York: Harcourt, Brace and World, 1964), 344–45, and Herwig, *The First World War,* 406.

4. General Ragueneau, Chef de la Mission Militaire Françaises pres l'Armée Américaine à Monsieur le Général Commandant en Chef les Forces Expédition-aires Américaines, 23 mars 1918, File 648, RG 120, NARA.

5. John J. Pershing, *My Experiences in the First World War,* 2 vols. (1935; reprint, New York: Da Capo, 1995), 1: 356.

6. Notes on conversation between General Pershing and General Pétain, 25 March [1918], File 657, RG 120, NARA.

7. Ibid.

8. Ibid., and Pershing, *My Experiences,* 1: 356–57.

9. Notes on conversation, Pershing and Pétain, File 657, RG 120, NARA, and Pershing, *My Experiences,* 1: 33–34.

10. Pershing, *My Experiences,* 1: 214. For details on the Allied Supreme War Council and the American role in it, see David F. Trask, *The United States in the Supreme War Council: American War Aims and Inter-Allied Strategy* (Middletown, Conn.: Wesleyan University Press, 1961).

11. Ludendorff, *Ludendorff's Own Story,* 2: 220–21.

12. Georges Clemenceau, *The Grandeur and Misery of Victory,* trans. F. M. Atkinson (New York: Harcourt, Brace, 1930), 38–39, and Jean Martet, *Georges Clemenceau* (New York: Longmans, Green, 1930), 195–96.

13. Clemenceau, *The Grandeur and Misery,* 38–39, and Martet, *Clemenceau,* 195–96.

14. Ferdinand Foch, *The Memoirs of Marshal Foch,* trans. T. Bentley Mott (New York: Doubleday, Doran, 1931), 264; André Laffargue, *Foch et la bataille de 1918* (Paris: B. Arthaud, 1967), 102–6; and B. H. Liddell-Hart, *Foch: The Man of Orleans* (Boston: Little, Brown, 1932), 278.

15. John Terraine, *To Win a War: 1918, the Year of Victory* (London: Cassell, 2000), 103–4, and T. M. Hunter, "Foch and Eisenhower: A Study in Allied Supreme Command," *Army Quarterly* 87 (1963): 33–52.

16. B. H. Liddell-Hart, *Reputations: Ten Years After* (Boston: Little, Brown, 1928), 154. Foch's military writings, which are numerous, constantly invoke the Napoleonic tradition as the proper method for waging war, although he is usually vague as to exactly what is meant by the term. See, for example, Ferdinand Foch, *The Principals of War,* trans. Hilaire Belloc (London: Chapman and Hall, 1918), and Ferdinand Foch, *De la conduite de la guerre* (Paris: Economica, 2000).

17. The best biographies of Marshal Ferdinand Foch are Jean Autin, *Foch* (Paris: Perrin, 1987), and Liddell-Hart, *Foch.* For intriguing portrayals of Foch by

members of his staff, see Maxime Weygand, *Foch* (Paris: Flammarion, 1947), and Charles Bugnet, *Foch Speaks,* trans. Russell Green (New York: Dial, 1929).

18. Jean de Pierrefeu, *French Headquarters, 1915–1918,* trans. C. J. C. Street (London: Geoffrey Bles, 1924), 22–23.

19. Pershing, *My Experiences,* 1: 364–65. In French: "Je viens pour vous dire que le peuple américain tiendrait à grand honneur que nos troupes fussent engagées dans la présente bataille. Je vous le demande en mon nom et au sien. Il n'y a pas en ce moment d'autres question que de combattre. L'Infanterie, l'artillerie, l'aviation, tout ce que nous avons est à vous. Disposez-en comme il vous plaira. Il en viendra encore d'autres, aussi nombreux qu'il sera nécessaire. Je suis venu tout exprès pour vous dire que le peuple américain serait fier d'être engagé dans la plus belle bataille de l'Histoire." Pershing confesses that this message was written up for the newspapers in far better French than he actually spoke at the time. This is probably true, as the French version that is reprinted in his memoirs contains several spelling and grammatical errors.

20. Pershing, *My Experiences,* 1: 364.

21. French carte postale, Box 349, Pershing Papers.

22. Confidential instructions from General Pétain, commander in chief of the Armies of the North and Northeast, to the liaison officers and officers acting as instructors with the American Expeditionary Forces, 8 May 1918, Box 349, Personal Correspondence, Pershing Papers, and *USAWW,* 3: 296–97.

23. Pétain, confidential instructions, Pershing Papers.

24. Ibid.

25. Handwritten note by John J. Pershing on his personal copy of ibid., 15 May 1918, Box 349, Personal Correspondence, Pershing Papers.

26. Eugène Savatier, "The American Doughboy Goes into Action," in *As they Saw Us,* ed. George Viereck (Garden City, N.Y.: Doubleday, Doran, 1929), 71.

27. GQG des Armées du Nord et du Nord-Est, Services Spéciaux, Service du Moral, "Le Moral Général de l'Armée en Janvier 1918," 16 N 1486, and GQG des Armées du Nord et du Nord Est, Services Spéciaux, Service du Moral, "Le Moral Général de l'Armée en Février 1918," 16 N 1486, both in SHAT.

28. Douglas MacArthur, *Reminiscences* (New York: McGraw-Hill, 1964), 54.

29. Field Orders, First Division, AEF, 20 April 1918, 4: 261–63, and Field Orders, First Division, AEF, 10 May 1918, 4: 268–69, both in *USAWW.* This part of the western front had previously been the sector for the British Fifth Army. The British had been heavily defeated there during March, and Pétain had shifted the French First Army north in late March and early April in order to plug the gap left by the retreating British.

30. *USAWW,* 4: 259.

31. George C. Marshall, *Memoirs of My Services in the World War, 1917–1918* (Boston: Houghton-Mifflin, 1976), 89.

32. General Charles Vandenberg [CG French X Corps] to General Eugène Debeney [CG French First Army], letter, 12 May 1918, 4: 270, and General Debeney, French First Army, to Commanding General X Army Corps [Vandenberg], memorandum, 15 May 1918, 4: 272, both in *USAWW.*

33. *Grand puissance de filloux* (high-powered ordnance materiel). These were French long-range 155mm guns designed specifically for counterbattery fire. Pétain had used these weapons with devastating effect against the German artillery batteries at Verdun.

34. Third Section, General Staff, French First Army, to Commanding General [French] X Army Corps, 14 May 1918, 4: 271–72, and First Division AEF Composition, on 28 May 1918, 4: 297, both in USAWW; and Allan R. Millett, "Cantigny, 28–31 May 1918," in *America's First Battles, 1776–1965,* ed. Charles E. Heller and William A. Stofft (Lawrence: University Press of Kansas, 1986), 169.

35. Field Order, X Army Corps, 15 May 1918, *USAWW,* 4: 272–73.

36. First Lieutenant Daniel Sargent, Fifth Field Artillery, U.S. First Division, "Cantigny," memoir, AEF USAMHI.

37. Ibid.

38. Marshall, *Memoirs,* 31, 87–99.

39. Account by an eyewitness of the attack on Cantigny, First Division, AEF 29 May 1918, *USAWW,* 4: 321–22, and Millett, "Cantigny," 172–79.

40. Sargent, "Cantigny," AEF USAMHI.

41. Ibid.

42. Colonel Hanson E. Ely, Twenty-eighth Infantry [Regiment], AEF, "Report of Capture of Cantigny and Consolidation of Position," 2 June 1918 *USAWW,* 4: 326–30.

43. Savatier, "American Doughboy," 84.

44. Ibid., 85.

45. Zabecki, *Steel Wind,* 80–85; Herbert Sulzbach, *With the German Guns: Four Years on the Western Front, 1914–1918* (London: Leo Cooper, 1998), 178–80; J. P. Muller, "The German Artillery at Chemin des Dames, 1918," *Field Artillery Journal* (March 1922): 154–62; and Guy Pedroncini, *Pétain: Le soldat, 1914–1940* (Paris: Perrin, 1998), 243–45.

46. Ludendorff, *Ludendorff's Own Story,* 2: 266–69; Crown Prince Wilhelm, *My War Experiences* (London: Hurst and Blackett, 1923), 318; and Rod Paschall, *The Defeat of Imperial Germany, 1917–1918* (1989; reprint, New York: Da Capo, 1994), 152–54.

47. Général Laure, *Le commandement en chef des armées françaises* (Paris: Éditions Berger-Levrault, 1937), 86–89; Jean Baptiste Duroselle, *La Grande Guerre des français, 1914–1918* (Paris: Perrin, 1994), 373–76; Pierrefeu, *Inside French Headquarters,* 269; and Crown Prince Wilhlem, *My War Experiences,* 318–19.

48. Rush telegram from General Francis J. Kernan to General Headquarters, American Expeditionary Force, 5 June 1918, File 650, RG 120, NARA, and Pershing, *My Experiences,* 2: 89–90.

49. Jean Jules Henri Mordacq, *Le ministère Clemenceau: Journal d'un témoin,* 4 vols. (Paris: Plon, 1930–1931), 2: 49; Clemenceau, *Grandeur and Misery,* 51; Jere Clemens King, *Generals and Politicians* (Berkeley: University of California Press, 1951), 228.

50. His statement is quite similar to that made by Foch regarding Amiens during the crisis brought about by Operation Michael earlier that year.

51. Assemblée nationale, *Annales de la Chambre des Députés, débats parlementaires, sessions ordinaire et extraordinaires de 1914–1918* (Paris: Imprimerie Nationale, 1918–1919), séance du 4 juin 1918; Georges Clemenceau, *Discours de guerre* (Paris: Presses Universitaires de France, 1968), 187–203; Laure, *Le commandement en chef*, 90; and King, *Generals and Politicians*, 229–30.

52. Memorandum for the commander in chief [Pershing] from Colonel T. Bentley Mott, U.S. military attaché to Foch's Headquarters, 29 May 1918, File 649, and Pershing's memo on redeployment of American troops in training with the British to Lorraine and the Vosges [n.d.], File 650, both in RG 120, NARA.

53. Mott, memorandum, and Pershing, memorandum, both in File 650, RG 120, NARA.

54. Third Bureau, General Staff, GQG [Pétain's Headquarters] to Headquarters, French Sixth Army, "Special Memorandum Relating to the Guarding of the Marne Crossings," 29 May 1918, File 649, RG 120, NARA; and Joseph T. Dickman, *The Great Crusade* (New York: Appleton, 1927), 49–51.

55. Journal of Operations, Second Division, AEF, 30 May 1918, *USAWW*, 4: 70–71.

56. Ministère des Armées, "L'action du service automobile dans les grands batailles de 1914–1918," *Revue historique des armées* 5 (September 1978): 85–92, and Robert B. Bruce, "To the Last Limits of Their Strength: The French Army and the Logistics of Attrition at the Battle of Verdun, 21 February–18 December 1916," *Army History* 45 (summer 1998): 9–21.

57. Robert Asprey, *At Belleau Wood* (1965; reprint, Denton: University of North Texas Press, 1996), 65.

58. James G. Harbord, *Leaves from a War Diary* (New York: Dodd, Mead, 1925), 288. Harbord is referring to Henry Wadsworth Longfellow's epic poem *Evangeline*, which tells the tragic story of the British expulsion of the ethnic French population from Acadia (Nova Scotia).

59. Quoted in Laurence Stallings, *The Doughboys: The Story of the A.E.F., 1917–1918* (New York: Harper and Row, 1963), 85.

60. Grand Quartier Général, Deuxième Bureau, "État de l'opinion en France 15 juin–15 juillet 1917," 7 N 867, SHAT.

61. The Third Division was rushed to the front piecemeal, with only token elements taking part in the initial battles along the Marne near Château-Thierry. The division was fully deployed and saw heavy fighting during the German offensive of 15 July and in the subsequent Franco-American counteroffensive that began a few days later. For details, see chapter 7.

62. Frederick Palmer, *America in France* (New York: Dodd, Mead, 1918), 240–41.

63. Pierrefeu, *French Headquarters*, 272–273.

64. Third Section, French Sixth Army, Special Orders no. 3156, for the American Second Division, 31 May 1918, *USAWW*, 4: 71–72. The U.S. Second Division was initially assigned to the French VII Corps but then almost immediately transferred by General Duchêne to the XXI Corps, as this was the sector most threatened by a possible renewed German drive. Duchêne's reputation was badly

marred by the near collapse of his army during the German offensive, especially as he had deployed the mass of his troops in exposed forward positions, directly contrary to Pétain's instructions. Pétain relieved Duchêne of command later that month and replaced him with Degoutte.

65. Oliver Lyman Spaulding et al. *The Second Division American Expeditionary Force in France, 1917–1919* (New York: Hillman Press, 1937), 38–40. This book was researched and written by a team of U.S. Army and USMC officers who served with the Second Division in the war as an official history of the division's service.

66. See for example Asprey, *At Belleau Wood,* and Stallings, *The Doughboys.*

67. A. W. Catlin, *"With the Help of God and a Few Marines"* (Garden City, N.Y.: Doubleday, Page, 1919), 97.

68. Third Section, General Staff, French XXI Army Corps, for the Generals Commanding the Second Division, AEF [and the French] Forty-third and 164th Inf. Divs., 2 June 1918, *USAWW,* 4: 96–97.

69. Headquarters, French XXI Corps, to Second Division AEF, 2 June 1918, 4: 105–6, and Journal of Operations, Second Division, AEF, 2 June 1918, 4: 106, both in *USAWW;* Spaulding, *Second Division,* 44–48.

70. Third Section, GS French XXI Army Corps, General Operations Order, 5 June 1918, *USAWW,* 4: 143–44.

71. Ibid.; Second Division, AEF Composition, 29 May–3 July 1918, 4: 350–51, and Field Order, Fifth Regiment, USMC, 6 June 1918, 4: 352, both in *USAWW.*

72. The U.S. Second Division remains one of the legendary formations of the U.S. Army and is noted for always being in the thickest part of the fight. This reputation is supported by the fact that it suffered the heaviest casualties of any American division in World War I; indeed, it also held this distinction for World War II and the Korean War. For more information on this splendid division during the Great War, see Spaulding, *Second Division;* James G. Harbord, *The American Army in France, 1917–1919* (Boston: Little, Brown, 1936); John A. LeJeune, *The Reminiscences of a Marine* (1930; reprint, Quantico, Va.: Marine Corps Assn., 1979); George B. Clark, *Devil Dogs: Fighting Marines of World War I* (Novato, Calif.: Presidio Press, 1999); and Asprey, *At Belleau Wood.* See also the semifictional work of John W. Thomason Jr., *Fix Bayonets!* (New York: Charles Scribner's Sons, 1926).

73. Field Order no. 3, Second Field Artillery Brigade, 6 June 1918, *USAWW,* 4: 363.

74. Ibid., Field Order no. 2, fourth Brigade, USMC, 6 June 1918, 4: 364–65.

75. Ibid., Second Division, AEF Operations Report, 7 June 1918, 4: 370–71; Spaulding, *Second Division,* 48–56; and Asprey, *At Belleau Wood,* 137–202.

76. General Ferdinand Foch, commander in chief, Allied Armies in France, to General John J. Pershing, commander in chief, American Expeditionary Forces, telegram, 12 June 1918, and General John J. Pershing, commander in chief, American Expeditionary Forces, to General Ferdinand Foch, commander in chief, Allied Armies in France, telegram, 13 June 1918, both in Pershing Papers.

77. Ibid., Georges Clemenceau to John J. Pershing, letter, 12 June 1918, Box 47.

78. Ibid., General Pétain to John J. Pershing, letter, 13 June 1918, Box 160.

79. Ibid., John J. Pershing to General Pétain, letter, 16 June 1918, Box 160.

80. Pierrefeu, *French Headquarters*, 287.

81. Smythe, *Pershing*, 22.

82. Harbord, *American Army*, 141.

83. Harbord, *War Diary*, 293–94.

84. Letter from First Lieutenant John W. Thomason Jr. to Dr. and Mrs. John W. Thomason Sr., 11 August 1918, John W. Thomason Collection, Newton Gresham Library, Sam Houston State University, Huntsville, Texas.

85. Pierrefeu, *French Headquarters*, 273.

86. Ibid.

87. Harbord, *War Diary*, 294. In addition, the regiments themselves were given Croix de Guerre battle streamers for their colors, an award the French issued much in the same way that the U.S. Army today issues Distinguished Unit Citations.

88. Commendation of Fourth Brigade, U.S. Marines, by General Degoutte, 30 June 1918, *USAWW*, 4: 656.

89. Letter from First Lieutenant John W. Thomason Jr. to Dr. & Mrs. John W. Thomason Sr., 7 July 1918, Thomason Collection.

90. Final report of General John J. Pershing, *USAWW*, 12: 292.

91. Interview of 19 May 1918 at Chantilly between General Pétain and General Pershing, File 657, RG 120, NARA.

92. Harbord, *American Army*, 201.

93. Ibid.

94. Pierrefeu, *French Headquarters*, 272.

95. Ibid.

Chapter 7. The Second Battle of the Marne

1. Erich Ludendorff, *Ludendorff's Own Story*, 2 vols. (New York: Harper Brothers, 1920), 2: 281. Although he was nominally subordinate both to Kaiser Wilhelm II and Field Marshal Paul von Hindenburg, by 1918 Ludendorff was the de facto commander of the German army and the virtual military dictator of the German Empire. See Gerhard Ritter, *The Sword and the Scepter: The Problem of Militarism in Germany*, 4 vols. (Coral Gables, Fla.: University of Miami Press, 1969–1973), and Martin Kitchen, *The Silent Dictatorship: The Politics of the German High Command Under Hindenburg and Ludendorff* (New York: Holmes and Meier, 1976). In addition to the two main offensives (Michael and Blücher) there had been two smaller German offensives in 1918. Georgette had been launched against the British in April and Gneisenau against the French in June.

2. Final report of General John J. Pershing, 1 September 1919, *USAWW*, 12: 140, and John J. Pershing, *My Experiences in the First World War*, 2 vols. (1935; reprint, New York: Da Capo, 1995), 2: 84. From August to November 1918 an additional 250,000 American soldiers arrived in France each month.

3. Erich Ludendorff et al., *The Two Battles of the Marne: The Stories of Marshal Joffre, General von Ludendorff, Marshal Foch, Crown Prince Wilhelm* (New York: Cosmopolitan, 1927), 219–20.

4. Georg Alexander von Müller, *The Kaiser and His Court: The Diaries, Note Books and Letters of Admiral Georg Alexander von Müller, Chief of the Naval Cabinet, 1914–1918,* ed. Walter Görlitz (New York: Harcourt Brace and World, 1964), 365; Hans Peter Hanssen, *Diary of a Dying Empire,* ed. Ralph H. Lutz et al. (Bloomington: Indiana University Press, 1955), 288–89; and Walter Görlitz, *History of the German General Staff* (Boulder, Colo.: Westview Press, 1985), 196.

5. Holger Herwig, *The First World War* (New York: St. Martin's Press, 1997), 416.

6. "Sickness in the German Army," from Intelligence Summary, 14 July 1918, in General Service Schools, *The German Offensive of July 15, 1918: Marne Source Book* (Ft. Leavenworth, Kans.: General Service Schools Press, 1923) (hereafter *German Offensive*), 746; Walther Reinhardt, "The AEF Halts the German Marne Offensive," in *As They Saw Us,* ed. George Viereck (Garden City, N.Y.: Doubleday, Doran, 1929), 98–99; and Robert B. Asprey, *The German High Command at War* (New York: William Morrow, 1991), 431.

7. J. W. Wheeler-Bennett, *Wooden Titan: Hindenburg in Twenty Years of German History, 1914–1934* (London: Archon Books, 1936), 154–55; Helmut Haeussler, *General Wilhelm Groener and the Imperial German Army* (Madison: State Historical Society of Wisconsin, 1962), 112–13; and Asprey, *German High Command,* 432–33. Of course, it is highly debatable that the Allies would have agreed to open peace negotiations along the lines that Kühlmann and others envisioned, as by summer 1918 both the Allies and the Central Powers were firmly committed to achieving total victory over their enemies, and neither side was really willing to discuss a compromise solution to the conflict.

8. Order no. 8685 from General Headquarters, chief of General Staff of the German Field Army to German Crown Prince Wilhelm, 14 June 1918, *USAWW,* 5: 175; see also Ludendorff, *Ludendorff's Own Story,* 2: 306–7.

9. Ludendorff, *Ludendorff's Own Story,* 2: 306–7, and Wilhelm, Crown Prince of Germany, *My War Experiences* (London: Hurst and Blackhurst, 1923), 326–28. The planned German offensive in Flanders, code-named Hagen, was supposed to be launched after Army Group German Crown Prince's attack had caused the Allies to move the bulk of their reserves from Flanders to reinforce the threatened French defenses in Champagne. Technically, the offensive against Reims was originally intended as a diversion to draw Allied attention and troops away from Flanders. Like Blücher before it, however, this diversionary attack quickly became a major offensive in its own right.

10. Ludendorff, *Ludendorff's Own Story,* 2: 306–7, and Barrie Pitt, *1918: The Last Act* (1962; reprint, New York: Ballantine, 1964), 196.

11. Ludendorff, *Ludendorff's Own Story,* 2: 280–82; Reinhardt, "AEF Halts German Offensive," 98–100; and Roger Parkinson, *Tormented Warrior: Ludendorff and the Supreme Command* (New York: Stein and Day, 1978), 165–66.

12. Ironically, this was the very day that Ludendorff first informed the German crown prince of his plans for the Marne-Reims offensive.

13. "Preparation d'actions offensives entre Aisne et Marne, 14 juin–12 juillet [1918]," 400-30.9, RG 165, NARA; General Foch, commander in chief of the Allied

Armies to General Pétain, commander in chief of the Armies of the North and Northeast, letter, 14 June 1918, *USAWW*, 5: 223, and Ferdinand Foch, *The Memoirs of Marshal Foch*, trans. T. Bentley Mott (Garden City, N.Y.: Doubleday, Doran, 1931), 339–41.

14. Foch, *Memoirs*, 352–54. Of the five remaining American divisions in the British sector, three were placed with the newly formed First Army in August 1918, leaving the U.S. Twenty-seventh and Thirtieth Divisions as the only American divisions actively to serve with the British during World War I.

15. Napoleon I, *The Military Maxims of Napoleon*, ed. David Chandler (New York: Da Capo, 1995), Maxim 29, 64.

16. Mission Militaire Française pres l'Armée Américaine, "Rapport sur les operations du Ier C.A.U.S. pour la période du 4 au 31 juillet 1918," 31 juillet 1918, 405-30.4, RG 165, NARA; U.S. Army War College, *Order of Battle of the United States Land Forces in the World War*, 3 vols. (1931; reprint, Washington, D.C.: CMH, 1988), 1: 193; and Hunter Liggett, *Commanding an American Army: Recollections of the World War* (Boston: Houghton Mifflin, 1925), 31.

17. Douglas Haig, diary entries for 1 October 1918 and 5 October 1918, reprinted in Douglas Haig, *The Private Papers of Douglas Haig, 1914–1919* (London: Eyre and Spottiswoode, 1952), 329–30.

18. Hunter Liggett, *A.E.F.: Ten Years Ago in France* (New York: Dodd, Mead, 1928), 85–88.

19. Allied intelligence officers had also deduced that the Germans were planning an attack against the British in Flanders, but they believed, correctly as it turned out, that the Germans would strike at Reims first.

20. Pétain had launched two limited offensives in August and October 1917, but these attacks were much smaller than the proposed operation, both in terms of the forces employed and the objectives sought.

21. Barthélemy Palat, *L'Année d'angoisse, 1917* (Paris: Berger-Levrault, 1927), 237 326; see also chapter 3.

22. Guy Pedroncini, *Pétain: General en chef, 1917–1918*, 2d ed. (Paris: Presses Universitaires de France, 1997), 406–9.

23. "Preparation d'actions offensives entre Aisne et Marne, 14 Juin–12 Juillet [1918]," 400-30.9, RG 165, NARA, and Pedroncini, *Pétain: Général en chef*, 380.

24. Douglas MacArthur, *Reminiscences* (New York: McGraw-Hill, 1964), 57.

25. James G. Harbord, *The American Army in France, 1917–1919* (Boston: Little, Brown, 1936), 312.

26. James J. Cooke, *The Rainbow Division in the Great War, 1917–1919* (Westport, Conn.: Praeger, 1994), 98.

27. Ibid., 103, and Henri Gouraud, "My Memories of the Rainbow Division," *American Legion Monthly*, November 1933, 56.

28. GQG, Armées Nord et du Nord-Est, "Note sur le moral des troupes d'apres le contrôle postal pendant la period du 22 juin au 3 juillet 1918," 16 N 1485, SHAT.

29. Ibid.

30. *AFGG*, tome 6, 2: 41–46, and Guy Pedroncini, *Pétain: Le soldat, 1914–1940*

(Paris: Perrin, 1998), 181–88. Various American historians have credited Foch with developing this defensive scheme. Yet the evidence from French sources demonstrates that Pétain developed and codified the ideas for this system of defense. This tactic clearly mirrors the methods that the Germans employed at Chemin des Dames and Passchendaele in 1917.

31. IV Armée, offensive allemande du 15 juillet 1918, 19 N 750, SHAT; General Barthélemy Palat, *La Grande Guerre sur le front occidental,* 14 vols. (Paris: Berger-Levrault, 1917–1929), vol. 14, *La capitulation de l'Allemagne* (Paris: Berger-Levrault, 1929), 2–3.

32. Georges Clemenceau, *Discours prononcé à Sainte Hermine le 2 octobre 1921* (Paris: Payot, 1921), 6–7.

33. Ludendorff, the German crown prince, and Hindenburg later blamed politicians, deserters, and loose talk among their officers and men for the compromise of secrecy regarding the operation. Although these charges may indeed be true, it is nevertheless difficult to discern why the German high command gave the code name Reims to an attack whose objective was to take Reims. It's as if Operation Overlord in World War II had been named Operation Normandy.

34. Operations report, Third Section, General Staff, French Fourth Army, 18 July 1918, *USAWW,* 5: 151–52.

35. Ibid., and David T. Zabecki, *Steel Wind* (Westport, Conn.: Praeger, 1994), 90.

36. Report of Colonel Douglas MacArthur, chief of staff, U.S. Forty-second Division, to GHQ AEF, 16 July 1918, *USAWW,* 5: 166–67.

37. Palat, *Capitulation de l'Allemagne,* 3.

38. Army Group German Crown Prince, Evening Reports, 15 July [1918], 532–34, and war diary, Army Group German Crown Prince, 15 July [1918], both in *German Offensive,* 539–41; Crown Prince Wilhelm, *War Experiences,* 334; and Zabecki, *Steel Wind,* 92.

39. Army Group German Crown Prince, Evening Reports, 532–34, and war diary, 539–41, both 15 July 1918, *German Offensive;* Crown Prince Wilhelm, *War Experiences,* 334; Zabecki, *Steel Wind,* 92; and war diary, German First Army, 15 July 1918, *USAWW,* 5: 183–86.

40. Personal journal of First Sergeant Norman J. Summers, Co. M, 167th Infantry Regiment, U.S. Forty-second Division, AEF USAMHI.

41. General Joseph Hellé and General Henri Berdoulat, "The A.E.F. in Their First Great Offensive," in Viereck, ed., *As They Saw Us,* 147; and MacArthur, *Reminiscences,* 58.

42. IV Armée, offensive allemande du 15 Juillet 1918, 19 N 750, SHAT.

43. Operations Report of French military mission with American Forty-second Division, 17 July 1918, *USAWW,* 5: 170.

44. Personal journal of First Sergeant Norman J. Summers.

45. Palat, *Capitulation de l'Allemagne,* 4–8.

46. Kurt Hesse, "The Battle of the 5th Grenadiers, 36th Division," *German Offensive,* 664–71, and Crown Prince Wilhelm, *War Experiences,* 334. Included in the heavy toll of German casualties was Colonel Unverzagt, commanding officer of

the German Seventh Army's *pioniers,* who was killed in action while overseeing the crossing of the Marne.

47. Report of Colonel Stacey Cromwell, commanding officer, U.S. Thirtieth Infantry Regiment, U.S. Third Division, 15 July 1918, *USAWW,* 5: 77–78.

48. U.S. War Department, *Histories of Two Hundred and Fifty-one Divisions of the German Army Which Participated in the War (1914–1918)* (1920; reprint, London: London Stamp Exchange, 1989), 180–83.

49. Report by Colonel Ulysses G. McAlexander on battle of 15/16 July 1918, 31 July 1918, *USAWW,* 5: 80–82.

50. Fifty-fifth Brigade, U.S. Twenty-eighth Division, war diary, chronological narrative of events, 15 July 1918, *USAWW,* 5: 106–14.

51. Report by Colonel Ulysses G. McAlexander on battle of 15/16 July 1918, 31 July 1918, *USAWW,* 5: 80–82, and war diary of the [German] Sixth Grenadier Regiment, 15 July 1918, *German Offensive,* 516. For a full account of the stand by the Thirty-eighth Infantry Regiment, see Jesse W. Wooldridge, *The Giants of the Marne* (Salt Lake City: Sea Gull Press, 1923).

52. "Report of [French] Lieutenant Marchand, Instructor of the 30th Infantry, upon the Events which took Place in the subsector Charteves-Fossy during the days of July 15, 16, 17, 1918," 405-30.4, RG 165, NARA.

53. Situation report, French XXXVIII Corps, 1145 hours, 15 July 1918, 5: 57–58; telephone message from General de Division Mondesir to Major General Dickman, 1140 hours, 15 July 1918, 5: 60–61; and French XXXVIII Corps, journal of operations, 15 July 1918, 5: 62–64, all in *USAWW.*

54. Hellé and Berdoulat, "The A.E.F. in Their First Great Offensive," 148–49.

55. Reinhardt, "The AEF Halts the German Marne Offensive," 108.

56. Crown Prince Wilhelm, *War Experiences,* 333–34.

57. Ibid.

58. General Pétain, commanding general of the French Armies of the North and Northeast, to General Fayolle, commanding general of the Reserve Army Group [GAR], telegram, 1000 hours, 15 July 1918, *USAWW,* 5: 241; Pedroncini, *Pétain: Le soldat,* 381–82; and Général Laure, *Le commandement en chef des armées françaises* (Paris: Berger-Levrault, 1937), 106–7.

59. Charles Bugnet, *Mangin* (Paris: Librairie Plon, 1934), 245.

60. General Ferdinand Foch to General Philippe Pétain, telephone message, 1225 hours, 15 July 1918, *USAWW,* 5: 242.

61. Message from General Pétain to General Fayolle, 1430 hours, 15 July 1918, *USAWW,* 5: 242–43, and Bugnet, *Mangin,* 245.

62. See, for example, Duroselle, *La Grande Guerre des français, 1914–1918* (Paris: Perrin, 1994), 389–90.

63. Pedroncini, *Pétain: le soldat,* 386–87; Jean de Pierrefeu, *French Headquarters, 1915–1918,* trans. C. J. C. Street (London: Geoffrey Bles, 1924), 279–81; Basil Liddell-Hart, *Foch* (Boston: Little, Brown, 1932), 336–37.

64. The best biographies of Mangin are Bugnet, *Mangin,* and Louis-Eugène Mangin, *Le Général Mangin, 1866–1925* (Paris: Éditions Fernand Lanore, 1986).

65. Foch, *Memoirs,* 10–37; Henri Philippe Pétain, *Verdun,* trans. Marshal

MacVeagh (New York: Dial Press, 1930), 65–90; and Alistair Horne, *The Price of Glory: Verdun, 1916* (New York: Penguin, 1993), 103.

66. Hellé and Berdoulat, "The A.E.F. in Their First Great Offensive," 156. The Moroccan Division was in actuality made up of Moroccan and Senegalese units as well as a French Foreign Legion regiment. While researching this book in Paris in summer 1999, I had the privilege of watching a company of Foreign Legion-naires and a company of Moroccan troops form up along the Champs-Elysées in preparation for their participation in the annual Bastille Day festivities. As the two companies waited for the parade to begin, they engaged in a contest of musical performances, taking turns singing the ancient battle hymns of their regiments and vying with one another for the applause of the crowd. It was a most entertaining, and moving, experience that all who witnessed it enjoyed.

67. Ibid., 158.

68. Allied order of battle for Aisne-Marne Offensive, *USAWW,* 5: 219, and Allan R. Millett, *The General* (Westport, Conn.: Greenwood Press, 1975), 382.

69. Foch, *Memoirs,* 361.

70. Hellé and Berdoulat, "The A.E.F. in Their First Great Offensive," 157.

71. Harbord, *American Army,* 317, and Douglas V. Johnson and Rolfe L. Hill-man, *Soissons, 1918* (College Station: Texas A&M University Press, 1999), 58–62.

72. Johnson and Hillman, *Soissons,* 60–62.

73. Pedroncini, *Pétain: le soldat,* 396–97.

74. M Company, Ninth Infantry, Second Division, south of Soissons, 18 July 1918, report written by L. T. Janda, CO, Co. M, AEF USAMHI.

75. Charles Mangin, *Comment finit la guerre* (Paris: Plon, 1920), 196.

76. War diary, Army Group German Crown Prince, 18 July 1918, 621–22, and Army Group German Crown Prince, morning reports, 19 July 1918, both in *German Offensive,* 624; and Palat, *Capitulation de l'Allemagne,* 33–36.

77. Letter from First Lieutenant John W. Thomason Jr., USMC, to Dr. and Mrs. John W. Thomason Sr., 26 July 1918, Thomason Collection.

78. Ibid.

79. Corporal Frederick Shaw, Eighteenth Infantry Regiment, U.S. First Division, AEF USAMHI.

80. Hellé and Berdoulat, "The A.E.F. in Their First Great Offensive," 160–61.

81. "A Study of Anglo-American and Franco-American Relations During World War I: Part II, Franco-American Relations," 7200 E, RG 165, NARA. Twenty-two percent of respondents either had no opinion or believed they had no basis to judge.

82. Johnson and Hillman, *Soissons,* 128–36, and Hubert Essame, *The Battle for Europe, 1918* (New York: Charles Scribner's Sons, 1972), 92.

83. Essame, *Battle for Europe,* 96–98.

84. War diary [German], Seventh Army, 18 July 1918, *German Offensive,* 613.

85. Shipley Thomas, *The History of the A.E.F.* (New York: Doran, 1920), 131.

86. Crown Prince Wilhelm, *Memoirs,* 191, 237, and 240.

87. Paul von Hindenburg, *Out of My Life* (London: Cassell, 1920), 386.

88. Martin Kitchen, "Ludendorff and Germany's Defeat," in *Facing Armaged-*

don: The First World War Experienced, ed. Hugh Cecil and Peter Liddle (London: Leo Cooper, 1996), 51–66, and Correlli Barnett, *The Swordbearers: Supreme Command in the First World War* (London: Cassell, 2000), 342–44.

89. Müller, *Kaiser and His Court*, 374.

90. Quoted in Edward Coffman, *The War to End All Wars* (New York: Oxford University Press, 1968), 247.

91. Mangin, *Comment finit la guerre*, 196.

92. Le Armée au QGA, Ordre général no. 318, 30 juillet 1918, reprinted in Charles Mangin, *Lettres de guerre*, ed. Stanislaus Mangin and Louis Eugène Mangin (Paris: Fayard, 1950), 284–85.

93. "Report of Lieutenant Marchand, Instructor of the 30th Infantry, upon the Events which took Place in the Subsector Charteves-Fossy during the days of July 15, 16, 17, 1918," 19 July 1918, 405-30.4, RG 165, NARA.

94. French military mission with the American army, American Thirty-second Division, "Lessons to Be Learned from the Offensive Operations of July 29 August 6, 1918, Between the Marne and the Vesle" [n.d.], 405-30.4, RG 165, NARA.

95. General Daugan, "On the Subject of the Americans: Report rendered after the Operation of July 18–22, 1918, by C.G. 1st Moroccan Division [General Daugan]," File 650, RG 120, NARA.

96. "Opinion française et les Américaines," 7 N 867, SHAT, and Jean Nicot, *Les poilus ont la parole: Lettres du front, 1917–1918* (Paris: Éditions Complexe, 1998), 465.

97. GQG, Armées Nord et du Nord-Est, "Note sur le moral des troupes d'apres le contrôle postal pendant la period du 14 au 24 août 1918," 16 N 1485, SHAT, and Nicot, *Poilus*, 465–66.

98. Statements of Sergeant Major Vernon C. Mossman, Eighteenth Infantry Regiment, U.S. First Division, Pfc James F. Shuff, Eighteenth Infantry Regiment, U.S. First Division, Corporal Frederick Shaw, Eighteenth Infantry Regiment, U.S. First Division, Private Ralph Clay, 168th Infantry, U.S. Forty-second Division, Pfc Edward L. Couron, 168th Infantry Regiment, U.S. Forty-second Division, all in AEF USAMHI.

99. Letter from First Lieutenant John W. Thomason Jr., USMC, to Dr. and Mrs. John W. Thomason Sr., 26 July 1918, Thomason Collection.

100. Nicot, *Poilus*, 465–68.

101. Pershing, *My Experiences*, 2: 168.

102. Ibid., 2:169.

103. Basil Liddell-Hart, *The Real War, 1914–1918* (Boston: Little, Brown, 1930), 419.

104. Pierrefeu, *French Headquarters*, 276–77.

Chapter 8. The Franco-American Armies in the Autumn Campaigns

1. Summary of conference at Bombon, 21 July 1918, *USAWW*, 8: 4, and John J. Pershing, *My Experiences in the First World War*, 2 vols. (1935; reprint, New York: Da Capo, 1995), 2: 168–69.

2. Summary of conference at Bombon, *USAWW*, 8: 4, and Général Eugène Debeney à Général Ferdinand Foch, letter, 22 May 1917, 403-30.1, RG 165, NARA.

3. Letter from General Foch, commander in chief of the Allied Armies, to General Pershing, File 657, Entry 267, RG 120, NARA.

4. Raymond Recouly, *Foch* (New York: Appleton, 1929), 25.

5. Notes on conversation between General Foch, General Pétain, Sir Douglas Haig, and General Pershing on 24 July 1918, at Château Bombon, 402-30.9, RG 165, NARA, and memorandum of 24 July 1918, from Allied commander in chief General Ferdinand Foch, reprinted in Ferdinand Foch, *The Memoirs of Marshal Foch*, trans. T. Bentley Mott (Garden City, N.Y.: Doubleday, Doran, 1931), 369–72.

6. Memorandum of 24 July 1918, from Allied commander in chief General Ferdinand Foch, reprinted in Foch, *Memoirs*, 369–72.

7. Premier Georges Clemenceau to General John J. Pershing, telegram, 27 July 1918, Box 47, Pershing Papers.

8. See chapter 5.

9. Pershing, *My Experiences*, 2: 215–16. The conversation is remarkably similar in tone and line of argument to the one Pershing had with George V in April 1917; see chapter 3.

10. Ibid., 2: 217–18. The U.S. Twenty-seventh and Thirtieth Divisions were left with the British and were formed into the U.S. II Corps. Although the British shipped over approximately 50 percent of the nearly 2 million American soldiers who served in Europe during World War I, these were the only two American divisions that actively served in the British sector of the western front.

11. Field Marshal Sir Douglas Haig, diary entry for Monday, 12 August 1918, in Robert Blake, ed., *The Private Papers of Douglas Haig, 1914–1919* (London: Eyre and Spottiswoode, 1952), 323.

12. Pershing, *My Experiences*, 2: 218.

13. David Lloyd George to Georges Clemenceau, telegram, 13 July 1918, File 651, RG 120, and David Lloyd George to Georges Clemenceau, telegram, 2 August 1918, File 651, RG 120, both in NARA.

14. Pershing, *My Experiences*, 2: 219.

15. Ibid., 2: 219.

16. Marshal Ferdinand Foch to General John J. Pershing, letter, 20 August 1918, *USAWW*, 8: 23.

17. Ibid., General Henri Philippe Pétain to General John J. Pershing, letter, 20 August 1918.

18. See Haig, *Private Papers*, 329–30.

19. Marshal Ferdinand Foch to General John J. Pershing, letter, 23 August 1918, Box 59, Pershing Papers, and John Terraine, *To Win a War: 1918, the Year of Victory* (London: Cassell, 2000), 131–32.

20. Marshal Foch, commander in chief, Allied Armies, to General Pershing, commander in chief, AEF, letter, 1 September 1918, Box 59, Pershing Papers.

21. See, for example, Paul F. Braim, *The Test of Battle*, 2d ed., rev. (Shippensburg, Pa.: White Mane, 1998), and Lawrence Stallings, *The Doughboys* (New York: Harper and Row, 1963).

22. Notes on conference between General Pershing, Marshal Foch, and General Pétain, 2 September 1918, 2: 589–92; Marshal Foch to General John Pershing, letter, 1 September 1918, 8: 46; Headquarters, Allied Armies, conference of 2 September [1918], 8: 47; and Headquarters, French Armies of the North and Northeast, Operation A, St. Mihiel, 2 September 1918, 8: 49, all in *USAWW*.

23. Notes, conference, Pershing, Foch, Pétain, 2 September 1918, 2: 589–92; Foch to Pershing, letter, 1 September 1918, 8: 46; Headquarters, Allied Armies, conference, 2 September [1918], 8: 47; Headquarters, French Armies of the North and Northeast, Operation "A ," St. Mihiel, 2 September 1918, 8:49, all in *USAWW*; Pershing, *My Experiences*, 2: 251–54; and Foch, *Memoirs*, 399–401.

24. Notes, conference, Pershing, Foch, Pétain, 2 September 1918, 2: 589–92; Foch to Pershing, letter, 1 September 1918, 8: 46; Headquarters, Allied Armies, conference, 2 September [1918], 8: 47; Headquarters, French Armies of the North and Northeast, Operation "A," St. Mihiel, 2 September 1918, 8:49, all in *USAWW*.

25. Donald Smythe, "St. Mihiel: The Birth of an American Army," *Parameters* 13, 2 (1983): 47–57

26. Order of Battle, U.S. First Army, 12 September 1918, *USAWW*, 8: 1–2.

27. Pershing, *My Experiences*, 2: 260–61.

28. GQG, Armées Nord et du Nord-Est, "Note sur le moral des troupes d'apres le contrôle postal pendant la period du 4 au 13 septembre 1918," 16 N 1485, SHAT.

29. Field order no. 11, from General John J. Pershing, 13 September 1918, 8: 261, and [German] General Fuchs, report of operations, Composite Army C, 19 September 1918, 8: 313–19, both in *USAWW*.

30. Douglas MacArthur, *Reminiscences* (New York: McGraw-Hill, 1964), 63–64; Hunter Liggett, *AEF* (New York: Dodd, Mead, 1928), 159–61; Edward Coffman, *The War to End All Wars* (New York: Oxford University Press, 1968), 283–84; and David Trask, *The AEF and Coalition Warmaking, 1917–1918* (Lawrence: University Press of Kansas, 1993), 112–13.

31. Pershing, *My Experiences*, 2: 271.

32. Marshal Foch to General Pershing, telegram, 13 September 1918, Box 59, Pershing Papers.

33. Ibid., General John J. Pershing to General Pétain, Commanding Armies of the North and Northeast, letter, 15 September 1918, Box 128.

34. GQG, Armées Nord et du Nord-Est, "Note sur le moral des troupes d'apres le contrôle postal pendant la period du 14 au 24 septembre 1918," 16 N 1485, SHAT.

35. Letter from Major Raymond Austin, Sixth Field Artillery, U.S. First Division, to his mother, 6 February 1918, AEF USAMHI.

36. This was a triumphant reference to "they shall not pass," the rallying cry of French forces during the battle, which symbolized French defiance and resistance at Verdun during the course of the struggle there. See Pershing, *My Experiences*, 2: 287.

37. Philippe Pétain, *Verdun*, trans. Marshal MacVeagh (New York: Dial, 1930), 14. Pétain called Pershing's speech "among the truest and finest words that have been said on the subject of Verdun."

38. Order of Battle, U.S. First Army, Meuse-Argonne Operation, 26 September–11 November 1918, *USAWW,* 9: 1–2.

39. The Meuse-Argonne campaign is a woefully understudied operation; to date, there have been only two books written on it, Braim's *The Test of Battle* and the dated account by the war correspondent Frederick Palmer, *Our Greatest Battle* (New York: Dodd, Mead, 1919). Though both of these works have merit, neither provides a definitive account.

40. Palmer, *Our Greatest Battle,* 76.

41. American Battle Monuments Commission, *American Armies and Battlefields in Europe* (Washington, D.C.: U.S. Army Center of Military History, 1992), 169, and Pershing, *My Experiences,* 2: 282–83.

42. Braim, *Test of Battle,* 86–87, and Barthélmey Palat, *La capitulation de l'Allemagne* (Paris: Berger-Levrault, 1929), 237–39.

43. Braim, *Test of Battle,* 89–103, and American Battle Monuments Commission, *American Armies and Battlefields,* 172–75.

44. Braim, *Test of Battle,* 89–103.

45. Ibid., and Coffman, *War to End All Wars,* 313–14.

46. André Laffargue, *Foch et la bataille de 1918* (Paris: B. Arthaud, 1967), 322.

47. Ministère des Armées, "L'action du service automobile dans les grands batailles de 1914–1918," *Revue historique des armées* 5 (September 1978): 85; Palat, *La capitulation de l'Allemagne,* 239; Coffman, *War to End All Wars,* 303–4; and Terraine, *To Win a War,* 156.

48. Général Pétain, Offensives D'Ensemble des Armées Alliées et Pousée vers la Meuse, 26 September–11 November [1918], 403-30.9, RG 165, and Général Pétain to Marshal Foch, letter, 30 September 1918, 403-30.9, RG 165, both in NARA.

49. Pétain, Offensives, 403-30.9, RG 165, NARA, and Basil Liddell-Hart, *Foch* (Boston: Little, Brown, 1932), 374–75.

50. Situation Report, Operations Section, Group of Armies Gallwitz, 28 September 1918, *USAWW,* 9: 519.

51. Report of First Army, German Army Order of Battle, 1–6 October 1918, *USAWW,* 9: 189.

52. Oliver L. Spaulding, *The Second Division, American Expeditionary Force in France, 1917–1919* (New York: Hillman, 1937), 167, and American Battle Monuments Commission, *American Armies,* 333. For details on the French battles in this region in 1915, see Général Barthélmey Palat, *La Grande Guerre sur le front occidental,* vol. 9, *Les offensives de 1915* (Paris: Berger-Levrault, 1922), 407–79.

53. Lejeune had seen service in the Spanish-American War and had served overseas in the Philippines, Panama, Japan, and Mexico. See John A. Lejeune, *The Reminiscences of a Marine* (Quantico, Va.: Marine Corps Assn., 1979).

54. Ibid., 340.

55. Ibid., 341–42, and Spaulding, *Second Division,* 168.

56. Lejeune, *Reminiscences,* 343, and Second Division, AEF Journal of Operations, 1 October 1918, *USAWW,* 9: 473.

57. Lejeune, *Reminiscences,* 364.

58. Second Division, AEF journal of operations, 10 October 1918, 9: 475;

Thirty-sixth Division, AEF field orders, 10 October 1918, 9: 475; Thirty-sixth Division, AEF field orders, 12 October 1918, 9: 475–76; U.S. First Army, operations report, 1–6 October 1918, 9: 228, all in *USAWW*, and Spaulding, *Second Division,* 179–91.

59. Lejeune, *Reminiscences,* 365–66.

60. Report of First Army, Order of Battle, U.S. First Army, *USAWW,* 9: 199.

61. Ibid., U.S. First Army, operations report, 1–6 October 1918, 9: 228, and Coffman, *War to End All Wars,* 324–25.

62. Braim, *Test of Battle,* 115–16; and Coffman, *War to End All Wars,* 325–27.

63. Braim, *Test of Battle,* 127–28, and Donald Smythe, *Pershing* (Bloomington: University of Indiana Press, 1986), 208–9.

64. Frank E. Vandiver, *Black Jack,* 2 vols. (College Station: Texas A&M University Press, 1977), 2: 972–73. I conducted a thorough search of the French army archives at the Service Historique de l'Armée de Terre in Vincennes, especially the Fonds Foch and Fonds Clemenceau, and found nothing to corroborate Vandiver's story. Indeed, Vandiver's accusation is discredited by most authorities on the AEF, including Trask, in *AEF and Coalition Warmaking,* 144.

65. Erich Ludendorff et al., *The Two Battles of the Marne* (New York: Cosmopolitan, 1927), 182–83. This book has a somewhat deceiving title in that the essays Foch and Ludendorff contributed cover not only the Second Battle of the Marne but also the overall course and major events of the entire 1918 campaign; thus it is an invaluable resource for any discussion of the final stages of World War I.

66. Recouly, *Foch,* 24–26, and Smythe, *Pershing,* 216–17.

67. First Army, AEF, field orders, 12 October 1918, 9: 257–58; First Army, AEF, general orders, 12 October 1918, 9: 260, both in *USAWW*; Hunter Liggett, *Commanding an American Army* (Boston: Houghton Mifflin, 1925), 95–96; Coffman, *War to End All Wars,* 327–29; and Allan R. Millett, *The General* (Westport, Conn.: Greenwood Press, 1975), 418, 423–25. Liggett officially took command of the U.S. First Army on 12 October 1918, but at his request Pershing retained tactical control until the ongoing battle subsided on 16 October.

68. Ludendorff et al., *Two Battles of the Marne,* 228.

69. Liggett, *Commanding an American Army,* 103–5.

70. Robert B. Asprey, *The German High Command at War* (New York: William Morrow, 1991), 482–84, and Roger Parkinson, *Tormented Warrior* (New York: Stein and Day, 1978), 182–83.

71. Paul von Hindenburg, *Out of My Life,* 2 vols. (London: Cassell, 1920), 437.

72. Helmut Haeussler, *General William Groener and the Imperial German Army* (Madison: State Historical Society of Wisconsin, 1962), 120–24.

73. General John J. Pershing to General Philippe Pétain, telegram, 11 November 1918, Box 128, Pershing Papers.

74. Ludendorff et al., *Two Battles of the Marne,* 228.

75. Max von Gallwitz, "The Retreat to the Rhine," in *As They Saw Us,* ed. George Viereck (Garden City, N.Y.: Doubleday, Doran, 1929), 286–87.

76. Pershing, *My Experiences,* 2: 396.

77. Ibid., 2: 397.

Chapter 9. Conclusion

1. American Third Army: Organization, Assembly, and Advance to the Rhine, *USAWW*, 11: 1–3.

2. "A Study of Anglo-American and Franco-American Relations During World War I, Part II: Franco-American Relations," 7200 E, RG 165, NARA. For a good analysis of varying American attitudes toward the Germans and the French in the immediate postwar period, see Jennifer D. Keene, *Doughboys, the Great War, and the Remaking of America* (Baltimore: Johns Hopkins University Press, 2001), 105–31.

3. In 1814 and 1815 the Prussians had been a part of the Allied Coalition against Napoleon and were joined in their invasion and occupation of France by Britain, Russia, and Austria.

4. "Report to Chief Liaison Officer on Conditions in Occupied Territory, 3 February 1919," appendix 5 to "A Study of Anglo-American and Franco-American Relations During World War I, Part II: Franco-American Relations," 7200 E, RG 165, NARA; Charles Bugnet, *Foch Speaks* (New York: Dial Press, 1929), 271–72; Charles Bugnet, *Mangin* (Paris: Plon, 1934), 267–304; Keith L. Nelson, *Victors Divided: America and the Allies in Germany, 1918–1923* (Berkeley: University of California Press, 1975), 110–13; and Jere Clemens King, *Foch versus Clemenceau: France and German Dismemberment, 1918–1919* (Cambridge: Harvard University Press, 1960).

5. See David Stevenson, *French War Aims Against Germany, 1914–1919* (New York: Oxford University Press, 1982), and King, *Foch versus Clemenceau.*

6. "Report to Chief Liaison Officer on Conditions in Occupied Territory, 3 February 1919," appendix 5 to "A Study of Anglo-American and Franco-American Relations During World War I, Part II: Franco-American Relations," 7200 E, RG 165, NARA, and the Rhenish Separatist Movement, Policies of American Military Authorities Regarding Changes of Civil Officials, *USAWW*, 11: 241–42. See also Bugnet, *Foch Speaks*, 271–72, and Bugnet, *Mangin*, 267–304. Mangin in particular persisted in scheming for an autonomous Rhineland until his mysterious death in 1925. Many believed that right-wing German extremists poisoned Mangin, for these groups particularly hated him. This was partly because of his activities in the Rhineland and also because he had advocated the use of African troops in the war and had used them extensively in the French occupation of the Rhineland. After the Germans captured Paris in 1940, Adolf Hitler ordered the statue of Mangin in the French capital, depicting him surrounded by his beloved colonial troops, to be destroyed.

7. "A Study of Anglo-American and Franco-American Relations During World War I, Part II: Franco-American Relations," 7200 E, RG 165, NARA.

8. Charles G. Dawes, *A Journal of the Great War*, 2 vols. (Boston: Houghton Mifflin, 1921), 1: 251. Although American soldiers have engaged in numerous wars overseas, more are buried in France than in any other foreign country.

9. Captain A. E. Dewey, "The Selection of the Unknown Soldier," report, US-AMHI.

10. Ibid.

11. Dewey, "The Selection of the Unknown Soldier," and *New York Times*, 24 October 1921.

12. *New York Times*, 24 October 1921.

13. Ibid.

14. Quoted in Gene Gurney, *Arlington National Cemetery* (New York: Crown, 1965), 41.

15. Dewey, "Selection of Unknown Soldier."

16. The United States had previously awarded the Medal of Honor to the Unknown Soldier of France.

17. *New York Times*, 26 October 1921.

18. The USS *Olympia* had been the flagship of Commodore George Dewey's Asiatic squadron during the Battle of Manila Bay in the Spanish-American War of 1898.

19. *New York Times*, 11 November 1921.

20. "President Harding's Address at the Burial of an Unknown American Soldier," *New York Times*, 12 November 1921.

21. Ibid.

22. Ibid., and James Edward Peters, *Arlington National Cemetery: Shrine to America's Heroes* (Kensington, Md.: Woodbine House, 1986), 280–82.

23. Joseph Joffre, *The Personal Memoirs of Joffre*, trans. T. Bentley Mott, 2 vols. (New York: Harper Brothers, 1932), 2: 580.

SELECTED BIBLIOGRAPHY

● ● ● ● ● ● ● ● ● ● ● ● ● ● ●

ARCHIVAL MATERIAL

Library of Congress, Manuscripts Division, Washington, D.C.

Newton D. Baker Papers
Tasker H. Bliss Papers
John J. Pershing Papers
Hugh L. Scott Papers

U.S. National Archives and Records Administration (NARA), Washington, D.C.

Record Group 120. Records of the American Expeditionary Forces, 1917–1923.
Record Group 165. Records of the War Department General and Special Staffs.

U.S. Army Military History Institute, Carlisle Barracks, Carlisle, Pennsylvania

Army Services Experience Questionnaires, WWI Research Project
U.S. Army Oral History Project

Service Historique de l'Armée de Terre (SHAT), Château de Vincennes, Vincennes, France

SÉRIE K:
Fonds Joffre

SÉRIE N:
Trosieme République (1872–1919)
4N Conseil supérieur de guerre interallié (1917–1919)
6N Fonds Clemenceau
7N État-major de l'armée (1872–1940)
14N Fonds Joffre and Fonds Foch (1912–1922)
17N Missions militaires françaises (1914–1923)
18N Groupes d'armées
19N Armées du front occidental

University of Virginia, Special Collections Department, Charlottesville

James Rogers McConnell Memorial Collection

Sam Houston State University, Newton Gresham Library, Huntsville, Texas

John W. Thomason Jr. Collection

NEWSPAPERS

Boston Herald
Chicago Daily News
Chicago Daily Tribune
Chicago Herald
New York Evening Post
New York Herald Tribune
New York Times
New York World
Washington Post

U.S. AND FRENCH GOVERNMENT DOCUMENTS

American Battle Monuments Commission. *American Armies and Battlefields in Europe.*
    1938. Reprint, Washington, D.C.: U.S. Army Center of Military History, 1992.
Ayres, Leonard P. *The War with Germany: A Statistical Summary.* Washington, D.C.:
    GPO, 1919.
Dastrup, Boyd L. *King of Battle: A Branch History of the U.S. Army's Field Artillery.*
    Washington, D.C.: U.S. Army Center of Military History, 1993.
General Service Schools. *The German Offensive of July 15, 1918: Marne Source Book.*
    Ft. Leavenworth, Kans.: General Service Schools Press, 1923.
Kreidburg, Marvin A., and Merton G. Henry. *History of Military Mobilization in the
    United States Army, 1775–1945.* Washington, D.C.: Department of the Army,
    1955.

Ministère de la Guerre. GQG 3e Bureau. *Manuel du chef de section d'infanterie.* Paris: Imprimerie Nationale, 1916.

———. GQG, des Armées du Nord et du Nord-Est. *Instruction sur le combat offensif des petites unités.* Paris: Imprimerie Nationale, 1918.

———. *Les Armées françaises dans la Grand Guerre.* 95 vols. Paris: Imprimerie Nationale, 1922–1939.

U.S. Army. *Manual for Commanders of Infantry Platoons.* U.S. Army translation of French Army's *Manuel de chef de section d'infanterie.* Washington, D.C.: GPO, 1917.

———. *World War Records: First Division, AEF Regular.* 25 vols. Washington, D.C.: GPO, 1928–1930.

U.S. Army War College, Historical Section. *The Genesis of the American First Army.* Washington, D.C.: GPO, 1938.

———. *Order of Battle of the United States Land Forces in the World War.* 3 vols. Washington, D.C.: GPO, 1931.

U.S. Department of the Army. *Final Report of General John J. Pershing: Commander-in-Chief, American Expeditionary Forces.* Washington, D.C.: GPO, 1920.

———. *The United States Army in the World War, 1917–1919.* 17 vols. Washington, D.C.: GPO, 1948.

U.S. War Department. *Histories of Two Hundred and Fifty-one Divisions of the German Army Which Participated in the War (1914–1918).* 1920. Reprint, London: London Stamp Exchange, 1989.

U.S. War Department, Army Infantry School. *Infantry in Battle.* Washington, D.C.: Infantry Journal Press, 1934.

Vigneras, Marcel. *Rearming the French: U.S. Army in World War II Special Studies.* Washington, D.C.: CMH, 1957.

PAPERS, LETTERS, AND DIARIES

Blumenson, Martin, ed. *The Patton Papers, 1885–1940.* 2 vols. Boston: Houghton-Mifflin, 1972.

Chapman, Victor. *Victor Chapman's Letters from France.* Edited John J. Chapman. New York: Macmillan, 1917.

Clemenceau, Georges. *Discours prononcé à Sainte Hermine le 2 octobre 1921.* Paris: Payot, 1921.

Corday, Michel. *The Paris Front, an Unpublished Diary: 1914–1918.* New York: E. P. Dutton, 1934.

Genet, Edmond. *An American for Lafayette: The Diaries of E. C. C. Genet, Lafayette Escadrille.* Edited Walt Brown Jr. Charlottesville: University Press of Virginia, 1981.

———. *War Letters of Edmond Genet.* Edited Grace Ellery Channing. New York: Charles Scribner's Sons, 1918.

Guéno, Jean-Pierre, and Yves Laplume, eds. *Paroles de poilus: Lettres et carnets du front, 1914–1918.* Paris: Librio, 1998.

Hanssen, Hans Peter. *Diary of a Dying Empire*. Edited Ralph H. Lutz et al. Bloomington: Indiana University Press, 1955.

Horne, Charles F., and Walter F. Austin, eds. *Source Records of the Great War*. 7 vols. Indianapolis: American Legion, 1923.

Kelly, Russell A. *Kelly of the Foreign Legion: Letters of Légionnaire Russell A. Kelly*. New York: Mitchell Kennerly, 1917.

Link, Arthur S. et al., eds. *The Papers of Woodrow Wilson*. 69 vols. Princeton: Princeton University Press, 1966–1994.

Mangin, Charles. *Lettres de guerre*. Edited Stanislaus Mangin and Louis Eugène Mangin. Paris: Fayard, 1950.

Müller, Georg Alexander von. *The Kaiser and His Court: The Diaries, Note Books and Letters of Admiral Georg Alexander von Müller, Chief of the Naval Cabinet, 1914–1918*. Edited Walter Görlitz. New York: Harcourt Brace and World, 1964.

Nicot, Jean. *Les poilus ont la parole: Lettres du front: 1917–1918*. Paris: Éditions Complexe, 1998.

Pedroncini, Guy, ed. *Journal de marche de Joffre: 1916–1919*, Vincennes: Service Historique de l'Armée de Terre, 1990.

Rockwell, Kiffin. *War Letters of Kiffin Yates Rockwell, Foreign Legionnaire and Aviator: France, 1914–1916*. Edited Paul Rockwell. Garden City, N.Y.: Country Life Press, 1917.

Roosevelt, Quentin. *Quentin Roosevelt: A Sketch with Letters*. Edited Kermit Roosevelt. New York: Charles Scribner's Sons, 1921.

Seeger, Alan. *Letters and Diary of Alan Seeger*. New York: Scribner's, 1917.

———. *Poems*. New York: Scribner's, 1917.

Seymour, Charles P., ed. *The Intimate Papers of Colonel House*. 4 vols. Boston: Little Brown, 1928.

Weeks, Alice S., ed. *Greater Love Hath No Man: A Collection of Letters from Americans Serving with the French Foreign Legion*. Boston: Bruce Humphries, 1939.

MEMOIRS

Alexander, Robert. *Memories of the World War, 1917–1918*. New York: Macmillan, 1931.

Baker, Newton D. *Why We Went to War*. New York: Harper and Brothers, 1936.

Barbusse, Henri. *Le Feu: Journal d'une escouade*. Paris: Flammarion, 1916.

Bliss, Tasker H. "The Evolution of the Unified Command." *Foreign Affairs* 1 (December 1922): 1–30.

———. "The Strategy of the Allies." *Current History* 29 (November 1928): 197–211.

Bugnet, Charles. *Foch Speaks*. Translated Russell Green. New York: Dial Press, 1929.

Bullard, Robert Lee. *Personalities and Reminiscences of the War*. Garden City, N.Y.: Doubleday and Page, 1925.

Catlin, A. W. *"With the Help of God and a Few Marines."* New York: Doubleday, Page, 1919.

Chaine, Pierre. *Les Mémoires d'un rat.* Paris: Éditions Louis Pariente, 2000.

Clemenceau, Georges. *The Grandeur and Misery of Victory.* Translated F. M. Atkinson. New York: Harcourt, Brace, 1930.

Davis, Richard Harding. *With the French in France and Salonika.* New York: Charles Scribner's Sons, 1916.

Dawes, Charles G. *A Journal of the Great War.* 2 vols. Boston: Houghton Mifflin, 1921.

Dickman, Joseph T. *The Great Crusade.* New York: Appleton, 1927.

Ettinger, Albert. *A Doughboy with the Fighting 69th.* Shippensburg, Pa.: White Mane, 1992.

Falkenhayn, Erich von. *General Headquarters and Its Critical Decisions, 1914–1916.* London: Hutchinson, 1919.

Foch, Ferdinand. *The Memoirs of Marshal Foch.* Translated T. Bentley Mott. Garden City, N.Y.: Doubleday, Doran, 1931.

Gouraud, Henri. "My Memories of the Rainbow Division." *American Legion Monthly* (November 1933): 26–27, 56–59

Harbord, James G. *The American Army in France, 1917–1919.* Boston: Little Brown, 1936.

———. *Leaves from a War Diary.* New York: Dodd, Mead, 1925.

Hindenburg, Paul von. *Out of My Life.* London: Cassell, 1920.

Hoffmann, Max. *The War of Lost Opportunities.* Nashville: Battery Press, 1999.

Joffre, Joseph. *The Personal Memoirs of Joffre: Field Marshal of the French Army.* Translated T. Bentley Mott. 2 vols. New York: Harper Brothers, 1932.

King, David Wooster. *"L.M. 8046": An Intimate Story of the Foreign Legion.* New York: Duffield, 1927.

Lansing, Robert. *War Memoirs of Robert Lansing.* Indianapolis: Bobbs-Merrill, 1935.

Lejeune, John A. *The Reminiscences of a Marine.* 1930. Reprint, Quantico, Va.: Marine Corps Association, 1979.

Liggett, Hunter. *A.E.F., Ten Years Ago in France.* New York: Dodd, Mead, 1928.

———. *Commanding an American Army: Recollections of the World War.* Boston: Houghton Mifflin, 1925.

Little, Arthur. *From Harlem to the Rhine.* New York: Corvici, 1936.

Ludendorff, Erich. *Ludendorff's Own Story.* 2 vols. New York: Harper Brothers, 1920.

Ludendorff, Erich, et al. *The Two Battles of the Marne: The Stories of Marshal Joffre, General von Ludendorff, Marshal Foch, Crown Prince Wilhelm.* New York: Cosmopolitan, 1927.

MacArthur, Douglas. *Reminiscences.* New York: McGraw-Hill, 1964.

Mangin, Charles. *Comment finit la guerre.* Paris: Plon, 1920.

———. *La force noire.* Paris: Hachette, 1910.

March, Peyton C. *The Nation at War.* Garden City, N.Y.: Doubleday, Doran, 1932.

Marshall, George C. *Memoirs of My Services in the World War, 1917–1918.* Boston: Houghton-Mifflin, 1976.

Mason, Monroe, and Arthur Furr. *The American Negro with the Red Hand of France.* Boston: Cornhill, 1920.

McConnell, James R. *Flying for France: With the American Escadrille at Verdun*. Garden City, N.Y.: Doubleday, Page, 1917.

Mitchell, William. *Memoirs of World War I: From Start to Finish of Our Greatest War*. New York: Random House, 1960.

Mordacq, Jean Jules Henri. *Le ministère Clemenceau: Journal d'un témoin*. 4 vols. Paris: Plon, 1930–1931.

Morlae, Edward. *A Soldier of the Legion*. Boston: Houghton-Mifflin, 1916.

Mott, T. Bentley. *Twenty Years as a Military Attaché*. Garden City N.Y.: Doubleday, Doran, 1937.

Painlevé, Paul. *Comment j'ai nommé Foch et Pétain*. Paris: Librairie Félix Alcan, 1923.

Parsons, Edwin C. *I Flew with the Lafayette Escadrille*. 1937. Reprint, Indianapolis: E. C. Seale, 1963.

Pershing, John J. *My Experiences in the First World War*. 1935. Reprint, with foreword by Frank E. Vandiver. 2 vols. in one. New York: Da Capo, 1995.

Pétain, Philippe. "A Crisis of Morale in the French Nation at War." Translated Rivers Scott. In Edward Spears, *Two Men Who Saved France: Pétain and De Gaulle*. New York: Stein and Day, 1966.

———. *Verdun*. Translated Marshal MacVeagh. New York: Dial Press, 1930.

Pierrefeu, Jean de. *French Headquarters, 1915–1918*. Translated C. J. C. Street. London: Geoffrey Bles, 1924.

Poincaré, Raymond. *Au service de la France*. 10 vols. Paris: Plon, 1926–1933.

Prince, Norman. *Norman Prince: A Volunteer Who Died for the Cause He Loved*. With memoir by George F. Babbitt. Boston: Houghton-Mifflin, 1917.

Raynal, Commandant. *Le drame du Fort de Vaux*. Verdun: Éditions Lorraines, 1996.

Rickenbacker, Edward V. *Fighting the Flying Circus*. Garden City, N.Y.: 1965.

Rockwell, Paul Ayres. *American Fighters in the Foreign Legion, 1914–1918*. Boston: Houghton-Mifflin, 1930.

Rommel, Erwin. *Infantry Attacks*. 1944. Reprint, London: Greenhill Books, 1990.

Serrigny, Bernard. *Trente ans avec Pétain*. Paris: Librairie Plon, 1959.

Snow, William J. *Signposts of Experience: World War Memoirs*. Washington, D.C.: U.S. Field Artillery Association, 1941.

Spears, Edward L. *Assignment to Catastrophe*. 2 vols. New York: Wynn, 1954.

———. *Liaison, 1914*. London: Heineman, 1930.

———. *Prelude to Victory*. London: Cape, 1930.

Tardieu, André. *France and America: Some Experiences in Cooperation*. Boston: Houghton Mifflin, 1927.

Thénault, Georges. *The Story of the Lafayette Escadrille*. Nashville: Battery Press, 1990.

Thomason, John W. Jr. *Fix Bayonets!* New York: Charles Scribner's Sons, 1926.

Viereck, George, ed. *As They Saw Us: Foch, Ludendorff and Other Leaders Write Our War History*. Garden City, N.Y.: Doubleday, Doran, 1929.

Wilhelm, Crown Prince of the German Empire. *Memoirs of the Crown Prince of Germany*. New York: Charles Scribner's Sons, 1922.

———. *My War Experiences*. London: Hurst and Blackett, 1923.

Winslow, Carroll Dana. *With the French Flying Corps.* New York: Charles Scribner's Sons, 1917.

Wright, Peter E. *At the Supreme War Council.* New York: G. P. Putnam's Sons, 1921.

York, Alvin. *Sergeant York: His Own Life Story and War Diary.* Edited Thomas Skeyhill. Garden City, NY: Doubleday, 1928.

SECONDARY SOURCES

Abrahamson, James L. *America Arms for a New Century: The Making of a Great Military Power.* New York: Free Press, 1981.

Ammon, Harry. *The Genet Mission.* New York: Norton, 1973.

Ardant du Picq, Charles. *Études sur le combat.* 7th ed. Paris: Chapelot, 1914.

Armstrong, David A. *Bullets and Bureaucrats: The Machine Gun and the United States Army, 1861–1916.* Westport, Conn.: Greenwood Press, 1982.

Arnold, Joseph C. "French Tactical Doctrine: 1870–1914." *Military Affairs* 42 (1978): 60–67.

Asprey, Robert B. *At Belleau Wood.* New York: G. P. Putnam's Sons, 1965.

———. *The German High Command at War: Hindenburg and Ludendorff Conduct World War I.* New York: William Morrow, 1991.

Audoin-Rouzeau, Stéphane. *Men at War, 1914–1918: National Sentiment and Trench Journalism in France During the First World War.* Translated Helen McPhail. Washington, D.C.: Berg, 1995.

Autin, Jean. *Foch.* Paris: Perrin, 1987.

Barbeau, Arthur E., and Florette Henri Barbeau. *The Unknown Soldiers: African-American Troops in World War I.* 2nd ed. New York: Da Capo, 1996.

Barnett, Correlli. *The Swordbearers: Supreme Command in the First World War.* 1963. Reprint, London: Cassell, 2000.

Beaver, Daniel R. *Newton D. Baker and the American War Effort, 1917–1919.* Lincoln: University of Nebraska Press, 1966.

Becker, Jean-Jacques. *The Great War and the French People.* Translated Arnold Pomerans. Providence, R.I.: Berg, 1985.

———. *La France en guerre, 1914–1918: La grand mutation.* Bruxelles: Éditions Complexe, 1988.

Berry, Henry. *Make the Kaiser Dance: Living Memories of the Doughboy.* Garden City, N.Y.: Doubleday, 1978.

Braim, Paul F. *The Test of Battle: The American Expeditionary Forces in the Meuse-Argonne Campaign.* 2d ed., rev. Shippensburg, Pa.: White Mane, 1998.

Bruce, Robert B. "America Embraces France: Marshal Joseph Joffre and the French Mission to the United States, April–May 1917." *Journal of Military History* 66 (April 2002): 407–41.

———. *Pétain: Soldier of France.* Dulles, Va.: Brassey's, 2004.

———. "To the Last Limits of Their Strength: The French Army and the Logistics of Attrition at the Battle of Verdun, 21 February–18 December 1916." *Army History* 45 (summer 1998): 9–21.

Buffetaut, Yves. *Paris menacé: 9 juin 1918, la Bataille du Matz*. Langres: Ysec, 2001.

Bugnet, Charles. *Mangin*. Paris: Librairie Plon, 1934.

Carrias, Eugéne. *La Pensée militaire française*. Paris: Universitaires de France, 1960.

Cecil, Hugh, and Peter Liddle, eds. *Facing Armageddon: The First World War Experienced*. London: Leo Cooper, 1996.

Challener, Richard D. *The French Theory of the Nation in Arms, 1866–1929*. New York: Columbia University Press, 1952.

Chambers, John W. II. *To Raise an Army: The Draft Comes to Modern America*. New York: Free Press, 1987.

Churchill, Winston S. *The World Crisis*. 5 vols. London: Thornton Butterworth, 1923–1931.

Clark, George B. *Devil Dogs: Fighting Marines of World War I*. Novato, Calif.: Presidio Press, 1999.

Clements, Kendrick A. *The Presidency of Woodrow Wilson*. Lawrence: University Press of Kansas, 1992.

Coffman, Edward M. "American Command and Commanders in World War I." In *New Dimensions in Military History*, 177–95. Edited Russell F. Weigley. San Rafael, Calif.: Presidio Press, 1975.

———. "The American Military Generation Gap: The Leavenworth Clique in World War I." In *Command and Commanders in Modern Warfare*. Edited William Geffen. Colorado Springs: USAF Academy, 1971.

———. "Conflicts in American Planning: An Aspect of World War I Strategy." *Military Review* 43 (June 1963): 78–90.

———. *The Hilt of the Sword: The Career of Peyton C. March*. Madison: University of Wisconsin Press, 1966.

———. *The War to End All Wars: The American Military Experience in World War I*. New York: Oxford University Press, 1968.

Contamine, Henry. *La victoire de la Marne*. Paris: Gallimard, 1970.

Conte, Arthur. *Joffre*. 1986. Reprint, Paris: Perrin, 1998.

Cooke, James J. *Pershing and His Generals: Command and Staff in the AEF*. Westport, Conn.: Praeger, 1997.

———. *The Rainbow Division in the Great War, 1917–1919*. Westport, Conn.: Praeger, 1994.

Cooper, John Milton Jr. *The Warrior and the Priest: Woodrow Wilson and Theodore Roosevelt*. Cambridge: Harvard University Press, 1983.

Corvisier, André. *Histoire militaire de la France*. Vol. 3. De 1871 à 1940. Paris: Presses Universitaires de France, 1992.

Crozier, William. *Ordnance and the World War*. New York: Scribner's, 1920.

Cuddy, Joseph E. *Irish America and National Isolationism, 1914–1920*. New York: Arno Press, 1976.

Darrow, Margaret H. *French Women and the First World War*. New York: Berg, 2000.

De Weerd, Harvey A. "The American Adoption of French Artillery, 1917–1918." *Journal of American Military Institute* 3 (summer 1939): 104–16.

Doughty, Robert A. "More Than Numbers: Americans and the Revival of French Morale in the Great War." *Army History* 52 (spring 2001): 1–10.

Dumur, Louis. *La Fayette nous voici.* Paris: Albin Michel, 1933.

Duroselle, Jean-Baptiste. *Clemenceau.* Paris: Fayard, 1989.

———. *La France et les Français, 1914–1920.* Paris: Richelieu, 1973.

———. *La Grande Guerre des français, 1914–1918.* Paris: Perrin, 1994.

Ellis, Jack D. *The Early Life of Georges Clemenceau, 1841–1903.* Lawrence: Regents Press of Kansas, 1980.

Essame, Hubert. *The Battle for Europe, 1918.* New York: Charles Scribner's Sons, 1972.

Falls, Cyril. *The Great War.* New York: Putnam, 1959.

Ferrell, Robert H. *Woodrow Wilson and World War I, 1917–1921.* New York: Harper and Row, 1985.

Ferro, Marc. *The Great War, 1914–1918.* Translated Norman Stone. London: Routledge and Kegan Paul, 1997.

Finnegan, John P. *Against the Specter of a Dragon: The Campaign for American Military Preparedness, 1914–1917.* Westport, Conn.: Greenwood Press, 1974.

Flammer, Philip. *The Vivid Air: The Lafayette Escadrille.* Athens: University of Georgia Press, 1981.

Foch, Ferdinand. *De la conduite de la guerre: La manoeuvre pour la bataille.* Paris: Economica, 2000.

———. *The Principals of War.* Translated Hilaire Belloc. London: Chapman and Hall, 1918.

Freidel, Frank. *Over There: The Story of America's First Great Overseas Crusade.* Boston: Little, Brown, 1964.

Frothingham, Thomas G. *The American Reinforcement in the World War.* Garden City, N.Y.: Doubleday, Page, 1927.

Fuller, J. F. C. *The Conduct of War, 1789–1961.* New Brunswick N.J.: Rutgers University Press, 1961.

———. *Decisive Battles of the U.S.A.* New York: Harper and Brothers, 1942.

Gamelin, Maurice. *Manoeuvre et victoire de la Marne.* Paris: Grasset, 1954.

Gaulle, Charles de. *France and Her Army.* Translated F. L. Dash. London: Hutchinson, 1945.

Genthe, Charles V. *American War Narratives, 1917–1918.* New York: David Lewis, 1969.

Gisclon, Jean. *De L'Escadrille Lafayette au Lafayette Squadron, 1916–1945.* Paris: Éditions France-Empire, 1975.

Görlitz, Walter. *History of the German General Staff.* Boulder, Colo.: Westview Press, 1985.

Grant, C. J. C. "Marshal Foch: 26th of March to the 11th of November, 1918." *Army Quarterly* 1 (January 1921): 263–89.

———. "Recollections of Marshal Foch in 1918." *Army Quarterly* 18 (July 1929): 325–34.

Grotelueschen, Mark E. *Doctrine Under Trial: American Artillery Employment in World War I.* Westport, Conn.: Greenwood Press, 2001.

Gudmundsson, Bruce I. *Stormtroop Tactics: Innovation in the German Army, 1914–1918.* Westport, Conn.: Praeger, 1989.

Haeussler, Helmut. *General William Groener and the Imperial German Army.* Madison: State Historical Society of Wisconsin, 1962.

Hagan, Kenneth J. *This People's Navy: The Making of American Sea Power.* New York: Free Press, 1991.

Hagan, Kenneth J., and William R. Roberts, eds. *Against All Enemies: Interpretations of American Military History from Colonial Times to the Present.* Westport, Conn.: Greenwood Press, 1986.

Hansen, Arlen J. *Gentlemen Volunteers: The Story of American Ambulance Drivers in the Great War, August 1914–September 1918.* New York: Arcade, 1996.

Heller, Charles E. *Chemical Warfare in World War I: The American Experience, 1917–1918.* Leavenworth, Kans.: Combat Studies Institute, 1984.

Hervier, Paul-Louis. *The American Volunteers with the Allies.* Paris: Éditions de la Nouvelle Revue, 1918.

Holley, I. B. *General John M. Palmer, Citizen Soldier, and the Army of Democracy.* Westport, Conn.: Greenwood Press, 1982.

Horne, Alistair. *The Price of Glory: Verdun, 1916.* Rev. ed. New York: Penguin, 1993.

Hudson, James J. *Hostile Skies: A Combat History of the American Air Service in World War I.* Syracuse N.Y.: Syracuse University Press, 1968.

Hunter, Thomas M. "Foch and Eisenhower: A Study in Allied Supreme Command." *Army Quarterly* 87 (1963): 33–52.

———. *Marshal Foch: A Study in Leadership.* Ottawa: Directorate of Military Training, 1961.

Jessup, Philip C. *Elihu Root.* 2 vols. New York: Dodd, Mead, 1938.

Johnson, Douglas V., and Rolfe L. Hillman. *Soissons, 1918.* College Station: Texas A&M University Press, 1999.

Johnson, Hubert C. *Breakthrough! Tactics, Technology and the Search for Victory on the Western Front in World War I.* Novato, Calif.: Presidio Press, 1994.

Kaspi, André. *Le temps des Américains à la France en 1917–1918.* Paris: Publications de la Sorbonne, 1976.

Keene, Jennifer D. *Doughboys, the Great War, and the Remaking of America.* Baltimore: Johns Hopkins University Press, 2001.

Kennedy, David M. *Over Here: The First World War and American Society.* New York: Oxford University Press, 1980.

King, Jere Clemens. *Foch versus Clemenceau: France and German Dismemberment, 1918–1919.* Cambridge: Harvard University Press, 1960.

———. *Generals and Politicians: Conflict Between France's High Command, Parliament and Government, 1914–1918.* Berkeley: University of California Press, 1951.

Knock, Thomas J. *To End All Wars: Woodrow Wilson and the Quest for a New World Order.* New York: Oxford University Press, 1992.

La Gorce, Paul-Marie de. *The French Army: A Military-Political History.* New York: George Braziller, 1963.

Laffargue, André. *Foch et la bataille de 1918.* Paris: Athard, 1967.

Laure, Général. *Le Commandement en chef des armées françaises: du 15 mai 1917 à l'Armistice.* Paris: Éditions Berger-Levrault, 1937.

Liddell-Hart, Basil. *Foch: The Man of Orleans.* Boston: Little, Brown, 1932.

———. "Pershing and His Critics." *Current History* (November 1932): 135–140.

———. *The Real War, 1914–1918.* Boston: Little, Brown, 1930.

———. *Reputations: Ten Years After.* Boston: Little, Brown, 1928.

Link, Arthur S. *Woodrow Wilson and the Progressive Era, 1910–1917.* New York: Harper and Row, 1954.

Luvaas, Jay. *The Military Legacy of the Civil War: The European Inheritance.* 2nd ed. Lawrence: University Press of Kansas, 1988.

———, ed. *Napoleon on the Art of War.* New York: Free Press, 1999.

Madelin, Louis. *La bataille de France: 21 mars–11 novembre 1918.* Paris: Plon, 1920.

———. *La deuxième Bataille de la Marne.* Paris: Plon, 1920.

Mahon, John K. *History of the Militia and the National Guard.* New York: Macmillan, 1983.

Mangin, Louis-Eugène. *Le Général Mangin, 1866–1925.* Paris: Éditions Fernand Lanore, 1986.

Marshall-Cornwall, James H. *Foch as Military Commander.* London: n.p., 1972.

Meigs, Mark. *Optimism at Armageddon: Voices of American Participants in the First World War.* New York: New York University Press, 1997.

Miller, John C. *The Federalist Era, 1789–1801.* New York: Harper and Row, 1960.

Millett, Allan R. *The General: Robert L. Bullard and Officership in the United States Army, 1881–1925.* Westport, Conn.: Greenwood Press, 1975.

Millett, Allan R., and Murray Williamson. *Military Effectiveness.* Vol. 1. *The First World War.* London: Allen and Unwin, 1988.

Millis, Walter. *Arms and Men: A Study of American Military History.* New York: G. P. Putnam's Sons, 1958.

———. *The Road to War: America, 1914–1917.* Boston: Houghton Mifflin, 1925.

Miquel, Pierre. *La Grande Guerre.* Paris: Fayard, 1983.

Muller, Commandant. *Joffre et la Marne.* Paris: G. Grès, 1931.

Nelson, Keith L. *Victors Divided: America and the Allies in Germany, 1918–1923.* Berkeley: University of California Press, 1975.

Nenninger, Timothy K. *The Leavenworth Schools and the Old Army: Education, Professionalism, and the Officer Corps of the United States Army, 1881–1918.* Westport, Conn.: Greenwood Press, 1978.

———. "Tactical Dysfunction in the AEF, 1917–1918." *Military Affairs* (October 1987): 177–81.

Newhall, David S. *Clemenceau: A Life at War.* Lewiston, N.Y.: Edwin Mellen Press, 1991.

Nouailhat, Yves-Henri. *France et États-Unis, aout 1914–avril 1917.* Paris: Publications de la Sorbonne, 1979.

Page, Arthur W. *Our 110 Days' Fighting.* Garden City, N.Y.: Doubleday, Page, 1920.

Palat, Barthélemy E. *La Grande Guerre sur le front occidental.* 14 tomes. Paris: Berger-Levrault, 1917–1929.

Palmer, Frederick. *America in France.* New York: Dodd, Mead, 1918.

———. *John J. Pershing: A Biography.* Westport, Conn.: Greenwood Press, 1948.

———. *Newton D. Baker.* 2 vols. New York: Dodd, Mead, 1931.

——. *Our Greatest Battle.* New York: Dodd, Mead, 1919.

Pappas, George. *Prudens Futuri: The War College, 1901–1967.* Carlisle, Pa.: U.S. Army War College, 1967.

Parkinson, Roger. *Tormented Warrior: Ludendorff and the Supreme Command.* New York: Stein and Day, 1978.

Paschall, Rod. *The Defeat of Imperial Germany, 1917–1918.* Chapel Hill, N.C.: Algonquin Books, 1989.

Paxson, Frederic. *American Democracy and the World War.* 3 vols. Boston: Houghton-Mifflin, 1937.

Pedroncini, Guy. "Le commandement unique sur le front occidental en 1918." *Guerres mondiales et conflits contemporains* 42, 168 (1992): 31–36.

——. *Les mutineries de 1917.* Paris: Presses Universitaires de France, 1967.

——. *Pétain: Général en chef: 1917–1918.* 2d ed. Paris: Presses Universitaires de France, 1997.

——. *Pétain: Le soldat, 1914–1940.* Paris: Perrin, 1998.

——. *Pétain: Le soldat et la gloire, 1856–1918.* Paris: Perrin, 1989.

——. "La Strategie du général Pétain." *Relations Internationales.* 35 (autumn 1983): 277–89.

Pitt, Barrie. *1918: The Last Act.* New York: Norton, 1962.

Porch, Douglas. *The French Foreign Legion: A Complete History of the Legendary Fighting Force.* New York: HarperCollins, 1991.

——. *The March to the Marne: The French Army, 1871–1914.* London: Cambridge University Press, 1981.

Rainey, James W. "Ambivalent Warfare: The Tactical Doctrine of the AEF in World War I." *Parameters* 13, 3 (fall 1983): 34–36.

——. "The Questionable Training of the AEF in World War I." *Parameters* 22, 4 (winter 1992–1993): 89–103.

Rearick, Charles. *The French in Love and War: Popular Culture in the Era of the World Wars.* New Haven: Yale University Press, 1997.

Recouly, Raymond. *Foch: My Conversations with the Marshal.* New York: D. Appleton, 1929.

——. *Foch: The Winner of the War.* New York: Charles Scribner's Sons, 1920.

——. *Joffre.* Paris: Éditions des portiques, 1931.

Renouvin, Pierre. *The Forms of War Government in France.* New Haven: Yale University Press, 1927.

Revue Historique de l'Armée. *Fraternité d'armes Franco-Américaine.* Paris: Ministère de la Guerre, 1957.

Roosevelt, Theodore. "Lafayettes of the Air: Young Americans Who Are Flying for France." *Colliers,* 29 July 1916.

Ryan, Stephen. *Pétain the Soldier.* New York: A. S. Barnes, 1969.

Schuman, Frederick L. *War and Diplomacy in the French Republic.* New York: Howard Fertig, 1969.

Seymour, Charles. *American Diplomacy During the World War.* 1934. Reprint, Westport, Conn.: Greenwood Press, 1975.

———. "Foch and Pershing." *Yale Review* 20 (June 1931): 805–9.

Smith, Leonard. *Between Mutiny and Obedience*. Princeton: Princeton University Press, 1994.

Smythe, Donald. "A.E.F. Snafu at Sedan." *Prologue* 5 (September 1973): 134–49.

———. "The Battle of the Books: Pershing v. March." *Army* 22 (September 1972): 30–32.

———. *Guerrilla Warrior: The Early Life of John J. Pershing*. New York: Scribner's, 1973.

———. "Literary Salvos: James G. Harbord and the Pershing-March Controversy." *Mid-America* 57, 3 (1975): 173–83.

———. *Pershing: General of the Armies*. Bloomington: University of Indiana Press, 1986.

———. "The Pershing-March Conflict in World War I." *Parameters* 11 (December 1981): 53–62.

———. "St. Mihiel: The Birth of an American Army." *Parameters* 13, 2 (1983): 47–57.

Spaulding, Oliver L. et al. *The Second Division American Expeditionary Force in France, 1917–1919*. New York: Hillman Press, 1937.

Spears, Edward L. *Two Men Who Saved France: Pétain and de Gaulle*. New York: Stein and Day, 1966.

Stallings, Laurence. *The Doughboys: The Story of the AEF, 1917–1918*. New York: Harper and Row, 1963.

Strachan, Hew, ed. *The Oxford Illustrated History of the First World War*. Oxford: Oxford University Press, 1998.

Taylor, A. J. P. *The First World War*. London: Hamish Hamilton, 1963.

Terraine, John. *To Win a War: 1918, the Year of Victory*. 1978. Reprint, London: Cassel, 2000.

Toland, John. *No Man's Land: 1918, the Last Year of the Great War*. Garden City, N.Y.: Doubleday, 1980.

Towne, Charles Hanson, ed. *For France*. Garden City, N.Y.: Doubleday, Page, 1917.

Trask, David F. *The AEF and Coalition Warmaking*. Lawrence: University Press of Kansas, 1993.

———. *The United States in the Supreme War Council*. Middletown, Conn.: Wesleyan University Press, 1961.

Vandiver, Frank E. *Black Jack: The Life and Times of John J. Pershing*. 2 vols. College Station: Texas A&M University Press, 1977.

Voisin, Général. *La doctrine de l'aviation française de combat: Au cours de la guerre, 1915–1918*. Paris: Éditions Berger-Levrault, 1932.

Watson, David Robin. *Georges Clemenceau: A Political Biography*. New York: David McKay, 1974.

Watt, Richard M. *Dare Call It Treason*. New York: Simon and Schuster, 1963.

Weigley, Russell F. *The American Way of War*. New York: Macmillan, 1973.

———. *The History of the United States Army*. New York: Macmillan, 1967.

———. *Towards an American Army: Military Thought from Washington to Marshall*. New York: Columbia University Press, 1962.

Weygand, Maxime. *Foch.* Paris: Flammarion, 1947.

Wildenberg, Thomas. "In Support of the Battle Line: Gunnery's Influence on the Development of Carrier Aviation in the U.S. Navy." *Journal of Military History* 65 (July 2001): 697–711.

Williams, T. Harry. *Americans at War: The Development of the American Military System.* Baton Rouge: Louisiana State University Press, 1960.

Williams, Wythe. *The Tiger of France: Conversations with Clemenceau.* New York: Duell, Sloan and Pearce, 1949.

Woolcott, Alexander. "Them Damned Frogs." *North American* (October 1919): 490–98.

Wooldridge, Jesse W. *The Giants of the Marne: A Story of McAlexander and His Regiment.* Salt Lake City: Sea Gull Press, 1923.

Wright, Gordon. *Raymond Poincaré and the French Presidency.* New York: Octagon Books, 1967.

Zabecki, David T. *Steel Wind: Colonel Georg Bruchmüller and the Birth of Modern Artillery.* Westport, Conn.: Praeger, 1994.

INDEX